The D.

The Drop Dead Funny '70s

*American Film Comedies
Year by Year*

DAN LALANDE

McFarland & Company, Inc., Publishers
Jefferson, North Carolina

ISBN (print) 978-1-4766-9254-8
ISBN (ebook) 978-1-4766-4974-0

LIBRARY OF CONGRESS AND BRITISH LIBRARY
CATALOGUING DATA ARE AVAILABLE

Library of Congress Control Number 2023020111

On the cover: Steve Martin as Navin R. Johnson in the 1979
film *The Jerk* (Universal Pictures/Photofest)

Printed in the United States of America

*McFarland & Company, Inc., Publishers
Box 611, Jefferson, North Carolina 28640
www.mcfarlandpub.com*

For Roger, with his cries
of "Let's go to the show, son!"

Table of Contents

Introduction

Many a book has been written about American film comedy. Scant are those devoted to the output of the 1970s, and yet, it was a period during which the form was, arguably, at a zenith. The hip, satirical comedy that had bloomed over the postwar period, whose popularity was furthered throughout the ensuing decade by an impressive string of bestselling novelists (Heller, Roth, Vonnegut) and on public stages by an equally popular roster of highbrow comics (Sahl, Allen, Nichols and May), was finally conquering cinema.

As the Hollywood studios were dying, so too were the big-budget comedies that had kept them afloat. Suddenly, a new style of humor was taking over North American screens: low-budget, New York–based character pieces, each expressing the angst of a hard-working, white-collar generation, largely Jewish, set unexpectedly adrift by the disruptive mores put into motion by anti-establishmentarian youth culture. In this context, a number of important directorial careers were spawned. Altman, Bogdanovich, Mazursky—experimental commercial artists who perfectly captured the vibe of the times by successfully hybridizing modern American discomfort with European cinematic technique.

As such, they were able to hold their own with a parallel generation (Coppola, Scorsese, Spielberg) that was simultaneously revitalizing drama. In the margins, a handful of quirky workmen (Zieff, Moore, Ross) were supplementing this with solid, likable successes that the upper crust critics, leading voices of that cinematically savvy time, continuously failed to take seriously.

With the progress of the decade, major wellsprings of national anxiety like Vietnam, the Nixon presidency and runaway inflation quelled. The cinematic scene, as a consequence, shifted from an ailing East to a post–Manson West, the first salvo of a renaissance that would revitalize the big studios in the resurgent 1980s. New York–based talent began to head to Hollywood, creating a bi-coastal limbo from which many a successful comedy was born.

By 1979, American film comedy had made an interesting cross-country (and cross-sensibility) transition: from low-budget, improv-based, Jewish-influenced ensemble cast social satire to respectably backed, carefully crafted, star-based WASP light-heartedness, largely devoted to the upper-middle-class folkways of a quotidian California populace.

The harbinger of the arrival of a usurping creative class, the Baby Boomers, appeared, with the enormously successful *Animal House* (1978) paving the way for a new mode of big-screen comic expression: the collegiate, TV-influenced, nostalgia-based humor of a hedonistic, post-political generation.

1

Threads ranging from the sentimental to the socio-political ran throughout: the bent for homage, a decade-long act of nostalgia born of a Film Studies–instilled reverence for Classic Film and a lament for the fall of the traditional studio (*What's Up, Doc?*, 1972, *Lucky Lady*, 1976, *Movie, Movie*, 1979); the influence of feminism, as championed by major screen comediennes including Barbra Streisand and Goldie Hawn, and its antithesis, the comic action flick, as the decade progressed into the "macho man" ethic of disco; and comedy's version of "blaxploitation" films, including titles such as *Cotton Comes to Harlem* (1970) and an enormously successful trio of black "buddy films" directed by African American icon Sidney Poitier.

If the '70s was a heyday for film, and film comedy, they were also a heyday for film criticism, then coming into its own as a legitimate literary genre. Kael, Canby, Gilliatt, Sarris and Simon, among others, ruled the roost, before intellectualism gave way, by decade's end, to populism, with the emergence of Siskel and Ebert. While the critical voice you will primarily be subjected to throughout this book will be mine, it would be a grievous error not to periodically quote American film criticism's greatest generation, if only to demonstrate just how many of their views seem showily overblown, curiously indifferent, or puzzlingly idiosyncratic in contemporary perspective.

Nothing comes out of a vacuum. If that bromide has a gold seal, it's the American comedy film catalogue of the '70s, distinct reactions and expressions of a deracinated time, the search for behavioral, romantic and economic comfort in the wake of crumbling values. Just as the Jews roamed the earth looking for a home, America's screen comics—mostly, in that era, Jewish—did the same, even if the journey was only from achingly ailing New York to pleasantly placid Los Angeles.

Take that journey here and enjoy—or, if you're a certain age, re-enjoy—what might have been American film comedy's greatest era since the screwball 1930s. Note, though, that not every film comedy released between 1970 and 1979 is represented. There's marginalia and then there's marginalia. Why expound on films whose distribution is limited to the point of non-existence?

That said, you'll find sub-classics, cult films, even a few "I've never heard of that one"s. So, relax. Read your way through this socio-critical look at the releases of each succeeding year, or use this book as an alphabetical reference whenever the need might strike to contextualize or compare opinion on, say, *The Hospital* (1972), *Foul Play* (1978) or some obscure comedy caught on DVD, YouTube or your streaming service of choice—showcases we only could have dreamed of back in the era of single-screen theaters, boxy art houses and three-network television.

Prologue

The Graduate (1967)

It would be simple-minded to attribute the entire comic tenor of the 1970s to a single piece of casting—or, rather, miscasting. But the substitution of square-jawed, all-American Robert Redford with the short, dark Dustin Hoffman, it can be argued, was the guiding light ensuing comic filmmakers followed. It altered the hippest, biggest comedy hit of the 1960s, Mike Nichols' *The Graduate* (1967), from its original intentions—a parody of the perfect postwar family, through sexual upset—into something much more universal: the imposition of the Jewish hero, the quiet-tempered but easily-rattled mensch, into self-aggrandizing WASP culture.

This new take on the old "fish out of water" formula, which had served screen comics from Charlie Chaplin to Jerry Lewis, deeply resonated with a growing youth culture. From the opening close-up, highlighting Hoffman's doleful eyes, we're brought face to face with the full sadness of a generation brimming with promise and vigor, faced with the prospect of daunting, empty conformity. A generation had been sold, under Kennedy, a solid future and a true, resonant voice in American and international life, only, after his unforeseen death, to feel achingly unmoored. Its members looked for role models and found but bluster, materialism and thinly veiled dysfunction. Ultimately, from such grand expectations, they became but cannon fodder (Vietnam) for indifferent and corrupt elders.

This was Nichols, older than said social sector, yes, but still suffering outlier's pangs. He remained, despite the heights he climbed on Broadway and in film, a Russian Jewish immigrant (with alopecia to boot) left to cluelessly cope in the American middle-class. Thus, the casting of Hoffman, a better representative of this relegation than Redford. (Beverly Gray, in her *Seduced by Mrs. Robinson*, devotes an entire chapter to the Hoffman usurpation.)

Nichols was conscious, too, that he shared his persona, in part, with the youth of the times. And so he set out, particularly in the film's zippy last act—in which the lead character, a clean-cut young shmuck secretly seeing a savvy seductress, stages a crazed elopement with her daughter as an act of generational one-upmanship—to boost the connection.

In so doing, many a critic, including Pauline Kael from her conning tower at the tony *New Yorker*, accused Nichols of throwing away a smart, hip bedroom farce to pander to the burgeoning Baby Boomers[1]—and indeed Nichols does. But the bias against

---

1. Pauline Kael, *5001 Nights at the Movies* (New York: Henry Holt, 1991), 299.

commercial filmmakers at that time of auteur mania was a standard posture among big-city critics.

Still, there's no arguing that the film's first half is rooted in Nichols' justly acclaimed stage work. It's composed, largely, of scenes between Hoffman and, as the flirtatious family friend cum femme fatale, Anne Bancroft. Their stolen moments, in her home, in a hotel lobby, in bed, share the same push me–pull you vibe as Nichols' cabaret work with former comic partner Elaine May. You can say it's the Nichols-May film that was never made (the popular duo broke up before the movies could snatch them): taut two-handed black-outs *à la* Second City, the University of Chicago–born sketch and improv collective founded in the late 1950s of which Nichols and May had been such a part, helping the outfit's behavior-based bits eclipse suit-and-tie stand-up as America's leading form of comic expression. Nichols even incorporates some of their best shticks (Hoffman stealing a prolonged kiss while Bancroft has a mouthful of cigarette smoke, for instance) into the early consummation of the mismatched lovers' cross-generational, world-shattering affair. Bancroft shot in profile with her dark hair down even physically resembles Nichols' old nightclub partner.

None of these scenes would have worked with the blonde, bland Redford. For one, Bancroft's attraction would have been perfectly explicable. With the nervous, diminutive Hoffman, we spend much of the film trying to read her malaise. What's with the any-man-will-do, we ask ourselves? The only clue we're genuinely afforded is when Hoffman's attentions turn to her daughter, latently triggering a Wicked Queen–Snow White dynamic.

Other comic highlights wouldn't have worked either: the famous wetsuit scene, for instance, in which Hoffman, made to look ridiculous in ill-fitting frogman's gear, sinks to the bottom of the family pool, a metaphor for the depth of his despair (water plays a symbolic role in the film). Give that moment to the athletic Redford and forgo its comic appeal and connotative quality.

Hoffman's terrified politesse is the engine of so much of the film's comedy. Arguably, it becomes the central male comic archetype for the remainder of the 1960s and, significantly here, most of the early 1970s. It establishes a behavioral mantle taken up, with the addition of idiosyncratic grace notes, by Bud Cort in *Harold and Maude* (1971), Charles Grodin in *The Heartbreak Kid* (1972) and Ryan O'Neal in *What's Up, Doc?* (1973), to name a few. It does owe something, though, to Billy Wilder's *The Apartment* (1960), wherein squeaky, submissive Jack Lemmon finds himself, like Hoffman's graduate, unwittingly complicit in a web of sexual complications, Oedipal ode included.

Like *The Graduate*, *The Apartment* served as a parody of the new sexual mores then sweeping America. Lemmon, Hoffman, *et al.* are America trying its hand at it, and proving clumsy and confused. As the '60s segued into the '70s, this template would hold, with interesting variations. The aforementioned *Harold and Maude* and *Heartbreak Kid*, while not the box office blockbusters *The Apartment* or *The Graduate* were, both went on to cult circuit success. *Maude*, in fact, plays as a *Graduate* parody, lampooning by darkening many of *The Graduate*'s conventions, from its May-December premise to its folk-pop, single-artist soundtrack and its moody montages.

The exploration of sex, while a major plaything of both the '60s and '70s, also ended up serving as a career-long motif of Nichols', even through to late work such as *Closer* (2002). Often considered a generalist, Nichols baffled auteur-happy critics. ("I find it

Dustin Hoffman and Anne Bancroft in *The Graduate* (Embassy, 1967). This classic instance of casting, or miscasting, paved the way for the character actor as star, establishing, inter alia, the behavioral template for the big-screen comic hero of the 1970s (Embassy Pictures/ Photofest).

hard to grasp a him in there, a movie director," David Thomson wrote of Nichols in his *New Biographical Dictionary of Film*. "Is there anything there more substantial than a high reputation and a producer's instinct for what smart people want to see?"[2]) But Nichols had his leitmotifs like anyone else, the fragile physical connection between men and women being as much a part of his life's work as it was that of literary contemporary John Updike's. Nor was Nichols given proper due for his cinematic savvy, the cognoscenti preferring, as Kael did, his stagey instincts to his work with cinematographers and editors.

But in both the film that introduced him to the moviegoing world, *Who's Afraid of Virginia Woolf?* (1966), and especially in the more cinematically sophisticated *Graduate*, Nichols and his teams demonstrated exquisite compositional sense and innovative use of sound. He took these practices to even greater heights in his next film, though sometimes to the point of obtrusiveness—more proof, perhaps, of the old axiom that one's genius is also one's flaw.

Back to *The Graduate*'s zippy ending, the one element responsible for universality, converting it from time-capsule comedy to time-tested classic, from Oedipal sex farce with counterculture overtones to manifestation of man's proverbial search for meaning.

---

2. David Thomson, *The New Biographical Dictionary of Film Updated and Expanded* (New York: Alfred A. Knopf, 2010), 704–705.

It wasn't wholly original; many a '60s comedy put people, climactically, in the same precarious place: eschewing establishmentarianism but unwilling to leap, as they thought they might, to hedonistic liberalism. They just know, these characters in these films, that there's *something* out there, some everlasting, all-rooting experience beyond lifestyle, romance, religion and other barriers. (Paul Mazursky, soon to follow in Nichols' actor-to-director footsteps, might have expressed this even better than Nichols in the screenplay he co-wrote for 1966's *I Love You, Alice B. Toklas*.)

And while few of these films, *The Graduate* included, never managed to classify this motivational malaise, much to the frustration of some critics (yes, Kael again), simply acknowledging it as the filmmakers did was enough for audiences. Unnamed as it went, it managed nonetheless to speak for the majority of moviegoers, to award shape and form to the spiritual itching powder that was finding its way into their souls.

Interestingly, though, the commercial comic films produced in the wake of *The Graduate* adopted these conventions—the outsider persona, the two-handed scenes, the spiritual discontent—to speak not, as this film did, to the youth movement but to those by whom the youth felt repressed; not for the Hoffmans of the world but the Bancrofts. The early '70s ushered in this new comic template to reflect the angst of what would become collectively called the Greatest Generation: middle-aged suburbanites raised in the Dirty '30s who built the idyllic '50s only to see the manic '60s immerse them in the soul-searching '70s. Let the kids stay in their communes, make their crazy music, and smoke their dope, producers seemed to have decreed; meanwhile, we'll borrow their dissatisfaction to reflect our own. The vibe, then, had been set—at least one that would last until the end of such acts of public madness as Vietnam, the Manson murders, Watergate and runaway inflation.

As for Nichols, he greeted the '70s by representationally taking on the former. It would be a much-anticipated project, deemed, by some, the perfect fit: the top anti-establishmentarian commercial filmmaker meeting the top anti-establishmentarian commercial novelist. But his complicated adaptation of Joseph Heller's complicated *Catch-22* (1970) would, despite more redemptive moments than it's been given credit for, prove both less hip and less accessible than *The Graduate*. Besides, as anti-war comedies went, another filmmaker, far chancier and much more cinematically inclined, handily bested him, stealing Nichols' crown as America's directorial darling.

And so, as the popular documentary TV series of the time would announce each week, here come the '70s…

1970

Social commentary, urban angst, the black experience, genre parody, marginalia. With its spectrum of the relevant, the rattled, the oppressed, the nostalgic and the quaintly weird, 1970 perfectly established the frameworks and themes that would run throughout the American comic film catalogue of the rest of the era.

It allowed climbing directorial talent, masters of the stage still relatively new to film, to keep climbing (Mike Nichols, Arthur Penn); it afforded the same break to Broadway-imported writers (Neil Simon, Bill Manhoff, the husband-and-wife team of Joe Bologna and Renée Taylor); it took in refugees from television (Carl Reiner, Bud Yorkin, Norman Lear, Mel Brooks); it brought comedy to blaxploitation (Melvin Van Peebles' *Watermelon Man*); it let sketch-based genre parody try to elongate itself (*Start the Revolution Without Me, The Twelve Chairs*); it introduced us to a new directorial voice that would continue to capture, albeit in hit-and-miss fashion, the woozy vibe of the era (Robert Altman) and one that would, after his flirtation with comedy, revitalize the horror genre (Brian De Palma).

Hollywood and big budgets were on their way out, New York and small budgets were on their way in. The big studios, out of touch with changing public tastes, gave way to maverick producers, independent financiers and distributors, and stars looking to control their own destinies. Broke, baffled and bested, the Big Boys largely gave way to an ad hoc system going against every convention they'd spent years holding up. Stars weren't glamorous any more, they looked like Walter Matthau and Barbra Streisand; lush, art-directed sets were deemed phony, traded for real-life locations; the boy and girl didn't kiss at the end, they had loveless sex throughout the picture; those who got shot didn't simply fall to the ground, they spouted realistic-looking blood; and comedy was no longer situational, genial or sophisticated. It was loose, edgy and proletariat.

Escapism, what American film had proudly offered since its infancy, had escaped. What audiences wanted to see instead was a reflection of their own confused times; they wanted their mixed feelings about everything that was changing—which was, well, everything—validated. Circumstances had gotten so dire, from urban decay to Vietnam to inflation to those goddamn long-haired hippies, that they needed to laugh about it. Finding no answers as to why the pristine, functional world they had built after World War II had proven unsustainable, they were happy to settle for a gag response.

Meanwhile, their successors, the kids, and their sympathizers were making their way into the movies, metaphorically criticizing the conflict in Asia, showing looser, even interracial sex, and going so far as to change filmmaking itself, using angles and editing techniques borrowed from European art films.

The comic hero, then, hitherto a bungling coward who falls into unwitting victory, became either a baffled, uptight everyman or a quirky young seeker.

Both would find solace as the decade progressed, leaving troubled New York for laid-back Los Angeles, trading crippling urban angst for sunny suburban empty-headedness. Before that, though, there was the early part of the '70s to get through….

Brewster McCloud

Plot: A bird-loving adolescent living in the Houston Astrodome becomes suspected of a series of bizarre, bird-related murders. **Director:** Robert Altman. **Script:** Brian McKay (uncredited), Doran William Cannon. **Cast:** Bud Cort, Sally Kellerman, Michael Murphy, William Windom, Shelley Duvall, René Auberjonois, Stacy Keach, John Schuck, Margaret Hamilton. MGM. 105 minutes.

Robert Altman, newly crowned industry darling with his groundbreaking *M*A*S*H* (1970), followed it up that same year with *Brewster McCloud*. If *M*A*S*H* showed us the brilliance of Altman's high-wire style, *Brewster* demonstrated for the first time just how precarious it was, how easily it could lead to uneven rhythms, wonky exposition and fuzzy statements. *M*A*S*H* had introduced us to the two Altmans who would share the rest of the 1970s: the bold satirist and the self-indulgent maverick. Here, the latter gets the better of the former. As his career progressed, it wouldn't be the last time.

The theme of *Brewster McCloud* is transcendence, flying away, both literally and figuratively. The idea is to flee America the Ugly, as personified in the Astrodome-set opening by the appearance of Margaret Hamilton, the iconic Wicked Witch of the West. She's in gaudy red, white and blue, singing an off-key rendition of the National Anthem into a cloudy nirvana. Is there any getting away from all this tacky, patriotic, overblown, institutional offensiveness?, Altman's film asks. As inquisitor, the film turns to its titular character: a bird-loving nebbish who, in the end, reveals himself to be a comic take on Icarus.

With his homicidal bent and his all-in identification with birds, McCloud suggests a comic Anthony Perkins in Alfred Hitchcock's seminal *Psycho* (1960). Unlike that shlock-influenced black comedy, however, *Brewster* does not perform double duty as a complex psychological character study.

The film is something simpler. For Altman, who had set such a precedent for virtuosity and bite with *M*A*S*H*, too simple: a counterculture revenge fantasy wherein abrasive American stereotypes—the corrupt cop, the shrewish, moralizing elder, the greedy, grumbling capitalist—are giddily gotten rid of. From a lesser talent, why not? But in 1970, from American cinema's new wunderkind? Both the critics and the public expected more, so much so that bird-brained Brewster ended up standing in for Altman himself: the colorful, left-leaning individualist with a penchant for virtuosity and violence brought crashingly to earth, exposed, in a public arena, as but an interesting-annoying failure.

If *M*A*S*H* constituted the back pages of the Screen Actors Guild's Who's Who, *McCloud* was cast from its footnotes. Altman needed the offbeat casting in the former to reflect the look and feel of the hippie generation; here, he's looking for the same unconventional quality for his heroes but just as much for his establishmentarian villains. The only member of the latter who hits the right note, however, is the most traditional looking: anonymously mannish Michael Murphy, whom Altman has good fun with as a parody of the stereotypically blue-eyed American hero.

And smoky-voiced Sally Kellerman, the hippie convert in *M*A*S*H*, appears again, this time with her clothes on, as a trench coat–clad mother-trickster guardian angel figure. It's a symbol Altman would employ again in his last film, the hit-and-miss *A Prairie Home Companion* (2006), as the prancing personification of the Beyond.

Altman then, with a single film, had gone from satire to silliness. It would relegate him to dreamy dramas for a while, until his funky comedy of manners *California Split* (1974), a woozily pleasant vacay from the dangerousness of his grander, showier instincts.

Catch-22

Plot: Anti-war satire in which a rattled World War II combat pilot tries desperately to leave his unit. **Director:** Mike Nichols. **Script:** Buck Henry, from the novel by Joseph Heller. **Cast:** Alan Arkin, Jon Voight, Bob Newhart, Orson Welles, Martin Balsam, Richard Benjamin, Peter Bonerz, Jack Gilford, Art Garfunkel, Buck Henry. Paramount. 122 minutes.

"It was very difficult," veteran screenwriter and cult comic Buck Henry admitted in Mike Sacks' *And Here's the Kicker*. "It doesn't have the same tone as the book; it has its own interesting kind of tone, which is surrealistic. The book isn't about surrealism. The book is a black comedy of another kind, but it was hard to figure out how to translate that."[1]

Many, in fact, before novelist Joseph Heller's bestselling black comedy hit the screen, had deemed the book unfilmable. But filmed *Catch-22*, by 1970, had to be; by then, the book was playing as the most popular commentary on the continuing mess that was Vietnam. Heller's episodic bestseller was a cautionary comedy about the plight of a respectable innocent—here a PTSD-afflicted World War II bomber pilot, Yossarian—whose impulses, in this case getting out of the Army, are thwarted by a subversively dysfunctional establishment aka the military-industrial complex. Who better to adapt such a property than Henry, master of black humor, and to film it than Mike Nichols, who, with *The Graduate* (1967), had proven the ultimate cinematic spokesperson for the book's narrative through-line?

In *The Graduate*, the bad guy was the WASPish, upper-middle bourgeoisie; in *Catch*, it's its fatigues-clad cousin, a military force headed by the war-mongering Nixon administration, busily (and tragically) chasing its tail at humanity's expense. The effect, however, is the same: a hapless hero ultimately martyred by a smug, bloated, self-absorbed culture, fueled by empty rituals and meaningless rewards. It conspires, by nature, to systematically diminish Yossarian's potential, intelligence and energy. And like Hoffman as the titular Graduate, the narrative's answer to this is to have Yossarian

---

1. Mike Sacks, "Buck Henry," *And Here's the Kicker: Conversations with 21 Top Humor Writers on Their Craft* (Cincinnati: F & W Media, 2010), Kindle, Location 273–274.

try and flee, an instinctual, ill-conceived form of transcendence. In the world of Mike Nichols, however, all running away can get you is a middlingly happy limbo state. In *The Graduate*, it's Hoffman and runaway bride Katharine Ross, the hard-breathing young lovers, at the back of the bus, with stultifying suburbia receding behind them; here, it's Alan Arkin as the AWOL Yossarian spread-eagle atop a raft, adrift in the vast Adriatic, free at last from the dictates of an unfeeling military. No one, not even Nichols, can offer a clue as to where any of these characters might end up. It's enough, though just, that they are free.

Yossarian, then, the cinematic edition, was yet another Graduate, unreasonably deemed dysfunctional by his oppressors for upsetting their precious social order. His kinship with the counterculture is reinforced by the pronouncement of the blustery Orson Welles, as the omnivorously officious General Dreedle, telling a defiantly naked Yossarian: "You're a very weird person." This from an authority as big as Welles served as the ultimate affirmation of the dividing line between the stuffy establishment and their looser, peace-loving offspring.

Yossarian's nakedness is yet another of the character's pleas to be deemed unfit for service, for banishment from the tribe. While his yellow streak, in the book, plays as a logical reaction to the mass manipulation that is the war effort, on screen, he's the continuation of a noble comic tradition: the cowardly, undersized, unwitting recruit, continually dwarfed by an immovably old-fashioned ideal of American manhood.

It's an archetype that harkens back to the days of the silents and that continued, just as successfully, all the way through the 1950s, with major comic personalities such as Bob Hope, Jerry Lewis and Danny Kaye assuming the mantle. As a result, on some level, *Catch-22* the film plays as but the next incarnation of the standard service comedy. It breaks with it, however, in the casting of Arkin, who would go on to be a comic screen stalwart throughout the '70s. The Hopes, the Lewises, the Kayes, while sufficiently challenged or threatened in their films, never yelled—other than the odd, infantile cry of pain or a prolonged monosyllabic plea for mercy. Arkin, on the other hand, vocally takes on his oppressors, externalizing his inner life to the point of pugnaciousness. It's the Jewish way ("Oy, am I thirsty!"), born of a life in the oppressed Eastern European shtetls where self-deprecation or communal dissent was the only style that was politically acceptable. Arkin was one of the first, on screen, to take the practice further, disrobing it from its veil of semi-secrecy to convert it to a battle cry, if a futile one.

Others, like Gene Wilder, would pick up on this style of rage until, collectively, it began to serve as comic man's primal scream against an unstoppable cosmic injustice, '70s-style.

That said, Nichols' *Catch-22* is no reduction of Heller's picaresque comic epic to populist, formulaic crowd-pleaser. The film demands a sense of structure above that offered by the book. European cinema, with its varied approach to narrative, may have been all the rage at the time, but it wouldn't have been enough to borrow that here. The service comedy had been such a venerable American tradition, it had instilled a deep, narrative expectation in American audiences, even in fans of Heller's book. This is a movie, they'd unconsciously cried, not a paperback; give us something simpler and more focused—but don't skimp on the intelligence nor the parts that we love. A tall task, to be sure. Kudos to screenwriter Henry who's mostly up to it, scoring particularly big on the last two fronts.

But Henry struggles, visibly, to provide a hero at once lovably familiar and contemporarily complex. Yossarian, yes, is Hope, is Lewis, is Kaye, but the running device of his unshakable, PTSD-instilling guilt over failing to aid a wounded young flyer on his first mission isn't enough to provide the latter. The on-screen Yossarian, then, is a dim echo of his predecessor, the Graduate.

Robbed of an all-pleasing character study as remedy for a cinematically unsteady narrative, we look to the original object of our anticipation: the grand metaphor for Vietnam. Could the narrative mess be standing in for the real-life mess? Hmmm … not quite. The biggest allusion to the Asian conflict is the bombing of the city of Ferrara, a killing for killing's sake, paralleling the tragically showy Mỹ Lai massacre. And the oppressive noise of the sound design, suggesting that Nichols had fallen too much in love with aircraft culture, can be assumed to be connotative—though it's hard to forgive the fact that it eats up a lot of the verbal humor.

But for all of this negativity—mine and, much more self-righteously, that of the critics of the day—the film, stripped of those expectations, is chockablock with comic highlights. They're Heller's, yes, but Henry has kept them, and Nichols has shaped them. In Heller's Marxian (as in Brothers) exchanges between ordinary, inquisitive soldiers and puffed-up, delusional bureaucrats, Nichols recognized a comic revue as good as any ever staged by the formative Second City. To wit, he gathered a veritable Who's Who of America's best comic actors and put up a clothesline of sharp, loopy two-handers *à la* Nichols and May. Some are literally Marxian (again as in Brothers), the faded 1930s and 1940s team which, at the time, was enjoying a cultural renaissance, their playful anarchy creating a spiritual kinship with the college protest movement. When Bob Newhart, as the memorably monikered Major Major Major Major, dons pith helmet and fake mustache to offer an idiosyncratic, bossy explanation of said disguise to lackey Norman Fell, it's hard not to note the allusion to Captain Spaulding of *Animal Crackers* (1930).

And *Catch-22* the film does have something to say, if not about Vietnam. Heller's book, printed in the early '60s, subscribes to a '50s mentality; its commentary on the labyrinthine character of bureaucracy appealed to veterans who had suffered it in the Army and were suffering it still postwar, behind the desks of the burgeoning, Brooks Brothers–wearing business world. But the film is more concerned about the inaccessibility of the American dream, and how it's reserved for a privileged few. It's a lot about dead ends, the bureaucratic and class (in this case, rank) barriers to the pursuit of life and liberty. Nichols, as an immigrant, could relate, as could, no doubt, screenwriter Henry (aka Zuckerman).

Again, it's the outlier, the Hoffman, looking to carve a happy sub-world within a larger, inaccessible one. And when these soldiers, led by Yossarian, can't, they go looney, as in the second half of the film, where it hits, both comedically and dramatically, its overdue stride. It becomes more concentrated and effective, building to a climax that ranks among the best work in Nichols' oeuvre: the long, slow, silent walk through the perfectly recreated streets of a shadowy Italian town, culminating in an event in turn surprising, humane and ironic (you'll get no spoilers from me).

Better films on the bungle that is high-level political bureaucracy had (*Dr. Strangelove*, 1964, *Hot Millions*, 1966) and would (*Brazil*, 1985, *Burn After Reading*, 2008) be made. And a better comic film about Vietnam, a European-influenced, multi-character, grand-scale pastiche with service comedy allusions, *was* being made: Robert Altman's *M*A*S*H*.

Cotton Comes to Harlem

Plot: Harlem detectives "Gravedigger" Jones and "Coffin Ed" Johnson chase down a corrupt spiritual leader. **Director:** Ossie Davis. **Script:** Ossie Davis, Arnold Perl. **Cast:** Godfrey Cambridge, Raymond St. Jacques, Calvin Lockhart, Redd Foxx. United Artists. 97 minutes.

If white urban angst enjoyed a comic voice, where was the one belonging to the even more beleaguered black community? Their anger, their issues, their prospective solutions had found a consistent showcase on the underground circuit. Low-budget, action-oriented, indigenous black films began to score big with their designated audience, spawning a genre labeled, largely due to their having white, money-hungry underwriters, "blaxploitation." Soon, dark-skinned vigilantes began to enact revenge, in martial arts–influenced, soul music–set slow motion, on their white oppressors and the misguided soul brothers in cahoots with them. These new heroes were takin' back the streets, one film at a time. Such would be the success of these films that the struggling mainstream studios would borrow their example as a means of financial rescue, starting with the sleeper-blockbuster *Shaft* (1971). And, once the genre began to integrate jokes, Hollywood would appropriate that too, financing a string of all-black ensemble comedies helmed by a surprise choice, the king of big-studio black gravitas, Sidney Poitier.

But the path to the Poitier films was *Cotton Comes to Harlem*, the first (and one of the only) blaxploitation comedies. It too was directed by a persona synonymous with sober integrity: character actor Ossie Davis. And like Poitier, Davis was out to expand his respective property's audience, with distinct designs to make the first black film for an integrated demographic.

Not that Davis had intentions of skimping on the conventions of the blaxploitation genre, from the cut of the characters and the nature of the narrative to the caliber of the production values. He wasn't out to mess with any of the mono-cultural questions either. Worried, perhaps, that he might be labeled a sell-out, Davis, in the film's first frames no less, adamantly affirms his identity and that of his primary viewership. The opening song is all about the question of being "black enough," a recurrent concern throughout the story.

And it demands to be re-posited, as the film's primary source of humor is a skewering of the major black movements and social remedies of the time. No faction is spared, from the overzealous militancy of the Black Panthers to the hyperbolic Back to Africa movement. Who else to expose the extremist or corrupt side of these self-promotional messiahs? Certainly not a white filmmaker, nor a talent as diplomatic as Poitier.

If these movements are lampooned, it is as part of a worthy and much-needed search—specifically, for exemplary black role models in a post–MLK-Garvey-Malcolm X universe. All the good ones, or at least diligently concerned ones, are gone. What remains, the film attests, are two-faced pastors and self-serving charlatans. The plot revolves around a smooth-talking preacher's secret skiving and his exposition at the hands of a diligent cop duo, admirably played by Godfrey Cambridge and Raymond St. Jacques. They are hard-working stiffs, out to raise the image of their race through professionalism, decency and self-possession. (As they put it, their mission is to "protect the black folk from themselves.") The film asks black culture to engineer its own functionality and dignity—qualities Davis and, on bigger screens, Poitier proudly promoted as actors.

Sounds good, right? It should have been. But Davis' eye on having a crossover hit compromises the film's socio-political integrity, not to mention its entertainment value. Davis was not a renaissance talent. Here, when he tries to do all things for all people, he seriously detracts from what he does best: drama—though it should be noted that he's a surprisingly respectable director of action; see the shoot-out in the junkyard. But as the tired, obtrusive sight gags demonstrate, Davis had no talent for broad comedy.

And there isn't much of the verbal variety either, leading us to suspect that he might have mistaken the comically physical for the exclusively universal.

But award him full marks for the one comedy bit that does click: the climactic striptease with the film's MacGuffin, a bail of cotton, parodying Deep South clichés. The film's only truly original sequence, it achieves, for a single moment, the tone the whole thing should have had.

That said, a pair of comic talents rise high above the lowly material, the testament being the bigger comic vehicles they would earn as a result: chitlin' circuit stand-up Redd Foxx, who, although he didn't know it, was auditioning here for the hit sit-com *Sanford and Son* (1972–77), with his portrayal of a chummy junk dealer, and the slyly energetic, perpetually underrated Cleavon Little, who would go on to usurp the higher-profile Richard Pryor as the lead in the decade's biggest and still most respected (discounting *Annie Hall*, 1977) comedy, *Blazing Saddles* (1974).

As for the film itself, its best legacy is as the opening salvo in a cannonade of commercially successful black screen comedies, from the aforementioned Poitier films to unheralded gems such as *The Bingo Long Traveling All-Stars & Motor Kings* and the blackified stage play *Norman, Is That You?* (both 1976). It may also have played a hand in the development of the black sitcom, having proven, financially, a Caucasian appetite for the concerns of an alternative culture.

Hi, Mom!

Plot: A Vietnam veteran moves into an apartment and plays Peeping Tom. **Director:** Brian De Palma. **Script:** Brian De Palma, Charles Hirsch. **Cast:** Robert De Niro, Allen Garfield, Jennifer Salt, Paul Bartel. West End Films. 87 minutes.

Before he found his niche as a Hitchcock-influenced horror king, Brian De Palma was slumming as a cheeky social satirist with an experimental instinct. Dark comedy would remain a part of his game, but over his hungry years, it was his primary mode of cinematic expression.

On an extremely low budget, young De Palma produced his own form of coming-of-age film, the sardonically titled *Hi, Mom!* (The "coming of age" genre, especially after the success of Britain's "angry young man" movement and the surprise success of 1967's *The Graduate*, resonated deeply with De Palma's generation. See Francis Ford Coppola's *You're a Big Boy Now*, 1966, and George Lucas' *American Graffiti*, 1973.)

Borrowing from Hitchcock—soon a trademark habit—De Palma situates his enterprising young hero in a discount New York apartment, from where he secretly films, *à la Rear Window* (1954), a kooky collection of 1970s cultural stereotypes: a pair of sexually liberated young women, some scheming revolutionaries, and an all–American family of squares. Each subject's actions are speeded up, silent movie style, for comedic enhancement (it sorta works). The hero's hope is to sell the juicier moments to a sleaze-bag porno king, played with ad-lib zeal by Allen Garfield, one of the busiest character actors of the decade. (Another one, Charles Durning, makes his cinematic debut in the film's opening moments.)

The film is about the tricky line between voyeurism and involvement, between passivity and activity, between apathy and morality—a common theme with the burgeoning Baby Boomers, weaned on JFK conspiracy theories, the backroom politics of Johnson and Nixon, and the influence of films like *Blow Up* (1966), a De Palma fave re-imagined later as his underrated *Blow Out* (1981). Mostly, though, it's a comedy about a failure to get with the times.

The busybody-dreamer mans his camera and sometimes falls asleep at it, only to imagine himself inside the life of one of his subjects—a nod to Buster Keaton's *The Cameraman* (1928). After he incompetently blows his chance to crack the then-booming porn industry, he participates in an interesting, if overlong, immersive theater production, in which the black militants and their young white supporters paint middle-class patrons in shoe polish and subject them to attempted rape and police brutality, so that they may suffer the urban black experience firsthand. (This culminates in the film's one true comic highlight: After this black and white, literally and figuratively, horror fest, the patrons all offer enthusiastic testimonials about the production.) Later still, after pseudo-settling down with his dream girl (met through spying), our hero tries his hand at guerrilla warfare, with mixed results.

This kind of elusive, complex male persona had been at work since the mid–1950s with the mold-breaking presences of Brando and Dean and had continued, in Anglicized form, through the Finneys and the McDowells. Now, in the early 1970s, it was taking on even stranger dimensions. More and more, thanks to films like *Hi, Mom!*, even the hippest of audiences were asking themselves: So, is the anti-hero still a hero?

This puzzlingly dimensional spokesperson for the malaise of the times—in *Hi, Mom!*, his actions are specifically attributed to urban decay, the porous social safety net, and the polarization over Vietnam—would become synonymous with a single actor, who gets the ball rolling here: a skinny, flop-haired Robert De Niro. While De Niro would soon solidify this on-screen identity in Scorsese's *Taxi Driver* (1976) and then, for the next four-plus decades, in a thick catalogue of gritty dramas, *Hi, Mom!* is, unfortunately, a comedy. De Niro was right to go the other way. Asked repeatedly here to carry scenes, he comes up painfully short, exhibiting little of the self-defeating neurosis and subversive hubris required, qualities a Charles Grodin could have provided with aplomb. (De Niro earned his comic stripes much later in his career, with 1999's *Analyze This*.)

Why, then, was De Niro cast? Perhaps for the odd exhibitions of raw rage his character is asked to display, like when he plays a racist cop in the militant theater piece. In a film about windows, it's the only window we have, years on, that proves interesting: a look at a seminal American actor in his professional infancy.

The Landlord

Plot: The son of a well-to-do family buys an inner-city (Brooklyn) tenement, only to become a champion for his low-income African American residents. **Director:** Hal

Ashby. **Script:** Bill Gunn, from the novel by Kristin Hunter. **Cast:** Beau Bridges, Lee Grant, Diana Sands, Pearl Bailey. United Artists. 113 minutes.

While it can only boast of a cult reputation, *The Landlord* remains the best film made on American race relations until Spike Lee's *Do the Right Thing* (1989). White talent may have been behind the film but like the same-year releases *Cotton* Comes *to Harlem* and *Watermelon Man*, *The Landlord* chased that two-toned Holy Grail: the first bi-racial box office success (even though it was primarily marketed as a blaxploitation film). Its deceiving slogan: "Watch the landlord get his."

It didn't achieve it; financially, the film flopped. Artistically, it suffers from a glaring unevenness. But what it did achieve is an impressively realistic portrayal of the sorrows and celebrations of urban black life, an earnest pronouncement on the inherently messy matter of reconciliation, and a handful of ambitiously artsy touches that help the material rise above the pugnacious or the polemic.

It must be remembered that this culture-clash comedy was made when the assassination of Martin Luther King Jr. was a fresh societal wound. Looking to heal the still-smoking racial divide, director Norman Jewison—an old hand at this collision-of-two-worlds thing, from *The Russians Are Coming! The Russians Are Coming!* (1966) to *In the Heat of the Night* (1967)—entrusted Bill Gunn's script, based on a 1966 novel, to the direction of Hal Ashby, the loose-cannon editor who had served Jewison so admirably.

Ashby, a convert to the counterculture and, *inter alia*, the black power struggle, recognized in the narrative an opportunity not just to send up a new American stereotype, the bleeding heart liberal, and to honor the script's wonky solution to the race problem but, with all his cinematic savvy, to seriously delve black culture: its vibe, verve and vulnerability.

Beau Bridges, playing the same shy rube roles as his brother Jeff at that time, is the poshly baptized Elgar Enders, a white-suited black sheep out to separate from his oppressively connected family by gentrifying an ailing brownstone in Brooklyn's Park Slope, then a predominantly black area. Elgar gets off on the wrong foot when the residents, looking to scare him off, play up on their stereotyped images, realizing, with giddy irony, that there's power over the white man in the images he has assigned them. Through Elgar, then, white America is shockingly immersed in the urban reality of black existence. Further, this puts the hero in a tug of war between two sets of freaks: the rich white eccentrics (they stage a costume ball where guests dress as iconic American figures) and the impoverished black militants.

Each culture is rendered in a distinct style: the whites, pure lampoon; the blacks, hip realism. And while it makes for a schizophrenic affair, the approach succeeds in exposing the true character of each subset, the whites naïve neurotics, the blacks earthy humanists. It's a distinction played up in other ways too—namely, the periodic, European-influenced moments of artistic high contrast interpolated throughout the film. The best of these, arguably, is a scene of interracial tenderness composed of black-white close-ups of intertwining body parts.

They're not Ashby's sole showy moments. Demonstrating that he still has his editing chops (he co-edited here), there's a smartly written rant conveyed through an impressive parade of cross-cut close-ups, ultimately positing Bridges against a white backdrop, like a man before a firing squad, as he's taken, metaphorically, to task for the white man's sins. Later in this sequence, Elgar, freed from the house party at which these arrows were slung, will throw up; the hangover as divine comeuppance.

The film's two major visual compartments preview the more celebrated work of cinematographer Gordon Willis, who went on to the dark tones of the *Godfather* films (1972, 1974, 1990) and the sun-dappled, brownstone-lined world of Woody Allen's relationship films. (A great cinematographer-to-be, Michael Chapman, helps out.) Boosting the film's duo culture is cult rocker Al Kooper, whose funk-blues soundtrack, aided by the irrepressibly spirited Staples Singers, brings additional life to the proceedings.

Though *The Landlord* contains many of the elements Ashby would later refine for his more focused *Harold and Maude* (1971)—the upper-crust white milieu, the eccentric, distant mother (Lee Grant here, too young for the part but at her energetic best), the buffoonishly hawkish father figure, the absurdist background business—it stands taller than *Maude* both ideologically and dramatically. As testament to the latter, there's the film's engrossingly volatile third act, focused on a sincere transgression with violent implications—further proof of the film's contention that America's melting pot will forever remain at a boil.

Little Big Man

Plot: Jack Crabb, the 121-year-old sole survivor of the Battle of the Little Big Horn, recounts his picaresque adventures as the product of two cultures, the white man and the Cheyenne. **Director:** Arthur Penn. **Script:** Calder Willingham, from the novel by Thomas Berger. **Cast:** Dustin Hoffman, Chief Dan George, Martin Balsam, Faye Dunaway, Richard Mulligan. Cinema Center Films. 147 minutes (uncut version).

Two instant classics were spawned in 1970: *M*A*S*H* and *Little Big Man*.

Both are anti-war films with large, quirky casts, deftly mixing satire and violence. But while the former singularly reflected, through the guise of the Korean conflict, Vietnam, the latter did the same through the veneer of the Western.

M*A*S*H eluded criticism for its semi-hidden ideological agenda; *Little Big Man*, conversely, did not. Perhaps Robert Altman's film was the more excused because his soldiers were still in fatigues. Put them in cowboy hats, and something more sacred and iconic appeared to be at stake.

That said, even the progressive critics took issue with *Little Big Man*'s metaphorical intention, citing the Asian look of the on-screen Cheyenne and the chilling reality of their slaughter. It spoiled, they collectively contended, much of the fun. Today, thanks to the erosion of cultural context afforded by the passing of time, the literary elite have been granted their wish. Separated from the sentiment of the day, the film stands on its own comic, dramatic and technical terms.

At once, *Little Big Man* is a hip, sweeping epic, a fun and fascinating character study, and a three-hour class in character acting. Given its picaresque exoskeleton—the roving reminiscences of 121-year-old Little Big Horn survivor Jack Crabb, told in stream-of-consciousness flashbacks—it's almost a whole cloth, yet another notoriously messy Arthur Penn production made uniform by faithful editor Dede Allen (who had also rescued Penn's *Bonnie and Clyde*, 1967).

Not that *Little Big Man*'s first political agenda, the one that still plays today, isn't in evidence. From the get-go, the film sets out to humanize what had long been a Hollywood stereotype. The film's Cheyennes, with whom Crabb, a man caught between two cultures, spends half his time, call themselves "human beings," an appellation emphatically endorsed by Penn.

Their portrayal, to a person, is realistic and reverent, a stark contrast to the exaggerated, loose portrayal of cowboy culture—Crabb's other world—composed largely of exacerbations of Western stereotypes: the medicine man, the schoolmarm, the preacher, the gunslinger *et al.* It's an ideological war of the worlds: the touchy-feely Indians vs. the self-serving cowpokes. As in so much of 1970s film comedy, it's the hip vs. the square, only here, the hip doesn't triumph. Penn's heroes, perpetually, are punished for taking a constructive interest in the oppressed, the way Bonnie and Clyde let that poor sharecropper and his black farmhand put a few rounds into the house the bank had repossessed before the establishment, in turn, put a few rounds (well, more than a few) into Bonnie and Clyde.

And again, as in *Bonnie and Clyde*, Penn puts a constructive premium on violence, making it, at least at first, at once funny and grisly—an ethos it shared with co-classic *M*A*S*H* which also set out, in its O.R. scenes, to remind us of bloodshed's simultaneous absurdity and reality.

As for the aforementioned cast. Dustin Hoffman's inherent incongruity, which he had to work against all film long in *The Graduate* (1967), fits here like a buckskin glove. Why wouldn't it? Crabb is a man who belongs to no culture, who lives in his own bewildered limbo. Who better than a versatile talent not handsome enough to be a traditional leading man (particularly in a "tall in the saddle" Western) nor cartoonish enough to be a supporting actor? He fares resonantly as both the half-cowboy and the half–Indian.

Further, he impressively distinguishes himself as Crabb the elder, in makeup that makes him look like a pontificating dumpling. *You* try emoting through that restrictive goop!

The rest of the cast is just as good, if not better: Jeff Corey, Martin Balsam and in particular, Robert Mulligan, about to become a mainstay in Blake Edwards' comedies. His Custer, in the climactic Little Big Horn battle, is the thinnest, cruelest of the caricatures the film offers and yet his manic simpleton becomes fixed in your mind. If he's restricted to psychotic buffoonery, it's no doubt because this Custer is Nixon in a cowboy hat, Custer's misguided tactical decision a clear parody of the president's plans of attack.

Penn has visual fun with it too, parodying Custer's saintly historical reputation by gracing him with an overdone visual effect standing in for a halo. Interestingly, a dramatic release that year would best this film for the presentation of Best Killer Clown: Franklin J. Schaffner's *Patton,* which brilliantly succeeded in both lionizing and lampooning its eponymous warmonger.

Just as commendable is the hypnotically even-tempered performance of Chief Dan George as Crabb's Yoda, his life coach–grandfather. Had George justly won the Supporting Actor Oscar for which he was nominated, one wonders if it would have negated the controversial industry snub engineered a few years later by Marlon Brando, in protest of Hollywood's perpetual portrayal of the American Indian.

I'd be seriously remiss if I didn't add the delicious touch offered by the dangerously playful Faye Dunaway, who, from her Bonnie forward, made a career of playing shallow, sexy bad girls. It's well-placed here, creating a funny dynamic: The film's women all subscribe to the new, looser sexual morals at work in 1970 America while straightjacketed in Puritan garb.

It's a testament to each of these actors, and Penn's legendary facility with them, that in all cases, they're caricatures but they're not. Why is that? Because together, Penn and his actors worked cleverly and hard to let us see, in the case of each character, the pain of their respective folly.

The ending: This being a 1970s film, we again come to the idea of transcendence. Here, in Calder Willingham's witty adaptation of the Thomas Berger novel, we get the best comic commentary to date on that notion: all-knowing Dan George lying down and preparing to die. Instead of his soul rising to the heavens, the heavens come down on him … in the form of rain. George, resigned, simply says, "Well, sometimes the magic works … sometimes it doesn't." A comic Carlos Castaneda.

Crabb, then, is left with but his two earthly factions. The war, inner and outer, will go on.

Lovers and Other Strangers

Plot: Cross-generational look at the validity of marriage through the lives of six different couples. **Director:** Cy Howard. **Script:** Joseph Bologna, David Zelag Goodman, Renée Taylor, based on the play by Bologna and Taylor. **Cast:** Michael Brandon, Bonnie Bedelia, Bea Arthur, Richard Castellano, Gig Young, Anne Jackson, Anne Meara, Harry Guardino, Bob Dishy, Marianne Haley. ABC Pictures. 104 minutes.

The battle of the sexes. It was an oft-used phrase in 1970, describing the war between patriarchy and feminism. Like all wars, there were casualties: The divorce rate soared, the marriage rate declined, and many a couple entertained questions a lot deeper than "And do you…?"

That nerve-wracking limbo state, questioning the validity of marital vows in an age of sexual upset, dominated much of the male-female dynamic of 1970s comic cinema. On-screen, long-standing couples found themselves re-examining their relationship, middle-aged men tried to stage affairs, and pairs of young lovers feared jeopardizing what they shared by making it official. The latter would look at their parents, their extended families, their parents' friends, even some of their own friends and fret. Too many of those relationships, if you examined them closely, were strictly products of social convention. Monogamy, the argument went, meant misery—but so, a little too often, did any of the alternatives. What were two people in love supposed to do?

Lovers and Other Strangers was adapted from an autobiographical play by the husband-and-wife acting team of Joe Bologna and Renée Taylor, both of whom went on to become busy big- and small-screen character actors. Who can forget the pugnacious Bologna's pseudo–Sid Caesar in *My Favorite Year* (1982)?

The circumstances surrounding their 1965 marriage, they realized, contained all the clashes then at large, from the roles of men and women and the ideological divide between the generations, to contrasts of class and ethnicity. And so, they dramatized it as, largely, a series of one-act plays within a larger framework.

Standing in for Bologna-Taylor are the charming Michael Brandon and Bonnie Bedelia, who find themselves on opposite sides of the marriage fence a mere three days before their wedding. They're the center of a storm raging over the integrity of sanctioned coupledom, as relatives and acquaintances alike weigh in while struggling within their pro or con stances.

As writers, Bologna and Taylor demonstrate an instinctive talent for the self-righteous logic, volatile music and deep-seated desperation of each of their characters. To their additional credit, they rarely, unlike others working in relationship comedy at the time, resort to one-liners for laughs and sentimentality for depth. These lovers and strangers are not witty, self-aware types; they're base and blind, spouting tired bromides in distinctive voices and eliciting pathos only when they're brought to recognize the flaws in their convictions.

It takes two things to rise to this caliber of talky, funny, performance-based material: a great ensemble and a director with serious stage chops. The former is in place and then some. The cast is a mix of some of the top character actors of the '70s (Richard Castellano, Bob Dishy, Anne Meara and a surprisingly hefty Bea Arthur), some old reliables having a great time (Gig Young and Anne Jackson), and a handful of notable newcomers (including Diane Keaton in her inaugural film).

The director is Cy Howard—no Broadway baby, surprisingly, but an old radio hand. (He also enjoyed middling success in B movies and TV.) Semi-retired at the time, he proves here, in his only film, that he retained a finely tuned ear for comic rhythms and a still robust facility for getting the best out of its practitioners.

The film enjoyed wide appeal back in the day, reflecting as it did the crazy-funny sexual zeitgeist by showing all sides. If it's forgotten today, it's no doubt due to that exact distinction. Products of their time, unless they're absolute classics, rarely last the ages.

As for Bologna and Taylor, they wrote one more autobiographical property (*Made for Each Other*, 1971), then called it quits as chroniclers of their relationship, which went on to last 50-plus years. That's right: Those who so questioned the institution of marriage ended up staying together for over half a century.

*M*A*S*H*

Plot: Black comedy about a manic medical unit during the Korean War. **Director:** Robert Altman. **Script:** Ring Lardner Jr., from the novel by Richard Hooker. **Cast:** Donald Sutherland, Elliott Gould, Sally Kellerman, Robert Duvall, Roger Bowen, Gary Burghoff. 20th Century–Fox. 116 minutes.

"'Altman loved organized chaos,' said Feiffer. 'That's what he was comfortable in.'" So pronounced the famed illustrator-humorist (first name Jules) in Dave Itzkoff's thorough biography of Robin Williams,[2] the comic whose ADD-style should have been in perfect sync with loosey-goosey director Robert Altman's. The failure of the Altman-Feiffer-Williams collaboration *Popeye* (1980), though, marked the end of Altman's heyday, forcing the director to prove himself as a strict adherer to script (mostly plays, if the offbeat variety) until he learned to split the difference and enjoy a second coming in the early 1990s.

For the best description of Altman's signature style, I offer another literary voice,

---

2. Dave Itzkoff, *Robin* (New York: Henry Holt, 2018), 140.

offering another literary voice: Jonathan Lethem in his *More Alive and Less Lonely*: "Dickens works to keep us aware of the variety he's met in the streets, and of the possibility that, if his eye happened to settle elsewhere, in place of the story underway we'd find another story going on. These methods anticipate film: the distended ensembles of Robert Altman."[3]

Altman had been a TV hack. In time, he grew constricted by the limited visual vocabulary of the form—wide shot, two-shot, close-up, over the shoulder—and its equally perfunctory approach to sound. When prospected as a last-minute choice for *M*A*S*H*, an episodic, slightly sexualized run-of-the-mill service comedy, Altman unleashed his inner hipster and went for broke, approaching it like it was the last job he might ever have. It almost *was*, as the cast, unaccustomed to both his cinematic and personal self-indulgences, conspired to have him fired.

When they saw the final product, however, they, like most of hip America, got it. Collectively, they realized that Altman was the first American director to successfully appropriate European filmmaking techniques to fashion something distinctly homegrown: an X-ray of contemporary USA.

For all of the film's reputation as the ultimate anti–Vietnam commentary, that conflict is metaphorically touched upon on only a handful of occasions: the introductory sequence in which helicopters deliver the wounded to the doleful "Suicide Is Painless," clearly labeling the war a suicide mission; bit player Bobby Troup's repeated expletive "Goddamn Army!"; and of course, the no-holds-barred operating room carnage, adding a shocking layer of realism to on-screen violence, hitherto bafflingly benign.

What *M*A*S*H* was, was a coming-out party for the new generational mores: explicit sex, drugs, long hair, disrespect for authority and, above all, an all-pervading camaraderie, echoing the bond of the then-burgeoning Baby Boomers.

Further reflecting this new, all-out universe is the film's style, with its non-stop crosscuts, overlapping dialogue and improvisational predisposition, the latter rooted, like Mike Nichols' work, in the legacy of Second City (to which the casting of that Chicago troupe's Roger Bowen, as the lax commanding officer Henry Blake, attests). Critic David Thomson this time, on Altman: "Altman seems less interested in structure than in atmosphere; scheme and character recede as chronic, garrulous discontinuity holds sway. ...[There's a sense] of people being like atoms whirling around to laws no one knows and thus part of a kind of play or hopeful gambling."[4] Such is the mania that the film's only plot consists of a systematic, prankish assault on its two establishmentarians: the all–Army Major Burns and his non-nonsense mistress Major Houlihan, until they're either removed (Burns) or converted (Houlihan).

And again, as in so much of '70s cinema, the influence of the resurgent Marx Brothers is there: Stars Elliott Gould and Donald Sutherland, as the film's primo pranksters, are made to look like a hippie-fied Groucho and Harpo. Further, their forced entry into a buttoned-down Korean hospital unabashedly references their comic forebears, echoing the Marxes' trademark habit of upsetting stodgy settings from dinner parties to opera houses. Then, there's *M*A*S*H*'s climactic football game, a remake, if you will, of the conclusion of *Horse Feathers* (1932).

Sports, as a whole—*M*A*S*H* also offers a golf sequence—plays a telling role in the

---

3. Jonathan Lethem, *More Alive and Less Lonely* (New York: Melville House, 2018), 33.

4. David Thomson, *The New Biographical Dictionary of Film Updated and Expanded* (New York: Alfred A. Knopf, 2010), 13–15.

film, representing an old-fashioned, all–American spirit ripe for the comic taking. It plays with humorous incongruity and may have set the tone for the same kind of pastime-based surrealism—in this case, surfing—that resurfaced later in the decade's best dramatic take on Vietnam, Francis Ford Coppola's darkly woozy *Apocalypse Now* (1979).

Back to *M*A*S*H* and its precedent-setting casting: Gould, Sutherland, those Second City refugees. With the star billing of the first two, the "weird kid" would become, industry-wide, the lead. Following the precedent set by Mike Nichols when he cast Dustin Hoffman in *The Graduate* (1967), *M*A*S*H* was almost singularly responsible for creating a new kind of celebrity, aided by the economic fall of the major studios which, for decades, had fed audiences the beautiful and the bland. For sure, the '70s would still have its male sex symbols—Redford, Reynolds, Caan, etc.—but now, shaggy hair, unconventional builds, bad postures, bulbous noses, quirky voices and buck teeth need apply. What had hitherto been deemed a freak show was now a star system.

And Altman, more than any other American director, was responsible for its perpetuation, continuously affording audiences like-it-or-not close-ups of Diane Arbus–worthy subjects like duck-faced Shelley Duvall and lantern-jawed John Schuck. At first, critics assumed this offbeat casting had been committed merely to reflect an offbeat war. But with Altman's repeat of the practice in subsequent films and its spill-over effect into those made by others, audiences were soon shelling out just as often to see Walter Matthau or Gene Hackman as they were Clint Eastwood or Paul Newman. Further, it helped to bring other directors into the comic film fold who had been doing the same in smaller arenas (for example, the underrated Howard Zieff, king of the quirky, personality-based TV commercial).

For now, though, it played as just one of many highly original, distinctly Altmanian touches, succeeding in winning him the critical crown of America's boldest, hippest, most cinematically savvy filmmaker. Of particular distinction was his approach to sound, the most innovative since that of another multi-talent, the radio-savvy Orson Welles. Hitherto, in comedy, sound had to be clean, if only to hear the jokes; here, you catch them as would a fly on the wall. Altman throws them away and in so doing, affords them new emphasis. He's the Phil Spector of screen sound, adding layer upon layer until the depth's the thing.

Unlike a lot of entries from that decade, much of *M*A*S*H* holds up admirably. That said, too much of it plays misogynistically. With the ethos of "free love" all but a memory, scenes such as the famed placing of the microphone under the Burns-Houlihan bed play as infantile male pranksterism, worthier of a film like *Porky's* (1981) than the work of a major American cineaste. Sexual humiliation is the film's primary weapon, with many a nurse—including, famously, Houlihan—pushily embarrassed at collective male behest.

It should be remembered that sex back then was a new societal, and therefore on-screen, plaything, regardless of how represented. It was enough that somebody was doing something with it, even if it favored one gender over another. Such was the premium on this one-time taboo that it's seen, in *M*A*S*H*, as salvific: When the camp dentist, Painless Potter, decides to end it all, it's the act of sex that brings him back to life.

Altman continued to apply his wild party/love-in/jam session style, sometimes brilliantly, sometimes disastrously—but never better than here, when he invents it. By the second half of the decade, his improvisational virtuosity started to fail to play, no longer serving as a mirror of the times as, post–Vietnam, the state of the nation become less fractured.

Altman spent the rest of the decade examining the war at home, skewing such Republican strongholds as Houston and, most famously, Nashville. But, thanks to him, anything could be cinematically skewered now, by anyone, anyhow.

The Out-of-Towners

Plot: An Ohio businessman and his wife come to New York and suffer every indignity the city has to offer. **Director:** Arthur Hiller. **Script:** Neil Simon. **Cast:** Jack Lemmon, Sandy Dennis. Paramount. 98 minutes.

By the 1970s, New York, America's shining urban jewel, was as desecrated as its iconic Statue of Liberty, then begging for a serious makeover. (It eventually got it, through the cause marketing of American Express.) The rampant crime committed by a disgruntled generation, the economic devastation inflicted by the costly war in Asia, a series of crippling labor strikes, and volatile, unsolvable racial tensions conspired to make New York City, literally, the most dangerous city in the world. No one suffered these slings and arrows more than the born-and-bred New Yorker, eyewitness to the widespread desecration of their nest. Once America's quintessential urbanites, New Yorkers found themselves pitied, mocked or both. After all, they could no longer walk their streets, ride their subways or frequent their haunts; their entire infrastructure had grown hazardous.

Here's playwright-screenwriter Neil Simon, from the first installment of his autobiography, reflecting on those years:

> By the early seventies, the innocence of New York had vanished. The drugs were now being used by the people who could least afford them, but who found their own ways of how to buy them.
> There were brazen daylight robberies of stores on chic Madison Avenue and killings that became a way of life from the West Bronx to any poorly lit neighborhood in the five boroughs. The news of crime now dominated our lives, with five-inch headlines in the *Daily News* and the *New York Post*. We doubled and tripled our locks, and Central Park became lost to us once the sun went down.
> If a child was ten minutes late arriving home, parents became frantic. Yankee Stadium was not where you'd want to be twenty minutes after a night game ended … cab drivers were being killed daily. It was not London during the blitz, but for an old woman walking home from the supermarket with her cart of food at 9 p.m., it might as well have been a war zone.[5]

In time, the city would be miraculously reborn; in 1970, the mere suggestion of such a possibility would have drawn deafening derisive laughter.

One native, more fed up than most, was inspired to divert from the opposites-attract formula that was fast making him a Broadway staple to try his hand, uncharacteristically, at social commentary. He was not as predisposed to it as his more intellectual stage and screen contemporaries—Jules Feiffer, Buck Henry *et al.*—sharing a TV pedigree as he did with Mel Brooks (an old collaborator and friend) and Bill Manhoff. Still, he had had enough. Uncertain as to how to paint this pitfall-strewn, angst-inducing urban landscape on the stage (he'd figure it out eventually, with *The Prisoner of Second*

---

5. Neil Simon, *Memoirs* (New York: Simon & Schuster, 1996), 257.

Avenue), the aforementioned Neil Simon, leading wit of the Great White Way, would instead bring his spirited dispiritedness to the big screen.

Again, our eyes are fixed on comedy's preferred type, the fish out of water: Jack Lemmon (fish), a good-hearted middle manager from Twin Oaks, Ohio, is lured to a job interview in New York (water). Along the way, he and wife Sandy Dennis endure every indignity the Big Rotten Apple has to offer. To wit: a re-routed flight, lost luggage, an overcrowded train, a city-wide transit strike, a canceled hotel reservation, a gunman, a carjacking, a dog attack, a false accusation, loss of property, physical assault, tinnitus, political protest and a skyjacking. So stacked is the shit sandwich, it prompts a fed-up Lemmon, in the middle of 65th Street, to yell: "Ya hear that, New York? We don't quit!" adding, "Persons are stronger than cities!"

But are they? According to the film, man is born free—free to travel, free to pursue economic opportunity, free to enjoy himself—and yet everywhere, he is in chains: flights forced to circle, hotels that won't hold reservations, streets that aren't fit to walk. In this, *The Out-of-Towners* sets the scene for a smaller, more popular kvetch-fest, TV's *Seinfeld* (1989–98), with its perpetual frustration over man's inability to control the most minute mechanics of the world he has so obliviously wrought.

In the comedy writing racket, there's an axiom as old as a pie in the face: Think Yiddish, write British. Here, Simon does just that, assigning the whining, worrying and wigging out worthy of an Alan Arkin to Lemmon, who translates it into perfect

Sandy Dennis and Jack Lemmon in *The Out-of-Towners* (Paramount, 1970). Early 1970s comedy was urban, neurotic and New York–based, with beleaguered middle-aged heroes reacting to the weight of a crumbling world (Paramount Pictures/Photofest).

WASPese. It's a facility the always willing Lemmon demonstrates with ease, his sweetly befuddled, slightly stammering style perfectly suited to its fluctuating rhythms.

According to the first volume of Simon's autobiography *Memoirs, The Out of Towners* was the first and only property that he ever wrote for a specific actor. No doubt he recognized in Lemmon's nervy style a more popular version of the Jewish verbal music by which he, Simon, had made his name. One has to think that this notion also extended to the eventual casting of Sandy Dennis, whose sweetly whiny style feminizes same. Lemmon and Dennis both look like out-of-towners, which is what the author wanted, but sound like lifelong citizens of Simonland.

And indeed, Lemmon's appearance in this, and in other Simon-penned properties (see *The Prisoner of Second Avenue*, 1975), helped to bring the Simon style to a wider audience, converting it from a tribal patois to the battle cry of the everyman. While Lemmon had demonstrated it, a bit, in Simon's *The Odd Couple* (1968), the bulk of it in that two-hander went to co-star Walter Matthau. Here it's all Lemmon's, with wife Dennis playing, largely, post-nasal Greek chorus. It also firmly cemented Lemmon in a carapace he had been wearing, on and off, for some time, that of the yakky, white-collar malcontent.

Lemmon would play it in both drama (most famously *Save the Tiger*, 1973, and *Missing*, 1984) and comedy (too many to mention) for the rest of his career, the sweetly sour, seriocomic Willy Loman, poster boy for a fallen generation of decent, hard-working, middle-class American businessmen. That said, he gives a tremendously energetic performance here, burning off the last drops of high-octane pluck from his early days as America's best light comedian.

The trick with Simon, which the famed playwright never fully learned, was the creation of the proper context for his non-stop one-liners and two-liners. *The Out of Towners* is one of two such properties (*The Sunshine Boys*, 1975, is the other) that qualify as properly framed. Sarcasm is what people come to when they are forced by particularly pushy circumstances—and *The Out of Towners* is all reaction (that and tracking shots, with Lemmon-Dennis perpetually running after trains and buses or away from thugs and dogs). It's what makes this most unpleasant visit to America's urban metaphor for national insanity a mostly enjoyable 97-minute excursion.

The Owl and the Pussycat

Plot: An uptight writer is coerced into living with a dysfunctional free spirit. **Director:** Herbert Ross. **Script:** Buck Henry, from a play by Bill Manhoff. **Cast:** Barbra Streisand, George Segal. Columbia Pictures. 95 minutes.

TV veteran Bill Manhoff's play *The Owl and the Pussycat* was produced in 1964. The odd coupling of an uptight, aspiring novelist and a loose-mouthed hooker with farcical acting ambitions (played on stage, interestingly, by an African American, an early example of color-blind casting) played on the carnal paranoia of the times, born of America's unease with the unstoppable growth of sexual liberation.

It subscribes to the classic two-hander formula familiar to those, like Manhoff, who had toiled in sketch comedy and sitcom: opposites forced into uneasy co-existence, negotiating their mile-wide differences through scattershot wisecracks.

Thanks to Manhoff and even more successful practitioners of the formula, like Neil Simon, this dynamic endured, on stage and in film, for a decade. Its popularity was, of course, testament to the prodigious joke-writing ability of those who subscribed to it. In addition, though, as the '60s and '70s progressed, it came to exclusively and resonantly represent, as it does in *Pussycat*, the battle of the Old World vs. the New. This becomes the leading narrative of early '70s film comedy: the conversion, witticism by witticism, of the unsuspecting square by the interloping hipster, from the art house hit *Harold and Maude* (1971) through to mainstream releases like *The Goodbye Girl* (1977). When Doris, the Pussycat, finally succeeds in seducing Felix, the Owl, modern mores triumph.

The characters, given the cloth from which they're cut, aren't much more than stereotypes. As such, each of the main actors—George Segal (Owl) and Barbra Streisand (Pussycat)—has to visibly rein in their natural intelligence. Still, it's evident that nevertheless, they're having a ball. Segal looks happy to be playing outside his Jewish everyman persona and Streisand is out to show another major side of herself. After having cracked the theatrical and cinematic mainstreams despite her type-defying looks, here she's on a new mission: to be the world's first bona fide Jewish sex symbol—and she pulls it off with aplomb, reinventing herself with raunchy relish. It was the first in a string of memorable, diverse performances—while yes, all relying here and there on ingratiating tricks—that would mark her, inarguably, as the leading comic actress of the '70s, not to mention the genre's premier feminist spokesperson.

Much of the credit for the on-screen chemistry belongs to director Herbert Ross, a name destined to grace many a well-performed comedy throughout the decade. (Veteran editor Paul Hirsch, in his *A Long Time Ago in a Cutting Room Far, Far Away...*, pronounced Ross "the best director of actors I ever worked with."[6]) Ross came from musicals and the theater. In short order, he became prolific producer Ray Stark's go-to guy to bring hit plays to the big screen. His job, or perhaps his wont, was to do so without messing them up, without adding any of the New Age cinematic technique that was then all the rage. Stark-Ross properties were always presented with the utmost reverence for the author and with a capital P premium on performance. The chanciest Ross ever gets here is a little hand-held camerawork; why mess with success? Besides, Ross was very good at getting the best out of his stars, as he ably demonstrates with Segal-Streisand, though less so with his supporting players; poor Robert Klein for instance. (Klein was one of the decade's best stand-up comics, but the movies never figured out how to utilize him.)

By the third act, the film hums on all cylinders, rising above the mantle of respectable adaptation (by Buck Henry) to demonstrate subtextual depth. It's here where Henry shines, using a voice as distinct as that of the film's Blood, Sweat and Tears soundtrack.

It begins with a few street-based vignettes. They vary in quality but still, they show a sound understanding of the emotional roots of the characters. Then Henry adds a nice bonding moment in a bathtub (where Segal, this time through his woozy, pleased reaction to incident-inciting marijuana, again represents the conversion of uptight America to modern ways), though it ends in bedroom farce cliché. Finally, there's the film's best scene, though the playing is spotty: a climactic confrontation set in snowy Central Park, where Owl Segal, putting on the brute, asks Pussycat Streisand whether or not this new, hipper, crazier America has bothered to make room for love or has that been

---

6. Paul Hirsch, *A Long Time Ago in a Cutting Room Far Away* (Chicago: Chicago Review Press, 2021), 195.

sacrificed for hedonism and neurosis? It's a question for the ages, the inquisitive piston of so much of the decade's comic engine: the quest for the genuine above the Right or Left's mile-high bullshit.

The couple's latent reconnection, their attempt to dig belatedly for something real beneath their madness, foreshadows the upcoming tempest in a cinematic teapot, *Last Tango in Paris* (1973). Had *Last Tango* been made first, this one might have been labeled a good parody. Instead, it serves as one of the more spirited stage-to-screen transfers of the times. Small wonder Stark and Ross would soon be toiling for Simon, with his impressive string of Broadway hits made from the same Manhoffian mold.

The Private Life of Sherlock Holmes

Plot: The Great Detective uncovers the secret identity of the Loch Ness Monster. **Director:** Billy Wilder. **Script:** Billy Wilder, I.A.L. Diamond. **Cast:** Robert Stephens, Colin Blakely, Genevieve Page, Christopher Lee. United Artists. 125 minutes.

With the coming of the sexual revolution and its influence, for better or worse, on American cinema, one-time Hollywood bad boy Billy Wilder began to appear as old hat as the signature accessory he wore atop his head. Like his mentor, Ernst Lubitsch, Wilder, throughout his long, fruitful career, was always looking to titillate, to goose the retentive posterior of the Puritan-bred American mainstream with the flirtatious fingers of a European hand. By the late '60s, however, his innuendos, his lascivious leering, his benign gender-bending were, comparatively, foreplay. Since the early 1940s, he'd been a dirty old man at a church picnic; now, he was a prude at an orgy. Further, critics didn't even bother to stop to award him his due as a pioneer. Poor, risk-taking Wilder had gone from vulgarian to antiquarian overnight.

He came too late, then, to this, a pet project: an investigation of the mysteriously suppressed sexuality of the world's most famous detective, enwrapped, by necessity, in a puzzle-based adventure story. Further, Wilder kowtows far too much to the Victorian vibe of the proceedings. The results, dry and genteel, made Wilder an anomaly anew, his conversion from crass to class failing to appease fans of either of his identities.

Separate the film from the times, though, and what do you get? An elegiac, inoffensively bemused homage to the talent and world of Sherlock Holmes, anchored on a delightfully absurdist plot.

Holmes & Co. (mostly Watson, of course) find themselves in scenic Scotland, where, clue by clue, they unveil the true identity of the Loch Ness Monster. Therein are, expectedly, all of the classic Wilderian leitmotifs: deceit, misogyny, anti–German sentiment (Wilder was an Austrian).

The film was one of the last gasps of the big-budget Studio Era, clearly conceived for a mile-wide screen (Holmes himself might have had a hell of a time trying to uncover a close-up or a medium shot). Alexandre Trauner's sets are long and large, echoing the white-collar depth of field he co-created for Wilder's influential masterpiece *The Apartment* (1960).

Such a big frame for such a small cast: not Peter O'Toole and Peter Sellers, as had been Wilder's desire, but Robert Stephens and Colin Blakely, a pair of classical stage actors who had made small splashes in mostly European films. The former gives us not

Wilder but Wilde, as in Oscar, playing Holmes as a foppish priss; the latter, to his credit, boldly breaks with stereotype, accentuating Holmes' sexual frigidity by virtue of contrast, serving up a robust, lady-killing Watson, whose energy Nigel Bruce couldn't have exhibited had he been chased by a pack of Baskerville hounds. As the signature Wilder heroine, the girl-woman object of desire in the Marilyn Monroe-Audrey Hepburn tradition, there is international sub-starlet Genevieve Page, demurely hypnotic with her hourglass figure, crown of russet ringlets, and wispy French elocution.

Holmes' next comic appearance would be the loopy-sloppy *The Adventure of Sherlock Holmes' Smarter Brother* (1975), though he'd fare far better in Herbert Ross' amusingly cross-genre *The Seven-Per-Cent Solution* (1976), based on the Nicholas Meyer bestseller. In the next decade, there'd be *Murder by Decree* (1980) and *Without a Clue* (1988), the last reinventing Holmes-Watson as a kind of Matthau-Lemmon. That's an idea which Wilder, of *The Fortune Cookie* (1966), *The Front Page* (1974) and *Buddy Buddy* (1981), might have had more success with, had he eschewed the aquatic beast and pursued that proposition instead.

Quackser Fortune Has a Cousin in the Bronx

Plot: In Dublin, a manure salesman experiences a life-changing encounter with an American exchange student. **Director:** Waris Hussein. **Script:** Gabriel Walsh. **Cast:** Gene Wilder, Margot Kidder. UMC Pictures. 90 minutes.

Quackser Fortune Has a Cousin in the Bronx has the feel and pace of British realist TV drama. Makes sense, given that that was the professional pedigree of director Waris Hussein. And the film probably should have played as British realist TV drama. But the team behind it had slightly broader ambitions, so it imported an up-and-coming American comic character actor for the titular role. His quirkiness, they hoped, might suit the nature of the property.

Gene Wilder tries his best. He tones down his trademark hysterics to fit the feel. He struggles here and there with the accent (at times, it sounds like the Yiddish one he'll use in *The Frisco Kid*, 1979) but it's a noble effort. And as his legacy goes, it will have to do: never again would the movies offer him the opportunity to interpolate his dramatic and comic chops in a single vehicle.

Quackser, the low-key tale of an Irish manure salesman who falls into a class-division relationship with a foreign beauty, both borrows and foreshadows many things: the work of Jacques Tati, with its theme of industrialization running roughshod over quotidian European life; *Harold and Maude* (1971), a more successful attempt at the cross-hatched lovers formula that would so mark the early part of the decade; and the Irish-Scottish film comedy movement of the 1980s and 1990s, featuring the dour charm of art house hits like *Local Hero* (1983) and *Waking Ned Devine* (1998).

Quackser is a kooky comedy of manners, with wanly weird Margot Kidder, an American intellectual free-spirit, largely playing straight person to Wilder's quirky ways, only to finally influence him. Having wormed their wily, woolly way into mainstream U.S. culture, the hippies (Kidder) were now converging on new turf—in this case, bleak, backward Dublin (Wilder), another polite (if unique) society ripe for cultural topsy-turvying. Then again, maybe this isn't a case, thematically, of same old, same old. Is this, instead, America disrupting the lives of ordinary foreign cultures *à la* Vietnam? Unconsciously, perhaps, if at all.

For this is no work of self-importance. It is, unashamedly, a curio: an offbeat romantic comedy short on the romantic, big on the offbeat. Besides, in the end, a happy compromise is struck: Quackser stays put in his quaint little backwater but assumes a job suited to a cosmopolitan milieu. (Yes, occasionally, I *will* play spoiler!)

The original choice as the film's director was the legendary Jean Renoir, whose poetic touch and resonant humanism might have elevated it to something grander. Certainly, it would have afforded it more publicity. The film is largely, though not justifiably, forgotten. Better exercises in this kind of thing fast followed—again, *Harold and Maude*—as well as better publicized Wilder vehicles, affirming the louder, much more loved persona he had set down in Mel Brooks' *The Producers* (1967).

Start the Revolution Without Me

Plot: During the French Revolution, two sets of twins, one common and cowardly, the other aristocratic and athletic, end up switching places. **Director:** Bud Yorkin. **Script:** Lawrence J. Cohen, Fred Freeman. **Cast:** Gene Wilder, Donald Sutherland, Victor Spinetti, Hugh Griffith, Billie Whitelaw, Orson Welles. Warner Bros.-Seven Arts. 90 minutes.

Start the Revolution Without Me helped to usher in the great age of cinematic genre parody. The talents overseeing the production had cut their teeth in the formative days of TV comedy when sketch comics regularly sent up Westerns, costume epics, even foreign films. The classiest of the bunch had been the multi-talented Sid Caesar, whose legendary whose legendary writers went on to distinguish themselves on Broadway and in film, particularly in the '70s.

Producer Norman Lear and director Bud Yorkin never worked for Caesar, but they'd written for many of his contemporaries—notably, the bafflingly popular Martin and Lewis, whose personas are, at least somewhat, borrowed in this film (though you'll also find a nod to their funnier predecessors, Hope and Crosby). When, in the mid–60s, TV talents, Caesar staffers included, began to transition to feature films, Lear-Yorkin followed suit. They scored a surprise hit with the underrated *Divorce American Style* (1967), a vocal look at the tensions raging within domestic America, foreshadowing their triumphant return to the small screen when, beginning with *All in the Family* (1971–80), they'd become the socio-political conscience of network television. Before that, though, with *Start the Revolution*, they'd have one last kick as purveyors of Old School comedy.

In eighteenth-century France, a lowly pair of mismatched twins (played by Gene Wilder and Donald Sutherland with, for some reason, semi–English accents) are conscripted into an underground movement to dethrone the monarchy, until they are mistaken for their uppity betters, a duo of Corsican fops with a facility for foils. The twins negate endless assassination plots until they manage to engineer statewide peace—only to see the revolution take place anyway.

It's another appropriation of the ol' *Prince and the Pauper* premise, having been employed regularly by comic personas from Danny Kaye (*Start the Revolution* borrows from Kaye's *The Court Jester*, 1956) to Mickey Mouse. Here, it's translated into a galloping gallimaufry, one of many comedies from the late, let-it-all-hang-out '60s and early '70s out to reflect, by its purposefully pell-mell nature, a world gone irreparably askew.

This type of filmmaking, with its handheld camerawork, its schizophrenic edits and its accelerated pace, had been pioneered by the influential French New Wave of the late 1950s, as an antidote to staid, stultifying studio work. Comedy had steered clear of it, convinced that the all-important jokes would get lost in the cinematic virtuosity. Then, Tony Richardson's *Tom Jones* (1963) became a mega-hit, demonstrating that instead, this technique, by then being practiced by England's Angry Young Man Movement and Beatles helmsman Richard Lester, could actually enhance the gags, even the most tried and true. The oldest form of comic expression, in fact, slapstick, benefited most, awarded a second life thanks to Arriflex lenses, choppy cuts and cheeky scores.

Tom Jones was certainly a visible influence on *Start the Revolution*. The latter's opening sequence almost replicates *Jones*' famed silent movie opening dramatizing the birth of its eponymous hero (though there are snatches of dialogue in this edition). Before that, over the opening credits, true silent films *do* play: a hasty assemblage of sepia-toned swashbucklers from the Fairbanks era, each mustachioed hero swinging from chandeliers, scurrying up sails, and skewering enemies. Pure, old-fashioned silliness, the film announces: that's what you're in for.

The film's next bent is now set into motion: parody. It begins with a self-amused appearance by the authoritarian Orson Welles, caricaturing on-screen narrators. Then, it's the serial intrusion of expositional titles, periodically reminding us of the story's place and time—the first, and most successful, of the film's countless running gags. (One, involving the Man in the Iron Mask, is relied on too much for an intellectual's joke.)

These self-referential, often literal tropes would pave the way for the man who would become the practice's top practitioner, Caesar alum Mel Brooks, who, after the so-so reception of his *The Twelve Chairs* (1970), veered away from character-based work to restrict himself to send-ups.

When not serving as a parody of historical epics, *Start the Revolution* is otherwise occupied as myriad things: a slapstick comedy, a bedroom farce, an offbeat two-hander. For a breather, there's owl-faced Hugh Griffith (another *Tom Jones* holdover) as the sweetly befuddled Louis XVI, offering a different type of humor, of the contrastingly quiet variety. As a consequence, Griffith walked away with the bulk of the reviews, though the film clearly belongs to Gene Wilder.

Wilder's distinctive style—focused, slow-mounting anger, whose larval state is a quiet neurosis—was first served in small dosage, back when Arthur Penn awarded him a cameo in his seminal *Bonnie and Clyde* (1967). It was enough, though, to suggest a comic voice perfectly suited to anxious times. (Pauline Kael on Wilder, in her *5001 Nights at the Movies*: "His self-generated neurasthenic rage is a parody of all the obscene bad temper in the world."[7]) Hitherto, this had been Alan Arkin's shtick, the stirringly internal made the incorrectly external. As the '60s and '70s exploded, though, so did Wilder, in film after film. The first to give us the full effect was Brooks' *The Producers* (1967), but *Start the Revolution* is truly Wilder's first legitimate showcase. There's no Zero Mostel, a figure even more "larger than life" than Wilder, with whom to share the screen; only subtle Donald Sutherland, doing his low-voiced best to hold his own (he does, but with gay jokes that play hollowly today).

---

7. Pauline Kael, *5001 Nights at the Movies* (New York: Henry Holt, 1991), 710–711.

While Wilder shines, this is far from a star vehicle. It's an ensemble piece, stocked with every nervy comic overplayer of the era. (Lester go-to Victor Spinetti is here, as is Blake Edwards bit man Graham Stark.) Even the glamour (Billie Whitelaw) is unconventional. But they're all working hard. The result may be labored buoyancy, but enough of the sweat glistens.

A comedy classic? *Non!* A guilty pleasure? *Oui!*

The Twelve Chairs

Plot: In the wake of the Russian Revolution, a trio of ne'er-do-wells cross paths in a goose chase over a chair stuffed with jewels. **Script/Director:** Mel Brooks, based on the novel by Ilf and Petrov. **Cast:** Ron Moody, Frank Langella, Dom DeLuise. UMC Pictures. 93 minutes.

One would never guess, judging by his first entry of the decade, that the sporadic Mel Brooks would go on to become one of the decade's leading comedy auteurs.

Brooks had been a cult artist, albeit a commercial one, starting in the early '60s when he enterprisingly parlayed a routine he performed at parties into a series of best-selling comedy albums. His largely ad-libbed *2,000-Year-Old Man*, in which he affected a borscht-thick Russian-Jewish accent and riffed wry reflections on his long and varied life, rescued him from the anonymity of writing for television—most famously, for Sid Caesar's *Your Show of Shows* (which regularly staged a similar routine between its star and the same straight man, Carl Reiner). The bit made Brooks a comic persona in his own, limited, right. It also established him as the leading—perhaps the sole—proponent of a distinctly un–Americanized Eastern-European Jewish wit. Where others were succeeding, wildly, by dressing the survivor's humor of the shtetls in a chic, cabaret-friendly veneer, Brooks was exposing the form's dirty roots, choosing, in his famous guise, crass over class, flip over hip, rage over refinement.

How to extend this character, though, beyond album-friendly bursts and bits? Might Brooks' Old Man, or at least, his manic emotional makeup, sustain itself in longer, more commercial form?

Brooks' first attempt at it was *The Producers* (1967), a small-budget comedy whose premise harkened back to an unproduced Marx Brothers film: a fallen impresario (sound like Groucho?) purposefully staging a no-doubt-about-it flop to bilk naïve investors. The film, particularly in the manic to and fro between larger-than-life stars Zero Mostel and Gene Wilder, revealed the 2,000-Year-Old Man as everyman; suddenly, anybody, from the operatic to the oppressed, could break into fits of fury or episodes of infantile hysteria.

Further, the premise's need for a bad play allowed Brooks to glaringly spotlight his irrepressible penchant for offensiveness—in this case, a jolly musical about the last days of Adolf Hitler. Brooks would spend the rest of his long, hit-and-miss career mixing and matching these two modes, his biggest successes coming when they'd be tempered by the rules of parody.

For now, though, he was again looking to expand on his bucolic, ruffian instinct. What better place to venture than the source? With that, the 18th film adaptation of the Russian literary classic *The Twelve Chairs* was put into modestly budgeted production in Yugoslavia.

As the film demonstrates, however, Brooks, as director, was still very much in his infancy. Too many scenes prematurely fade to black, too much physical comedy is speeded up to approximate silent cinema. So much so, it becomes obvious that Brooks is working around the casting—namely, Ron Moody as a fallen, frustrated aristocrat and Frank Langella as the roguish ne'er-do-well that he falls in with. Together, they're sent on a wild goose chase over a set of missing chairs, one of which is pregnant with a bevy of pre–Revolutionary jewels.

Moody and Langella, while commanding, are no Mostel and Wilder. Tasked with periodically exploding into episodes of bellicose Brooksian badinage, they are dutiful but not inspired, energetic but not loose. Both were creatures of the stage, slaves to directorial discipline. Asked to be more playful, they are largely lost at Balkan Sea.

It's particularly obvious when contrasted to the performers who *do* get it: Brooks, in a too-small cameo, finally captures the magic of his 2,000-Year-Old Man on film, and Dom DeLuise, as a two-faced clergy out for the jewels himself. Both are products of a sketch-comedy background, able to take a simple scene to comic heights with an innate facility for physical abandon and a shameless repertoire of groans, guffaws and grimaces.

As the estimable Walter Kerr maintained of Chaplin in his definitive *The Silent Clowns,* Chaplin made films memorable simply by walking on screen enough times, defining him as "essentially a man who liked being bound by a tight frame."[8] If *The Twelve Chairs* is anything, it's because of Brooks-DeLuise subscribing to that same ethos.

Like *The Producers, The Twelve Chairs* is about the extremes of capitalism, its tragicomic effect on the sadly susceptible human soul. But this is not a political metaphor, no dressed-up reflection of the Cold War then (1970) raging. Brooks is not a polemicist but a humanist; it's simple brotherly connection he chooses over politics, as his ending (Moody and Langella make up after a falling-out) makes clear. To quote Maurice Yacowar in his *Method in Madness: The Comic Art of Mel Brooks,* "Brooks' central point is man's need for adult community."[9] Routinely, pride and position are forcibly sacrificed for the necessity of companionship.

Despite *The Twelve Chairs'* best intentions—including its largely unheralded cinematography, by location native Djordje Nikolic—it's clear that, like *The Producers,* it relies on a thin plot and, more detrimentally, a blind investment in performance. Brooks' self-penned opening theme, looking to capture the sadly ironic core of Russian-Jewish folk philosophy, advocates: "Hope for the best, expect the worst." Had he been able to foresee the final result of his film, he might have adjusted it to "Hope for the best, expect the here and there."

Watermelon Man

Plot: A bigoted insurance broker wakes up to find that he is now black. **Director:** Melvin Van Peebles. **Script:** Herman Raucher. **Cast:** Godfrey Cambridge, Estelle Parsons. Columbia. 98 minutes.

---

8. Walter Kerr, *The Silent Clowns* (New York: Alfred A. Knopf, 1975), 250.
9. Maurice Yacowar, *Method in Madness: The Comic Art of Mel Brooks* (New York: St. Martin's Press, 1981), 89.

Watermelon Man was written, improbably, by Herman Raucher. In a few short years, Raucher would boast the biggest sentimental hit since *Love Story* (1970) with the autobiographical *Summer of '42* (1972). Meanwhile, he had decided to do his part in aid of the black power movement, crafting a comedy exposing the hypocrisy of the white, suburban pseudo-liberals who supported it: the tale of a respectable, middle-class businessman who wakes up one morning to find that he has mysteriously changed pigment.

For all of its political intentions, the aim of the film might have been a maudlin morality tale about political conversion. A white, commercial-minded liberal would certainly have made that film. But the directorial task went, appropriately, to an African American director: cult filmmaker Melvin Van Peebles, interested, yes, in going mainstream but not by too great a compromise. The result was a tug of war between author and director, with Van Peebles ultimately winning. (Raucher, still looking for the upper hand, went on to novelize his initial draft)

So, the film is "blacker" than was Raucher's. In a concession paralleling Ossie Davis' in *Cotton Comes to Harlem* (1970), however, Van Peebles gives the white audience its jokes—not slapstick in this case, like *Cotton*, but ones just as sorrily facile: every hokey, Caucasian-generated play on the genetic misfortune of being black, from lounging too long under a defective sun lamp to redemptively bathing in a tubful of milk. It's a dictionary of moldy bad taste, delivered without cleverness or subtlety.

So why watch?

Because though Van Peebles might have settled for the ass-kissing jokes, he didn't settle for anything else. While the film is, unmistakably, an all-audiences comedy comedy, at the same time, it's an unabashedly black-driven polemic, using the same ethos, energy and, occasionally, technique (restless, alternative editing; crazed, colored filters; eclectic, cheeky music) as the blaxploitation pictures of the day. It even ends with the hero's conversion to militancy, endorsing black anger and take-no-prisoners advocacy.

It's a bold, significant alteration. The intended ending was that the hero's unwitting conversion, leading to the good-natured ire of colleagues and co-workers that dominates the film, would end up being but a dream (not *that* old cliché!). In its defense, it certainly would have conveyed the film's central conviction that black life in modern America is indeed a nightmare. Instead, Van Peebles opts to introduce white audiences to the full, organizational anger of the black community, hitherto known only, cinematically, to the blaxploitation set. *Watch out, whitey, we're comin' for ya!*

But in the end, such admirable single-mindedness isn't enough. *Watermelon Man* should have been important. It isn't, remaining, as it was upon its initial release, but a curio.

Where's Poppa?

Plot: A troubled lawyer can't extricate his cloying mother from his life. **Director:** Carl Reiner. **Script:** Robert Klane. **Cast:** George Segal, Ruth Gordon, Trish Van Devere, Ron Liebman. United Artists. 82 minutes.

As *The Out-of-Towners* (1970) attested, by 1970, the world, aka New York City, had truly gone off the rails. While Neil Simon continued to serve as that turn of events' commercial comic spokesperson, smaller voices were joining the chorus. One of them was comic novelist and screenwriter Robert Klane. Klane specialized in taking long-standing Jewish jokes—bad summer resorts, clinging mothers, ill-planned arsons—and elongating them with dark wit, frank language and over-the-top sight gags, balls he juggled with underrated agility.

Carl Reiner, yet another Sid Caesar–schooled multi-talent, had joined the fray of those transitioning from TV to the movies in the mid–1960s. His would be a hit-and-miss film career, interrupted by periodic returns to the small screen. While he served largely as a kingmaker—helping to create film careers for TV talents Dick Van Dyke, Steve Martin and John Candy—his best films would professionally pad innovative, if thin, premises, mostly by mining their best moments for all their worth.

This capacity demonstrated a deep, abiding respect for the writing, a quality no doubt instilled during his years at the behest of Caesar's legendary sketch-grinders. "Let's get the most out of what's on the page" seems to have been Reiner's ethos, "then we'll add what little else might be required." Simply compare the exemplarily written *All of Me* (by Phil Alden Robinson, 1984) to the largely improvised John Candy vehicle *Summer Rental* (1985). End of argument.

Reiner the script lover had a beauty in *Where's Poppa?* It's tight, swift and consistently funny, giving a wide range of humor impressively egalitarian due. There's even a little sweetness to it: the critically appreciated scene wherein the hero, a mustachioed George Segal, sings softly to Trish Van Devere, the film's love interest. Reiner gets sentimental without taking us out of Klane's cockeyed universe.

By today's enlightened standards, the idea of the burden of the elderly as comic fodder seems bold and callous. It must be remembered that Klane's novel-script was the continuation of an age-old joke, that of the disruptive Jewish mother, which stage and TV comics had been throwing at audiences for eons.

So ingrained was the idea that the film hardly has to develop it. Awarding Ruth Gordon a few unexpected eccentricities (like kissing her son's bare butt in polite company) is enough. She can spend the rest of the film in a state of oblivious sweetness and we'll still consider her, as her son does, a genuine pain in the ass. She doesn't have to yell, dish out guilt trips, or look unsightly—a stark contrast to when this premise was essayed again in *Throw Momma from the Train* (1988). Still, she's a handful—so much so that her son, a lawyer, can't get the kind of sleep required to serve his clients, can't win the wan woman of his dreams, can't rely on his brother to help him out. It doesn't help that, whenever called, this brother (Ron Liebman) finds himself trapped in a running gag where a gang of street toughs put him through his paces in the middle of Central Park. It's one of the film's many jokes that, through its mix of nervous energy and outright absurdity, successfully captures the electric dysfunction of early 1970s New York. If *The Out of Towners* was a sincere but light-hearted look at that phenomenon, *Where's Poppa?*, gag by gag, restores its rightful grit and tension.

The film is teeming with frank language too, at least by 1970 standards. To Klane's ear, the errant is the direct. Polite, even logical society is a long-forgotten idea. As the world has gone awry, so too has communication between its citizens. Everyone speaks in their own wonky music, and yet, because they all inhabit the same off-kilter universe, they can all understand each other. Sometimes, though rarely, they even manage to connect. Part and parcel of this circumstantial patois is the periodic use of expletives, each of which comes at you like a clown from a perfectly timed jack-in-the-box. It's never gratuitous, never for effect. It's just another symptom of cripplingly contemporary urban existence. Best example: the best-yet comic take on the generational divide, wherein Reiner's son Rob, as a verbose conscientious objector defended by Segal, goes after Barnard Hughes, an obliviously hawkish general. (Eagle eyes will spot Rob's then-wife, Penny Marshall, as an extra in this scene. So, one scene, three directors.)

Mom, then, bad as her offspring might contend, isn't the trouble. The true culprit is our surroundings, screams Klane, ever demanding, barely salvageable. By the time the movies again visited Planet Klane (*Fire Sale,* 1977), this sub-world had lost its function as a mirror of society. Instead, it resembled a sloppy, offensive one of its own making.

1971

American film comedy circa 1971 was almost entirely New York–based. With the Hollywood studios in financial hot water due to a fractured demographic, a steady diet of maxi-budget mega-flops, and the decline or death of the directorial Old Masters, film comedy would come to be monopolized by the most troubled metropolis in America.

American comedy had been, for many years, largely Jewish, a culture whose legendary, self-deprecating wit came out of the economic and political oppression of the Eastern European ghettos—which, if you replaced mud with concrete, New York was fast becoming.

It still wasn't enough, though, to motivate the indigenous talent to hightail it to higher, safer ground, i.e., the Hollywood Hills. And so, at least for the time being, they'd stay, recognizing voluminous comic material, mostly of the sour variety, in the unstoppable deterioration of their universe. They would go down joking.

And it wasn't only their physical world that was unraveling. Most, born in the 1920s, had now reached middle age (this was before 50 had been deemed the new 40). Hairlines were receding, backs were aching, marriages were growing staid. Built into the comedy, then, was a pervading sense of nostalgia: a lament for the dissipation of their youth, the geographical context in which it had taken place, and the gilded era over which it had flourished. A constant comparator was at work, the old, more innocent world contrasted with the inexplicably complicated new.

Later, one of this set's literary spokespeople, novelist Philip Roth, labeled it the journey from the American Pastoral to the Great American Berserk. It was David vs. Goliath, only David (note the Jewish name) was growing too old to work his slingshot; the best he could fling was a one-liner.

The heroes (if you can call them that) of these pieces were largely businessmen, a hard-working, anonymous army of Willy Lomans, usually with generational monikers like Mel or Harry or Murray. They were trapped in well-worn suits, walked with pronounced stoops, and offered tired smiles.

Their long-suffering wives were sympathetic creatures, loving shrews who, when pressed, showed a quicker understanding of this crazy new world than their simple, sentimental exteriors suggested. These couples lived in spacious apartments of bland, pleasant design, where they spent most of their time talking in an up-and-down comic singsong. It would be the last time the movies' primary comedy audience would focus on them. Come the end of the decade, ticket buyers would be younger. Major comic vehicles for actors over 40 would become exceptions, not rules.

These characters would first appear, more often than not, on Broadway. Film producers had rightly discerned that that was where the best stuff was, comedy-wise, TV's first generation having migrated there. Those writers could now stretch out what they had learned over two (intermission included) hours. Of all of the templates to which they subscribed, it was the two-handed, domestic-based sketch that transferred best to the legitimate stage, given its relatable characters, universal concerns and modest economy of scale, though the odd genre or historical spoof (like Larry Gelbart and Burt Shevelove's *A Funny Thing Happened on the Way to the Forum*, 1962) was occasionally chanced.

Neil Simon alone, having scored his first stage success in 1961 (*Come Blow Your Horn*), became a veritable machine, mounting a hit a year—a streak not enjoyed since the heyday of George S. Kaufman, with whom he was regularly equated. Others interpolated stage work with alternate assignments, from screenplays to essays to comic strips. Those, happy to be making movies but still aspiring to the stage (aka Mel Brooks), would have to wait their turn.

Added advantage: As movies went, these kinds of stage-born properties were cheap to make. So, you were going to transfer the latest Broadway hit, circa 1971, to the big screen; what was it going to cost? You could use, largely, real-life locations; yes, there'd be actors to pay but no Alan Arkin is going to cost what Paul Newman might. Post-production? A little "street tone"—screaming ambulances, screeching buses, yakky pedestrians. A minimalist music score that wouldn't offend the pre-rock sensibility—is Dave Grusin or Marvin Hamlisch available? And a guy from *Mad* magazine, like that Mort Drucker, to do the poster. Even with a limited release, you would recoup your investment and then some.

New York may have been, literally, the most dangerous place on Earth, but comedically, it was the best. Hollywood still gambled on the odd entry, but it was largely busy with the reinvention of drama, turning, slowly, to a new film school–based vanguard to revitalize venerated genres: the gangster picture (Francis Ford Coppola's *The Godfather*, 1972), the horror film (Brian De Palma's *Carrie*, 1976), the sci-fi epic (George Lucas' *Star Wars*, 1977). New York City, comedy-wise, was the place, and the demographic Hollywood no longer had the infrastructure to appease was the audience.

Bananas

Plot: A heartbroken nebbish gets involved in a Latin American revolution. **Director:** Woody Allen. **Script:** Woody Allen, Mickey Rose. **Cast:** Woody Allen, Louise Lasser, Carlos Montalbán, Howard Cosell. United Artists. 82 minutes.

In 1969, Woody Allen transitioned from groundbreaking stand-up comic to aspiring filmmaker with *Take the Money and Run*. The film, while distinctly Allenesque, owed a lot to the cinema of another stage comic cum auteur: the publicly loved, critically maligned Jerry Lewis. Lewis, in fact, was slated to direct *Take the Money and Run* until Allen decided he wanted complete control. Lewis' oeuvre, in turn, owed a lot to the silent film comics. Like them, Lewis had built a reputation on stringing gags of varying quality on a simple narrative clothesline. In *Take the Money and Run,* Allen did the same. To provide *some* cohesion, he framed the jokes within a parody of true crime documentaries.

In *Bananas,* while again the gag is decidedly the thing, Allen comes even nearer to a genuine story, creating the thin but sweet tale of an undersexed nebbish romantically influenced to "man up" by unwittingly joining, then leading, a ragtag group of Latin American revolutionaries.

If that premise sounds like political satire, it isn't. That said, *Bananas* certainly starts off that way, with the then ubiquitous (and much imitated) Howard Cosell calling the assassination of a banana republic's power-mad dictator like a Saturday afternoon sports event. (Little did Allen know he was also predicting the exploitative future of television when the CNNs and Fox Newses of the world would make this style of coverage a reality.)

While the film returns to comically comment on the unstoppable lunacy of Latin American politics and America's subversive role in it—a real concern at the time—its intentions are much more old-fashioned.

Few knew at this time what would later become much more obvious, even appreciated: that Woody Allen, the hippest comic going, was a diehard worshipper of one

of the left's worst public nightmares, veteran comedian Bob Hope. Hope had been what Allen was becoming: the most respected comic voice of his generation. From the mid-1930s to the early 1960s, Hope enjoyed a cross-platform career, back when "cross-platform" meant radio, movies and TV.

By 1971, though, Hope was down to a series of bi-monthly TV specials, where he read stale jokes off of cue cards and verbalized his unwavering support for the disruptive shenanigans of the Nixon administration. As a result, there would be protests at his appearances and requests to defend himself on TV talk shows. To anyone under 30, many of them Allen fans, Hope was comic and cultural anathema.

Small wonder Allen rarely wore his worship on his sleeve; then again, a proud recluse, he rarely granted interviews. Still, much of Allen's early on-screen

Woody Allen in *Bananas* (United Artists, 1971). Allen had been part of the legendary writing staff for TV's Sid Caesar, along with Mel Brooks and Neil Simon. By the '70s, they constituted American comic cinema's Big Three (MGM/United Artists/Photofest).

persona—his cowardice, his sex drive, his hubristic bravado—is of Hope-ian lineage. Kept secret, it played fresh and original.

And so, we have *Bananas*, the ambitious Allen's attempt at the kind of service comedy Hope had ground out during World War II when the young Allen would have been looking up at him admiringly from his seat in a Brooklyn movie house. *Bananas* is chockablock with fumbled rifles, wisecracks about Army chow and other staples of the genre, each measuring the spindly, outlier hero against the traditional ideal of American manhood. True to form, it has the hapless hero unwittingly rising to unprecedented heights, winning public acclaim and, of course, the girl (in this case, Louise Lasser, Allen's ex-wife). Allen being Allen, though, he'd add a third act in which, true to his pessimistic persona, the hero would be disgraced, then criticized by his romantic prize.

Outside of Hope, other icons of comedy are also mined: the aforementioned Lewis (look for episodes of spastic yelling and running) and the much-loved Marx Brothers, with a tribute to their *A Night at the Opera* (1935) and a climactic courtroom scene whose manic nature owes much to Groucho and his brethren.

There's even a small preview of the Allen-to-be in the exchanges of interpersonal psychobabble between himself and Lasser, as they negotiate their brittle union. Allen returned to this in subsequent comedies, before expanding it into a sober-faced subgenre. That transition classified him as a master of the relationship film, with movies such as *Bananas* labeled "the early funny ones." Even aliens would pledge their affinity for them in Allen's *Stardust Memories* (1980).

Maurice Yacowar, one of Allen's first serious scholars, framed *Bananas* this way in his *Loser Take All: The Comic Art of Woody Allen*: "*Bananas* satirizes the kinds of ways that man conspires to exploit others—politically, religiously, culturally, and romantically, the sense that this exploitation is a lunatic waste of life gives this chaos of comedy its remarkable and sober cohesion."[10] Hmmm...I don't know about "sober." The film doesn't have a serious bone in its body. It's all gags, and they're almost all good.

Cold Turkey

Plot: Residents of a small Iowa town nervously agree to go smoke-free. **Director:** Norman Lear. **Script:** Norman Lear, William Fox Price. **Cast:** Dick Van Dyke, Pippa Scott, Vincent Gardenia, Tom Poston, Jean Stapleton, Bob Newhart, Bob and Ray. United Artists. 101 minutes.

Cold Turkey, with its great comic hook—a small town volunteers to stop smoking as an act of civic amelioration—was made in 1969. Sensing a limited international audience, it was given an ah-what-the-hell release two years later.

The town in question is Eagle Rock, Iowa, population 4006. A Republican, white-picket-fence stronghold. In other words, in 1971, ripe for satirical picking. Writer-director Norman Lear, whose struggles with the film's distribution helped prompt his jump back to television, would zoom from dabbler to magnate by continuing to examine the effects of political, cultural and economic wear and tear on the American

10. Maurice Yacowar, *Loser Take All: The Comic Art of Woody Allen* new expanded edition (Oxford: Roundhouse, 1979), 135.

fabric. His seminal *All in the Family* (1971–80) pioneered a new style of TV sitcom: struggling class, socio-political, high-minded—attributes found in *Cold Turkey*, the final film that bore his name.

Lear and Bud Yorkin are interesting to contrast. Like Yorkin when he helmed *Start the Revolution Without Me* (1970), Lear too gives in to the rushed, obtuse film fashion of the day; better to cutaway, insert or speed up than to give a scene or a performance its proper due. Lear had had added incentive, though: Focusing as it does on an entire populace, *Cold Turkey* is a panoramic work, a form that always favors pace over performance.

Still, Lear does make some welcome concessions: Dick Van Dyke, rescued from facile family fare yet again by the Lear-Yorkin team (they had also awarded him the lead in their *Divorce American Style,* 1967), has a handful of good moments as the pillar of this quaint, quirky community, a parody of the sweaty small-town moralists then flourishing in the shadow of TV staple and presidential crony Billy Graham. On the whole, though, Van Dyke's a little too sober, perhaps considering this, a rare casting against type, an opportunity to demonstrate his dramatic side.

Bob Newhart, on the other hand, is perfectly placed as the middling tobacco rep out to upset the apple cart, as, in his popular stand-up, he had long been imitating the sober shills that consumer advocates like Vance Packard had been exposing. And though Newhart has but one scene with but half the duo, what a thrill it must have been for him to work with his idols, cult radio comics Bob and Ray, in a succession of roles (and hairpieces) sending up the pompous newsmen of the day. The film, while a broad, accessible indictment of military-industrial big-thumb, is just as much a satire of the state of news in 1971's three-channel universe, an early taste of the knee-jerk, hyperbolic character that factual media took on in more recent years.

As for the rest of the good citizens of Eagle Rock, they became Lear's TV stock company; the film plays like an audition tape for top-rated 1970s sitcoms. Jean Stapleton (*All in the Family*) is here as a nervous housewife, along with Vincent Gardenia (same) as the mouthy mayor; docile Paul Benedict (*The Jeffersons*, 1975–85) appears as a stop-smoking guru, while Graham Jarvis (*Mary Hartman, Mary Hartman,* 1976–77) helps Lear expose the yahoo fringe organizations making up the marginal Right. The rest, from Barnard Hughes to Barbara Cason, might not have landed Lear-produced TV leads but they went on to appear regularly in half-hour showcases generously sweetened by cloying laugh tracks.

As his TV canon would also demonstrate, Lear, when again contrasted to Yorkin, was the more political animal—and staunch moralist to boost. The tension in the film is attributed to tobacco withdrawal—one must remember what an intrinsic middle-class ritual smoking once was—but it's representative of the nervous state of 1971 America. When the minister's wife, played by sober-faced Pippa Scott, screams her indignation over the change in the town's character, as it converts from moral exemplariness to crass opportunism, it's America's scream, the whole country on a rooftop, giving primal voice to the soul-wrenching anguish instilled by what it's unwittingly become.

The conversion too is smartly reflected in Randy Newman's opening and closing song, "He Gives Us All His Love," a wry reference to America's two great overseers, often synonymous: God and the president. Both the song and the film are about how the former, the deity behind the country's Puritan roots, has been forsaken for the latter, the military-industrial king. The film ends, as a result, with a socko punchline, again proving that Lear was better suited to sketch comedy and sitcom than film: After a nervous, slapstick-filled month without its top vice, Eagle Rock is generously chosen by the White House as the site of a new missile plant. The film ends with an aerial shot of the town, the smoke-emitting towers of the plant resembling lit cigarettes.

It's an interesting criticism because for once, aside from a small concession to some teenage protesters, this isn't the youth movement calling the older generation on its contradictions. They're being knocked here by one of their own. On film as on TV, Lear scored laughs by politically and morally framing the demographic to which he belonged, often as patriotic simpletons marching to a misguided moral code.

A high-concept, one-joke movie is always a risk (though often, monetarily, a good hook is enough to garner an audience) but this one is better sustained than most, thanks to Lear's clever script and the memorable ensemble playing. Still, it might have played better as a writers' room picture. Here, Lear tries to be one all by himself. With more contributors, the gags would likely have been more varied and the few sustained moments a lot stronger.

The slapstick, while ubiquitous, is welcome but sloppy; Lear's a dialogue man (even though he wrote for many years for the very physical Jerry Lewis) as *Divorce American Style* and his ensuing TV work affirmed. And as a filmmaker, he's no Altman. He doesn't have an innate film sense, being too much the Old School commercial artist, despite the modernity of his politics.

The film's climax, which takes place over a triumphant celebration in the town square, includes, awkwardly, some surprise assassinations. They're uneasy moments bordering on the tasteless, with their echo of the then still-fresh Kennedy shootings—though they're categorized, quite rightly, as consequences of an America gone mad. So the moralist, in the end, goes mad too, shooting himself in the tonal foot—though he's rescued by his sight-gag denouement.

The Gang That Couldn't Shoot Straight

Plot: A power struggle develops between mobs over a bicycle race. **Director:** James Goldstone. **Script:** Waldo Salt, based on the novel by Jimmy Breslin. **Cast:** Jerry Orbach, Lionel Stander, Robert De Niro, Leigh Taylor-Young. MGM. 96 minutes.

...by the crew that couldn't shoot comedy.

This adaptation of legendary New York columnist Jimmy Breslin's comic novel about a mob rivalry fraught with incompetence is a veritable tutorial on how not to direct a comedy. Only a handful of Breslin's best gags survive: the nervous mob boss who gets his dutiful wife to start his car, the hysteric who makes a living at mob funerals as a professional mourner, the vain gunmen who remove their designer shoes before hunting down their marks. The rest are lost, largely due to a director, the enigmatic TV-film hybrid James Goldstone, painfully uneducated in the fundamentals of cinematic gag-telling. Every rule is violated: how to set up a joke, how to sustain it, how to pay it off, how to top it. Instead, we get throwaway audio, a gag-obscuring allergy to inserts, a paucity of reaction shots, and joke-killing jump cuts.

It's likely kind to attribute all of this to an effort to replicate the rambling tone of Breslin's novel, which set out to expose Brooklyn-based mob culture while simultaneously making fun of it. Many years later, TV's *The Sopranos* (1999–2007) did it to perfection, albeit by subscribing to a darker, more organic form of humor, capitalizing on the underworld's natural absurdity.

Gang is also a catalogue of every over-the-top, Italian-American stereotype there is: the gravel-throated mob boss, the double-crossing hit man, the pious-dangerous mama—plus a sprinkle of outrageous outliers thrown in for kookiness' sake (including a dubbed Hervé Villechaize of TV's *Fantasy Island*, 1977–84). As one, these primping, pinstriped, pugnacious underdogs are supposed to serve as a criminal version of the then-burgeoning counterculture, and their Damocles, the boss on whom they seek their perpetually ill-wrought revenge, as the white-haired establishment. But we can't root for them as intended; we're too busy trying to decode the comedy.

Screenwriter Waldo Salt, coming off of *Midnight Cowboy* (1969) no less, tries hard to make something uniform of Breslin's busy, bombastic book but he's usurped at almost every turn by Goldstone. Both are momentarily redeemed, however, by the insertion of a central love story—between a bicyclist-crook parading as a priest (a skinny young Robert De Niro) and a mobster's sister (where have you gone, Leigh Taylor-Young?), wherein two broken souls find healing through an unwitting union. It's a familiar dynamic in Salt's work (*Midnight Cowboy* and *Coming Home*, 1978) which, here, affirms Goldstone's greater facility with drama.

Had the film been made a year or two later, right after the mega-hit *The Godfather* (1972), it would have had better context and, sloppy as it is, might even have piggybacked on it to the piggy bank. It even boasts a central assassination attempt in an Italian eatery that would have played as a parody of Michael Corleone's first, formative hit.

Why wasn't *The Gang That Couldn't Shoot Straight* tried again, when, post–*Analyze This* (1999), producers were scrambling for mob comedies?

Harold and Maude

Plot: A suicidal teenager and an aged free spirit develop an unlikely, and shocking, relationship. **Director:** Hal Ashby. **Script:** Colin Higgins. **Cast:** Bud Cort, Ruth Gordon, Vivian Pickles. Paramount. 91 minutes.

Of all the films subject to the trickle-down effect of *The Graduate* (1967), none resonated more than Hal Ashby's *Harold and Maude*. Much of it plays like a dark send-up of its obvious inspiration, though screenwriter Colin Higgins, responsible for taking it from Masters' Thesis to novel to play to screenplay, never so much as afforded its forebear a nod.

The first parallel is, of course, the core dynamic: the young, lost soul falling in with the life-altering older woman. Older indeed. Maude, played by veteran character actress and sometime screenwriter Ruth Gordon, was 79. Maude teems with *joie de vivre*, croons happy tunes (written by Cat Stevens, the shaggy, whispery folk God *du jour*) that champion individualism, defies highway etiquette on a motorbike, and reveals veritable universes in the small and the self-contained; a hippie-era Goddess, on earth to give the young her all-embracing blessing. Harold, by contrast, is barely out of his teens and as obsessed with death (though mostly as a snub to his snobbishly oblivious mother) as

Maude is with life. They "meet cute" at a funeral, the beginning of Harold's cockeyed, sentimental education.

With its dark stateliness and shock-value wit, the film owes just as much to cartoonist Charles Addams as it does to Mike Nichols. And in the same way that Addams' work enjoyed a unique position among his single-panel brethren, the made-you-look sight gags of *Harold and Maude* (Harold's comic suicide attempts) distinguish themselves in the canon of film slapstick.

M*A*S*H (1970) had made the inclusion of gore permissible in film comedy and *Harold and Maude* took it a step further, using it not as an insertion of realism or as an agent of political commentary but as a joke in its own right.

That said, these scenes also serve, though secondarily, to frame the youth generation as items of the grisliest disposability, underlining its devaluation at the hands of the political engineers of Vietnam. And it's hard not to take in Harold's backyard immolation—the funniest, most memorable of his cleverly masterminded near-goodbyes—without the famous image of the gasoline-doused Vietnamese monk running simultaneously through your mind. Nevertheless, you laugh—and not simply because of the appeasingly benign payoff.

If the film's political agenda has a prime agent, it's the presence of Harold's pushily patriotic uncle, who encourages his meek, taciturn nephew's conversion from wide-eyed kook to red-eyed killing machine. Rewarding as some of their exchanges are, they constitute the film's few concessions to obviousness, breaking with its otherwise singular tone.

So yes, the film violates itself here and there. But it's a strong (if slim) script, serendipitously aided by Ashby's unobtrusive though not indifferent direction and that happiest of film accidents, perfect casting. Gordon, as the free-spirited earth mother from the high-living 1920s who grew uncorrupted by postwar affluence and suburban sterility, plays her part with poised relish. She is effective but never excessive, reminding the dispirited young of the time that if they looked hard enough, there were old, bohemian role models to be found. A major studio would have cast some pat, mouthy iconoclast like Katharine Hepburn in the part, strangling the film's charm and message.

And Bud Cort, as Harold, with his pale, staid unease, suggests a hipster Peter Lorre. It's not a layered performance but that's exactly why it works. Depth would have killed it with sophistication; added restraint would have made it caricature.

And it's more than just a hippiefied two-hander. There's genuine substance, just enough of it, in the scenes where each lead gets to relate their respective backstories—not to mention in that all-important, lightning-fast cutaway during the surprise proposal scene (a direct parallel to *The Graduate*) when Ashby allows us to catch the concentration camp number on Maude's wrist, turning the heat up under the film's central theme.

As Ashby's second film, after *The Landlord* (1970), a directorial upgrade is the expectation. But he sticks to his guns, seemingly staid but surprisingly smart. Ashby's trademark reliance on wide shots (ironic for an ex-editor) creates not, as it should, an affirmation of amateurishness or indifference but a hypnotic vacuity that speaks of the emptiness and disconnect at large in the material world. (Added bonus: It allows the sight gags to properly play out.) Stanley Kubrick went on to use these shots for much the same effect, as did Ashby's arguable heir, Wes Anderson.

It must be remembered that wide shots were, after all, the norm in the days of performance-based silent comedy, and very effective too. They went on to prove their surrealistic comic value in the work of that catalogue's direct descendent, French pantomimist-auteur Jacques Tati. A venerable but valuable tradition then, often misinterpreted as lack of sweat equity by the supposedly savvy film critics of Ashby's era.

They weren't crazy about much else in the film either. Vincent Canby, in *The New York Times*, spoke for most of them when he called it "creepy and off-putting."[11] And check out *Variety*: "*Harold and Maude* has all the fun and gaiety of a burning orphanage."[12] But the film was not made for the white-collar working stiffs for whom the Canbys of the world toiled at their corporation-issued typewriters. *Harold and Maude* was, from the get-go, art house fodder. It enjoyed a dozen solid years on that circuit, the small cinema's leading American comic commodity until *The Rocky Horror Picture Show* came along in 1975.

The Hospital

Plot: Murder breaks out at a New York teaching hospital while the suicidal Chief of Medicine begins an affair with a patient's bohemian daughter. **Director:** Arthur Hiller. **Script:** Paddy Chayefsky. **Cast:** George C. Scott, Diana Rigg, Barnard Hughes, Richard Dysart, Don Harron. United Artists. 103 minutes.

In 1955 when *Marty* was released, all hailed its celebration of the common stock. By 1971, that triumph, trumpeted by screenwriter Paddy Chayefsky, was a cry of defeat. Institutions long held dear, from the brick-and-mortar to the socio-political, had crumbled, the result of a ravaged economy, labor strife, changing mores and generational friction.

The 1971 poster boy for the personal cost of all of this was not a hard-working, happy-go-lucky Bronx butcher (Marty) who finally finds love but another "Marty": an embattled white-collar professional, bitterly divorced, alcoholic, estranged from his children, suicidal even.

Making matters worse, the Manhattan teaching hospital at which he is Chief of Medicine is the next ol' reliable in a state of unstoppable disarray. Protesters are disrupting its expansion, fellow doctors are either unforgivably self-serving or dangerously incompetent, and both patients and staff are mysteriously dying. The only possibility of redemption is a brainy, shapely free spirit offering, in her New Age way, to take our poor hero away from all of this—an ideological leap posing a serious challenge to his old-fashioned sense of responsibility.

With this May-December dynamic, Chayefsky sexualized the generational divide then prevalent. As was his wont, it's expressed largely through blood-and-thunder exchanges of long, literate, accusatory monologues, disrupted by shocking episodes of heated sex, 'til December calms down and nobly leaves May to her idiosyncratic agenda. (Chayefsky used all of this again in *Network*, 1976.)

But the film is much more than a generational tug of war fronting as a kooky love story. This "Roman farce" and "Gothic horror story," as it calls itself, is just as much a Grand Guignol satire, a cheeky murder mystery, and a broad commercial comedy. Further, it's a grand showcase for the formidable George C. Scott.

---

11. Vincent Canby, *Harold and Maude* review, *New York Times*, Dec. 21, 1971.
12. *Harold and Maude* review, *Variety*, Dec. 16, 1971.

By 1971, moviegoers had had a bellyful of Method-trained macho men, with their look-at-me scenery-chewing and their epigrammatic (if often illiterate) self-righteousness. Though Scott was never a formal product of that school, with both *Patton* (1970) and *The Hospital*, he reminded audiences of just how effective that style could be, at least when applied with maturity, intelligence and rhythmic aplomb.

With these twin turns, Scott rivaled Marlon Brando for the mantle of America's greatest actor, a glory that would prove, alas, all too brief. A series of flops, coupled with a difficult on-set demeanor, diminished, in shockingly short order, his critical and commercial cachet.

Chayefsky wrote the part specifically for Scott. He wanted as rabid a dog as he could find for the rage and despondency stirring inside his white-coated avatar. Like most of his generation, Chayefsky was, to quote a phrase he made famous five years later, "mad as hell" and unwilling to take it any more—so much so that the film crudely parodies the primary source of his ire, the growing counterculture, presenting them as a kind of mealy-mouthed absurdist theater company. Diana Rigg's hippie Goddess, the love interest, was exempt by little more than her kittenish sexuality.

It's one of the few shortcomings in what is otherwise one of the decade's best comedy scripts—nay, one of the best scripts, period: adult, brainy, messianic.

The result was Chayefsky's second Oscar for Best Original Screenplay (there'd be a third, for *Network*). But the real prize was the clout it afforded him. Chayefsky's win was a major agent in the new esteem developing toward screenwriters, a class of creative contributors hitherto parked, permanently it seemed, on the lowest rung of the moviemaking ladder. The reversal had started with the then high price ($325,000) that had been paid for William Goldman's script for *Butch Cassidy and the Sundance Kid* (1969), another Oscar winner.

By the time of *The Hospital*, there was no doubt about it: American screenwriting was getting more literate, deeper, and increasingly clever, busting genres and editorializing with resonant insight. Freed with the fall of the studios from roles as producers' stooges and privy to a college-educated, film-savvy moviegoing demographic, the Goldmans, the Chayefskys and, soon, the Robert Townes of the world became, improbably, names as bankable as those of the stars for whom they wrote. Plus, they were finally in on the big money, able to negotiate their own deals. On his next film, Chayefsky cut himself in for a whopping 23 percent of the profits.

That didn't mean that their woes were over. After *Network* came *Altered States* (1980), a messy take on drug culture that Chayefsky divorced himself from, going so far as to remove his name (sort of: he used his proper first and middle ones).

It was Chayefsky's turn to learn, as the self-interested doctors in *The Hospital* had, that money can't buy professional respect.

Kotch

Plot: A quirky senior citizen develops a relationship with a pregnant teenager. **Director:** Jack Lemmon. **Script:** John Paxton, based on the novel by Katharine Topkins. **Cast:** Walter Matthau, Deborah Winters, Felicia Farr. ABC Pictures. 113 minutes.

Throughout his career, Jack Lemmon was periodically accused of laying it on too thick, in both of his on-screen modes: as neurotic urban everyman and as sour-faced middle-aged martyr. The anticipation come *Kotch*, his sole directorial foray, was that the film would suffer from same.

And indeed, from its opening sequence, in which Walter Matthau, as the eponymous senior citizen, enjoys a sentimental frolic with his grandson through gauzy cinematography, we are immediately parachuted into operatic territory. A dramatic separation, we instinctively recognize, is mechanically afoot, one that will unfairly tear guardian from charge with Chaplinesque aspirations. But in an interesting bait and switch, that's not exactly what we get. Instead, poor, kindly Joe "Kotch" Kotcher invests his devalued paternalism in a wayward free spirit, creating a desexualized May-December romance aimed at reconciling the establishmentarian-hippie divide.

Kotch, then, is no mere senior citizen. Shave a few years off his shaggy white head and remove his ice-thick specs and what have you got? A spokesperson for Lemmon's generation (Lemmon was 46 at the time) who, given the Dylanesque a-changin' of the times, probably felt like 100. To director Lemmon's credit, he was not out, through Kotch, to play disgruntled mouthpiece. The film, instead, is a kind of peace offering, an ambling, low-key search for common ground between old and young. (For the senior citizen as hippie cheerleader, audiences that year had Hal Ashby's *Harold and Maude*.) Is there still room, the film asks, for the patently patriarchal?

Matthau, as the titular character, tries hard to bring something authentic to the proceedings, though yes, he flirts with caricature. It was a big year for the pickle-nosed actor, with three releases (the others were *Plaza Suite* and *A New Leaf*). Throughout this period, he was clearly out to eschew type, to replace irascibility with versatility. Hence, his uncharacteristically low-key Kotch, a commendable if semi-interesting commitment for which he was rewarded with an Oscar nomination. (Matthau earned his next one as a senior citizen too, and in far more convincing makeup: *The Sunshine Boys*, 1975.)

The hope, of course, was that the same electricity the Lemmon-Matthau combination had provided as actors (up to this point, they had made two films together; in the end, there would be eight) would sustain itself with the former behind the camera and the latter in front of it, especially given the film's "odd couple" premise. Another bait and switch: *Kotch*, its reputation to the contrary, is no commercial comedy.

Excuse the film the occasional gag (you'll be hard-pressed to; Lemmon has a limited talent for them) and what you're watching is a genteel character study—a rather actorly exercise, with petty pretensions of social relevancy.

Little Murders

Plot: A young spinster brings her nihilist boyfriend to meet her dysfunctional family. **Director:** Alan Arkin. **Script:** Jules Feiffer. **Cast:** Elliott Gould, Marcia Rodd, Vincent Gardenia, Elizabeth Wilson, Lou Jacobi, Donald Sutherland. 20th Century–Fox. 108 minutes.

In the late '60s, with American mass anxiety on the rise, who better to help the theater and film worlds reflect its crippling effect on the soul than Jules Feiffer, the intellectual cartoonist whose deeply introspective heroes adultized the funny papers?

In 1966, Feiffer, frustrated with his popular strip for *The Village Voice*, attended Yaddo, one of America's legendary writing schools. There, a novel he was refining revealed itself as a play. If Feiffer could not awaken America to the root causes of its tears and rages through cartooning, he would do it through another means. In his 2010 memoir, *Backing into Forward*, Feiffer wrote: "I had been lamenting for some months that my cartoons had become too popular, too readily accessible. I wanted to use theater to clear up the confusion about my subversive content. What I would demand of this play that I now passionately embarked upon was attention, controversy, and a famous failure."[13]

Feiffer got all three, until Alan Arkin successfully revived the brilliantly oblique yet shockingly direct *Little Murders* a short time after its ill-received 1967 Broadway premiere. Come 1971, Arkin was directing (and appearing in) the film version.

As the adjective in the title suggests, *Little Murders* is about the trivialization of violence. In Vietnam, innocent civilians were being slaughtered at the hands of America's military-industrial complex; at home, political assassination was widespread and the urban crime rate, particularly in New York, was peaking. Increasingly, violence was becoming a way of life, until families, like the one at the center of the film, were becoming absurdly inured.

Enter into that family's tasteful apartment Elliott Gould, as a lanky, Nikon-wielding nihilist who disinterestedly gives himself over to their vivacious daughter. After a lot of the psychological circuitry that passes for courtship in the world of Jules Feiffer, Gould is brought out of his defining indifference to give the tenets of human decency—love, marriage, family—a try ... only to have it all turn to his favorite photographic subject: shit.

Next, another houseguest: director Arkin as a deliriously apoplectic cop, reduced to a stammering mess by the burden of having to bring logic and order to his beat's unstoppable bloodlust. He comes, of course, to no tidy conclusions. As Vincent Gardenia, in his first big splash as the perturbed paterfamilias, asks the indifferent heavens, "What have I left to believe in?"

Given these kinds of questions, as well as the film's predictable propensity for towering soliloquies, you'd think we were in the hands of Paddy Chayefsky. (Soliloquy-wise, there are three beauties, each in impressively long takes: Lou Jacobi as a messianic judge, Donald Sutherland as a hippified minister, and Gould over a long, dark night of the soul.) At rival cinemas, Chayefsky's *The Hospital* was also finding the funny in the frustratingly fallen. Black comedy, that year, was *in*—big time. Other entries included *Harold and Maude* and *The Ruling Class*. But *Little Murders* was the funniest and the most challenging, coming across as an American screwball comedy of the '30s directed by Sam Peckinpah.

Civilization, Feiffer unabashedly declares, has indeed decayed. Worse, its only recourse is to join the barbarians. "Why bother to fight back?" Gould asks his fiancée, played by the sadly forgotten Marcia Rodd. "It's dangerous to challenge the system unless you're at peace with the thought that you're not going to miss it when it collapses."

All one can do, then, is go out with a bang.

Made for Each Other

Plot: Pandora and Giggy meet at a group therapy session, then strive to overcome their issues as romance blooms. **Director:** Robert B. Bean. **Script:** Joseph Bologna, Renée

13. Jules Feiffer, *Backing Into Forward* (New York: Doubleday, 2010), 351.

Taylor. **Cast:** Joseph Bologna, Renée Taylor, Paul Sorvino, Olympia Dukakis. 20th Century–Fox. 101 minutes.

"It's not my fault!" So screams Gig, the fallen Italian-American macho man, from the floor of the group therapy session he was reluctant to attend, his fellow neurotics cradling him like an overgrown child. "Who am I now?" sings, off-key, Pandora, the Jewish-American shrew still convinced, at middle age, that she can make good on all of the show biz promise her cloying mother convinced her she possessed. Two lost, tortured souls, desperately trying to transcend their psychological inheritances in the bumpy journey to the self. Can they get their shit together while trying to make a go of it as a loving couple?

Such was the fate of a lot of would-be lovers throughout the '70s, when the analysis craze of the '50s grew heads (shrunken heads?) and people signed up en masse for everything from Gestalt to EST. Everybody in America under the age of 40, it seemed, was "off to find the real me," looking to shed the restricting carapace that was keeping them from uncomplicated self-expression so that they could accept themselves and others. Otherwise, the thinking among the introspective movement went, people would be perpetually plagued by their Jungian shadow, one cast by those sticky enemies of peace, love and happiness: their parents.

The Gordian knot of love and family was the specialty of husband-wife acting-writing team Joe Bologna and Renée Taylor, first with the expansive *Lovers and Other Strangers* (1970), then with the smaller *Made for Each Other*. Husband-and-wife teams had been a comedy staple since the days of vaudeville, from the much-loved Burns and Allen to the lesser-known Phil Ford and Mimi Hynes. In the '60s and '70s, it took on a hipper inner quality, as duos like Jerry Stiller and Anne Meara contrasted their ethnic pedigrees and traded personal issues.

Taylor-Bologna brought that sensibility to the big screen, which, in its own quiet way, had been waiting for it. In so doing, they helped to pioneer the relationship comedy, a staple of the '70s whose distinguished practitioners included Woody Allen, Paul Mazursky and James L. Brooks.

Back to our lava lamp–era Punch and Judy, Gig and Pandora: He of the bar shop-owning bully and the devoutly Catholic mama, she of the pushy, astrology-loving stage mother and perpetually preoccupied father. Small wonder Gig and Pandora find themselves participating in that encounter group, then, Freudian patterns being Freudian patterns, reluctantly attracted to each other. Tragicomically, their only commonality, aside from obtrusive primal chemistry, is that they're hopelessly unmoored, a pair of self-loathing seekers sustained only by their illusions. In *Lovers*, writers Taylor and Bologna spread this poisonous pixie dust over an entire cast. Here, the film being mostly a two-hander, we get it in concentrated form.

So, it's more volatile, more personal, more resonant. Unable to say "I love you" to one another, or to anybody else for that matter, Gig and Pandora scream, cry and otherwise carry on. Bologna and Taylor, as actors, are out to put on a show (it was the bombastic Bologna's debut) and they're more than up to the task. To paraphrase the type of sports cliché Howard Cosell might have made on *Monday Night Football* (then just hitting its stride), if this were a fight, it would have been stopped by now.

Bologna and Taylor also award each other some great showcases: her crude, offbeat nightclub act and Bologna's climactic rant, prompted in part by the hysterical (in both senses of the adjective) holiday gathering at his home, which today, feels like *Moonstruck* (1987) on uppers. Olympia Dukakis is even in attendance.

Director Robert B. Bean (talk about a footnote; just try looking him up on the Internet!) has no idea how to frame all of these hot-tempered histrionics. If it's true, as the Hitchcockian bromide has it, that there's only one proper place to put the camera, Bean plays hide-and-seek with it all film long. One suspects this amateurishness is supposed to create a kind of raw, documentary feel. But this is not *cinéma vérité*; it's *cinema manqué*. Still, it matters little.

Bean compensates with a deep-set appreciation for his actors, even if all he probably did was let them strut their stuff. He's rewarded not just with Bologna and Taylor but with Helen Verbit (who?) as Taylor's difunctionally doting mother and, more recognizably, Paul Sorvino and the underrated Dukakis as Bologna's apish parents. They're stereotypes, unapologetically, but stereotypes with bleeding souls.

Most on-screen couples spent the '70s wondering if they should just live together or get married. These two are too traumatized and terrified to even get to simple connection. It takes a kind of synchronized primal scream therapy, in the end, for them to get there. Another paraphrase, this one from a nursery rhyme: First comes catharsis, then comes marriage.

A New Leaf

Plot: Henry, a broke, self-centered fop, plots to wed and dispose of Henrietta, an accident-prone botanist. **Script/Director:** Elaine May, based on a story by Jack Ritchie. **Cast:** Elaine May, Walter Matthau, Jack Weston, David Rose, James Coco. Paramount. 102 minutes.

The film's history is legendary: a four-hour cut resized to a tidy hour and a half by mega-producer Robert Evans. Next, a lawsuit, resulting in the release of the studio cut. Positive reviews, hailing writer-director-star Elaine May as America's first female comic auteur and Hollywood's newest problem child.

May's next film, *The Heartbreak Kid* (1972), would prove a case of *déjà vu*, sowing the seeds of an implosion that would relegate her to a catch-as-catch-can career, robbing audiences of a sizable cinematic talent and a much-needed feminist icon.

Then again, May's shyness, personified in *A New Leaf* in the character of Henrietta, a gawky, socially inept botanist, might have prevented that from happening anyway. A young single mother in the uptight 1950s, May, for all of her intelligence, wit and brio, was a decided outlier. It was only by teaming with a fellow outsider, the immigrant Mike Nichols, that she began to publicly shine. A lot of *A New Leaf* is about just that: how two hermetic people can, through an unlikely coupling, bring out the best in one another.

The other half of the film's romantic (if you can call it that) arrangement is Henry, a haughty millionaire with a palpable contempt for anything common. When his trust fund exhausts, poor, untalented Henry must marry rich to maintain his Upper East Side lifestyle. To maintain it in peace, he must subsequently murder his bothersome betrothed.

A mix, then, of 1930s screwball and 1940s Hitchcock. As the original script and first cut would have it, a lot more of the latter than the former: Henry would knock off a few members of Henrietta's unsavory house staff before getting to her. None of those murders take place in the final film. Henry and Henrietta settle into an uneasy but promising union, literally walking off into the sunset.

This is May cinematically re-examining her brief, rushed and ill-fated marriages (the second, another whirlwind affair, effectively broke up Nichols and May), letting us in on the comic, painful search for a man suited to her smarts and aloofness. She'd be at it again in *The Heartbreak Kid*, another tale of disastrously premature wedlock.

Henry is played by Walter Matthau, miscast as a young, blue-blooded upstart. Still, in fighting trim and foppish coiffure, the old pro gives it everything he's got, using his hangdog face to new purpose: not to affiliate with the common man but to separate from him. And the supporting cast is top-notch: David Rose as Henry's sage of a butler (how ironic is it that Rose was actually murdered?), James Coco as his contemptuous uncle, William Redfield as his flustered attorney, Jack Weston as a mealy-mouthed rival, and a young (i.e., middle-aged) Doris Roberts as a high-living housekeeper.

The highlights in this small, consistently funny fable are many. It's no surprise that the Second City trained May specializes, like one-time partner Nichols, in two-handed set pieces. Matthau and Redfield have a very funny scene, as do Matthau and May when he tries to undress her on their wedding night.

To May's credit, while all of the characters are closer to caricature, even stereotype, a beating heart lurks within each personage. This is sketch, even farce, delicately humanized.

Next, *The Heartbreak Kid* and then … sigh. As Alexandra Heller-Nicholas has written in *The Films of Elaine May*, "[T]he hackneyed phrase 'hidden in plain sight' applies to her perhaps more than any other pioneering artist of her generation."[14]

Again: …sigh.

Plaza Suite

Plot: Three male-female encounters, all set in the same suite at New York's Plaza Hotel. **Director:** Arthur Hiller. **Script:** Neil Simon, from his play. **Cast:** Walter Matthau, Barbara Harris, Maureen Stapleton, Lee Grant. Paramount. 114 minutes.

Neil Simon, Broadway's comic Golden Child, made an unlikely entrance on the 1970s movie scene: an original screenplay, one, in the end, of his few. He'd spend the bulk of the decade "opening up" his stage hits, i.e., adding extraneous bits of business for the simple sake of varying the stifling geography of play-based material. Occasionally, he'd suffer fits of nostalgia for his sketch-writing days and extend that form into all-star genre parodies bereft of the moroseness that passed, too often throughout his work, for depth. *Plaza Suite*, then, was the 1970s-era moviegoer's proper introduction to Simonland, a hermetic, simmering universe wherein the populace, mostly world-weary, New York–based mid-lifers, trade hit-and-miss (mostly hit) one-liners

---

14. Alexandra Heller-Nicholas and Dean Brandum, *The Films of Elaine May* (Edinburgh: Edinburgh University Press, 2019), 1.

till the big issue behind the badinage bubbles, melodramatically, to the middle-class surface.

It was Simon's first work to utilize the sketch form for full-length purposes. As he explained in *Rewrites*, his 1996 memoir: "The idea was to vary the styles ... so that the entire evening could comprise a drama, a satire, a comedy, and a farce."[15] Admirably ambitious, but a long evening. In time, the play (and film) was trimmed to a trio. And it subscribed to an additional gimmick: all three would be played by the same pair of actors—George C. Scott and Maureen Stapleton—allowing them to demonstrate their respective versatility.

While the film adaptation is faithful to the form (confessed Simon, "I have to accept some of the blame for the film. I kept all the action in one room"[16]), it breaks from its supporting innovation. While Simon argued for a varied cast, Paramount envisioned it as a star vehicle for Walter Matthau, then a bankable comic commodity looking, despite his signature persona (hangdog, avuncular, crafty-flirty), to stretch.

Selected as director was Arthur Hiller, who, the previous year, had not only helmed the soggy megahit *Love Story* but also Simon's original screenplay *The Out-of-Towners*. Both films demonstrate a thematic affinity with *Plaza Suite*: an examination of the effect of extenuating circumstance (in the case of *Love Story*, premature death; in the case of *The Out-of-Towners*, everything else!) on romantic coupling, a Hiller leitmotif since the days of his first hit, the Paddy Chayefsky–penned *The Americanization of Emily* (1964). (The bugaboo in that one, by the way, is war.)

And so we have Matthau, trim and mustachioed, as a businessman breaking off with his wife of 23 years (Stapleton, retained from the play); Matthau, in a russet shag cut, as a movie-producing lothario, seducing a renewed acquaintance from suburban New Jersey (Barbara Harris); and Matthau, topped by a silvery widow's peak, as a comic strip–torn father grouchily sparring with his wife (Lee Grant) while salvaging their daughter's wedding—all in the same expansive suite in Manhattan's iconic Plaza Hotel. (The play-film is a form of valentine to it. The Plaza was another New York City landmark that had been prospectively slated for demolition, part of a planners vs. people tug of war that had started with the still controversial modernization of Penn Station in 1965.)

The play-film, purporting to be a three-part battle of the sexes, is just as

Throughout the early '70s, the prolific Neil Simon served as a major mouthpiece for the midlife malaise of modern moviegoers (**Photofest**).

15. Neil Simon, *Memoirs* (New York: Simon & Schuster, 1996), 229.
16. Turner Classic Movies, *Plaza Suite*, June 15, 2006.

much an examination of male sensitivity, in the tradition of the work of Frank Capra and John Cassavetes. While the women's roles, to Simon's credit, certainly aren't underwritten, the tragedy behind the comedy is unevenly spread. In all cases, the bulk of the brunt is borne by Matthau (exacerbating, in all cases, his postural stoop). Collectively, the scenarios constitute a male mid-life crisis, the climactic subtext of each a war between waning prowess—sexual, patriarchal or generational—and the upper hand of time.

Simon had issues with the conversion of his play to a one-man show. There is a modicum of merit to the author's protestation. Matthau is very much at ease in the film's bookends, as a fidgety 50-year-old and the bullhorn-throated father figure. His unforced ease with Simon's major modes, conservative self-pity and outright outrage, serve both particularly well. Matthau's at his most rewardingly clownish in the climactic farce, as the disasters pile up on himself and the equally high-strung Grant. It's the Sid Caesar-Imogene Coca couple battles from *Your Show of Shows* (1950–54) on which Simon was a staffer, polished and perfected. But Matthau is miscast in the film's middle episode. No ladies' man, he plays it as a sexual vaudeville, coating his "boy wonder" (?) big shot in sibilant glibness, in a role requiring a quality akin to Scott's foxy gravitas. It hardly helps that the underrated Barbara Harris counters with a thoroughly credible performance.

Discouraged by what he saw, Simon reacted by trying his hand at another kind of adaptation—a property originated by somebody else. The result, *The Heartbreak Kid* (1972), would prove one of the true comic gems of the era, leaving those with little appreciation for the film versions of his plays asking why he didn't make a habit of the practice.

Who Is Harry Kellerman and Why Is He Saying Those Terrible Things About Me?

Plot: A popular folk singer is plagued by a mysterious stalker. **Director:** Ulu Grosbard. **Script:** Herb Gardner. **Cast:** Dustin Hoffman, Jack Warden, Barbara Harris, Dom DeLuise. Cinema Center Films. 108 minutes.

It was called, semi-comically, "the great folk scare." With the advent of the 1960s, a deep interest in indigenous American music took root. Young people across the country were picking up acoustic guitars and imbuing music clubs and coffee houses with folkloric chestnuts attributed to Stephen Foster and Woody Guthrie. The crew-cutted Kingston Trio became a deity. In time, with the assassination of America's youngest president, the civil rights debacle and the escalation of Vietnam, a kindred spirit writing angrier, original material, Bob Dylan, became the movement's Zeus. You could grind any ax with your ax. Better still, you didn't have to know how to sing; technique had become synonymous with gloss aka superficiality. If you could warble, whinge or whine, as long as you were subscribing to the right politics, you could call yourself that exalted anti-establishmentarian hybridization: the singer-songwriter.

Late in the decade, spawned by Simon and Garfunkel's bestselling soundtrack to *The Graduate* (1967), the movies came calling. At the end of 1971, Cat Stevens' voice became synonymous with *Harold and Maude*; a few months before that, though, parodist-poet Shel Silverstein put his stamp on a cult film manqué, Ulu Grosbard's *Who*

Is Harry Kellerman and Why Is He Saying Those Terrible Things About Me? (Silverstein enjoys an energetic cameo in the film, heading his folk-rock ensemble Dr. Hook and the Medicine Show.)

That said, the film's hero, Georgie Soloway, is a post–folk boom folkie. He's a household name now, gracing the covers of *Time* and *Life* and living in a cavernous, ivory-colored penthouse—trapped not just by money and success but by all of the other pressures that the times were doling out, the same ones other heroes in other movies were going through and would continue to go through until the decade crossed the mid-point. It's divorce, it's New York, it's aging, it's the corrosion of a kinder, gentler time— oh, and the elusiveness of that all-saving commodity, love.

The anxiety that went unnamed by Benjamin Braddock in *The Graduate* is given, here, a million labels. There's even one supposedly unique to Georgie: an eponymous nemesis, a mysterious besmircher making poor Georgie's name mud, driving him to a shrink (Jack Warden) and depriving him of sleep. He's metaphorical, of course, this stalker, a phantasmic embodiment of the aforementioned ennui.

Harry Kellerman, then, is the mid-life, urban malaise being suffered on other screens by gray-haired, establishmentarian comic protagonists of the early '70s attributed to a younger, contemporary spokesperson. It's an affirmation, according to writer Herb Gardner, that that particular manifestation of angst is a more universal commodity than the world had been led, at that time, to believe.

As in Gardner's hit play and film *A Thousand Clowns* (1965), our guitar-strumming hero is a sociologically oppressed showboat. He has no recourse from life's stifling b.s. but to cocoon himself in his sneery code, even though he knows it's a faulty mode of operation that will only allow him to function so much. Unlike his predecessor, however, a staff writer for a children's TV show, his primary language isn't sour epigrams. Being a singer, he's cut from more poetic cloth. And so he speaks and acts with a lithe muscularity, making for a more quiet, reflective kind of comedy. As a result, there's a pleasant vacuity to the film, a hip form of understatement, unique for the product of a brash genre looking to appease an equally brash (i.e., young) demographic. Further, it's broken up nicely, if belatedly, by healthy bits of backstory: set pieces of Jewish-American life devoted to Harry's Portnoy-ish coming of age, wherein Gardner gets to affirm that his folk-singing superstar is himself, a middle-aged playwright, and not some serio-comic riff on Dylan.

It's done freestyle, *à la* Fellini, with touches of surrealism both welcome and obtrusive. Many of the scenes foreshadow (or did they directly influence?) *Annie Hall* (1977). All they do in the end, though, when contrasted to the stronger, longer scenes, is affirm that this is a creative team composed of members of an older generation—Gardner, 47, director Ulu Grosbard, 52, and star Dustin Hoffman, 34—attempting to speak for the subsequent one.

Like the film adaptation of *A Thousand Clowns*, with its endless, dead-end, edit-happy montages superimposed over the flagship scenes of the play, the veneer of faux hip here fools no one.

Nevertheless, it's commendably, if only semi-successfully, experimental. There's Gardner's writing—he's a deeper, less pushy Neil Simon—and Hoffman's performance. Coming off of three big hits—*The Graduate*, *Midnight Cowboy* (1969) and *Little Big Man* (1970)—this film, and his low-key turn in it, was considered a puzzling letdown.

Maybe he wasn't a bona fide member of the new fraternity of male actors—Pacino,

Hackman and Nicholson, soon to be joined by De Niro and Duvall—that was restoring Method-born integrity to the screen after the crash of Brando and the popularity of detached minimalists like Steve McQueen. Soon, though, Bob Fosse's *Lenny* (1974) would help restore critical faith in Hoffman.

Meanwhile, there was his Georgie Soloway, essentially Ben Braddock in mustache and curls. It's all there, the actorly wonts introduced back in '67 and fast, by '71, becoming familiar: the head-shaking despair, the seductive gentility, the schleppy smarm. And for a singer, even an acceptably bad one, he doesn't croon very much, leaving it to Silverstein and company (though Hoffman does have a charming duet with Barbara Harris, in an impactful supporting role). It isn't slumming. Actors of Hoffman's caliber don't know what that is. Still, it doesn't break new ground either.

The film, however, tries hard to.

1972

Starting in 1973, American film comedy began its slow but inevitable concession to the Baby Boomers, re-welcoming a sizable population that, in their collective coming of age, had abandoned the movies to join communes, cross the country on Harleys, and picket the White House. The dramas wooed this demographic first, albeit cautiously, as a new generation of filmmakers, the first to emerge from America's collegiate film programs, were being afforded sizable budgets and wide releases.

Thus, a new cinematic reflection of America—realist, leftist, energized—was making its way onto the screen, developing a growing audience and revitalizing the long-suffering box office. It was only a matter of time before comedy got with the groove.

First, though, there was 1972. It was the year of *The Godfather*, much talked about then and, it ended up, in perpetuity. The unprecedented amount of money it made paved the way for the advent of the blockbuster, a seismic industry shift that was furthered by *Jaws* (1975) and *Star Wars* (1977). With its spotlight on the Mafia, *The Godfather* served as cinematic affirmation that all of the trouble that was going on in the world was, at its core, institutional. And who was going to right it for you, the corrupt cops in *Serpico* (1972)?

Trapped in this dead-end universe, it's small wonder that the troubled, middle-aged everyman remained, in both drama and comedy, a dominant archetype, as did its younger version, the befuddled seeker. Add to that, at least behind the camera, the nostalgist, looking to create the world and cultural sensibilities of a time that may have been just as difficult but that steeled one's soul instead of stealing it: the 1930s.

Avanti!

Plot: An American businessman travels to Italy to claim the body of his deceased father, only to fall into a relationship with the English priss whose mother perished in the same accident. **Director:** Billy Wilder. **Script:** Billy Wilder, I.A.L. Diamond. **Cast:** Jack Lemmon, Juliet Mills, Clive Revill, Edward Andrews. United Artists. 142 minutes.

Throughout the Studio Era, émigré Billy Wilder made a career of pitting American puritanism against European rakishness. Sometimes he sided with the Americans, making the French, the Germans and the Italians look like Old World buffoons subscribing to 19th-century manners and political rigidity. Other times he pined for his homeland, portraying Americans as brash, proud simpletons who viewed hedonism as the ultimate violation of national character.

Avanti! is a marathon of both practices, running close to two and a half hours—and yes, often, Wilder grows visibly tired. Sixty-six at the time, he had been at this game a long time. The protagonists are overly familiar, the central romance predictable, the supporting types caricaturists' caricatures. Plus, the film was shot widescreen (presumably to showcase its lush location, Ischia), giving the jokes, as does the running time, an overinflated quality.

That said, it's not bad—simply slower of walk and croaky of voice.

Jack Lemmon (who else?) plays Wendell Armbruster Jr., a harried American industrialist forced to travel to Italy to claim the body of his mentor-father, killed in an automobile accident. While traveling, he practices his eulogy into a tape recorder. He is overheard by Juliet Mills aka Pamela Piggott, a porcelain frump off to claim the body of her mother, killed, unbeknownst to Armbruster, in the same mishap.

Lemmon, the American, is shocked by the revelation of his father's secret sexual identity; Mills, the European, lauds the whole episode as magically romantic. When the bodies of the deceased lovers go mysteriously missing, Lemon and Mills are forced, albeit waaaayyyyy too slowly, to bond—and so history repeats itself. Quite a meet-cute. As per late Wilder, at once light and dark.

By 1972, Wilder's European-American war takes on, *inter alia*, a second front: the battle between the Greatest Generation and the hippies. Lemmon is the former, forced to confront the sexual revolution through Mills, champion of the latter. Strangely, this new, semi-incidental agenda dates the film more than many of Wilder's earlier, black and white productions. Lemmon's shock over his father having been a "dirty old man," a leading cultural stereotype of the '60s and '70s, seems almost baffling in today's anything-goes age, while much of the lingo, including "dig," "chic" and "groovy," makes the beatnik-speak in *The Apartment* (1960) comparatively forgivable. (You'll find plenty of period name-dropping too, from Ralph Nader to Christiaan Barnard.)

Lemmon, on the whole, tries too hard, as he was wont to do mid-career. Mills, who, to her credit, gained 40 pounds for the role and appears nude to boot, counters him as best she can, but her light touch is often too light. On occasion, you almost forget she is there.

When it comes to ministerial morass, a European point of pride, Wilder still has his snap. The bureaucratic barriers to the bodies, related in long diplomatic monologues by character actor Clive Revill as Lemmon's dapper Italian dogsbody, echo the better political machinations in Wilder's Cold War comedy of manners *One, Two, Three* (1961).

In the end, though, even Wilder must have felt he was propelling this kind of exercise on fumes. It would be his last kick at the romcom can. Next, he would turn to the tried and true, written by somebody else in fact—*The Front Page* (1974)—only to affirm yet again that while there was still a certain bounce in his step, the knees had decidedly stiffened.

Butterflies Are Free

Plot: A blind man befriends a free-spirited neighbor, much to the consternation of the former's concerned, conservative mother. **Director:** Milton Katselas. **Script:** Leonard Gershe, based on his play. **Cast:** Goldie Hawn, Edward Albert, Eileen Heckart. Columbia. 109 minutes.

Nineteen sixty-nine. A time of liberation: African Americans, women ... and finally, people with disabilities. Helping to pave the way for the latter, artistically, was writer Leonard Gershe. Gershe, who had started his career as a lyricist, scored his first true show biz success in the button-down 1950s with his screenplay for the hit film musical *Funny Face* (1957). Reusing that Oscar-nominated screenplay's central dynamic—savvy man mentors innocent coquette who wins, improbably, his heart—in the name of disability rights advocacy, Gershe fashioned *Butterflies Are Free*, a seriocomic three-hander in which a 20-year-old blind man, trying to function independently, falls under the unlikely influence of a girlish free spirit, i.e., a sexy hippie, much to the consternation of his overprotective, establishmentarian mother.

Butterflies was a smash on Broadway, running for close to three years; it's still performed on the regional theater circuit. The reasons were myriad: for the genre, it is well-crafted work. Said critic Clive Barnes in his original *New York Times* review, "If a committee had sat down and meticulously worked out what it takes to produce a hit Broadway comedy, this is almost precisely the expertly packaged product that might have emerged."[17] Two, the play offered substantial roles to its actors, providing just enough range and depth to each Broadway comedy archetype so that they might, given their due performance, stand a decided cut above the white-collar, one-liner spouting New Yorker neurotics then dominating the scene.

Three, the play, while messianic, isn't overloaded with bleeding-heart puffery or political self-importance. It's adamant, yes, but low-key. Last, it boasted cross-generational appeal, validating the misgivings of both young and old, bringing down the judgmental hammer on equal sides but with just enough force. In so doing, *Butterflies*, in its original run, struck paydirt, presenting an audience-pleasing détente between society's warring factions.

If the film version, three years on, proved just as popular, it was due to a producer's decision to retain much of the play. *Butterflies* the film is not much more than a series of single-set (the blind hero's discount apartment) takes, broken up, for breaking up's sake, by token excursions into San Francisco's Haight-Ashbury district, a geographical reset aimed at adding an extra layer of youth-appeal and a break from the on-screen ubiquity of New York City. This isn't just another wisecracking, smart-mouthed, small-budgeted Broadway import about unhappy American Easterners, the film wants to shout—only it doesn't shout it; it cursorily suggests it.

They needn't have bothered. The respect for the writing—formulaic but well-intentioned, and sufficiently lively to boot—is enough, as are the spirited performances.

The true butterfly set free here is Goldie Hawn, as the improbably 19-year-old (she was 26 at the time) Jill, the vivacious come-and-go neighbor of Don's (the hero, Edward Albert). This was Hawn's first true vehicle; she's asked to fully carry the commercial ball

---

17. Clive Barnes, *Butterflies Are Free* review, *New York Times*, Dec. 13, 1970.

(after all, who were Edward Albert or Eileen Heckart, his on-screen mother?), unrestricted by bigger name co-stars.

What she demonstrates, in her comet-like rise from TV's go-go dancing dumb blonde on *Laugh-In* (1969–73) to this, her third feature film, is a complete awareness of the audience-appeasing tools at her disposal: her silent film star eyes; her nubile dancer's body (she spends half the film in bra and panties); her anticipatory smile; her little-girl-lost, no, found, no, lost again, vibe. There's a knowing inventory of every individual piece in her toolkit and a quietly calculated command of each. It's a Pavlovian performance, yet it flows and amuses and excites; an overriding naturalism plays Zeus over the lesser gods.

As such, Hawn began to make a serious place for herself among the female film firmament of the time. Nineteen seventy-two gave us Liza Minnelli in *Cabaret*, Diana Ross in *Lady Sings the Blues*, Cicely Tyson in *Sounder* and Barbra Streisand in *What's Up, Doc?* A forefront of feminist-influenced women, making major inroads on American screens. In time, many of them came to constitute the first generation of Hollywood-based females to shape their cinematic destinies, obtaining creative control over their projects and molding, thereby, their professional images as they saw fit.

Hawn accomplished this as well, and, arguably, better than most. That said, she would never be taken as seriously as, say, a Fonda or a Streisand, an ignominy largely due to the "bubble-headed" aspect of her characters, a bread-and-butter quality she refused to refute.

Milton Katselas, the Elia Kazan protégé who directed the play, was awarded the honors for the film. He knew the property inside and out, and proves here, assisted by cinematographer Charles B. Lang, that he also knew how to frame it. And like all theater-based directors, he could be counted on to draw out strong performances: Hawn, for sure, but also Albert, given the toughest assignment of the lot, and Heckart, repeating her stage role.

Free love ain't so bad, the film announces, as long as it's tempered with good ol' fashioned decency. The butterflies, then, aren't exactly free. They're happily caged.

Every Thing You Always Wanted to Know About Sex* *But Were Afraid to Ask

Plot: A series of sketches based on Dr. David Reuben's bestselling primer on human sexuality. **Script/Director:** Woody Allen. **Cast:** Woody Allen, Louise Lasser, Anthony Quayle, Lynn Redgrave, Gene Wilder, Lou Jacobi, John Carradine, Tony Randall, Burt Reynolds. United Artists. 88 minutes.

It was a good hook: the controversial bestseller on sexuality interpreted (well, at least select sections of it) by the short, myopic TV and film comic positing himself as America's anti-sex symbol. (There'd be a cameo, though, by the nation's genuine sex symbol: Burt Reynolds.)

After securing film rights to the book from then-star Elliott Gould (Lord knows what he was planning to do with it), Woody Allen borrowed but a few of the book's inquisitive chapter headings—e.g.: "Do aphrodisiacs work?"—and used them as springboards for a series of outrageous black-out sketches. Foregoing the allusions to narrative he'd been entertaining in *Play It Again, Sam* (1972) and, to a lesser degree, *Bananas* (1971), Allen returned to his sketch writing roots. This time, he introduced clinical sexuality to the form, largely in the way of his facility for parody and his bent for over-the-top surrealism. The result is an uneven comic revue whose highlights, gratifyingly, dwarf the noble misses.

It's also a showcase for Allen's comic versatility. The film's episodes range from the old-fashioned—an opening sketch about a medieval fool pursuing a prudish queen, a kind of sexualized Bob Hope vehicle—to the pains-takingly parodied—the vintage game show *What's My Line?* (1950–67), re-imagined in all its kinescopic glory as *What's My Perversion?* (Look for Regis Philbin as one of the panelists, long before his two-decade TV ubiquity.)

Under the latter banner resides the film's least successful entry, though it constitutes Allen's first serious stretch as a film director: a send-up of Antonioni, in which a cool customer cannot bring his equally removed wife to orgasm. It's strong, studied work, dressed in the Italian filmmaker's arcane Euro glam, replete with its showy, geometric framing, its distinct color palette, and its terse verbal rhythms, comically betrayed here by boyish subtitles. Curiously, though, the episode subscribes to no culminating punchline. Where's the obligatory rimshot? (Allen co-stars in the episode with then-wife Louise Lasser. They appear to have had bad luck together making this one; another sketch, in which they played spiders, failed to make the final cut.)

Allen distinguishes himself, however, whenever he trades his parodic pen (though a spoof of horror films, starring genre staple John Carradine, has its moments, largely thanks to a series of oversized props) for a more original, character-based form of comedy. The first serves as a perfect vehicle for the distinct comic persona of Gene Wilder, who, with his pleading blue eyes, small, gaping mouth, and knee-jerk blood pressure spikes brings hyperkinetic humanity to the absurdist tale of a respected doctor who falls for a sheep. (It helps too that the sheep's organic docility provides a perfectly contrasting deadpan.) Then there's Lou Jacobi, American cinema's Jewish uncle, chancily transitioning from avuncular kvetch to improbable transvestite, another sketch made memorable by perfect casting.

The climactic piece, interestingly, must have made a sizable imprint on the filmmaker: a look at the human body as a busy command center, negotiating a prospective sexual encounter (with Erin Fleming, Groucho Marx's sometime-actress caregiver, soon to make headlines as a practitioner of elder abuse). It's rendered in futuristic whites and flashing thingamabobs, clearly foreshadowing *Sleeper* (1973). Like a lot of what precedes it, it's fundamentally funny, though peppered with jokes and asides that in today's politically enlightened age might be classified as crude or sophomoric. (Allen later confessed to a sense of deep embarrassment over some of the film's material.)

Still, the film helped to affirm that sex had come to American film comedy, and that all forms of humor were welcome to it.

The Heartbreak Kid

Plot: On his honeymoon, a young Jewish man falls for a WASPy beauty. **Director:** Elaine May. **Script:** Neil Simon, based on a story by Bruce Jay Friedman. **Cast:** Charles Grodin, Jeannie Berlin, Cybill Shepherd, Eddie Albert. 20th Century–Fox. 106 minutes.

I wouldn't be the first critic to make a comparative study between Mike Nichols' *The Graduate* (1967) and Elaine May's *The Heartbreak Kid*. Could it have been possible that May, Nichols' former partner in comedic crime, in a fit of jealousy, envy and one-upmanship, decided to remake Nichols' mega-hit? Or perhaps, egotistically, improve upon it, largely by adding the Jewishness Nichols' version could but subliminally (largely through the casting of Dustin Hoffman) suggest?

The Heartbreak Kid, based on a short story by satirist Bruce Jay Friedman, boasts one of the best comic hooks of the era, firmly rooted in the universal male fantasy— namely, the transformative hunt by the invisible everyman for the great golden goddess (put more colloquially, the blonde, blue-eyed cheerleader).

Lenny Cantrow is a New York nebbish who, too quickly, acquiesces to the behavioral template of his culture: He marries a nice, if blowsy, Jewish girl, then heads to Miami Beach (where else?) for the honeymoon. There, a mere three days into his marriage, the hairpin essence of his character is revealed: He decides to leave his unsuspecting bride for an all–American Amazon from WASPy Minnesota.

Like a lot of late 1960s-early 1970s comic heroes, Lenny, by way of the anything-goes sexual revolution, is out to find a romantic form of spiritual fulfillment. In the end, though, all he'll be left with is a bad case of the nagging, unnamed ennui first introduced to cinematic audiences in *The Graduate*.

There's more borrowed here from Nichols' landmark comedy, much more in fact: the narrative dynamic—young, uncertain interloper makes a play for respected family's daughter, upsetting all and sundry; an angry, judgmental father figure as formidable foe; a third act in which Lenny pops up at his paramour's college, hoping to make the improbable, at long last, probable.

It's the Jews vs. the Protestants, marriage vs. experimentation, the moderns vs. the traditionalists—all of the battles then being fought, on-screen as in life. Familiar territory, cinematically, even as early as 1972, though a lot of it would continue to play out throughout the decade. Few films, however, would do it as successfully, benefiting as *Hearbreak Kid* does from a trio of top-tier talents seeped in the befitting sensibility: Friedman, Neil Simon and May.

The first two shared such an inherent comic and thematic kinship, it forced the latter to respect their narrative. Simon had but to interpolate, not impose, the nerve-fraught male-female badinage by which he was making his name. Two hours of Simon is an acquired taste, bordering on the laborious. Simon kept short and sweet renders an audience, conversely, hungry for more. After a while, the film begins to operate like a thriller: We anticipate the coming dangers, eager to see how our hero wrangles his way out of each.

May certainly recognized a good scene when she read one, and there are many here: Lenny lying to his wife *ad infinitum*, the big break-up in the seafood restaurant, Lenny's climactic face-to-face with his prospective father-in-law. She also recognized its place. The credits may start with Simon's name but note how rapidly "An Elaine May film" appears after it. With wisdom and pride, May frames Simon's scenes within bittersweet documentary pretensions, purporting to present a quirky episode from contemporary Jewish life.

When not showing off her facility with actors, she's busy trying to make the implausible plausible, largely through her detailed eye for the comically quotidian (the plinky piano at the opening wedding scene, for example, sounding a then-popular Coke jingle over the mazel tovs and huzzahs).

She had a more than willing accomplice in Charles Grodin, then an up-and-coming character actor in his first starring role. (Sad to say, it remained one of his few). Appearing in one of his most fertile toupees (there'd be others), Grodin's miniaturist style is perfectly suited to the ethos of the property. He never once stomps on a line, as too many do when playing Simon. Instead, he approaches them sheepishly, like he's scared of saying them, like the joke or the sentiment therein might be too big for him, might dare to express him in totality, thus robbing him of his essence. When contrasted with a bigger player, like Jeannie Berlin here as his shrewish wife, or later, the ever-stewing Robert De Niro in *Midnight Run* (1987), it brings that quality out all the beneficially more.

Let's go back to contrast, what comedy is, largely, all about. How so expert a comedy writer as Simon then, by arguing for WASPy Diane Keaton in the Berlin part, could have forgotten it is puzzling. Perhaps he feared, with May's casting, accusations of anti–Semitism, the film being prospectively reduced to a lay-off-my-man tug of war between an unattractive JAP and a Breck Shampoo model. And in his defense, Berlin (May's daughter) spends the film as a homely stooge. But a simple brunette-blonde, Veronica-Betty grudge match would have comedically upset the film, castrating Lenny to mere kook and softening or even exorcising the all-important culture clash. Instead, we have a comedy that operates on all cylinders, as much a sociological comparative study as a behaviorally based bedroom farce.

Charles Grodin and Cybill Shepherd in Elaine May's *The Heartbreak Kid* (20th Century–Fox, 1972). With the rise of feminism, 1970s film comedy ached for a female auteur. May filled the bill but for a few short years (20th Century–Fox/Photofest).

As far as Hollywood's Jewish New Wave went, May, with *Heartbreak Kid*, had clearly reached the summit. It seemed a sure bet that she was on her way to becoming American comic film's first bona fide female auteur, ready to hold her own with Woody Allen and Mel Brooks, then also on the rise. But that imploded, due to a combination of ego, self-indulgence, questionable choices and studio tussles. (Many a director would follow suit, ending the American auteur movement by decade's end and ushering in the age of the producer-driven blockbuster.) Instead, May went on to a hit-and-miss career as an industry Renaissance woman.

Heartbreak indeed.

Last of the Red Hot Lovers

Plot: A middle-aged man, out to get in on the sexual revolution, tries staging affairs with three different women. **Director:** Gene Saks. **Script:** Neil Simon, based on his play. **Cast:** Alan Arkin, Sally Kellerman, Paula Prentiss, Renee Taylor. Paramount. 98 minutes.

Every season has its Simon—so went a Broadway bromide that endured from the early 1960s 'til the advent of the 1990s. And every play, in turn, its cinematic adaptation. What moviegoing audiences were treated to, mostly, were filmed records of Simon's stage plays, well cast, energetically played, and only semi-apologetically hermetic. Brought before the cameras, Simon's properties were opened up but a little: a token street scene here, a to-and-fro in a coffee shop there. Then it was back to the apartment or the hotel room where most of the action—a man and woman, usually, warring wittily as a result of changing times—took place.

The film *Last of the Red Hot Lovers*, adapted from the 1969 stage play, was the embodiment of the practice. It's three big scenes, all taking place in the same location: the tasteful apartment of the hapless hero's mother as he tries, with a trio of troubled women, to conduct an affair if only to get in on the sexual revolution of which he is, thanks to the rigid values that remain the pride of his generation, exempt.

The wrapping and the ribbons over all of this—a little *cinema verité*, accompanied by a morose mumble of a voiceover—are particularly execrable. The play's the thing. Why have Gene Saks, director of so many of Simon's stage productions, purport membership to the *nouvelle vague*?

But distinguish himself, once comfortably within four walls, Saks does, with his unabashed reverence for Simon's dialogue and the fire he sets under his actors. He even manages to give what little depth the property has its proper due, likely sharing Simon's Act One lament about the invisibility, sexual and otherwise, of the middle-aged male (Saks was 50 at the time). Alan Arkin, in the lead, is even made to resemble his director, sporting Saks' horseshoe hair and stern-faced mustache. So, call it autobiographical.

Saks probably didn't have to work with Arkin too much, one imagines, as cinema's top neurotic before the reign of Woody Allen delivers, largely on instinct, a comic *tour de force*, switching gears from vegetable to animal and back again like an on-off power surge. Part of the trick to playing Simon is to make audiences sense the human behind the caricature. Some don't even bother, happier to simply put on a show. Arkin, though, while as happy to ham it up as anyone else awarded a Simonesque opportunity, succeeds and then some, giving us *Death of a Salesman* as bedroom farce.

The most pleasant surprise is the women. While only Renée Taylor, as a doubting housewife looking to avenge a cheating husband, seems like a fit, both Sally Kellerman, as a leggy Italiano, and Paula Prentiss, as an off-key chatterbox, fall into the swing of things with educated aplomb, occasionally even upstaging Arkin and preventing the property from becoming a one-man show. The Arkin-Kellerman exchange is such a fair fight, the audience may begin to wonder if Simon would have been better off spending less time at his typewriter and presenting a One-Act play.

All of this to say that for all of the critical pushback about the bulk of Simon's cinematic work being little more than filmed theater, such complaints overlook the careful caliber of the casting and the hard reality that it takes a decidedly theatrical hand, like Saks', to make Simon's brand of urban comic angst function properly. The badinage, the neurosis, the hysteria are geographic by-products; it's the convention of confinement that wrings them out of Simon's otherwise buttoned-down characters. Let loose into the world—other than for a minute-long stroll or a stop at a coffee shop—these characters are but uninteresting stereotypes.

Play It Again, Sam

Plot: A neurotic film critic, guided by the spirit of Humphrey Bogart, romances his best friend's wife. **Director:** Herbert Ross. **Script:** Woody Allen, based on his play. **Cast:** Woody Allen, Diane Keaton, Tony Roberts. Paramount. 87 minutes.

No post–Studio Era icon enjoyed an echo as lasting as Humphrey Bogart's. There were endless deserving candidates, both male (Edward G. Robinson, James Cagney, Spencer Tracy) and female (Bette Davis, Katharine Hepburn, Joan Crawford)—and yet it was Bogie, growlingly lisping under his trademark fedora, who lived, posthumously, largest. Today, his very presence symbolizes the entire American film period from the 1930s to the mid–50s. And yet, in his lifetime, despite regular star billing, he was considered by public and press alike to be an acquired taste. Why him, then, as the gilded icon of a bygone heyday?

The answer lies in the persona he perpetuated throughout his largely black-and-white career: the smart-mouthed outlier pulled into a subversively corrupt society. There, it seemed, his purpose was to direct a searchlight on its Jungian shadows and to hold the rogues he exposed accountable for their actions. While often bruised in the end, Bogie almost always managed to walk away, buoyed by a cynical, self-preserving code stitched from the folly of writing wrongs.

As such, Bogie was adopted by a swath of other self-appointed shit disturbers, the counterculture. Life-size posters of him began to be taped to dormitory doors, art houses began to play his movies, and his gravelly pugnaciousness was imitated by all.

This new audience had picked him, in effect, out of the garbage: the ruins of the old Studio System, the Hollywood-based production factories that, for almost seven decades, had ground out films the way that Detroit had made wheels or Milwaukee, beer cans. Disgruntled 20-somethings had caught this catalogue on late-night TV and had picked out a number of stars with whom they could identify. Foremost were Bogart and the Marx Brothers, all celluloid practitioners of needling the establishment until it imploded. (The Marxes' 1930 *Animal Crackers* got a theatrical re-release in 1974.)

Bogie represented something else, too: an old-fashioned definition of manhood that was being reshaped by feminism. By 1972, the female population had begun to advocate for a post-patriarchal male, not someone in the mold of their right-wing, taciturn businessmen-fathers but a leftist, responsive egalitarian. He'd have a public avatar, mid-decade, on network TV, in the form of anti-violence, pro–ERA poster boy Alan Alda. Meanwhile, though, American men were struggling to conform to this new, feminism-formed image without violating a gender-based sensibility they considered nobly intrinsic, something Bogartesque. A widespread male identity crisis was on.

Who better to comedically represent said crisis than Woody Allen? In his hit stage play *Play It Again, Sam*, he presented a pleasant, probing contrast of patriarchal, alpha male masculinity with the self-aware, confessional variety.

Allen, circa 1972, was at the height of the development of his comic persona: the sexually obsessed, hopelessly insecure, physically frail nebbish. He'd hang on to it 'til it was long past its due date but here, it's fresh and complete. He's Alan Felix, one of those Bogart-loving film nuts then at large, only this one can't get women—a situation that magically invokes the ghost of his idol, who lends him enough of his persona to see him through a *Casablanca*-influenced affair with Felix's best friend's wife.

It's not only Allen at his verbal finest, it's one of his last ditches as a physical comedian. Periodically, he gives himself opportunities to enhance his social awkwardness with laugh-out-loud slapstick, an amalgam of traditions old and new that resurfaced in even better balance in *Love and Death* (1975). By the time he made what is generally considered his masterpiece, *Annie Hall* (1977), the verbal and the cinematic took over from the physical—the beginning of his career conversion from ambitious movie comic to experimental auteur.

Speaking of *Annie, Play It Again, Sam* is Allen's first on-screen pairing with the perfectly complementary Diane Keaton. Together, they constituted the most successful male-female comedy combo since Nichols and May, filling the gap until the emergence of Tom Hanks and Meg Ryan. It's New York Jew meets Midwestern WASP. In almost all other comedies of the time, these types are rivals.

But here, and in later Allen-Keaton films, their commonality is almost instant; by the first plot point, she recognizes that there's a lot more of him in her than she thought and he begins to borrow some of her soul-saving stalwartness. Yes, it always ends; Allen may be the only major film comic who never got the girl. (There was Tati too but that was because his trademark persona, Mr. Hulot, was such an indifferent creature.) With so much comedy at that time devoted to warring worlds, Allen's, refreshingly, is about the sweet if brief possibility of fusion.

For Allen, it was a break too from his home base (*Play It Again, Sam* is set and shot in San Francisco, which serves as a geographic metaphor for the film's "love is an uphill struggle" theme) and from the responsibility of directing. He conceded that to Herb Ross, who again does great service to the property, chopping it up into smaller scenes and keeping the actors on their toes. He even manages to wring some Chaplin-esque sympathy for the lead character, finding a human heart in Allen's caricature.

Plus, Ross playfully uses some *au courant cinema verité*, to commendable effect. One wonders, after a fashion, about this film's influence on Allen as a filmmaker. Many of the compositions suggest Allen's later work, as does the cinematography—and there's a parody of foreign cinema which, while conceived by Allen, is accomplished enough that Allen tries it again himself in his *Every Thing You Always Wanted to Know About Sex* *But Were Afraid to Ask* (1972).

No run-of-the-mill stage-to-screen adaptation, *Play It Again, Sam* helped to unleash several 1970s comic film Best Practices—namely, the habit of characters wearing their subconscious selves on their sleeves. Early practitioners, like Alan Arkin and Gene Wilder, had to be circumstantially brought to it; here, it's like breathing. And by 1972, with the re-election of warmongering, economy-ravaging Richard Nixon, it became more and more difficult for anxious America—subversively, through the movies—to keep its insecurities to itself. What was once a cry was now a conversation.

With Allen too, particularly here, sex comes to American comic cinema, just as he had brought it, years earlier, to stand-up comedy. The new frankness that was permeating drama was finally crossing over. Who better to lead the charge for a physical act that had always represented traditional manhood than the poster boy for the new, confused male, trying to enjoy its hedonistic pleasure while separating it from the outdated stereotype that valued it just as much?

The War Between Men and Women

Plot: A nearsighted misanthrope inherits a wife and daughter, forcing him to face his misogyny. **Director:** Melville Shavelson. **Script:** Melville Shavelson, Danny Arnold, based on the work of James Thurber. **Cast:** Jack Lemmon, Barbara Harris, Jason Robards, Lisa Gerritson. National General Pictures. 110 minutes.

In 1969, industry veteran Melville Shavelson, who had cut his teeth fashioning comic vehicles for Bob Hope and Danny Kaye, brought to television the work of *New Yorker* humorist-illustrator James Thurber, a 1940s-50s literary darling. The series was an inventive mix of live-action and animation called *My World—and Welcome to It*. The result was critical acclaim, an Emmy for Outstanding Comedy Series—and almost immediate cancellation.

So, try, try again.

Buoyed by the series' critical reception, Shavelson refashioned some of the material into a screenplay. The resulting film, *The War Between Men and Women*, feels, predictably, like an extended edition of the sitcom, bigger in cinematic scope and deeper in content.

It concerns the conversion of a mouthy, myopic misogynist—humorist-cartoonist Peter Wilson, a character clearly based on the bespectacled, curmudgeonly Thurber—to family man, the unwitting overlord of a landscape littered with his pet peeves: women, children, dogs. (Thurber was the thinking man's W.C. Fields.)

While the film retains many of the conventions of the TV series, plus some tried-and-true romantic comedy traditions, it comes into its own in the second act, when husband and ex-husband enjoy a long, boozy convo on the nature of women. Thus, the revelation: that Thurber, in 1972, had gained renewed relevance, his misogyny representing the battle then raging between the sexes. Further, the sequence climaxes with some clever interplay between man and cartoon, with Wilson drawing an army of Rubenesque warrior-women that he and his drinking buddy proceed to take on, guns literally blazing.

With the release of other comic films that year occupying the same thematic territory, including Neil Simon's *Last of the Red Hot Lovers*, Woody Allen's *Play It Again, Sam* and Elaine May's *The Heartbreak Kid*, not to mention Archie Bunker's frequent anti-feminist rants on primetime TV, it's safe to say that this was the year that the traditional American male made, in all forms of major media, his Last Stand, Custer-style. He ranted, he railed, he pitied himself. The more he did these things, the more he approached outright buffoonery.

"Mother," the daughter (played by Lisa Gerritson, retained from the TV series) asks after the aforementioned Scotch-soaked man-cartoon stand-off, "there's women all over the walls. Why would men draw something like that?" Answers her mother: "It's the only way they can win."

The film, then, is a political-sexual concession, the hero's impending blindness (the subplot) a metaphor for the loss of his outdated view of the opposite sex. Well ... a near-concession. In the end, Wilson is still classified "the same mean old son of a bitch." Nevertheless, he's been visibly humbled. So still, it's the TV series put to sociological use.

As such, the film should simply serve as a timepiece. To its credit, it's more than that. Shavelson's one-liners out–Simon Neil Simon, while reflecting a greater intelligence and pithiness; DePatie-Freleng's classy hand with Thurber's loopy, lumpy caricatures, culminating in a winning "living storybook," take on his famed short story "The Last Flower"; the cast: Jack Lemmon as Wilson, Barbara Harris as the object of his love and ire, and Jason Robards as her ex-husband, all play it with the perfect light-dark touch, rescuing the film from such prospective adjectives as "preachy," "cloying" and "noisy."

Award it, at least, the same cult status as the series.

What's Up, Doc?

Plot: A married musicologist is doggedly pursued by a kooky college drop-out. **Director:** Peter Bogdanovich. **Script:** Buck Henry, David Newman, Robert Benton. **Cast:** Barbra Streisand, Ryan O'Neal, Madeline Kahn, Kenneth Mars, Austin Pendleton, Michael Murphy. Warner Bros. 94 minutes.

"A screwball comedy. Remember them?"

So asked the poster for this unapologetic throwback. The answer was a resounding "Yes!" as the film went on to become the third-highest grosser of the year (behind the instant classic *The Godfather* and "disaster film" granddaddy *The Poseidon Adventure*).

It was the inevitable brainchild of Peter Bogdanovich: Inspired by the critics cum filmmakers who modernized French cinema in the 1950s, he had grandiosely committed to parlaying his reputation as a literary exponent of the studio system, prolifically interviewing heyday directors and actors, into a career as a bona fide director. After an apprenticeship under fast-buck artist Roger Corman—a low-paying mentorship that became a generational baptism—Bogdanovich developed a cult reputation with *Targets* (1968). Then he took the world by storm, Orson Welles–style, as the *enfant terrible* behind the impressively atmospheric *The Last Picture Show* (1971).

While *Targets* drew, perversely, on Hollywood's Golden Era, Bogdanovich had yet to fully promote the kind of cinema closest to his heart: full-scale homages to Classic Film.

Now, with box-office clout, he could. It was time to indulge in the genres, storylines and archetypes he had been keeping alive through articles, documentaries and books, elements for which an older demographic still hungered while the younger one, mostly through collegiate Film Studies programs, were intellectually dissecting.

Star Barbra Streisand's people came to Bogdanovich first. The then-vaunted screenwriting team of Robert Benton and David Newman were directed to devise an old-fashioned screwball comedy, with plenty of star quality. Though other writers came on board, the Benton-Newman imprint remains on the film. A lot of it, in fact, particularly the third act, plays like a parody of their acclaimed *Bonnie and Clyde* (1967): two young, offbeat lovers enjoying the Heaven-Hell of being on the run. Buck Henry also contributed, no doubt adding form (Benton-Newman had a reputation for loose narrative) by borrowing from the film's clear inspiration: Howard Hawks' manic *Bringing Up Baby* (1938).

Bringing Up Baby was a flop in its day, but was rechristened Grade A after a later generation discovered it on television. Cary Grant starred as a befuddled paleontologist stalked by a free-spirited scatterbrain. In *What's Up, Doc?*, Ryan O'Neal is a befuddled musicologist stalked by a free-spirited scatterbrain. In *Baby*, Grant is drawn into a wild goose chase for a missing bone. In *What's Up, Doc?*, O'Neal is drawn into a wild goose chase for a missing rock. All of this—and many other parallels—to say that you can almost call the latter a remake of the former (many did) or, in modern parlance,

Peter Bogdanovich directs Barbra Streisand and Ryan O'Neal in *What's Up, Doc?* (Warner Bros., 1972). Early 1970s cinema was rife with 1930s nostalgia, the era in which the primary moviegoing audience had come of age and whose films were now being intellectualized by the younger demographic. One of its prime practitioners was journalist-cum-auteur Bogdanovich (Warner Bros./Photofest).

a re-imagining. We're much more forgiving about that kind of thing these days. Bogdanovich, unfairly, was exonerated only by the box office. The Old School highbrows called his film an act of hubristic heresy, the messy, forced infantilization of a greater work; the young intellectuals lamented the loss of an original cinematic voice, one who blinded a keen, reflective eye on marginal America to make crowd-pleasing, derivative claptrap. In their defense, *What's Up, Doc?* is very much a love letter to Warner Bros., whose archive was its inspiration (mostly) and who were paying the bills besides, from the assaulting use of their music catalogue to the references to their classic stars (including Bogart) and the use of titles and gags from their signature cartoons (and finally, the cartoons themselves). Cloying to some, but mainstream audiences, looking for pure throwback entertainment, loved it. They won: Today, stripped of comparative study due to the erosion of interest in the black-and-white era, the film stands as a spirited star vehicle, energetic and endearing, if engineered.

Like in so many films of the early part of the era, *What's Up, Doc?* runs on an Establishment vs. Counterculture, WASP vs. Jew dynamic, with the latter, incident by incident, winning. Perhaps, in RKO's *Baby*, Bogdanovich recognized the precursor of something that would play even better in contemporary times while still maintaining its nostalgic feel. So, once again, it's politesse vs. shtick.

Streisand, having been a musical comedy star, a legitimate actress and a sex symbol, was now ready to be all three at once. And she is, distinguishing herself, if at times a little too indulgently, in each capacity. She's a bit old for the part—a struggling student? Babs, who are you fooling?—negating any true counterculture vibe.

But the film has no real political pretensions; the hipification of Streisand is just a quick, easy way to update the material. They're looking for a yakky, obtrusive, energetic, offbeat lost soul, which she delivers with show biz aplomb. So formative was the role that Streisand made a mini-career of it, playing a well-meaning, man-fixated, accident-prone gamin again in *For Pete's Sake* (1974), a kinder, gentler version of *Doc*.

O'Neal, as her straight man, tries hard but as a reactor, he can't bring to things what Cary Grant did. So, it's a one-woman show. Well, almost.

There's the supporting cast, most caught up in the film's B plot, an elongated farce about the misappropriation of matching suitcases, one of which contains the elusive rock, the other important government papers—the Hitchcockian MacGuffin of which the reverent Bogdanovich, self-appointed Hollywood nostalgist, had waxed about in print. Bogdanovich pulls off the endless comings and goings with control and relish, even tipping things, occasionally, into Marxian madness. He was later afforded a chance to try his hand at this kind of exercise again, with the 1992 film adaptation of the hit play *Noises Off*. Both cases are testaments to his brief apprenticeship, pre–literary career, in the theater.

Oh yes—that supporting cast. There's Kenneth Mars as a Germanic fop, reminding Classic Film fans of Hans Conried; Austin Pendleton as a blushing nebbish; and, in her film debut (disregarding *The Duva*, 1968, an amusing Bergman parody), Madeline Kahn as the operatic frump Streisand must liberate O'Neal from. Who would have known, seeing her here, that one of the sexiest comic stars of the era was hiding in that bouffant and baby doll wardrobe? Also, in a Capra-esque turn as a quirky, beleaguered judge, diminutive Liam Dunn, who never had as meaty a role again (despite small, memorable stints in Mel Brooks' *Blazing Saddles*, 1974, *Young Frankenstein*, 1974, and *Silent Movie*, 1976).

Given the success of *What's Up, Doc?*, only the third film under Bogdanovich's belt, how could he have known that this was the beginning of the end? Audience nostalgia for a bygone era would remain strong for the next few years (the following year, the 1930s-set *The Sting* swept the Oscars), but Bogdanovich never again successfully capitalized on it. A hit-and-miss career would ensue, positing his reputation just outside the Winner's Circle in the arena of great 1970s directors.

1973

In 1973, Watergate came to cinema. It would take another three years, which would include the fall of Nixon and a bestselling account of the chicanery he clumsily masterminded, before drama could do the whole messy affair proper justice (*All the President's Men*, 1976) But it would come to comedy early. With that appropriation, what was fast becoming a staid comic formula—the conversion of the befuddled WASP at the hands of hippies—would begin to disappear.

The converters, the anti-heroes, remain such, only they work in greater solidarity and target not individuals but systems. Armies on both sides of the battle line grew bigger. Further, the overall comic tone of things changed. No one was out to simply disrupt any more. No longer were the weapons of underdog choice slapstick, social embarrassment or sexual impropriety. A single weapon would do: The Big Gun was the con, playing the naïve or the equal to infiltrate Command Central, then, subvert it via back-room engineering. Nixon, by bugging and breaking into the headquarters of his Democratic rivals, had done same, to political scandal and public shame. Now, the counterculture was going to send him up by comically mirroring his tactics, incompetence included. The yield, though, would be different: widespread acclaim.

This new emphasis also helped to unite a hitherto divided audience. For the most part, the adults had their films and the kids had theirs; the big chain cinemas vs. the art house. Rare was the crossover hit, aside from the odd *succès de scandale* (like *The Exorcist*, 1973). Now, though, with the scandalous serendipity of a common enemy, anti-hero momentum was a universal phenomenon. Finally, in life as on-screen, the hippies had succeeded in converting the WASPs.

The new comic hero was an entity: a gang of raggy misfits, out to wreak havoc not with 1960s-style anger or aspirations of socio-political reform but with a knowing wink and a sly nod. After all, we were all in this together now, right?

No film caught this wave as well as George Roy Hill's surprise hit *The Sting*. But there was also the equally charming *Paper Moon* and the messy but well-intentioned *Steelyard Blues*. While Serpico was martyring himself, trying to expose corrupt police culture (drama again proving what comedy was already figuring out: that it's easier to fight as part of a united front), the equally frustrated heroes of *Cops and Robbers* were doing same as his comic equivalent. Even the films that weren't out to subvert anything, like George Lucas' busily innocent *American Graffiti*, had subsectors as central heroes.

The nostalgia thing, meanwhile, still played but it wasn't just the FDR 1930s that were being sentimentalized any more; the 1950s and early 1960s were joining the fold. Mainstream movies were beginning, slowly, to acknowledge the maturing of a new demographic, the Baby Boomers. Formative rock'n'roll was enjoying a renaissance in record shops and on the radio, while network TV, hot on the heels of the success of *American Graffiti*, was grinding out *Happy Days* (1974–84).

Meanwhile, though, the con was on!

American Graffiti

Plot: The night before they're slated to go east for college, a collection of small-town California kids indulge in teenage pastimes one final time. **Director:** George Lucas. **Script:** Willard Huyck, Gloria Katz. **Cast:** Richard Dreyfuss, Ron Howard, Cindy Williams, Charles Martin Smith, Paul Le Mat, Candy Clark, Mackenzie Phillips, Wolfman Jack. Universal. 112 minutes.

"*American Graffiti* is still fun," critic–film historian David Thomson asserted 36 years after its release, "and still an honest teenage picture from a time when teenagers kept their fun and their anguish decently to themselves in the certainty that they weren't worth a hill of beans anywhere else."[18] In this same entry in his *Have You Seen…?*, Thomson noted the film's "sly charm," interpolating nods to its sobriety and modesty.

Justified assessments, yes, but decidedly revisionist. Upon its debut, *Graffiti* was considered an electric act of cinematic bombast, equally crowned and questioned for its all-out celebration of teenage hijinks. Never before had the Baby Boomers, then still called War Babies, been so cinematically celebrated. The idle, indulgent life they led while creeping up, semi-silently, on adulthood—a life of cruising the main drag, hanging out in burger joints, and benign acts of delinquency—was suddenly presented not as an empty, self-indulgent life stage but as a definitive model of existence. The movies, at this time, were still busy trying to squeeze a dollar out of the previous generation. That year's other foray into nostalgia was *The Way We Were*, a star-based romance covering the gamut from the Dirty '30s to the McCarthy portion of the 1950s. *Graffiti* was out to validate the lives of that generation's children. As such, it captured something universal (pun intended; Universal produced): a realistic record of the American teenage experience.

It's Steven Spielberg, generally, who is credited as the father of the "Hollywood Renaissance": the emergence of an exciting new crop of young American filmmaking talent, most mentored by B-king Roger Corman or generational elder statesman (and *Graffiti* producer) Francis Ford Coppola. But credit for the movement rightly belongs to a quiet, small-town California car nut, George Lucas. Lucas, first by parlaying his own experiences (along with co-screenwriters Willard Huyck and Gloria Katz) into *Graffiti*, then by regurgitating one of his generation's guilty TV pleasures—B studio sci-fi serials—into *Star Wars* (1977), led the Boomers, Moses-like, into the Promised Land, delivering them to the major studios as the cash-happy moviegoing audience to be primarily appeased.

Graffiti is a likable cross-stitch of teenage troubles circa 1962 (though really, it's the late '50s) taking place over a long, single, high beam–lit night. To a decade's worth of Top Forty chartbusters, mixed so that they sound like they're coming out of a car radio,

18. David Thomson, *Have You Seen…?* (New York: Alfred A. Knopf, 2009), 28.

Charles Martin Smith and Candy Clark in *American Graffiti* (Universal, 1973). *Graffiti* not only reflected a deep-set collective nostalgia for more innocent times, but also ushered in a new filmgoing demographic: the Baby Boomers (Universal Pictures/Photofest).

a collection of stereotypes—the males: an everyman, a mensch, a tough guy, a nerd; the females: a goody-two-shoes, a tart, a gawky pre-teen—cruise the central strip, try to get laid, and second-guess their next life, whether it be college, romantic commitment or death. While celebrating the best of times (as all of America was: poisoned by Vietnam and the growing Watergate scandal, a collective wish was at work for a time machine that would bring the country back to the serenely sterile), the film subscribed to a subversive fatalism. They are not long the days of wine and roses—neither, maintained Lucas, those of an illegally acquired pint of Old Harper or of peeling out of Mel's Drive-in.

Much ballyhooed was the cast—all, except for Ron Howard (who soon, thanks to *Graffiti*, would be cast in TV's more sanitary version of *Happy Days*, 1974–84), had been unknown. It's little remembered that the prospective Golden Child, according to the critics, was the largely forgotten Paul Le Mat as the dime store James Dean. Even the bestselling soundtrack's liner notes single him out. The lesson: America loves, above all types, a rebel.

Speaking of soundtracks and rebels, where the hell is Elvis? Not only has Elvis left the building, but he's also left the era in which he came to fame. RCA, it ended up, wanted too much money for his tunes. So Lucas settled for Bill Haley, Chuck Berry, the Big Bopper, et al.—not bad for second prize.

Second prizes, in fact, abound: Ron Howard's character, slated for a promising college career, settles for small-town domesticity; Charles Martin Smith, filmdom's first realistic nerd, spends the night with a blowsy blonde out of his league (the sexy-sweet Candy Clark, giving the film's only Oscar-nominated performance) only to confess that he is not as he had purported; Le Mat, the drag race king, wins the climactic game of chicken against his cowboy-hatted rival (a skinny, shadowy Harrison Ford) but knows, nevertheless, that his days are numbered; Richard Dreyfuss, in a deceptively low-key debut (he'd played bit parts before), suffers a double whammy: first, by being brought to realize that the God to which the kids bow—DJ Wolfman Jack—is but a fabricated persona, then, by never catching up to that blonde in that gleaming white T-Bird. In all cases, the lesson is the same: that there is no God, no silver loving cup, no adolescence in perpetuity. Diane Jacobs poetically wrote in her 1977 book *Hollywood Renaissance*, "It is Eve yearning for her apple, innocent and precocious and scared all at once."[19])

Life, in the end, is a walk through an automotive graveyard, like the one to which Le Mat takes the underaged date he is trying to shake (a perfectly punky Mackenzie Phillips). All of us, like America as it weaved its dangerous, crazy way from 1962 to 1973, are destined to end up ghosts of glory.

Blume in Love

Plot: A lawyer tries to win back his ex-wife from her bohemian boyfriend. **Script/ Director:** Paul Mazursky. **Cast:** George Segal, Jennifer Anspach, Kris Kristofferson, Marsha Mason. Warner Bros. 116 minutes.

As feminism continued to take root, Woody Allen wasn't alone in comedically examining the anxieties and value of the unseated American male. Another New Yorker with a pedigree in television, Paul Mazursky, was doing same. Though he had also enjoyed a stint as a Method-era actor (a capacity he would return to after his directorial days), Mazursky, in his films, gave himself but bit parts. He had scant interest in developing his own comic persona. His designs were grander than the kinds of vehicles that could accommodate that. Mazursky was out to examine the once sacred union of marriage, its fragility in changing times and, in an act of admirable egalitarianism, its effect on both men and women.

His first big splash, the controversial ensemble *Bob and Carol and Ted and Alice* (1969), did its best to spread the psychological wealth. Further, it helped to bring the frank, looser sexuality of European cinema to its American counterpart, a long-overdue crossover for which Mazursky was never given his due. A few misses later, Mazursky revisited the same thematic territory with *Blume in Love* (the title is a play on the Tin Pan Alley ditty *Love in Bloom*) with avatar George Segal as the poster boy for male, mid-life marital unmooring.

It's a cute premise: a divorce lawyer who triggers his own divorce, then can't win his wife back. It's worthy, with a little cleaning up, of the romcoms of old (think Cary Grant and Irene Dunne). And fundamentally, that's what the film is, only turned inside out. Yes, Blume succumbs to his male sexual instinct (a blind-eye peccadillo with

---

19. Diane Jacobs, *Hollywood Renaissance* (South Brunswick, N.J.: A.S. Barnes, 1977), 26.

a mini-skirted secretary) necessitating a sad-sack sojourn to Venice, Italy (the site of his honeymoon), to stew. But he's also a victim of turbulent times, the free love ethic that was still at large, insinuating its way into the middle-class marital bed. And, like Bob, Ted, Carol and Alice, he's a victim of that other Venice—California, where, in a nice irony, the film's domestic scenes are set. Perpetually at the forefront of any cultural trend or major movement (it's a point of pride over there), the West Coast was leading the charge in conjugal disruption and sexual experimentation while the East, at least in comic film, was still busy fretting over corrupt cops and garbage strikes. Mazursky, as a product of the latter, brought the right foreign eye to the California charge, capturing that culture's loose, woozy, semi-surrealistic vibe and its hermetic hold on those caught up in it. (Non–New Yorker Robert Altman, in work like *The Long Goodbye*, 1973, and *Short Cuts*, 1993, managed it too.)

Examinations of male sensitivity, while never really a genre, weren't new. As Diane Jacobs made plain in her 1977 *Hollywood Renaissance* (the first major work on America's new generation of filmmakers [Spielberg, Lucas *et al.*]), Old School populists like Frank Capra had been doing it for years, as had experimentalist John Cassavetes. But on the whole, exercises in emotional inventory had been the domain of female-oriented cinema. Bette Davis, Barbara Stanwyck and Joan Crawford had been its prime promulgators, with films like *Diary of a Mad Housewife* (1970) and *Klute* (1971) coming along to perpetuate and modernize the practice. In time, Mazursky joined the fold with his *An Unmarried Woman* (1978), a rare example of an American male writer-director making a female character study authentic and sincere enough to be embraced by the feminists—the counterpoint, if you will, to *Blume in Love,* adjusted for gender and tone.

Blume, like other Mazursky heroes (back to *I Love You, Alice B. Toklas,* 1966) is a seeker, a lost soul looking for a happy alternative to worlds either too stifling (marriage) or too far-out (non-marriage). Further, those worlds are literal—the two Venices—though Mazursky recasts them with a nice, quiet irony: The chaste scenes are set in Europe, the sexed-up ones in America.

There's another contrast: Segal vs. romantic rival Kris Kristofferson, carving out his early on-screen career as a viable version of the hippie romantic alternative: a macho man-guru persona making the guitar-playing, dope-smoking, free-lovin' generation palatable to the Puritans—in this case, Segal's ex, played by the perpetually tense Susan Anspach. Segal and Kristofferson meet, and the tectonic plates of early '70s male identities are triggered into an act of friction.

Segal, an older, modernized version of the proverbial "nice Jewish boy," gets the worst of it, setting into motion an interesting love-hate "bromance" (long before the term was coined) reflecting Mazursky's, and male America's, ambivalence over persona and purpose. In one of the film's nicer scenes, Segal and Kristofferson croon "I'm Sick and Tired of Beating Down the Devil in Me," endorsing, male-wise, the "let it all hang out" war cry of the times while simultaneously parodying it. In the end, though, Mazursky the seeker finds what it is he is looking for—namely, a happy compromise: that each type can borrow, constructively, from the other.

Segal, it should be reiterated, is a great lightweight. His winning naturalism goes a very long way. (He even gets away with a rape scene—a shocking and inexcusable plot insertion by contemporary standards) with nary a trace of material-killing self-pity. Put in proper properties—not too shallow, not too deep—he would continue to distinguish himself, as he does here, throughout the decade.

The film's shaggy tone—a kind of aspirational realism influenced by fractional European storytelling—was all the rage at the time (again, think Robert Altman) though it's gone on to baffle many a first-time viewer in our age of Robert McKee mania. Some, though, adopted and adapted it. Quentin Tarantino became one of the film's big fans. Other aspects of *Blume in Love*—its deeply introspective relationships, its small cast, its autumnal colors—might have paved the way for Woody Allen's more serious efforts, wherein, with his slapdash classicism, he simplified and starched them.

The film's central triangle was visited again, often by Mazursky himself. We'd even see exactly the variation presented here, hairy-interloper-charming-the-man-of-the-house-while-semi-secretly-seducing-the-woman, in his comeback hit *Down and Out in Beverly Hills* (1986), itself an Americanization of Jean Renoir's *Boudu sauvé des eaux* (1932).

"In Mazursky's best films," wrote Pauline Kael, "craziness gives life its flavor and a little looseness hardly matters."[20] Fortunately, as both the times and cinematic storytelling stiffened, Mazursky, unlike too many members of the counterculture with whom he semi-sympathized, never cut with his fundamental values.

Cops and Robbers

Plot: Two frustrated New York cops pull off a heist during a parade. **Director:** Aram Avakian. **Script:** Donald E. Westlake. **Cast:** Joseph Bologna, Cliff Gorman. United Artists. 89 minutes.

In the 1930s, it had been the gangster, despite government intervention to romanticize his antithesis, the G-man. Jimmy, Kid or Duke was on the wrong side of the law and yet, in those cockeyed times of mile-long breadlines and pencil-hawking, seemed to be the only cinematic archetype able to cling to that eroding personal commodity: dignity. Diehard subscription to a gutsy, self-made morality was his secret until, America being, after all, a Puritan society, he had to be struck down for protecting it with a machine-gun.

After World War II, this philosophical mantle was passed on to the P.I. Silver screens were awash with a pugnacious population of trench coat–clad wiseacres, setting deluded dames straight, bringing down small empires built by little round men, and going *mano a mano* with their lunkheaded muscle. And what did they ask for in return? Not much. A modest fee per day plus expenses and the right, above all, to hold their heads high, to proclaim themselves the last scions of morality in an otherwise irreversibly corrupt universe.

By the 1970s, it was the cop, the boy in blue, the man on the beat. Ironic. A few years earlier, he had been the enemy, the anonymous, societal stooge, the pig, the fuzz, doing an old-fashioned, oppressive government's bidding: lobbing tear gas at crowds advocating for peace, love and understanding, or putting bullets into Kent State college kids. Now, though, the world, and New York City in particular, had really gone to Hell—and not just '60s-style Hell. Cities were unsafe, labor strikes were a daily occurrence, and drugs had become big business. Where once we might not have liked the cop very much,

---

20. Pauline Kael, *5001 Nights at the Movies* (New York: Henry Holt, 1991), 88.

now, by sheer necessity, he was what the gangster and the P.I. had been: the last line of defense against all-out chaos.

And like the gangster and the P.I., he had problems of his own. Big problems. By the early '70s, police corruption—again, particularly in New York—had hit an all-time high. In the '60s, the cops couldn't beat 'em so they joined 'em. They traded payoffs for blind eyes the way kids were trading bubble gum cards of Tom Seaver for Pete Rose, until a fellow cop, Frank Serpico, dared to blow the whistle. He got his own book and film, *Serpico* (1973) as compensation for the resulting loss of his career.

Serpico, book and movie, converted all of America to an internal investigation unit. Suddenly, through this gritty rise-and-fall parable centered around a modern-day Jesus, the world was made aware of just how widespread the compromise, coupled with crippling budget cuts, was among those responsible for everyday civic justice. Further, the film made us feel their pain. We became fully aware of just how tough the job was, of the depth of their challenges on the streets and at the office. They were no longer the dime-a-dozen, stone-faced pigs of yore, nor the pleasantly bland do-gooders of TV shows like *Adam-12* (1968–75). They were as vulnerable as those whom they protected and those whom they busted, maybe more so.

And so, public sympathy grew. An ex-cop with a pulpy way with words, Joseph Wambaugh, rose to the top of the crime fiction bestseller list; the cop-based TV series became, as much as then-stodgy TV would allow, more realistic, with procedurals like *Police Story* (1973–77; Wambaugh again) and sitcoms like *Barney Miller* (1975–82). Big-screen comedies accentuated the dangerous absurdity of cops' lives while again, pointing out their pain.

Enter *Cops and Robbers*, a low-budget, low-key comic caper in which a pair of hard-working boys on the beat, Joe Bologna and Cliff Gorman, are portrayed as just another set of good-hearted working stiffs. Their lives have plateaued. They're stuck in lower-middle-class New York, their common decency, both the professional and the personal, societally devalued. But they're New Yorkers—a touch of larceny lives within. Over the opening credits (featuring the worst entry of the film's mish-mash of a score, an eponymous light soul theme, penned by Michel Legrand no less, that sounds like *Shaft* on downers), one of them, in uniform, robs a liquor store. He confesses to his partner one sweltering August afternoon on the jam-packed Long Island Expressway, and a mutual spark is set off—and a quirky crime caper is put into motion.

The big heist, despite the earnest performances by the brotherly, ballsy Bologna and granite-faced internalist Gorman, is the film's true star. What else to expect in a film penned by master plotter Donald E. Westlake? Throughout his long, schizophrenic career, Westlake wrote comic capers under his own name and equally involving darker ones under pseudonyms. Hollywood didn't call on him nearly enough but when they did, the results were usually successful. His *Point Blank* (1967) was a solid hit and remains much revered by the cognoscenti.

Predictably, the central crime is both clever and curious; a more staid, anti-cinematic master theft you couldn't find: the coercion of a pretty secretary (Charlene Dallas, a former Miss California) into the procurement of bearer bonds, the simple act of freeing them from one of the deposit boxes in an anonymous midtown office tower. Guns don't blaze, car tires don't screech, squibs don't squirt. And yet, in a film where directorial amateurism attempts to pass for gritty realism (director Aram

Avakian had been a hit-and-miss documentarian), the tension, if only by way of reverence for the writer, is there. Further, just when it runs its course, there's a small series of cheeky toppers—testament again to the unrelentingly inventive Westlake.

The third act, sad to say, gives way to familiar territory: a good guy-bad guy stand-off in which the bonds are exchanged with the Mafia, culminating in that most overworked of crime conventions, the car chase (and at that, not much of one).

Still, the film works—just. Further, it does its part in upholding the working-class hero who bravely walks the beat, guarding the line between ourselves and civic madness. Later in the year, Woodward and Bernstein broke the Watergate scandal, and the cop, as heroic enforcer of behavioral accountability, was eclipsed. To the journalist, the spoils.

Paper Moon

Plot: An itinerant con man and his alleged daughter scam their way through the American Midwest. **Director:** Peter Bogdanovich. **Script:** Alvin Sargent, from the novel *Addie Pray* by Joe David Brown. **Cast:** Ryan O'Neal, Tatum O'Neal, Madeline Kahn. Paramount. 102 minutes.

Paper Moon—starring Ryan and Tatum O'Neal, adapted by Alvin Sargent, directed by Orson Welles. *Orson Welles*? Well, sort of.

As *Paper Moon* went into production in 1972, Peter Bogdanovich's friendship with Welles, fated to go sour, remained strong. As such, the great Welles provided valuable advice on the title, the storyline and the cinematography. Duly heeded. To wit: *Addie Pray*, the name of the novel from which the script was crafted, remains only as the moniker of the pint-sized pain in the fast-talking hero's side; the central relationship, a blustery father figure undone by a young protégé, is right out of such Wellesian classics as *Chimes at Midnight* (1966); László Kovács' cinematography, with its extended takes and depth of field, flogs innovations pioneered in *Citizen Kane* (1941).

Bogdanovich was, of course, a notorious borrower. After lionizing his heroes in print, resulting in the sweet-and-sour relationship with Welles, he set out to remake, effectively, their films. *Paper Moon* alone, while marginally Wellesian, owes just as much to Chaplin's *The Kid* (1921), King Vidor's *The Champ* (1931) and, closer to the times, Arthur Penn's *Bonnie and Clyde* (1967). In each, we have an odd couple—here a handsome, mealy-mouth grifter and an enterprising young orphan—negotiating hard times, dubious employment and, of course, their own love-hate relationship.

That Bogdanovich enjoyed outsized success as a professional sycophant didn't do him any good with his elders, most of whom, like Welles, went on to ostracize him. With the public, though, it was a different story. Bogdanovich regularly ignited their sense of nostalgia for the era in which most of them had come of age; he restored the innocence, pace and spirit that the movies, by 1972, had forsaken for European-influenced technique and New Age moral lassitude.

Paper Moon, like Bogdanovich's pseudo-screwball *What's Up, Doc?* (1972), played to the old-fashioned moviegoer, in this case, right down to the black-and-white cinematography. Not to say that the film, in its day, wasn't in any way modern. It was released at the height of the Watergate scandal; nine-year-old Tatum O'Neal's searing eyes, as she scrutinizes the behavior of her con man protector, serve as America's, pronouncing damning judgment on its dirty-dealing paterfamilias.

Over the period in which the film is set, the gangster, in Hollywood, was king, even though, given the Christianity of the times, a dramatic comeuppance was strictly enforced. Now, in 1973 (the film was released that May), he was a sour joke, not fast-talking Edward G. Robinson but pratfall-prone Ryan O'Neal—and his punishment wasn't death by machine-gun but by the imposition of family.

The little girl in question, Tatum O'Neal (the star's daughter, in a chancy bit of stunt casting), steals the show. Her pugnacious precociousness made her Oscar's youngest-ever recipient. Even her dad, hitherto an all–American *objet d'art*, fares well, holding his own with her as best he can. For a little extra fun, there's Madeline Kahn, delivering, as a blowsy showgirl, a monologue that expertly exploits all of the right dynamics, rendering her at once sexy, shrewish and sad.

Screenwriter Sargent was the master of the adapted screenplay. He had a well-earned reputation for affording movie-friendly pace to literary works without reducing the novelistic fullness of their characters. As a result, he worked well into his final years, one of the few seasoned screenwriters to be adopted by the Marvel Comics generation. (His brother Herb left his mark on the '70s too, as the elder statesman on the *Saturday Night Live* [1975–present] writing staff.)

While another 1930s-set ode to chicanery, *The Sting* (1973), bested it in all ways, the less original *Paper Moon* held its own. Today, in fact, it comes across as the better film: its setting strikes us as more authentic, its characters as more real, its themes—family, survival—more universal. Its moon is no longer paper.

Fun fact: For one brief season, 1974, *Paper Moon* was a TV series. Its Addie: a pre-teen Jodie Foster.

Sleeper

Plot: A health food store owner, cryogenically frozen for 200 years, awakes to find himself embroiled in an anti-government rebellion. **Director:** Woody Allen. **Script:** Woody Allen, Marshall Brickman. **Cast:** Woody Allen, Diane Keaton. United Artists. 87 minutes.

After a series of films ranging from strings of gags to sketch-length episodes, Woody Allen came up with his first sustained narrative, a sci-fi spoof aspirationally titled *Sleeper*. (It *was*, too, grossing over $18 million on a $2 million budget.) As such, the film announced that Allen was a comic presence with cinematic staying power, the first such personality in American comic cinema since the fall of Jerry Lewis.

For all of its distinctly Allenesque touches—comic speculations on God, sex and death; the use of Diane Keaton as the love interest; the jazz-based soundtrack (a break from the sonorous silliness of most sci-fi films)—the film is equal parts lampoon and homage.

Intelligent, high-concept sci-fi had been the rage for some time, from the popularity of intellectual darling *2001: A Space Odyssey* (1968) through to *The Andromeda Strain* (1971), *The Omega Man* (1971) and *Silent Running* (1972). Here, Allen borrows from them all (the spare, ivory-toned sets; the hordes of anonymous scientists rattling off expository gobbledygook; the gadgets and devices aimed at promoting domestic convenience and hedonistic quick-fixes), affirming his instinctive talent as a sharp, dedicated parodist. The storyline, meanwhile, playing on the 1960s-born, Communist-influenced underground militant movement then still at large, is borrowed from the populist comedies of Allen's idol, Bob Hope, another peddler of plots in which a cowardly hero is unwittingly forced to measure himself against the standard.

Allen is Miles Monroe, a health food store manager, jazz clarinet player and modern Rip Van Winkle, who wakes up from a procedure for a peptic ulcer 200 years into the future. He is cryogenically thawed back to life by an interest looking to overthrow the authoritarian government, ruling a world out of *1984* and *Fahrenheit 451*. With heroism his only option for survival, our hero coerces an uppity-nervy socialite into assisting him. (This precedes the kidnapping and conversion of heiress Patty Hearst, just a few months away. Could the Symbionese Liberation Army have been Woody Allen fans?) In the end, they save the day and fall in love—one of the few traditional endings in Allen's oeuvre. Starting with his next film, *Love and Death* (1975), he went back to affirming his reputation as the only major American comic figure to insistently offer narrative resolutions firmly opposed to the dictates of the genre.

Sleeper is an extremely well-balanced comedy, using clever verbal gags to set up the equally clever sight gags; the new (Allen) and old (Hope, the Marxes, silent film comics) schools working hand in hand, generationally gapping the art of comedy.

Critics, having settled for the messy and the compromised since the fall of the major studios, the generational changing of the guard, and the influence of European filmmaking, had been long waiting for a comic messiah, someone to bring narrative muscle, inobtrusive technique, consistently strong gags and a bankable personality back to the screen. Hitherto, they had settled for a writer who wrote foremost for the stage (Neil Simon) and a pair of auteurs who, while funny and original, continued to struggle with the fundamentals of feature-length storytelling (Mel Brooks, Elaine May). Now, they finally had their bona fide comic auteur.

Over time, with Allen's conversion to the seriocomic (from which you can ax, on occasion, the "comic"), *Sleeper* would be reframed as a prime example of one of his "early funny ones," a famous classification serving both as praise for the catalogue by which he made his name and as criticism for his comparatively limited talents as a dramatist.

It's also Allen and Diane Keaton in embryotic form, the first populist on-screen coupling since the heyday of Tracy and Hepburn. Here, writing expressly for and directing her for the first time (though they had worked together on stage and on film in *Play It Again, Sam,* 1972), Allen relies strongly on her Midwestern simplicity while giving her a little range as the brittle, pseudo-intellectual doyenne. Most memorably, he uses their natural chemistry in a sweet stairway scene in which, as two politically opposed personalities, they finally bond and flirt, a compatibility setting the precedent for their definitive collaboration, *Annie Hall* (1977).

Early in '74, Allen the comic auteur had company, when Mel Brooks got it together to form a one-two big-screen comic punch. Account for Simon, though not a director, and you have American Comic Cinema of the 1970s' Big Three, the presences by which all other practitioners of the genre were dwarfed. (It was a shame that Elaine May's career imploded; there could have been a Mount Rushmore.)

Slither

Plot: An ex-con and a free spirit, after a stash of stolen money, are stalked by a pair of mysterious black vans. **Director:** Howard Zieff. **Script:** W.D. Richter. **Cast:** James Caan, Sally Kellerman, Peter Boyle, Louise Lasser, Allen Garfield, Richard B. Schull. MGM. 96 minutes.

He's the nervy, soft-spoken macho man, out to enterprise but with ease. Unfortunately, there's a busy, deracinated world out to weigh on him, forcibly bringing out his animal instincts until, despite his best efforts, he becomes an everyman, prone to madness.

If you've guessed Mel Gibson, you're ahead of the time continuum. Try this, our mystery man's signature look: low button shirt displaying his hairy, V-shaped upper body, tight pants accentuating his cocky strut, hats worn at a jaunty, contemptuous angle. Add his offhand, whispery delivery, making indifference a defiant posture. In short, a disco Brando.

Shout out "James Caan!" and you win. He's perfecting the look here in Howard Zieff's *Slither*, written by another minimalist eccentric, the equally underrated W.D. Richter. It's the film that converted Caan from hotheaded sex symbol to quiet comedian, the lesser of the two capacities by which he'd make his career. Zieff, in fact, in this simple, offbeat road movie disguised as a comic suspense thriller, uses Caan, largely and wisely, as straight man. When Caan delivers funny lines, too often, they're forced. Much of what he has to do here, though, is react—that's what makes him funny.

And there's a lot to react to, a mini-universe of cream-of-the-crop comic character actors: Sally Kellerman (this time as a kind of hippie Lauren Bacall), Alex Rocco, Louise Lasser, Peter Boyle, Allen Garfield and Richard B. Schull.

Together, they're an extension of the signature casting instinct by which Zieff, hitherto a commercial photographer and TV ad man, made his name. His legacy was the introduction of ethnicity into mainstream advertising. Who could forget his smiling Eskimo, holding up a traditional Jewish nosh under the banner "You don't have to be Jewish to enjoy bagels"? Not to mention his avuncular Italian, interrupting *Gunsmoke* (1955–75) or *Kojak* (1973–78) to announce, "That's some spicy meatball!" He was a product of melting pot Chicago, so it was only natural that Zieff would reflect that city's panoramic culture, comedically, yes, but with enthusiasm and reverence. He's at it again in this, his first film. The poster, in which he must have had a hand, gushed, "Kopetzky and Kanipsia—Together at Last!" a reference to the colorful, un–American names of the film's two leads.

But this is not, as so many releases of the time were, the twisted tale of yet another Square Peg looking for an all–American hole, nor of that other overly familiar formula, the Square Peg forced into the anti–American hole. By sending the Jewish but WASPY-looking Caan on a wild, MacGuffin-based goose chase through a loony landscape, Zieff simultaneously sends up both the counterculture (represented, primarily, by the seductively askew Kellerman) as well as its counterpart, the ugly American middle class (represented, primarily, by the offensively askew Peter Boyle). Caan is Zieff, happily scratching his amused head over both sides.

It's an all-encompassing embrace. In the world according to Zieff, appreciation usurps anger. Later in the decade, another filmmaker would come along, subscribing to the same ethos: Jonathan Demme, whose comic canon would kick off with *Citizens Band* (1977). Demme too would repeatedly demonstrate an expansive appreciation for humanity's faults, foibles and follies, disempowering class or cultural division to promote a lovably lost universe. Collectively, Zieff and Demme can be held unwittingly responsible for the overuse of such empty, go-to adjectives as "wacky," "zany" and "madcap" by the nation's film critics, forever challenged by their descriptive duties when faced with character-based comedy of the Zieff-Demme caliber.

Not to say that Zieff-world isn't dangerous. Caan is a car thief looking for a stolen stash, a revelation imparted in a memorable opening scene which, like a lot of the film, promises cliché only to veer left. While the film, in the fashion of the day, rambles amiably, the narrative anchor of suspense is sustained successfully. This is thanks to the repeat appearance of a pair of mysterious black vans, chilling cameos introduced by a bass-based theme—an introductory style that was later afforded two other anonymous, iconic '70s villains: the insatiable shark in *Jaws* (1975) and evil overlord Darth Vader in *Star Wars* (1977). Perhaps, too, these vans explain why the film is called *Slither*; it's the vans slithering up on people, is that it? (Otherwise, you tell me!) And there's violence too, though only the quirky Zieff would stage the twin climaxes the way he did: a fistfight in a Bingo tent and a shoot-out at a vegetable stand.

Did I mention the music? That's eclectic too, mostly trad jazz, paralleling another comedy released that year Woody Allen's *Sleeper*.

It's a comparison worth continuing, at least a bit: Both filmmakers, while one made TV commercials and the other wrote sketches, were still, despite Allen's already mounting film catalogue, making episodic work. What are *Bananas* (1971) or *Every Thing You Always Wanted to Know About Sex* *But Were Afraid to Ask* (1972) but cinematic clotheslines dripping with one-off gags and ten-minute scenes? But 1973 marked the year of Zieff-Allen's mutual maturation. With, respectively, *Slither* and *Sleeper*, both successfully graduated to long-form narrative, greater depth of character, sophisticated subtext and tone, and proof positive of cinematic staying power.

Zieff's films are about the burden of adaptation to circumstance (*Hearts of the West*, 1975, *The Main Event*, 1979, *Private Benjamin*, 1980, etc.) and the pursuit, traditionally futile, of the American dream—thematic threads rooted, again, in the ethnological experience. While it's hardly new territory, Zieff nevertheless stands out, setting it as he does to Homeric laughter instead of bittersweet banter.

As the decade progressed, Zieff would be back—though not often enough.

The Sting

Plot: Two grifters target a mob boss as part of "the big con." **Director:** George Roy Hill. **Script:** David S. Ward. **Cast:** Paul Newman, Robert Redford, Robert Shaw, Ray Walston, Harold Gould, Jack Kehoe, Eileen Brennan, Charles Durning. Universal. 129 minutes.

Where's Archie Bunker? Kojak? Fred Sanford and his "big dummy" of a son?

Audiences searching for summer reruns of their favorite TV shows in 1973 were instead subjected to panels of stern-looking "suits," wearing horn-rimmed glasses and extremely stern expressions. These interrogators were searching—night after night after night—for answers, ones that could lead to a circumstance more improbable than any devised by the sitcoms or dramas they were interrupting. Could the break-in at Democratic National Headquarters, conducted during Richard Nixon's bid for a second term, have been engineered by … the president?

Big-time chicanery, as a result, was on everybody's mind. So when a lackey at Universal read a slush pile–buried script about a pair of 1930s grifters attempting to pull off a "big con," it wasn't hard to see the green light at the end of the tunnel. The premise, after all, suggested a benign or reverse Watergate. On TV, you rooted against the crooks; on the big screen, you could root *for* them.

The Sting sanitized, glossed even, that country-shaking scandal in other ways too, and with it, an earlier scourge, the Great Depression, taking much of the "Dirty" out of the Dirty '30s: Edith Head's classy costumes, which, for a time, brought fedoras and flat caps back into fashion; Henry Bumstead's sets, owing, with *noblesse oblige*, to the Warner Bros. gangster catalogue; Jaroslav Gebr's imitation *Saturday Evening Post* title cards, serving the film up as cinematic canapes; Marvin Hamlisch's adaptation of Scott Joplin's bouncy rags, from the wrong period, okay, but still, fitting the on-screen shenanigans like well-buttoned spats. (The soundtrack sold reams of sheet music, and the main theme, "The Entertainer," cracked that year's rock-heavy Top 40.)

The film, then, was lauded just as much for its design as it was for its timely premise and clever screenplay. There was something else at work, though, too: director George Roy Hill's man-boy playfulness, a quality, in the earnest times over which he worked, either overlooked or devalued by the critics. Serially, Hill set his heroes out on missions that were bigger than they could handle. Most became legends in the end—not because they succeeded but because they came so close. *Butch Cassidy and the Sundance Kid* (1969) was Hill's best manifestation of this interesting and surprisingly commercial (given how much America loves a winner) variation on the genre. *The Sting* was a close second.

The Sting owes a lot more to *Butch* than just that, including, most obviously, the re-twinning of Robert Redford and Paul Newman. They were reprising, effectively, the same archetypes as before: cynical young hotshot and vulnerable visionary-mentor. Plus, the film is full of the same good-natured macho-ribbing, relieved by episodes featuring some of the most colorful character actors on SAG's A-list, each appearing to be having a grand ol' time: Harold Gould, Ray Walston, Jack Kehoe, Charles Durning and Eileen Brennan.

The villain is Robert Shaw, who almost pulls off the improbable and steals this much-ornamented picture. Playing it low-key, he's the Irish racketeer who gets the film's diegesis going after avenging an $11,000 skim, forcing Redford-Newman to attempt to take him down. Shaw makes for a formidable opponent, rivaling his equally taciturn villainy in *From Russia with Love* (1963). His steely gaze, basso brogue and X-ray stare can exude stature and menace with but the lamb's share of the lines. There may be a lot of pretty scenery to be chewed but Shaw has put himself on a strict diet.

Indeed, the high spirits are palpable (catch Newman in the poker scene)—which may be why the film today strikes us as strangely self-amused, a lot of smirky to-do about not very much. We, as a result, find ourselves nostalgic not for the 1930s but for 1973, and the context that had made the film such an enormous success.

A Touch of Class

Plot: An American businessman and a British divorcée stage an affair, only to find themselves falling in love. **Director:** Melvin Frank. **Script:** Melvin Frank, Jack Rose.

Cast: George Segal, Glenda Jackson, Paul Sorvino. Avco Embassy Pictures. 106 minutes.

By 1973, but a few of the Old Masters were still at it. Their self-appointed mission was to continue to give audiences what they had always given them, while keeping with the times. No easy task. But one Studio Era talent pulled it off on a grand scale: Melvin Frank.

Frank, with original partner Norman Panama, had been responsible for the better Bob Hope and Danny Kaye vehicles. Frank's *The Facts of Life* (1960), in fact, is often considered the prolific Hope's best film. Why not remake it, then, in a contemporary context? And so George Segal and Glenda Jackson find themselves in the same sticky situation as did Hope and Lucille Ball: trying to stage an affair despite perpetual impediments, including the biggest one of all, their contrasting temperaments.

Segal is Steve, a married American shipping executive working in London. Jackson is Vickie, a harried couturier who is newly single. They "meet-cute," of course, then engineer a week-long tryst in Spain. They weather logistical roadblocks, banter in bed, have slapstick sex, fight like an old couple, then reconcile. If that sounds more like modernized Tracy-Hepburn than Hope-Ball, you're right. Jackson approximates Hepburn very much, right down to the feminist fire and the exaggerated cheekbones. Segal lacks the avuncularity to be Tracy but counters Jackson's haughty-hither act pound for pound with his casual-neurotic shtick. In other words, a perfectly fair fight, akin to the Ali-Frazier dust-up that same year. No one is underwritten, nothing is played as homage or camp, and no moralism spoils the fun—thus, Tracy-Hepburn, in polyester jackets and silky pant suits, duly updated. Despite a few familiar conventions, the film, per Frank's (and co-writer Jack Rose) intentions, is at once old-fashioned and very 1973. So, by today's standards, old-fashioned and old-fashioned.

Unlike other relics working, if sporadically, at the time, Frank goes easy on the gas. Very little is forced, bitter, editorial or any other of those flaws to which his brethren, like Billy Wilder, became prone. It's as if he and Rose had been dying to throw Tracy-Hepburn into the sexual revolution, dying to have them love and hate and love again by looser, more adult rules.

But all good things must come to an end—in this case, a rushed and dour one. The film's final minutes are devoted to the end of the affair, casting an unexpected invasion of dark London clouds over energetic American sunniness. Grandiose, ill-fated romance was a big thing that year—the bombastically elegiac *The Way We Were* was the second-highest grosser—as America's divorce rate continued to climb. Pity, though, that Frank hadn't taken notice of the critical rabidness unleashed on the previous hit romcom, *Pete'n'Tillie* (1972), when its third act made the unwelcome transition from comedy to tragedy.

Nevertheless, that climactic pivot did nothing to hurt *A Touch of Class*, either at the box office or at the Oscars, where it was nominated in all the major categories (Jackson won). It would also prove Frank's final hurrah. With his next, and last, films—*The Prisoner of Second Avenue* (1975), *The Duchess and the Dirtwater Fox* (1976), *Lost and Found* (1979) and *Walk Like a Man* (1987)—Frank at last joined the mechanical, dispirited Old School he had miraculously eschewed.

1974

In 1974, many of the threads that had been running through American film comedy began to interweave. It was the year that marked the cinematic height of Mel Brooks, who brought box office legitimacy to Old School, sketch-show genre parody; the year in which black-audience comedies went mainstream; the year that Barbra Streisand re-affirmed her monopoly on feminist film comedy; the year when a pair of old hands, Billy Wilder and Blake Edwards, made commercially successful comebacks, perpetuating audience appetite for studio system–style content. But new ground was broken too, with the first concession to a new, coming audience via low-budget, underground satirical-sophomoric efforts that set the table for the 1975 debut of TV's *Saturday Night Live*.

Something old, something new…

The Apprenticeship of Duddy Kravitz

Plot: A brash young hustler stops at nothing to secure a plot of land. **Director:** Ted Kotcheff. **Script:** Mordecai Richler, Lionel Chetwynd, from Richler's novel. **Cast:** Richard Dreyfuss, Jack Warden, Micheline Lanctôt, Denholm Elliott, Randy Quaid. Paramount. 120 minutes.

Oh, Canada, he lamented.

After World War II, when Europe was facing the flood of a four-year backlog of American movies threatening to monopolize its theaters, the Brits, the French and the Italians entered yet another conflict—this time, in the name of cultural protectionism.

By establishing quotas on imported films, each country was able to rebuild its national cinema, ravaged and repressed at the hands of Huns, while still enjoying the eye-opening likes of *Citizen Kane* (1941), a flood of film noir (as the French would come to call it) and other Hollywood commodities. Canada, while it had nothing to rebuild (save for the work of a handful of rogue filmmakers), was also looking to establish a feature film industry. It had distinguished itself throughout the war by producing documentaries under the government-subsidized aegis of the National Film Board and felt ready, postwar, to take the leap from fact to fiction.

Two factors conspired against it, one enemy internal, the other from the outside. The first was John Grierson, head of the NFB, who lobbied hard for a national commitment to the form by which the institution had just made a name. Then there was the country's nearest neighbor and largest trading partner, the U.S., which had held a claim on Canadian theaters since the days of vaudeville. The idea of surrendering but an acre of moneymaking territory to yet another outside market, albeit a chummy one, proved, for capitalist America, too much. Instead, it appeased a culturally oblivious Canadian government with cockeyed concessions (promoting cross-border tourism, for instance, through token references to Canada in American features) and the threat of economic sanctions. Hollywood had saved its skin by skinning Canada.

Enter the '60s and '70s and nationwide enthusiasm spawned by Canada's centenary as well as a celebratory World's Fair (Montreal's Expo '67). For the first time in history, Canada, unlike the Vietnam-plagued U.S., was the safe, hip place to be. Looking to remain in the international spotlight, the country finally gambled on the establishment of a feature film industry, though its access to theaters remained limited.

The idea was to develop properties at once distinctly Canadian and internationally appealing. Inevitably, the country's eyes fell on its fiction writers, then making strides after years of imitating Mother Britain's arch Victorian style. This practice, book to film, would remain Canada's go-to whenever it aspired to enter a new visual market—to wit, the advent of the streaming age and the smash success of Margaret Atwood's *The Handmaid's Tale* (2016). Enter Mordecai Richler, the mordant Montrealer who, from his second home in England, had crafted a seriocomic examination of Canadian-Jewish culture, at once affirming and criticizing its behavioral penchants: his 1959 novel *The Apprenticeship of Duddy Kravitz*.

"It's moneygrubbers like Kravitz that cause anti–Semitism," comments a rival of the eponymous hero. And indeed, in his Duddy, Richler had exaggerated the longest-standing bias against his people. Get-rich-quick scheme after get-rich-quick-scheme, cocky, enterprising Duddy, looking to transcend his working-class roots, makes his way up the proverbial ladder. The rungs, however, are the decent-hearted people who stand by him, each crushed under the weight of his ambition. For all of its Jewishness, then, *Kravitz*, book and film, is more Bible than Torah: What profit it a man, etc.—thereby the property's American appeal. It's another case of hucksterism gone awry, a narrative—the rise and fall of a self-made, stumblebum capitalist—which America never seems to grow tired of, in art (*Citizen Kane*, 1941, *The Godfather*, 1972) or life (Donald Trump).

The title role of Duddy was played by Richard Dreyfuss, just off the runaway success of *American Graffiti* (1973). Dreyfuss is an actor who epitomizes the theory that one's genius is also one's most sizable demerit. His inherent zeal, his desperation to be liked, and his self-serving laugh can bring life to a property or overwhelm it. (For a further examination of this dichotomy, see *The Goodbye Girl*, 1977.) Here, however, it's perfectly placed, as every action Duddy commits cries "Look at me!" Duddy, like Dreyfuss, is chutzpah, the "for better or worse" variety, personified.

For a Jewish film, that's a lot of ham—plus, there's more: Jack Warden as Duddy's deluded mouthpiece of a father, full of tall tales and shortcomings; gravel-voiced Joe Silver as Duddy's first benefactor, a self-made junkman who plays blue-collar sage; Denholm Elliott as a fallen filmmaker Duddy lures into recording bar mitzvahs, an uppity downer. Ironically, it's the French-Canadians, a colorful, hardy type, who play it down, as does, smartly, a young Randy Quaid, as an American-born, epileptic innocent on whom Duddy preys, his cornpone vulnerability a nice contrast to all of that Yiddish energy.

It's a peppy character study, if a little coarsely handled, by director (and fellow Canuck) Ted Kotcheff. Canadian cinephiles, in fact, still consider *Duddy* the best Anglo film ever made on native soil. The proof? A commemorative stamp issued in 1996.

Blazing Saddles

Plot: A parody of Westerns in which a black sheriff parachutes into a small town. **Director:** Mel Brooks. **Script:** Norman Steinberg, Andrew Bergman, Alan Uger, Richard

Pryor. **Cast:** Cleavon Little, Gene Wilder, Madeline Kahn, Harvey Korman, Slim Pickens. Warner Bros. 93 minutes.

"Never give a saga an even break." Comedy writers never had, the parodic instinct going as far back as the silent cinema. Among its seasoned practitioners during the early days of TV was Mel Brooks. Later, as a film force, he had but a lampoon of film musicals, as part of *The Producers* (1967), under his cardboard belt. (Lovers of *The Producers*, that reference was for you!)

Now, though, approached with a Western comedy borrowing a gun-totin' hero from blaxploitation films, Brooks had cinematic license to skewer every cliché the horse opera had ever spawned.

To both spoof the Western and accommodate his African American protagonist, Brooks hired writers from across the spectrum. He not only instructed them never to give his saga an even break, but to imbue the script with all of the colors—black, blue, red, whatever—constituting comedy *à la* 1974, a time when "ethnic humor," as it was then called, was at its height. While the final result unsettled many a critic, the film created an audience as diverse as its writing staff. *Blazing Saddles* became only the tenth movie in history to surpass the $100 million mark.

The premise—from an initial draft called *Tex X*, playing on the black militancy movement—sends a railroad-working slave to the dusty whistle-stop of Rock Ridge as the town's new sheriff. He's a "token" in more ways than one, a stooge sent to placate the populace while secret plans to plow the place over are afoot. By racializing the fish-out-of-water formula, the script exposes the inherent biases of small-town America, with its unabashed resistance to the new resident—until, of course, the new sheriff redeems himself by protecting (with the aid of an ailing gunslinger) the town's interests. The film, then, is a comic revenge fantasy, wherein Black America ultimately gets the best of those whose simple-minded understanding of marginalized cultures has yet to modernize.

It's the hicks vs. the hip. As Gene Wilder, in a sly, subdued turn as the fallen gunslinger, asks Black Bart, the new sheriff, "What's a dazzling urbanite like you doing in a rustic backwood like this?" It's cosmopolitan New York–Los Angeles having one over on Middle America, but, as it's Brooks, with burlesque instead of bitterness.

But *Blazing Saddles* had allusions beyond the benign boundaries of burlesque (and its partner, vaudeville). It was the first commercial release to fully play the ethnic-racist humor card, a style of comedy practiced at the time by TV and nightclub staples Don Rickles and Redd Foxx. It's perhaps wisest to classify that movement, in today's politically enlightened age, as an integrational baby step; a good-humored first dialogue. But where others baby-step, Brooks goose steps. *Blazing Saddles* took to the practice without reserve, offering attitudinal extremism and frank language—a genre-busting shock effect that wouldn't be chanced again until TV's *Deadwood* (2004–06).

Just as controversially—and loved—was the equally generous display of Brooks' sophomoric sensibility. While other comic auteurs—Allen, May, Mazursky—were offering increasingly sophisticated sexual comedy, Brooks was infantilizing it. In his cameo as the state's obliviously enterprising governor, he rests his cross-eyed head on bulbous breasts and offers up seductress Madeline Kahn as a "Teutonic twat."

The film broke ground. In time, "collegiate," a negativism the "crickets" (Brooksian for "critics") would affix Brooks, not only became a compliment, it became a genre, with hits like *Animal House* (1978) and *There's Something About Mary* (1998). In his later years, whenever Brooks criticized things he deemed low humor, friends would be quick to remind him that he was the practice's granddaddy.

You're waiting for the segue to the fart scene, aren't you? Okay, here it is: Brooks' ultimate manifestation of this sophomoric instinct was the famous-infamous fart scene, perhaps alone responsible for the film's gargantuan success. He argued genre-busting, he argued realism. There was a little something to both defenses, but in reality, ordering his bean-eating, fireside cowpokes to break wind was but a big, noisy concession to the shameless schoolboy within. In so doing, he exposed the one in us all. Many of us went on to become Brooks' base, indulging him, gag after shameless gag, through the rest of his hit-and-miss career.

It wasn't simply the film's broad strokes with which the "crickets" took issue. Many felt, with this multi-writer, scattergun approach, that Brooks had turned his back on something that was not only unique but still forming: the caricature-based, improvisational style by which he had made his name, first on record, then in his memorable cameo in his own *The Twelve Chairs* (1971). Brooks was no longer riffing, some lamented, he was making "writers' room" movies, returning to his sketch roots.

It's a valid criticism and, yes, something giddily electric and perpetually surprising may well have been lost. But would it have sustained itself film after film? *Blazing Saddles* is one of American comic cinema's few genuinely consistent entries, and one even more consistent would follow.

Brooks took heat too for his casting of Cleavon Little as Gucci-wearing Black Bart

Throughout the 1970s, genre parody was a popular form. Mel Brooks had two such hits in the same year, 1974: *Blazing Saddles* (Warner Bros.) and *Young Frankenstein* (20th Century–Fox), the former with Cleavon Little (pictured) (Warner Bros./Photofest).

over popular co-writer and comic Richard Pryor—but it was a smart choice. Pryor's nervy, reactive style would have only served the scenes of small-minded societal oppression. The savvy slickness also required would have rung, in his hands, hollow. Little's cool, lithe, physical style fit that latter capacity to a T, creating a genuine character arc that provides much-needed narrative unity.

With *Blazing Saddles*, Brooks set into motion his professional legacy as keeper and perpetuator of comedy's Borscht Belt school, expanding its scale, diversifying its palette, and bringing it to the widest, most diverse audience it had ever enjoyed.

California Split

Plot: A pair of gamblers set out to score the big win. Director: Robert Altman. **Script:** Joseph Walsh. **Cast:** George Segal, Elliott Gould, Ann Prentiss, Gwen Welles. Columbia. 109 minutes.

Starting in 1974, the word "California" begins to appear in more and more film titles. It's not that the West Coast was being posited as a happy if loopy alternative to Eastern urban decay—though that uppity notion was most assuredly on its way. The primary filmgoing audience, at least for quality, character-based comedy, remained, circa 1974, New York–based. The genre still belonged to them, those defeated white-collar subway-riders railing against the rigors of everyday existence. The California reference is cheekily pejorative, the comic films set in that state offering long-suffering Easterners a look at a woozy, preoccupied culture even weirder than their own.

Robert Altman became the prime purveyor of this perspective, through films like his 1973 modernization of Raymond Chandler's *The Long Goodbye* and this, his subsequent effort. *The Long Goodbye*, in fact, opened in California first, to predictably mediocre reviews. Nobody who lived there had the objective wherewithal to note the surrealism of their sunny but strange surroundings. When the film played in the East, it drew raves, that audience (in particular the highbrows) correctly identifying it as a deft mix of gawk and grit, aimed primarily at the exposition of the dark, explosive underbelly of the sun-and-sand set.

Having tried his hand at the war film (*M*A*S*H*, 1970), the Western (*McCabe and Mrs. Miller*, 1972) and the detective flick (*The Long Goodbye*), Altman continued his genre studies by tackling its newest entry, the buddy movie. The buddies here are George Segal and Elliott Gould, the former an antsy businessman who falls into gambling culture (a card-based variation on the counterculture) at the hands of the loose-talking latter. It's *The Sting* (1973) only, as hippie culture–Altman would have it, the Big Con here is the establishment (comprised, in this case, of back rooms and casinos). The best mortal man can do is to slip away with a fuzzy personal victory instead of the purse.

Gould walks through the film's opening frames like he not only owns the picture (which he does) but contemporary American cinema—and rightly so. By this time, he was its crown prince, the shaggy sharpie who, in a succession of films, suffered blows at the hands of the corrupt higher-ups but survived to outsmart them through a loose bravado that he wore like a badge. Sound like Bogart? You bet! Gould convinces you that had Bogie lived, he would, by this time, have traded his trench coat and cigarette for a Hawaiian shirt and a doobie. Gould had also already done two Altman films and was very comfortable working by Altman's directorial dictates, which fit Gould like a three-day growth and a bad hangover.

Segal, as he who must be converted to the other side (yes, that premise was still very much in play), is practically buried here. There is scant evidence of his naturally winning personality; but then again, he is playing a loser. The improvisational bonhomie between him and Gould, buoyed by Altman's love of overlapping dialogue, repeatedly scores.

It's hardly Altman's only bragging right. He's at the height of his signature style here until the film—a subcultural etude, one of the many Altman would attempt—takes on an almost documentary quality. The layered, atmospheric realm of pennyante gambling is right up Altman's eavesdropper's alley, a milieu populated by eccentric underdogs, singsong verbosity, and

Maverick director Robert Altman helmed a number of successful, groundbreaking comedies throughout the 1970s (Photofest).

fun, fragile friendships. So much so that though the action is purportedly dependent upon games of chance, we seldom see the cards, even in the climactic stand-off. It's all about behavior. That's what Altman wanted us to peek at, the way we might the gamblers' hands. And he developed a device that served him well throughout the rest of his career: convenient cutaways to a singer (in this case, smoky-voiced lounge lizard Phyllis Shotwell), allowing him to conveniently bridge action without continuity worries. This methodology resurfaced repeatedly in his masterpiece *Nashville* (1975) and his near-masterpiece *Short Cuts* (1993).

This was also the first time Altman had used an eight-track recording system (other tracks would be added over his next films), allowing him to mix-and-match the aural comings and goings. Just as studio execs, and a few audience members, had had issues with this in *M*A*S*H*, the practice weighed just as contentiously with screenwriter Joseph Walsh, who considered it an unholy violation of his autobiographical script. But, hey, screenwriters were just learning at that point that to Altman, a script was but a starter's pistol. (Walsh has a cameo as Sparkle, an enterprising bookie.)

As in most buddy movies, the climax is the prospective break of the bond. That's what's really at stake in our increasingly askew universe, Altman declares, not solvency but humanity. And the threat is an all–American value known as avarice—a contention that went on to serve as one of his major leitmotifs.

For Pete's Sake

Plot: A young housewife goes to a loan shark to secure money for a stock market tip. **Director:** Peter Yates. **Script:** Stanley Shapiro, Maurice Richlin. **Cast:** Barbra Streisand, Michael Sarrazin, Estelle Parsons. Columbia. 90 minutes.

"A screwball comedy. Remember them?"

So asked, as aforementioned in this book, the poster for *What's Up, Doc?* (1972). In case that film hadn't sufficiently refreshed audiences' memories, Barbra Streisand's ensuing comedy, two years later, posed the question yet again. The '70s marked her last decade, in fact, as a comedienne (let's leave *Meet the Parents,* 2000, out of this), climaxing in her reunion with Ryan O'Neal in *The Main Event* (1979). Unlike *What's Up, Doc?* and *Main Event, For Pete's Sake* has Babs romantically entangled with a less bankable, if more affable (slightly) talent: blue-eyed B-movie beefcake Michael Sarrazin, the next in her long line of goyish boy toys (goy toys?) aimed at elevating her sexual status. Streisand hardly needs the boost, her form-fitting turtlenecks, skin-tight jeans and gender-busting short hair alone affording her sufficient magnetism.

But while she might look like the proverbial "woman who has it all" (the new feminist ideal, soon to be the new feminist cliché), in truth, her character has little. She's an age-old archetype in *Ms. Magazine* wear: a harried housewife. Due to an economic pinch, she sets out on all kinds of crazy schemes to procure her much-loved husband money for a cash cow stock, one that just might allow him to stop compromising his college education by driving a cab. Most of these schemes end in slapstick disaster. Sound like something out of *I Love Lucy* (1951–57)? Well, it is and it isn't, in the same manner that *What's Up, Doc?* was a Howard Hawks comedy but wasn't.

The jokes may be old but the subtext was new: a reaction to widespread inflation. By 1974, it stood at a whopping 12.4 percent. The result was rising food costs, skyrocketing rents and a dangerously flighty market. It wasn't enough that people could be mugged on the streets; now, they were being mugged at the check-out counter.

Pete and his shapely, irrepressible missus, like a lot of couples young and old at the time, just want their piece of the rapidly thinning pie. The premise appealed to both generations: the old, trying to hang on to what they had, and the new, just beginning to put their hippie ways behind them and establish a nest egg. "Selling out," i.e., giving up on the leisure-based counterculture to take one's place in the Old School's rat race, was fast becoming a new catchphrase. After all, those preparing to enter it explained, the war is over, Nixon's gone … why keep playing the protest card? As role models for this kind of conversion went, Streisand was leading the charge. She and her much-loved Pete were comic film's first hippies attempting to go yuppie, previewing the mass cultural conversion that took place in the '80s. Materialism is cool now, the no-longer-so-young were beginning to declare. It's the new long hair, the new feel-good plaything. *For Pete's Sake,* then, was still anchored on an age-old hippie theme: the absurdity of pursuing the American dream—only now, it was being held up as an agent of undue frustration for entirely different reasons.

Peter Yates, a hit-and-miss director, specialized in alien heroes desperate to re-enter the establishment, only on their own terms—so, a perfect choice for this playful little comedy, despite his pedigree in action-oriented properties. And while he still made this, in part, a Peter Yates movie, adding a motorcycle here, a car chase there, he also created a sweet-tempered, well-paced, commercial crowd-pleaser. That said, it's a bit forced—particularly over its bedroom farce-ish middle act. But then, most situational humor, as opposed to the character-based variety, is prone to the contrived.

As for Babs, still on her mission, at this time, to single-handedly feminize screwball comedy (the still-rising Goldie Hawn eventually took her place), she remains an indefatigable and accomplished comic actress, full of Groucho-esque delivery (the result of that aging comic icon having visited her on the set of the previous year's *The Way We Were* with its Marx Brothers–themed party sequence?) and shapely-ass-over-teakettle flights of physical comedy. But what's building below is the Streisand who, in due time, would begin to seriously annoy. Caution: healthy exhibitionism, cloying delivery and maudlin theme songs ahead!

In the end, all of these things combined to send her back to her original, establishmentarian audience. In 1974, though, she belonged to the world, as both the classic female stereotype—the good wife, doing all she can for her hard-working man (is there a Freudian root to this, given Streisand's public sentimentalization of her taken-too-young father?)—and the new feminist superhero, taking on the repressive, white male–dominated universe, guns blazing.

The 1970s marked the multi-talented Barbra Streisand's most sustained period as a comedienne, making her comic film's primary feminist icon. *For Pete's Sake* (Columbia, 1974) (Columbia Pictures/Photofest).

Freebie and the Bean

Plot: A pair of brawling San Francisco cops attempt to take down a crime boss. **Director:** Richard Rush. **Script:** Robert Kaufman. **Cast:** Alan Arkin, James Caan, Valerie Harper, Loretta Swit, Jack Kruschen. Warner Bros. 113 minutes.

Screenwriter Robert Kaufman: "All my films are about commitment. Somehow. The moral was, love is better with a monster who'll make a commitment than with a nebbish who won't."[21]

And so, the comic buddy film was born.

The truth is, in the same way that *The Graduate* (1967) spawned the 1970s coming-of-sexual-age film, *Butch Cassidy and the Sundance Kid* (1969) gave birth to the comic buddy movie. Hitherto, Westerns had often indulged in comic episodes of two-man tension (see John Ford's *Two Rode Together*, 1961) but largely as grace notes. The true bonding agent was the team's mutual commitment to their mission and, in a conservative concession to sentimentalism, each other's survival. *Butch* reversed the practice. Its box office popularity (not to mention its ancillary reputation as a screenwriting template, perpetuated by William Goldman) solidified giddy-up goading to a genuine genre, known first as the "buddy movie," then as the "bromance."

Butch and Sundance were the last successful on-screen heroes of the Old West. When urban blight, such as the kind New York City had been increasingly suffering, began to prove veritably uncontrollable, the cowboy, long America's homegrown shining knight, came to be replaced with a modern Eastern champion: the cop. In this, TV led the way. There were only three major networks at the time but there were thousands of small screen policemen, plainclothesmen and private detectives. So crowded was the law-abiding landscape that it soon became necessary for showrunners to distinguish their brainchildren by signature characteristics. There was the slovenly detective (*Columbo*, 1971–78), the fat detective (*Cannon*, 1971–76), the bald detective (*Kojak*, 1974–78) ad infinitum.

The most tired convention of all of these ubiquitous cop shows was usually introduced by a line like, "You're a good cop, Frank—but you're too close!" Then, climactically, "I'm taking you off the force!" said by some sweaty, middle-aged character-actor in an off-beige leisure suit. Cut to the commercial for Clairol hair permanent or Paul Masson wines. And so, for an act or maybe even a couple of episodes, the eponymous hero went rogue, a gesture of good-hearted vigilantism ultimately deemed, even by those who had relegated him to it, admirable.

The message was that humanity was better off taking matters into its own hands. The worst that could happen to the TV cop, for instance, would be a long speech before reinstatement. In film, the stakes were slightly higher; for example, the Jesus-like martyrdom suffered by the messianic title character of *Serpico* (1973).

Frank Serpico aside, the movie version of the rogue was rarely a cop. The vigilante *dramatis personae* of the times included folk heroes (*Walking Tall*, 1973), martial arts practitioners (*Billy Jack*, 1971) and ordinary working men done over by society (*Death Wish*, 1974). Each film was extremely popular, helping a certain, fed-up faction of America vicariously avenge itself against the new enemy: the corrupted hippie ethos. By the

---

21. "Robert Kaufman: Comedy Writer for Movies and TV," *Los Angeles Times*, Nov. 23, 1991.

early '70s, the cultural premium on mind-altering drugs, loose sexual mores and disrespect for your elders had mutated, some crazy how, from the harmless love-in to a harmful hate-on.

A lot of that had been spawned by the notoriety of hippie-gone-wrong Charles Manson. The Manson gang's shocking, grisly crimes, committed on the cusp of the '70s, had played as affirmation of the older generation's worst suspicions: that all of the kids' peace-and-love stuff was a sham, a model for living that could both implode and explode. Once the bulk of that movement was associated with Manson, whom justice did not corral accordingly, it was time to take those kids down. Cue Dirty Harry.

Contrast being an essential component of comedy, screenwriter Robert Kaufman thought it might be funny, *Butch*-style, to pair the Old School cop with the new, hotheaded model. He set them in that hippie den of inequity San Francisco and called them, memorably, *Freebie and the Bean*.

Freebie and the Bean takes the conventions of ubiquitous TV and film cop entries and attempts to revitalize them via hysteria. Foremost among these are the reprimand, but also the car chase (popularized by *Bullitt*, 1968, as well as B-movie-makes-good *The French Connection*, 1971) and street violence (see *Death Wish* and, yep, *Dirty Harry*, 1971). Hysteria was a big part of film comedy at that time, the emotional climax of the angst movement that began in the oppressive 1950s. It had always belonged, though, to the ordinary citizen.

Times were getting so bad now, however, that even those in charge were feeling the mania-inducing pinch. The lunatics were taking over the asylum and the asylum keepers were getting as unmoored as the lunatics.

A lot gets lost, that said, when this kind of barely controllable hysteria breaks out. *Freebie and the Bean* is full, too full, of overlapping dialogue and intrusive physical aggression. That's what happens when you ask actors like Alan Arkin and James Caan, each prone to showy fits, to play over-the-top parodies of themselves. The latter is a comic Sony Corleone; the former the voice of reason who keeps losing his grip, largely through the squeeze of circumstance. So, signature shticks gone operatic. In '70s-style offices of *faux* mahogany paneling and spiky plastic plants, the two snipe and spar, at odds with themselves just as much, if not more, than with the world. It becomes such a mode of life for them that when Caan berates his girlfriend for bothering to read a book, it serves as the film's central message: that street smarts—the instinctive, the brutish, the personal—might be a messy commodity but they remain the best kind of smarts, you sorry, susceptible intellectuals. It wasn't enough to laugh at the Keystone Cops any more; now, we were being asked to idolize them, faults and all.

Director Richard Rush, a two-hit wonder, was very forgiving in this respect. His unscrupulous, manipulative on-screen avatar in his other big film, *The Stunt Man* (1980), equally lionizes invasive, questionable authority figures. And it too subscribes to the same central dynamic: a deranged despot trying to control an equally deranged underling. Call it good cop-bad cop, as *Freebie and the Bean* does, but skewed through the historic lens of comedy, it's something more universal: father-son, the continuation of a grand tradition in which a mature, strait-laced (more or less) moralist beratingly educates an infantile, misbehaving lesser. Laurel and Hardy...Martin and Lewis...Freebie and the Bean.

Which begs the question (and the digression): Why don't we have two-man comedy teams, at least popular ones, any more? Answer: feminism. When men, prompted by the women's movement, eschewed the all-knowing paternal authority figure shtick, out went the identity embodied by the traditional straight man. Alternate answer: the Baby Boomers. When, in turn, a generation came to the fore refusing to yield to maturity, what was left of the father figure-straight man archetype became virtually indistinguishable from the comic.

Without that father-son tension, the interpersonal friction essential to the success of the two-man comedy teams was dismantled. *Freebie and the Bean*, produced when feminism was hitting full stride, came close to giving us what would become the new version: two misbehaving children, with but a thin wall of common sense left between them. In time, that wall would crumble entirely, bringing on the bromance movement of *Dumb and Dumber* (1994) and *Wedding Crashers* (2005). *Freebie and the Bean*'s one semi-poetic moment puts the central relationship in perfect perspective: Caan steals Arkin's gun and they childishly go after one another in a public park, demonstrating that, fundamentally, these are no more than a pair of boys at play.

Rare is the comedy that makes us laugh (or at least, tries to) and goes serious toward the end yet still becomes a hit. Usually, switching gears like that plays as a violation of contract, the unspoken but important one between filmmaker and audience. But *Freebie and the Bean* got away with it, big time. Its bloody climax, set against that all–American event, the Super Bowl, suggests that blood sport is America's true pastime. It was, and remains, an effective and resonant message, especially as it features the film's one genuinely moving scene: Arkin's surprise death, where both director and principal actors prove that, when push literally comes to shove, they can stop their tomfoolery and offer up good work.

The Front Page

Plot: A wanted criminal hides in a busy newsroom. **Director:** Billy Wilder. **Script:** Billy Wilder, I.A.L. Diamond, from the Ben Hecht-Charles MacArthur play. **Cast:** Jack Lemmon, Walter Matthau, Susan Sarandon, Carol Burnett, Harold Gould, Vincent Gardenia, Austin Pendleton. Universal. 105 minutes.

The success of *The Sting* (1973) created a voracious appetite for properties set in the 1920s and '30s. Universal, which had collected a slew of Oscars for reteaming Paul Newman and Robert Redford as Depression-era con men, was, understandably, eager to play the next card. In 1974, they dusted the rust off of Ben Hecht and Charles MacArthur's venerable play *The Front Page*, and, *inter alia*, another relic, writer-director Billy Wilder.

By 1974, Wilder "was not just a survivor," as David Thomson reminded us in the final edition of his *New Biographical Dictionary of Film*, "but *the* survivor, our last link with the merry, wicked talk of the golden age."[22] Who better, then, to oversee the merry, wicked talk of *The Front Page*, a hermetic examination of newspaper culture circa 1928, with its catty chorus of mealy-mouthed ambulance chasers rattling off sour, hyperbolic updates on the unraveling plot—a prospective hanging gone ridiculously awry—at a speed looking to shatter the sound barrier?

---

22. David Thomson, *The New Biographical Dictionary of Film Updated and Expanded* (New York: Alfred A. Knopf, 2010), 1043–1045.

The play had made it to the big screen in '31 and again, with a gender-bender twist, as the much-loved *His Girl Friday* (1940), helmed by another old reliable, Howard Hawks. Both films were critical-commercial successes, making *The Front Page*, producer-think went, infallible.

But Wilder wasn't interested in sticking, literally or figuratively, to script. Ever eager to add his own touches to his periodic adaptations, Wilder violated what is otherwise an affirmation of one of the best plays ever produced in America. His film is fine when it sticks to the source but when Wilder attempts to open it up, he and Diamond fill it with the kind of cardboard characters and tired jokes they took hell for in their hit-and-miss Cold War comedy *One, Two, Three* (1961). Witty as Wilder once was, by 1974, his acidic obviousness was not on par with the more robust sapience of Hecht-MacArthur. Wilder went so far as to prove it again over the end credits, updating us, *American Graffiti*–style (1973), on the fate of the characters. Fortunately, it's not enough to disprove that this is a dense, spirited, mechanically sound play with a working man's sincerity and a crass, quotable wit, energetically capturing a profession, a time, a city.

For reasons cited in the introductory paragraph, Wilder's *The Front Page* was presented as a period piece, a decision both commercially and artistically sound. (Just *how* sound was definitively proven in 1988, with the attempt to update it to the world of TV news: the disastrous *Switching Channels*.) Another smart decision: the pairing of Jack Lemmon and Walter Matthau, the result of a search for male-on-male chemistry as proven as that of Newman and Redford. It was Wilder's idea, of course: He had pioneered the pairing in his dark, underrated *The Fortune Cookie* (1966). To boot, he had even tested, in that film, Matthau's talent for mile-a-minute dialogue, as well as the dynamic that would come to define the Matthau-Lemmon relationship: the fast-talking bully and the nervy go-along. (Audiences would remember it primarily when it was imported, seamlessly, into Neil Simon's *The Odd Couple*, 1968, which Wilder had aspired to direct.)

Lemmon is Hildy Johnson, the Dapper Dan ringleader of the rogues' gallery of reporters housed in central Chicago's criminal court building. Matthau is his take-no-prisoners editor, who repeatedly schemes to keep the resigned Johnson on his paper's beat until the story cools. They play their roles with a tremendous amount of commitment and verve. It's obvious that, in contrast to Wilder, a great reverence for the property is afoot. That said, the film's climax—a search for the escaped man, hiding in the newsroom—is left largely to pinch-faced Vincent Gardenia (his hair and eyebrows dyed to go with Henry Bumstead's oily, auburn sets), who brings all of his rattled glory to it. The remainder of the characters are played by an assortment of mid–70s character actors (Charles Durning, Herb Edelman, Austin Pendleton, Allen Garfield, etc.), all equally thrilled to be there.

The lone bad note, infamously, is sung—nay, screeched—by Carol Burnett, riding high at the time on her top-rated variety show and trying to build a dual career in film. Burnett, to the shock and dismay of almost every critic in America, gave a shrill, one-note performance, depriving her role, the prostitute who sympathizes with the victim, of its emotional necessity: resonant humanity. She was given the heart of the property but, like a bad cardiac patient, rejected it. The film would have benefited greatly from awarding her part to Susan Sarandon, in the film as, incongruously, Lemmon's serially jilted fiancée (Lemmon is far too old for her). Seeing that she was just an up-and-comer at the time, and Burnett a commercial commodity, one doubts that this was even a consideration.

Over time, almost everyone associated with this *Front Page*, including Wilder himself, denounced it. It proved to be his last commercial success.

The truth, in retrospect, is that it isn't all bad, a bumpy record of one of America's great comic plays, enacted with just enough reverence and relish.

Uptown Saturday Night

Plot: A pair of working-class heroes have their winning lottery ticket stolen, and go after the criminals themselves. **Director:** Sidney Poitier. **Script:** Richard Wesley. **Cast:** Sidney Poitier, Bill Cosby, Calvin Lockhart, Flip Wilson, Richard Pryor. Warner Bros. 104 minutes.

It was TV's *The Jeffersons* (1975–85) who, around this time, were musically "movin' on up." On the big screen, another commodity aimed at black audiences was going upscale: the blaxploitation film. It had already, of course, with big studio releases such as *Cotton Comes to Harlem* (1970) and *Shaft* (1971). Now, though, its distinct mix of action, advocacy and low comedy was goin' uptown, on a Saturday night no less. That title in and of itself was a metaphor for the genre's geographical evolution from small, discount cinemas in marginalized neighborhoods to mainstream showcases in the heart of major metropolises.

Looking to broaden the genre's appeal, *Uptown Saturday Night* put comedy in the front seat and the other elements, those rooted in anger, in the back. And who better to class up the black comic image than the man who had classed up the black drama

Blaxploitation's mix of high energy and low comedy went legit with Sidney Poitier's *Uptown Saturday Night* (Warner Bros., 1974), the first of a trio of mainstream comedies made by African American talent that became cross-cultural hits (Warner Bros./Photofest).

image: the universally respected Sidney Poitier? To some, it seemed a leap—Poitier, the king of African American gravitas (keeping the seat warm for Morgan Freeman), starring in and helming a comedy? To most, though, it was a welcome sign that on-screen black comedy had finally been rescued from hands that had restricted it to derogatory, slapstick-based relief in mainstream releases and/or the same in low-budget niche market fare, even if the latter had been directed by black talent.

Besides, for a guy synonymous with class, Poitier had always shown a healthy on-screen affinity for the common man—first and foremost black but any working-class hero would do. There's a pair of them here, fashioned from the classic, contrasting two-man comedy mold, played by Poitier and the beloved, buffoonish Bill Cosby (ubiquitous at this time—records, TV, animation—before the shocking revelations that betrayed his family-friendly image).

Poitier and Cosby venture uptown on the sly, only to get robbed of a winning lottery ticket. Tracking it down, they get unwittingly caught up in a mob war. Written by Drama Desk–winning black playwright Richard Wesley, the script borrows many of the classic blaxploitation conventions (as does some of the casting, including one of the genre's most recognizable stalwarts, the underrated Calvin Lockhart), attempting to keep their grit while leaving plenty of room for guffaws.

Poitier is a much better director here than he was in his first film, the clever but messy *Buck and the Preacher* (1972). This effort is simple, clean and well-sustained, though it settles for a staid third act with, inevitably, that post–*French Connection* (1971) staple, the car chase (and a bad one to boot). Had Poitier simply learned from his sloppy sophomore effort? Or is this film's winning directness attributable to the fact that he was new to comedy and, willing but out of his element, feared screwing it up? Testament to the latter of these theories is the number of dependable comic stars in the film, the black comedy fraternity of the time. There's not only Cosby, there's Flip Wilson and Richard Pryor. Whether it's attributable to savvy or fear, or both, director Poitier is smart enough to get out of the way of his comic betters and to simply allow them to do their thing: Cosby is all pseudo-improv, his best bit being his attempt to get out of a barroom brawl with a pint-sized, Bruce Lee–influenced kung-fu mobster (Studio Era dancer Harold Nicholas, displaying a new kind of physicality). Wilson, as a fast-talking preacher (a crossover character from his hit 1970–74 variety show) has an amusing monologue on "loose lips." Pryor, meanwhile, enjoys a forced but self-amused moment as a nervous private eye. Poitier the actor even tries his hand at this kind of showy, playful comedy, hollering arcane obscenities and contorting his usually focused visage into a series of uneasy mugs. Some critics picked up on these attempts to extend his range; others thought it an unholy desecration of his trademark dignity.

While the film has its moral drive—it's a lesson on the extent to which decent-hearted, hard-working black folk have to go to get a break—the real star is the tone. The whole thing has a happy, peppy vibe. The players are having fun doing what they do best; the instinct to cut loose on all parts rules the roost. Take away the plot and it's a comic jam session. Enjoying it most, it seems, is the guy who plays it the most straight: singer-actor Harry Belafonte, in a parody mixing Marlon Brando with Little Caesar.

By the way, for you lexicographers, it may be of interest that this film is also a veritable dictionary of vintage 1970s jive talk, the patois that played precursor to today's rap-based language. (Suggestion: Make a drinking game out of it, imbibing every time someone says "turkey" or "chump.")

The happy tenor spread. The film proved, as was its unabashed intention, a cross-over hit. The Holy Grail had finally been secured: the first black comedy to imprint itself on a mainstream audience. In that era where, thanks to the success of the second *Godfather* film (1974) the numerical affixation "2" was just beginning to be attached to everything, the film spawned two successors—not sequels technically but made in the same spirited vein.

Young Frankenstein

Plot: The grandson of the notorious Dr. Frankenstein returns to Transylvania and creates another monster. **Director:** Mel Brooks. **Script:** Mel Brooks, Gene Wilder. **Cast:** Gene Wilder, Marty Feldman, Peter Boyle, Teri Garr, Madeline Kahn, Kenneth Mars. 20th Century–Fox. 105 minutes.

The big question re: *Young Frankenstein* is, How was it, thereafter, that Mel Brooks never produced a film as focused or as disciplined?

Theories abound: it was star Gene Wilder's story and screenplay (his first) and, in spite of the invitation he extended to Brooks to help him shore it up, Wilder protected his work with an actor's integrity (to wit, he later forbade the fourth-wall–breaking Brooks from appearing in it)—and Brooks, in a surprise episode of *noblesse oblige*, dutifully acquiesced, proving that the father-son leitmotif running through his films (it's here again, between the creator and the monster) came from a real place; while the film pays homage to the breadth of the *Frankenstein* film catalogue (specifically, 1931–39), narratively, it sticks closest to *Son of Frankenstein* (1939). Therefore, *Young Frankenstein* is not a generalist's parody, as was *Blazing Saddles* (1974, the same year, incredibly), borrowing archetypes, scenes and clichés from across the Western film spectrum, but a send-up, more or less, of a single film, necessitating an unerring strictness; the cast. It's perfect. In addition, it too conforms to the premium on self-discipline, every member giving us just the right serving size of their signature shtick: Wilder as the notorious Dr. Frankenstein's shame-faced ancestor, unleashing his inner monster at carefully selected intervals; Marty Feldman as the hunchbacked dogsbody who welcomes him to his ancestral home, whose small episodes of banjo-eyed impishness serve as Old School grace notes; Peter Boyle, a great comic reactor (as the sitcom *Everybody Loves Raymond*, 1996–2005, later attested), bringing instant sympathy to the monster which the doctor is prompted to create, even though Boyle has but grunts, and a badly warbled song, for lines; Cloris Leachman as the sober-faced hausfrau, slyly encouraging the doctor's efforts; Madeline Kahn as the doctor's distanced fiancée, being as delicate with her perkily repressed animalism as she is, sexually, with her frustrated paramour; Kenneth Mars, one of the era's greatest (and most underused) comic character actors, as Inspector Kemp, the sneering policeman who warns the residents of the Transylvanian village to whom the doctor has relocated to be on their guard.

Set within the reverently sober restrictions of 1930s film horror (kudos to Gerald Hirschfeld's fuzzy, luminous cinematography), these well-proportioned and equally well-spaced episodes of signature behavior, along with Brooksian jokes running the gamut from vaudeville ("Walk this way!") to burlesque ("What knockers!"), stand out like bolts of lightning in a dark sky. In other Brooks films, they'd simply be lost in the shuffle.

Maurice Yacowar, in his *Method in Madness: The Comic Art of Mel Brooks*, pulls *Young Frankenstein*'s primary theme from Brooks' earlier *The Twelve Chairs* (1970): "In both the moral is the same: man must seek his salvation in human fraternity, not in hope of divine intervention."[23] Put simply: Don't play God, play with your friends. And indeed, Dr. "Fronk-en-steen" finds consolation, in the end, not in the failure-based folly of pursuing scientific achievement but in the fact that through it all, a small, eclectic group of cohorts has stood dedicatedly alongside him. It can also be argued, however, that *Young Frankenstein* is foremost about the pain and thrill of procreation, from the high-low imparted by the "birth" and release of the monster to the sexual humor, if infantile, that abounds.

Almost universally, critics were delighted that Brooks, even if it took the bitch-slapping of Wilder, had eschewed his scattergun ways and come out with a film which, while being distinctly Brooksian, demonstrated narrative discipline and tempered wit. Even John Simon, the *bête noire* of the then all-important New York film critics circle (Simon made Pauline Kael look like a shrinking violet), anointed it the comedy of the year.[24]

Many since have called it the comedy of the decade.

1975

In 1975, American cinema hit an undisputed peak. Consider that year's five Best Picture candidates (yes, it was a mere five in those less saturated times): *One Flew Over the Cuckoo's Nest, Dog Day Afternoon, Nashville, Jaws* and *Barry Lyndon*. Except for the stately, soulless *Barry Lyndon*, each film is its respective director's masterwork. American auteurism was in full, impressive bloom; the Film Program generation, influenced by Studio Era and underground fare as well as by Europe's Old Masters, had hit its stride. And that was just the domestic talent. Imports, whose quality matched or exceeded that of the homegrown practitioners, were just as likely to pack them in. Thanks to the ever-enterprising Roger Corman, their work was even playing mainstream showcases like drive-ins. Bergman under the stars!

One of the biggest names of that era, Jack Nicholson, later paralleled those film-happy times to the explosion of European cinematic product that had taken place a decade earlier: "For ten years we expected to see a new masterpiece every week, and for ten years we did see a new masterpiece every week."[25] Nicholson's equation was no exaggeration. By 1975, the movies had become, as a vast college-educated, cinematically in-tune generation came of ticket-buying age, America's—nay, the world's—top cultural plaything. Not only were the movies again worth going to, such was their quality and integrity that they'd become on par with literature as an intellectual chew toy.

23. Maurice Yacowar, *Method in Madness: The Comic Art of Mel Brooks* (New York: St. Martin's Press, 1981), 96.

24. John Simon, "Our Movie Comedies Are No Laughing Matter," *New York Times*, June 29, 1975.

25. Stephen Hunter, "Nicholson, Revved Up to Full Throttle? Sorry, But You Don't Know Jack," *Washington Post*, Dec. 2, 2001.

Jaws was the throwback of 1975's lot, rooted as it was in classic, more innocent genres, such as the horror film and the adventure story. In a few short years, *Jaws* and *Star Wars* (1977) would unwittingly dismantle the intellectual movement and, for better or worse, help American movies reclaim their original identity as grand, innocuous entertainments. With the added, and inevitable, integration of CGI, film would ultimately be equated with video games and thrill rides. Psychology and ideology, long the twin engines of on-screen drama, would be replaced by technology and virtuosity. Marketing, based on record-breaking grosses, would play more and more of a part too, until males aged 14 to 25, who liked to blow their minimum wages on T-shirts and action figures, would become be the primary audience. The big-budget action flick would rule the roost.

Such would be the effect created by *Jaws*, the big-concept big bang. Public pools, the summer of its release, were crowded with kids pretending to be sharks, slyly immersing themselves below the water's surface to grab the pale, thin legs of fellow bathers—the same kids who would grow up to buy all of those aforementioned action figures. It was the first of a succession of signs that a new industry convention was, like those shark-like arms, taking hold: the summer blockbuster. Hitherto, the June-September period was considered a soft time for cinema. Everyone, it had always been assumed, was away from the theater-strewn urban core, at a campground or the beach or overseas. Summer was the time for small, feel-good films only, like a nice little comedy.

Those "nice little comedies" continued to be released in tandem with *Jaws*, at least until the indifferent New York interests who had taken over what had been left of the smoldering studios got wise to the new reality: that there was just as much money, if not more, in the motion picture as there was in commodities like sugar and pork. Still, film comedy was in for a change. The long-standing "New York-the-bad" thing that had played for the first half of the decade was beginning to feel forced. The proof: Neil Simon's *The Prisoner of Second Avenue*. The play, the ultimate commentary on the human price of the rotting Big Apple, had resonated deeply with both audiences and critics—but that was in 1973. Two years later, when it was translated to film, it seemed only somewhat relevant and overly familiar.

The new gold mine, the mile-deep motherload of comedic raw material, was Los Angeles, a crazy, sunny oasis ripe for good-natured ribbing, with films like *Shampoo* and *Smile*. Slowly but surely, La La Land was becoming the new sandbox for the comedically inclined, with a looser, more playful vibe much fresher and more fun to capture. Thus far, it had almost always been skewed through a New Yorker's (or another unhappy outsider's) perspective, criticized, often in on-screen dialogue, as a lazy, hedonistic, surrealist landscape populated by mellow egotists too geographically isolated and/or self-absorbed to play by recognizable rules. Now, though, that was no longer a minus; it was a plus. The West Coast was usurping the East as the place to be. Time to shed one's Eastern angst and join the fray—or maybe, at least, an EST class.

For those who weren't entirely ready to embrace this notion, the coolest thing to become was "bi-coastal," an arrangement permitting one to enjoy the hustle and bustle of the east at the same time as the feel-good indulgences of the west.

The uptight outlier who always had to be converted to the looser life, the dominant dynamic of American comic film since the late '60s, was now a real-life mass movement.

The Adventure of Sherlock Holmes' Smarter Brother

Plot: The Great Detective's brother, a sleuth in his own right, chases down a royal document that foreign powers are eager to acquire. **Script/Director:** Gene Wilder. **Cast:** Gene Wilder, Madeline Kahn, Marty Feldman, Dom DeLuise, Leo McKern, Roy Kinnear. 20th Century–Fox. 91 minutes.

Smarter? How about wilder, as in Wilder? As in angry, fallible, romantic and not too shabby with a sword?

After the comic mega-hits *Blazing Saddles* (1974) and *Young Frankenstein* (1974), studios offered multi-picture deals to two associated talents to try their luck as comic auteurs in their own right, on the proviso that they reward them with, more or less, the same style of humor.

Gene Wilder, foremost an actor, would borrow more from the performance-based *The Producers* (1967), while Marty Feldman, hitherto a gag man, would borrow from Brooks' later "writers' room" pictures. Neither, however, would entirely capture nor sustain the Brooksian idiom, proving just how hard it is to consistently hit a target with a scattergun. Nor would Wilder or Feldman succeed in developing a sufficient quotient of their own touches to boast signature styles. The results in each instance, while occasionally pleasurable, are best classified "baby Brooks."

As Pauline Kael pointed out in her original review, the prospect of Sherlock Holmes having a smarter brother "has mouth-watering possibilities."[26] But if he's smarter in Wilder's script, it's only according to the character himself. While it's a point of periodic pride that his famous older brother, when baffled, is forced to lean on him, the truth is that the youngest Holmes, Sigurson, is more often than not used as a dupe—as he is in this case, wherein a *Maltese Falcon*–inspired heroine leads him on a lie-littered quest for a document that could very well force England into war. As plot goes, however, that's it. Kael again: "There's no mystery, and as you can't have a parody of a mystery without a mystery, there's no comic suspense."[27] Note the word "parody." Brooks' biggest successes, including the Wilder-generated *Young Frankenstein*, were just that. Here, Wilder is flying without a template; all he's borrowed are Arthur Conan Doyle's characters and a handful of Victorian archetypes. Instead of plot, there's premise; instead of scenes, business.

The result is an exercise in light, behavior-based absurdism. As in *The Producers*, everyone, no matter how prim or proper, is prone to puncturing politesse or protocol with fits of idiosyncratic madness. Some of it works. Wilder, as writer, shows an easy facility for the comic strengths and verbal rhythms of his cast: his own, ever-reliable mounting anger shtick, Feldman's genteel absurdism and heroine Madeline Kahn's snooty-sexy to and fro. (In addition, Wilder takes great advantage of her opera-based singing ability.) But they can't completely buoy his thin plot nor elevate the schoolboy sexuality that passes for much of the wit.

There are a handful of inspired moments—a coach chase involving oversized props, a formal introduction marred by a box of gooey chocolates, a ballroom waltz featuring a pair of bare behinds—but in the context of so much unformed material, their success gives

---

26. Pauline Kael, *5001 Nights at the Movies* (New York: Henry Holt, 1991), 6.
27. Pauline Kael, *5001 Nights at the Movies* (New York: Henry Holt, 1991), 6.

the illusion that they're happy accidents. The unhappiest accident of all occurs when the whole thing climaxes with an opera number aspiring to the one in the Marx Brothers' *A Night at the Opera* (1935), failing miserably by comparison.

Low marx.

Cooley High

Plot: On Chicago's South Side in the early '60s, two black youths and their brethren indulge in adolescent hijinks. **Director:** Michael Schultz. **Script:** Eric Monte. **Cast:** Glynn Turman, Lawrence Hilton-Jacobs, Garrett Morris, Cynthia Davis. American International Pictures. 107 minutes.

American International's Samuel Arkoff, king of the exploitation film, jumps again onto the "blaxploitation" bandwagon in an attempt to cash in on the lingering success of *American Graffiti* (1973) by revamping it for a niche audience. Should be terrible, right? But what ended up being created, thanks to writer Eric Monte and director Michael Schultz, was an authentic look at the black urban experience circa 1964, just before the politicizing advent of the emancipation movement. The film didn't end up bilking black audiences (producer Arkoff's sole intention) but validating their experiences, creating a connectivity seldom offered by action-oriented blaxploitation films or even the well-subsidized comedies of Sidney Poitier.

Proof: On a budget of $750,000, *Cooley High* grossed over $13 million—and this almost exclusively from an audience on limited incomes, as the film was no crossover cash crop.

For all of its authenticity, this playful, moving tale of coming-of-age in dodgy Chicago, shot entirely on location, did make concessions to commercialism. It unabashedly piggybacks on TV sitcoms: its geographic opening, for one, mirroring those of the Norman Lear-MTM-James Toback series; then the casting of tall, toothy Lawrence Hilton-Jacobs of *Welcome Back, Kotter* (1975–79) fame, whose restless style works even better here.

The film even morphed *into* a sitcom: the much more contrived *What's Happenin'?* (1976–79); and Monte ended up working on the Lear comedies *The Jeffersons* (1975–85) and *Good Times* (1974–79). There's also a nod to sketch comedy with the insertion of Garrett Morris, then riding high as the token black cast member of a hot new late-night staple *SNL* (1975–present day). Here, his inherent dignity, more often a hindrance on that Baby Boomer showcase, serves him in good stead as a sympathetic teacher.

But *Cooley High* is not a three-set exercise in writers'-room–generated wise-cracking. It's brotherly jivin', class-cutting, street corner crooning and tenement hall make-out sessions—authentically replicated rituals of Monte's own adolescent experiences growing up in the North Side projects.

Like *American Graffiti*, the film revels in the low-cost, after-dark pastimes of a high-flyin', horny young population trying to get their kicks in a hermetic American milieu. And while it does its due diligence to many of *Graffiti*'s plot conventions—the prospect of college, the gas-guzzling hijinks, the unattainable girl—they play just as organically. Teenagers, in Caucasian California or the projects of Chicago, will be teenagers.

As we indulge in these energetically quotidian rites of passage, set to a Motown soundtrack paralleling *American Graffiti*'s greatest hits of the '50s, we are privy to the up-and-down relationship of Preach and Cochise, the first studious and writerly, the second truant and street-savvy. With its premium on male bonding, the film, while heavily rooted in *American Graffiti*, serves as a black *I Vitelloni* (1953). It's an important distinction. *American Graffiti*'s focus was, gender-wise, more of an even split. In addition, this focus set the precedent to which more earnest black films ultimately subscribed, bringing the plight of young black males to a wider, cross-cultural audience. Best example: wunderkind John Singleton's *Boyz n the Hood* (1991).

Cooley High breaks with *American Graffiti* again in its third act, truly its comic high point, when one of its heroes hides in a diner's minuscule ladies' room to avoid a muscly pair of vengeful types. It's a rare leap from the organic to the contrived. But while it suggests, yes, sitcom, and also the sloppy, simple-minded slapstick comic relief historically provided by black actors in mainstream Hollywood releases, it plays as neither incongruous nor derogatory. And despite its low budget, there's cinematic fancifulness in the film too, when it boldly turns a riotous scene in a movie theater into an impressively elaborate shadow play.

Thereafter, the film shifts into serious mode, with the dramatic death of Cochise. To the filmmakers' credit, both the death and the heartfelt eulogy aren't overplayed, as they certainly would have been in a blaxploitation picture or a maudlin WASP drama. Then it's back to *American Graffiti,* borrowing Lucas' iconic denouement featuring on-screen updates of the characters' post-film futures.

Forgive it, as its intended audience did at the time, its knock-off roots and penny-ante production values (the location sound, particularly indoors, is a perpetual problem). *Cooley High* is a rewardingly indulgent piece of urban American authentica, sociologically important and comedically high-scoring.

Death Race 2000

Plot: A bloody transcontinental road race becomes prime-time TV entertainment. **Director:** Paul Bartel. **Script:** Robert Thom, Charles B. Griffith, based on a story by Ib Melchior. **Cast:** David Carradine, Sylvester Stallone, Simone Griffeth. New World Pictures. 80 minutes.

The year 1975 was the height of American cinema: *One Flew Over the Cuckoo's Nest, Nashville, Jaws* ... oh, and the father of drive-in fodder, Roger Corman, remained at large. With *Death Race 2000*, he punched above his weight thanks to a clever cornerman, cult satirist Paul Bartel. *Death Race 2000* purports to be a "car movie," the high-octane chronicle of a transcontinental road race akin to the Super Bowl, staged by rivaling, larger-than-life cultural stereotypes. But it's a spiky spoof of a grab bag of American cultural pet peeves: gas-guzzling, bloodthirstiness, religious and political zealotry and media-based mega-hype. It even incorporates recent events, like the abduction and conversion of heiress Patty Hearst by the Symbionese Liberation Army.

For all of its pretensions as a social satire, the film's primary influence is clearly cartoons, specifically, Chuck Jones' Road Runner shorts and Hanna-Barbera's *Wacky Racers* (1968). It should have been a smartly sustained satire—likely Bartel's intention. But it quickly settles for its crassest elements, likely Corman's intention: over-the-top violence and proudly gratuitous nudity.

One question: Did star David Carradine's get-up, perhaps itself influenced by old *Flash Gordon* serials and cult Mexican wrestlers, influence the look of the coming Darth Vader?

The Fortune

Plot: Two inept con men plot to fleece a kooky heiress. **Director:** Mike Nichols. **Script:** Adrien Joyce. **Cast:** Warren Beatty, Jack Nicholson, Stockard Channing. Columbia. 88 minutes.

After the crazily ambitious *Catch-22* (1970), Mike Nichols gave the world the sourly seriocomic *Carnal Knowledge* (1971); then, exchanging the urban for the aquatic, the eco-thriller *The Day of the Dolphin* (1973). While both deserved higher praise than they received, the critical disappointment for both prompted Nichols to cash in on the 1920s–30s craze set loose by the runaway success of *The Sting* (1973). Hence *The Fortune*, part screwball comedy, part Laurel and Hardy.

Standing in for the aforementioned duo are two of the biggest stars of the era: Warren Beatty as, effectively, Ollie—in his case, a towering, stiff-backed Dapper Dan—and Jack Nicholson, crowned by clownish coiffure, as Stan. For a busy, swift-moving 90 minutes, these enterprising, incompetent, Gatsby-era fortune hunters molest and murder, sort of, a cinematic newbie: Stockard Channing, a kooky heiress with a feminine hygiene empire. It all takes place on a surprisingly small scale (was Nichols still reeling from *Catch-22* and *Dolphin*?) in a brown-beige California geographically reduced to an adobe bungalow complex and a small stretch of beach.

It was a chance, then, for Nichols to return to his theatrical roots, an opportunity to stage extended scenes short on editing, long on acting. In between, there'd be episodes of slapstick: fights on kitchen floors, lovemaking on undersized furniture, car accidents on bridges.

Needless to say, given the caliber of the talent, critics expected a lot more than sexualized low comedy. Ultimately it was categorized as Nichols' third consecutive misfire, and he sheepishly returned to his roots, the stage, for seven years.

But the film has its merits: first and foremost, Nicholson. It's his film. You can sense him, scene after scene, unabashedly trying to steal the picture. If his evident enthusiasm for such a slight property seems disproportionate, one must remember his previous catalogue. He was accustomed to playing the smartest guy in the room; here was a rare, fun opportunity to play the dumbest.

In his Larry Fine hair and silent comic's baggy pants, Nicholson repeatedly rolls his eyes back into his head and his upper lip into his nose. Further, he pours on the lasciviousness, the way a Valentino wannabe might apply too much Old Spice. In short, it was the first role that informed us that beneath the compromised intelligence and seething vengeance that was fast becoming his trademark, a big, fat clown was waiting to reveal himself. This, then, is Jack-in-the-box. Future roles allowed him to unleash this part of his game even more unabashedly, to both detrimental (the self-directed *Goin' South*, 1978) and legendary (*Batman*, 1989) avail.

Beatty is given far less to play. For the comic contrast to function, Nichols had to set Nicholson loose while keeping Beatty tightly chained. Still, Beatty plays good soldier and dutifully acquiesces the spotlight. Channing in the Madeline Kahn role of the sexy, kooky shrew impresses, if just. She's attractive in the proper vintage way—there's a sexy 1920s androgyny to her, in her boyish clothes and foppish, boy-band hair—but, in Adrien Joyce (aka Carol Eastman)'s slim screenplay, she's hardly more than a device. It's as if the gold dust in *The Treasure of the Sierra Madre* (1948) could innocently seduce and dance a mean tango.

The final act, in which the boys, unable to access the heiress' fortune, decide instead to ice her, plays like a first draft of *Weekend at Bernie's* (1989), again buoyed by the comic energy of the performances.

But it was Nichols who was the one put on ice—Boy Wonder Grows Prematurely Decrepit—while the others, in short order, re-established reputations, foremost Nicholson. Later that same year came his bravura performance in *One Flew Over the Cuckoo's Nest* (1975), imprinting him forever as moviegoing America's bad guy on the good side.

Hearts of the West

Plot: A wannabe Western writer gets an education in Hollywood politics when he becomes a fixture in B-Westerns. **Director:** Howard Zieff. **Script:** Rob Thompson. **Cast:** Jeff Bridges, Blythe Danner, Andy Griffith, Alan Arkin. United Artists. 102 minutes.

The Western, that most venerable, distinctly American of genres, was at a crossroads. The traditional male audience that had always ensured its popularity was, due to a combination of aging and the feminism-influenced redefinition of manhood, in its death throes—as was, literally, the genre's icon, cowboy deity John Wayne. (Wayne's last film was released in 1976, the dour, small-scale *The Shootist*.) A handful of filmmakers still put them out but even those, the work of reverent revisionists like the savage-sentimental Sam Peckinpah and the quirkily sober Clint Eastwood, had an elegiac quality to them. The genre was clearly being eulogized.

But last rites need not always be so doleful. Enter the underrated Howard Zieff, late of *Slither* (1973), to offer the fondest of farewells, alive with a nostalgic, boyish sense of wonder and a winning simplicity.

Hearts of the West was the brainchild of screenwriter Rob Thompson, a later contributor to the cult TV hits *Northern Exposure* (1990–95) and *Monk* (2002–09). He was a perfect pairing with director Zieff, given their mutual love of offbeat societies. The society here may be cowboy culture but of a marginally urban kind. In Capraesque fashion, a small-town rube—in this case, an aspiring Zane Grey—packs up the trusty Underwood with which he spins his grandiose notions of the Old West and ends up in California, only to find, after falling in with a rogues' gallery of ranch hands slumming in movie serials, that all he had held true was false. The song had it right: It's only a paper moon. Fortunately, a classy-sassy production assistant falls for his boyish ways and, aided by his fair-weather mentor, they chase a MacGuffin all the way to a happy ending.

There's a lovely nostalgic hue to it all, greatly boosted by Mario Tosi's cinematography. Better still, unlike most efforts to recapture, pay tribute or downright rip-off the innocent, entertaining fare of the Big Studio Era, there's nothing forced about

While the attention was concentrated on major comic auteurs, the 1970s also featured the work of quirky, underrated yeomen, including Howard Zieff, seen here behind director of photography David M. Walsh (Warner Bros./Photofest).

it—though some critics, high on the exemplary character work, lamented the imposition of the goose chase plot, forgetting that convention's necessity in American commercial cinema. Zieff, though, had heard it before. The same snobby lot had expressed it over *Slither.*

Still, you could hardly blame Kael, Canby *et al.* Zieff's eye for character manifests itself here in all ways, both major and minor.

Major:

- Jeff Bridges as the whistle-stop hick thrown in with the cosmopolitan sharpies dressed in kerchiefs and chaps. He's everything the part should be, almost to the point of parody.
- Blythe Danner as the Jean Arthur character. Never before had her wan ways so risen above miscasting.
- Andy Griffith as Bridges' paternal, homey mentor, teeming with clandestine desperation, a mellower version of his smiley-sad shit heel in *A Face in the Crowd* (1957).
- Alan Arkin as the hack serial director. This was perhaps his quintessential role, the very definition of "Arkinesque" (though Arkin claims the performance was an amalgam of three directors under which he'd worked).
- Marie Windsor—yes, *that* Marie Windsor, one-time Queen of the Bs, in a welcome cameo.

Minor:
- The extras. Zieff displays a magic way even with them. He knows just which ones to put where—an eavesdropper in a diner, an old man on a set of stairs, a few dead German soldiers on a back lot—enhancing each of the film's atmospheres with minimalism, immediacy and color.

Hearts is one of the true little gems of the '70s. If it's gone unheralded, it's in part due to the emergence of a more commercial version of the same film, Billy Crystal's *City Slickers* (1991), which, while a fine, if slicker (pun intended) commercial comedy, unabashedly borrows much of the heart of *Hearts*.

Let's Do It Again

Plot: A pair of blue-collar workers attempt to save their fraternal lodge by rigging a prizefight. **Director:** Sidney Poitier. **Script:** Richard Wesley. **Cast:** Sidney Poitier, Bill Cosby, Jimmie Walker, John Amos, Calvin Lockhart, Denise Nicholas. Warner Bros. 113 minutes.

In October 1975, one of the most anticipated boxing matches in pugilistic history took place: the legendary "Thrilla in Manila," the third confrontation between Muhamad Ali and Joe Frazier. The sport was at its height. The 42-minute confrontation, a brutal 14-round affair, was watched by over one billion people around the world.

That same month, in theaters across America, another hyperbolic bout was taking place: 40th Street Black vs. Bootney Farnsworth. Bootney, thin as a licorice whip, didn't stand a chance against his hard-punching opponent. And so, two sly, working-class heroes broke into his hotel room while he was sleeping and hypnotized him into believing he was Ali's middleweight equivalent. They then placed a small bet on him that would multiply, they were certain, into enough to save their ailing fraternal lodge. It all went according to plan, until the gangsters with whom they'd entrusted the money got wise. It had been easy to outwit Bootney; now, they had to best the mob.

The heroes in question are Sidney Poitier and Bill Cosby, who, after the success of *Uptown Saturday Night* (1974), said, "Let's do it again." And so they did, with, largely, the same cast, embellished (or diminished, depending on your perspective) by some of the top African American talents on TV. That included Jimmie Walker, the skinny, gawky self-aggrandizer whose catchphrase "Dy-no-mite!" was being spread like gospel through Norman Lear's hit sitcom *Good Times* (1974–79). It's a big, easy central joke, the undersized coward as muscle man—an old one, too, harkening back to the days of silent cinema.

A lot of *Let's Do It Again*, in fact, errs on the side of easy. While the film manages to give off a lot of the jolly, jive vibe that had made its predecessor a hit, everyone seems to have grown a tad too comfortable, self-satisfied even. The plot is thinner, the gags more base, the direction wonkier. Audiences, however, hardly noticed. It brought in more money than the crazy-headed duo of Poitier-Cosby did by rigging fights.

Despite Walker's presence, Cosby remains the big comic puncher. Put him in frame enough times, let him ad-lib (presumably) and you have a handful of highlights. This time around, they even dress him up in gaudy get-ups—a parody of blaxploitation's iconic haute couture—as comic insurance.

The fun stopped here. The next time Poitier and Cosby made a film, they traded high-spirited buffoonery for unabashed sanctimoniousness (see *A Piece of the Action*, 1977). Ali-Frazier gave us three pairings to remember; Poitier-Cosby two.

Love and Death

Plot: During the Napoleonic Wars, a cowardly Russian finds himself involved in a plot to assassinate France's famed emperor. **Script/Director:** Woody Allen. **Cast:** Woody Allen, Diane Keaton, Harold Gould, James Tolkan, Jessica Harper. United Artists. 85 minutes.

Between *Sleeper* (1973) and his next film, *Love and Death*, the expectation from Woody Allen was a career's worth of solid comedies, a canon akin to those of his idols from both the pre-war and wartime years: Charlie Chaplin, W.C. Fields, the Marxes, Bob Hope. But Allen had other dimensions, ones he would start incorporating into comedy forthwith, even taking sabbaticals from the genre altogether. As a result, *Love and Death* stands as the climax of his film comedy career. Never again would he prove so concerned with showcasing the on-screen comedy persona he had spent years grooming; never again would he exhibit his considerable skills as a cinematic parodist; never again would he investigate his pet subjects—sex, death, God—using purely farcical criteria.

Wes D. Gehring, in his *Genre-Busting Dark Comedies of the 1970s*, describes the film best: "*Love and Death* is essentially Bob Hope caught in Ingmar Bergman land."[28] Like *Sleeper*, *Love and Death* is first and foremost a pseudo–Hope vehicle: Boris (played by Hope … uh, sorry, Allen) is the runt of a hale, 19th-century Russian litter. To his grand dismay, he's coerced into fighting the unstoppably militaristic Napoleon. After an act of accidental heroism, he wins (in a hard-earned victory, of course) the hand of the fair Sonya, the cousin with whom he has long been infatuated. When war resumes, Sonya coerces him into agreeing to assassinate France's otherwise unstoppable emperor—a slapstick attempt that earns poor Boris the death penalty. While Boris stews in his cell, an angelic vision appears, promising him that God will spare the rod. But the deity disappoints.

So concludes Allen's Bergmanian search for a protective hand, affirming instead the Kafkaesque contention that man is but a squishable insect, destined to live an all too brief life filled with cosmic ennui.

While the twin influences of Hope and Bergman (strange bedfellows or what?) are consistently referenced, Allen does not stop there. Comedically, the film is a veritable catalogue of the various styles of comic cinema's trademark talents: Chaplin (when a hapless Allen, in a scene right out of *Soldier Arms*, 1918, saves the day by being fired from a cannon); Fields (thanks to an obtrusive sword that keeps fumblingly disrupting a stuffy social occasion); and the Marxes (with its playful snatches of repetitive dialogue suggesting *Duck Soup*, 1933, and *A Night at the Opera*, 1935).

Nor does Allen spare honoring-ribbing favorite filmmakers past and present— not just Bergman, whose *The Seventh Seal* (1958) and *Persona* (1966) are sent up but,

---

28. Wes D. Gehring, *Genre-Busting Dark Comedies of the 1970s* (Jefferson, NC: MacFarland, 2016), 139.

more fittingly, Russian master Sergei Eisenstein. (*Love and Death*'s score is composed of snatches from the one Prokofiev wrote for Eisenstein's *Alexander Nevsky,* 1938). The film is also stocked with literary allusions to Dostoyevsky, Kafka and Emily Dickinson, from which it forms its insistently atheistic philosophy. As Allen joked in a promotional piece he penned for *Esquire*, "A comedy about death and one's existence in a godless universe. The commercial possibilities were immediately apparent to me."[29]

Not to suggest that the film is entirely imitative. It is also just as full of Allen's signature wit, then also on display through his bestselling short story collections. There are well-developed monologues, duologues and syllogisms, parodying the gobbledygook of the intellectually exploratory 1970s. The result of combining these two approaches is an extremely well-balanced work, in which middlebrow and elitist sensibilities play together in perfect harmony. By appeasing, in equal measure, the mainstream and the intellectuals, Allen ended up elevating the classic comic archetype—the undersized underdog, measured against the muscle-bound (and muscle-headed) American male—to its loftiest status: as metaphor for man's cosmic insignificance. Here, Man is the overmatched, the vulnerable, the unfit, while God is the impossibly capable, invulnerable and unmatchable type against which he is contrasted.

Diane Keaton is here, too, of course (as Sonya, though the constant references to her as a "great beauty" strike us as overstatement). She speaks largely in Allenesque jokes. Not until Allen's next film, two years on, did he bother to give the actress her proper due, tapping into her real-life personality to create the film still considered his masterpiece. That dramatic gamble also constituted the first step Allen took on a journey toward recognition as one of international cinema's foremost writers of dimensional women, a mantle he inherited from—who else?—Ingmar Bergman.

Lucky Lady

Plot: The story of a *ménage à trois* between rum-runners in the 1930s. **Director:** Stanley Donen. **Script:** Willard Huyck, Gloria Katz. **Cast:** Liza Minnelli, Burt Reynolds, Gene Hackman. 20th Century–Fox. 118 minutes.

As originally conceived by writers Willard Huyck and Gloria Katz, of *American Graffiti* (1973) fame, *Lucky Lady* was a kooky, sassy relationship comedy interpolated with action sequences. Come the cutting room, the notion took to convert it to the opposite.

That might have passed as a sound idea had its intended director, Steven Spielberg, been the helmsman. Unfortunately, the script was assigned to the venerable Stanley Donen, whose history with non-musicals was, at best, dodgy (Andrew Sarris, in his seminal *The American Cinema*, calls Donen's non-musical works "either relentlessly trivial or nervously over verbalized."[30]) Worse, Donen had rarely made a punch land or a gun blaze.

And so, the sea-crossing first-time bootleggers at the heart of the film—a *ménage à trois* consisting of Liza Minnelli, Burt Reynolds and Gene Hackman—fire

29. Woody Allen, "Woody Allen on Love and Death," *Esquire*, July 1, 1975.

30. Andrew Sarris, *The American Cinema: Directors and Directions 1929–1968* (New York: Dutton, 1968), 126.

weapons, fashion Molotov cocktails and otherwise combat the competition and the law in sequences that don't build and with slapstick that falls flat.

Underneath all of this, the romantic merry-go-round of Minnelli-Reynolds-Hackman is allowed but to peek through. A shame. Judging by the few moments where the film bothers with it, there was definitely something there. Huyck and Katz had had a grand time, it's evident, spicing their 1930s dialogue with sass and snap, and the performers an equally grand time delivering it. Wise innocents were Minnelli's specialty, and she's spot-on as the middling, russet-haired chanteuse playing the uneducated mastermind. And like in *Cabaret* (1972), despite her pipe-cleaner physicality, she gets all the sexuality she can out of the role. Reynolds plays the first of two consecutive chummy dopes (the next was in *Nickelodeon*, 1976), and though it's a schizophrenic performance (he falls into Burt the macho posturer in the middle act), he plays the clown with relish. Hackman, as the wisest of the trio, gives it his cool-gruff all, and when they're on land together, living high off their illicit spoils, the picture clicks. When, as climax, they're put out to sea again, they're … well, out at sea again.

Better their company, though, than that of the supporting cast. It's universally awful—a glaring rarity in '70s film when there were so many good character actors around. Cold, classy John Hillerman is badly miscast as a broad-shouldered gangster, old reliable Michael Hordern goes through the motions as a sympathetic sea captain, and '70s heartthrob Robby Benson is at his bland, Bambi-eyed best (or worst) as the trio's supposedly savvy cabin boy.

The picture bloated to a cost of $22 million, ultimately recouping less than half. At that, the producers were lucky.

The Prisoner of Second Avenue

Plot: A middle-aged business executive suffers a mid-life crisis, brought on by the oppressive weight of his New York City existence. **Director:** Melvin Frank. **Script:** Neil Simon, from his play. **Cast:** Jack Lemmon, Anne Bancroft, Gene Saks. Warner Bros. 98 minutes.

Still suffering the slings and arrows (aka muggings and labor strikes) of urban suffocation after the hate letter to New York that was his original screenplay *The Out-of-Towners* (1970), Neil Simon took what remained of his angst back to the stage. The result, the poetically titled *The Prisoner of Second Avenue*, concentrated more deeply on the human cost of a changing world, specifically its effect on that most privileged of species, the middle-aged, white-collar Caucasian male.

His name is Mel. He's a business executive who's let go, triggering every other form of indignity a comfortable New Yorker can suffer. It culminates in a nervous breakdown, which includes visits to an inattentive shrink, fights with his long-suffering wife, and verbose self-talks while toying with a baseball. Mel, stripped of his creature comforts, posits pained rhetorical inquiries ("Is the whole world going out of business?"), rails against the urban gods ("It's my city! They're not going to kick me out of my city!"), and waxes philosophical to the point of martyrdom ("The deterioration of the spirit of man…"). This is New York City as a microcosm of the decay of civilization. What to do? According to Simon, you let it break you down completely, until you're forced to find the last vestige of your deeply hidden survivor's spirit. It's the classic American cry of "Can do!" only in comic form. It's not much, but it's the best a pessimistic wit can offer as a course in urban survival.

While both the play, produced in 1971, and the film took a shit-kicking by the critics, one can still argue that this is the quintessential Simon property, best displaying his love-hate relationship with his geographic birthright and affirming his status as the leading comic spokesperson for the modern melancholic man.

It played better on the stage, of course, restricted to a homegrown audience, at a time when New York the Bad was a teeming comedic gold mine. By '75, that notion, while still true, had grown staid and overly familiar. So too, then, is the movie version of *Prisoner*.

The stage leads were Peter Falk and Lee Grant; the film's, Jack Lemmon and Anne Bancroft. The first smack of up-from-nothing tenacity and realistic resignation; the latter of pat playfulness and calculated self-pity. Simon once said of Lemmon, who does most of the heavy lifting, that he could innately find the funny in the sad man and the sad in the funny man. True, but as he aged, Lemmon's "sad man" took on a desperately redemptive quality, too often souring the comedy. It took a latent re-pairing with frequent co-star Walter Matthau (*Grumpy Old Men*, 1993, *Out to Sea*, 1997, *The Odd Couple 2*, 1998) to restore balance. Lemmon and the film, however, have their moments.

Some of Lemmon's exchanges with Bancroft, as his wistful vessel, hit the proper Simonesque notes, and he's smart enough not to compete with Gene Saks as his antsy, avuncular older brother (a Simon dynamic destined to resurface in succeeding properties). Saks was perhaps the most well-steeped member of Simon's stage-film stock company, having appeared in and/or directed many of his plays and films. He not only knows where the jokes are (okay, that's not hard) but where the sub-jokes are, in the set-ups, the pauses and the reactions.

Once reverence for a writer kicks in, directing becomes but an exercise. Old hand Melville Shavelson—mind you, never exactly Orson Welles—affirms it here. It's largely a question of following whoever has the most lines like a hockey puck, with odd cutaways to whoever's playing straight man. As an editor, you interpolate these flagship scenes (which were shot in Burbank) with the grace notes that the second unit shot in New York. (One of them, a mugging gone awry, features a beefy unknown who, in less than a year, would become a household name: Sylvester Stallone.) For music, you alternate minor-key horn work with a light acoustic march, creating something akin to what was then known as "elevator music" (a distinct step down for the popular Marvin Hamlisch, who was slumming between the mega successes of *The Sting* and *The Way We Were*, 1973, and *A Chorus Line*, 1985). If all of this suggests that the film is seriously, and incongruously, lacking in edge, move to the front of the Media Studies class.

Prisoner was a summer release. Come Christmas, Simon was commercially if not critically redeemed. Another stage adaptation was released, this one in a distinctly feel-good vein. ("For the price of a movie," the ad campaign for *The Sunshine Boys* promised, playing on the ailing economy, "you'll feel like a million.") Simon the angry young man—make that the angry middle-aged man—was done. He spent the rest of the decade, at least cinematically, in a generally more buoyant mood before, come the 1980s, he collected his last huzzahs as a devout nostalgist.

Rafferty and the Gold Dust Twins

Plot: An ex–Marine Corps sergeant, living in Hollywood, is kidnapped by a pair of hitch-hikers who take him to New Orleans. **Director:** Dick Richards. **Script:** John Kaye. **Cast:** Alan Arkin, Sally Kellerman, Mackenzie Phillips, Alex Rocco. Warner Bros. 91 minutes.

Never, in 1970s American comic film, had a movie established the generational divide so quickly or so obviously: In the opening moments of *Rafferty and the Gold Dust Twins*, Alan Arkin is introduced as a World War II veteran cum disgruntled driving instructor, semi-coerced into escorting two hippie-era free spirits, Sally Kellerman and Mackenzie Phillips, from Los Angeles to New Orleans. If the transition strikes us as too fast or too easy, it should be noted that it is not forced nor unexpected. That's because hero Arkin is, philosophically, already there, or mostly there, so fed up with an America whose proud, exemplary past has fallen into disrepair, he's oh-so-close to resigning himself to the other side, ready to fall in line with its dysfunctional hedonism, knee-jerk sex and petty crimes against what's left of the workaday establishment.

It was an affirmation, via screenwriter John Kaye, that by 1975, the square vs. hip battle that had been raging for so long had clearly been settled, the decision going to the shaggier side. Thus, Kaye advised the older audience, there is no going back; unleash your inner bohemian and learn to go, bumpy as it may prove, with the flow. Arkin, as the put-out ex–gunnery sergeant, does just that. As added encouragement, there's the stoop-shouldered Vinny, played by character actor Alex Rocco, a Vegas-based casino rat who, over the central trio's stop in that surrealistic city, advocates life lived large. Call Rocco's Vinny, then, an American Zorba. Sure, he warns, it can be dangerous, but you'll laugh, you'll love, and most of all, you'll learn, the development of a personal code being the only thing worth anchoring a life on these days.

And so, along the dusty byways of Arizona and Nevada, Arkin, Kellerman and Phillips form a new, looser kind of family. The arrangement holds but just. Still, the film maintains, it beats the traditional variety—a claim it makes plain when Kellerman, visiting her cowboy father, is rejected outright over her wanton ways.

By mid-decade, "road movies" such as these, wherein a duo or trio of marginalized characters fall in with one another over a rambling journey into the unknown, had become a bona fide subgenre. And while the concentration was foremost on the central characters, a supporting agenda was at work: a microscopic examination of quotidian America. What better way to investigate the state of the union than an extended road trip? As the country's Bicentennial neared, this cinematic, socio-geographical census seemed especially important. Commercial, too. A year earlier, Paul Mazursky had scored a sizable hit by affixing wheels to Art Carney and cat in *Harry and Tonto* (1974). In all cases, comedy or drama, the collective conclusion seemed to be that in a place that had grown ideologically, economically and politically bereft, hunch, whim and only the simplest form of human connection were the only sensible things left in which to invest.

If this philosophy sounds strictly political, it needs to be said that it is just as much a personal one, a leitmotif of director Dick Richards.' The obscure Richards, a top advertising man who graduated to feature films, could rightfully be labeled the most underrated director of the decade. He followed the amiable *Rafferty* with one of the best Raymond Chandler adaptations, his acclaimed *Farewell My Lovely*. That film (also 1975) recognizably boasts many of the same strengths as *Rafferty*: a screenplay that zigzags without veering off course, a palpable feel for time and place, perfect casting and, getting back to that leitmotif, a seasoned, disillusioned hero resigned to life's bumps and grinds as an alternative to emotional and professional stagnation.

And yes, you did read that little-used encomium "perfect casting." The role of Rafferty is ideally suited to Arkin's introspective hysteria; the kookily controlled Kellerman is her charming, seemingly unfettered self; and Phillips remains the perfectly punky lost lamb we came to know in *American Graffiti* (1973) and on TV this same year, in the original version of Norman Lear's *One Day at a Time* (1975–84).

Phillips here is reunited with *American Graffiti* co-star Charles Martin Smith, in one of the film's few predictable turns: He's a bumpkin-soldier whom she rolls for money, on the pretense of fast sex. It's excused only by the fact that it sets up the bar-based climax.

Rafferty was a modest hit, critics and audiences deeming it, at best, sufficiently pleasant. What few noted were its merits as a sociological barometer and what it had to offer as remedy for what it recognized.

The Return of the Pink Panther

Plot: In a search for the Pink Panther, bumbling Inspector Clouseau again goes after Sir Charles Litton. **Director:** Blake Edwards. **Script:** Blake Edwards, Frank Waldman. **Cast:** Peter Sellers, Christopher Plummer, Catherine Schell, Herbert Lom, Burt Kwouk. United Artists. 114 minutes.

By 1975, slapstick had gone the way of Charlie Chase, Chester Conklin and other forgotten heroes of the silent era. Dwarfed by Broadway-born verbal wit and Second City–spawned behavioral comedy, it had come to be deemed overdone, predictable and facile. Let the less developed minds, those of children, enjoy it. The only place you could find it was in Disney's live-action fare. Even those practicing it on the small screen, like perpetual *Carol Burnett Show* (1967–78) guest star Tim Conway, seemed anachronisms, wild cards included to upset the pack. One long-time fan, though, badly fallen from the filmmaking firmament, not only never lost his taste for it, he remained convinced that it might be the very thing to resuscitate his once flourishing career.

British talent magnate Lew Grade, who represented Julie Andrews, suggested that her husband Blake Edwards re-establish a relationship with another one of Grade's ailing clients, the diverse but difficult Peter Sellers. The idea was to create a third vehicle for the fondly remembered Inspector Clouseau, the accident-prone French detective who hadn't appeared on screen in a dozen years. The Edwards-Sellers relationship had grown into a tense affair but the promise of Grade's brassy ballyhooing and an enthusiastic distribution deal with United Artists swayed all parties. Bygones would be bygones. The result would bring new, professional life to Edwards, Sellers and, yes, slapstick, paving the way for much-loved modern practitioners like Jim Carrey and Will Ferrell.

The Return of the Pink Panther even opens with unabashedly announced returns. First, the eponymous diamond, including the panther-shaped flaw that awards it its value and a brief history of the role it has played in the cat-and-mouse game that began in *The Pink Panther* (1963) between Clouseau and Sir Charles Litton, the sly, sophisticated jewel thief.

Director Blake Edwards, one of a handful of Old School talents still working at the time, would resuscitate not only his own career but that of Peter Sellers and the art of slapstick with his big-budget re-introductions of the much-loved Inspector Clouseau (United Artists/ Photofest).

Then, that other Pink Panther: the sleek, showy cartoon one. (He had been holding the fort with his own Saturday morning TV series [1969–73], shared with a character based on Clouseau.) The Panther appears in a cheeky credit sequence featuring odes to the great silent comics whom Edwards and Sellers will soon be emulating. And the primary talents' names don't just appear matter-of-factly. They're on animated marquees, in giant letters that glitter like comets. *We're back!* the names scream, bigger and better than before. The accompanying classy-brassy theme, with its famous saxophone riff, is by Henry Mancini, another fallen talent—disregarded, in the rock era, as a staid sentimentalist; thanks to this film, he too enjoyed a career revival (arena power trio Emerson, Lake and Palmer even covered his theme to an earlier Edwards-Mancini collaboration, the TV series *Peter Gunn*, 1958–61).

Then, daringly for a comedy, the film proper doesn't open with a laugh. Instead, we get a prolonged, sober-faced caper sequence: the theft of the diamond. It's Edwards, in short order, out to remind us that he didn't just make comedies but was, and remains, capable of all kinds of things. Finally, we see Clouseau embroiled in an argument with a mouthy organ grinder over his filthy monkey, while a robbery takes place behind their backs. We are prompted to remember what had been so funny about Clouseau; to remember why, for 12 years, we had held him so dear: his utmost professionalism, completely misplaced.

Cue, minutes later, Cato, the Asian manservant whose primary responsibility is to keep Clouseau's self-defense skills sharp by ambushing him when and where Clouseau least expects it. (Surely there's a Film Studies student out there who's written an essay about Clouseau's fumbling as a metaphor for the French's bungled grip on Vietnam, America's love of his epic failures as a form of hate for the French for leaving them with such a mess, and Cato's high-kicks and karate chops as a Vietnamese revenge fantasy?)

In all cases, these returning conventions are, from when we last indulged in them, nicely broadened—most famously, Clouseau's accent, which has taken on an elongated, nasal quality. Over time, Edwards and Sellers, high on its success, would repeat the practice until it robbed the character of his hubris and vulnerability. But that's sequels away. Most exaggerated of all is Clouseau's trademark floundering. Where once he might have leaned on a spinning globe to be sent to the carpet or obliviously slipped a burning lighter into his pocket, now he wrecks entire rooms and crashes through walls. Not too long before, '70s audiences might have classified this kind of humor as condescending or bombastic; this time around, they relished every second of it. While most of the gags are very old indeed, they're accomplished with such expertise and affection, they practically read as new. Even the running gags, predictable as they are, are welcome. It helps too that they're perfectly framed by Edwards and cinematographer Geoffrey Unsworth, the perspective always managing to get the most out of a joke. So many score that, as a result, the film conforms to that most valued and elusive commodity that we look for in a big, commercial comedy: consistency.

Even the film's second agenda, the contrasting caper, fails to break the comic tempo. And parts of it are enjoyable. Christopher Plummer, as Litton, is infectiously enjoying himself, as is his on-screen wife, the sweetly smug Catherine Schell, who suggests a less forced Julie Andrews (though her decision to repeatedly giggle at Clouseau's antics is annoyingly overdone). Edwards even throws in a small ode to *Casablanca* (1942), setting a white-jacketed Plummer to banter with Peter Lorre–like Graham Stark while "As Time Goes By" tinkles on lounge piano. It's just tolerable enough, bringing us to the brink of a cry for the next Sellers-centric set-piece, wherein he'll fiddle with a misbehaving gadget (unlike James Bond, they are not his friend) or play victim to an undetected booby trap.

If we love and, in a twisted way, admire Clouseau, it's because, as those moments repeatedly affirm, he's the ultimate beneficiary of blind luck. His failings may be many, but they are, miraculously, enveloped in providence. We'd all be so lucky!

Shampoo

Plot: An L.A.–based hairdresser-playboy juggles multiple women. **Director:** Hal Ashby. **Script:** Robert Towne, Warren Beatty. **Cast:** Warren Beatty, Julie Christie, Goldie Hawn, Lee Grant, Jack Warden, Carrie Fisher. Columbia. 110 minutes.

It takes 20 years for nostalgia for any given period to kick into high gear. (All sociology aside, that's how long it takes a generation to bloom into a moneyed demographic, eager to buy back its youth through movies, music and mementos.) But when it came to looking back at the free-wheelin' 1960s, a practice that would dominate the American cinema of the 1980s, a handful of films were, chancily, ahead of the curve. Poor, worthy *I Wanna Hold Your Hand* (1978), a frantic adolescent comedy about the importation of the Beatles, suffered from a bad case of premature exhibition. It hardly helped that the film, produced on a modest budget and overseen by industry newbies, suffered from a complete lack of star power (discounting its all–Fab Four soundtrack).

Shampoo was made three years earlier (so, separated by a mere seven years from its setting, the eve of Nixon's 1968 landslide election) and operated with the safety net of an all-name cast: actor–co-writer–producer Warren Beatty and a teeming bag of eye candy: Julie Christie, Goldie Hawn and Lee Grant. (Another bonbon was an amateur making her film debut: a plain-faced, nubile Carrie Fisher, two years away from Princess Leia, the Puritan Barbarella.) Further, the latter were all sexualized up the proverbial yin-yang, adorned in period mini-skirts and chest-hugging sweaters, which they shed for beefy Beatty in bohemian bedrooms, at swank soirees and in suburban shower stalls. It all made for a "kaleidoscopic farce" (Pauline Kael in her *5001 Nights at the Movies*[31]) that was "boastfully risqué" (David Thomson in his *New Biographical Dictionary of Film*[32]).

That said, the film ingratiated itself to its intended audience prior to the revelation of a single body part. Long before the practice became ubiquitous, *Shampoo* eschewed music composed expressly for the screen for Baby Boomer jukebox fodder, immediately positing the film as a commodity for the hipper, younger demographic. Further, the opening tune, the catchy-kitschy "Wouldn't It Be Nice?" by the corny but much-loved Beach Boys, perfectly framed the film's major themes. Famously, the song entertains the transition from adolescent-style relationship to adult commitment, going on to equate personal happiness with the notion of marriage.

The film, then, is about the free-for-all '60s giving way to the confused '70s before settling for the monogamous '80s. Beatty, in a mix of self-parody and self-pity, is George, a free-wheeling Beverly Hills hairdresser whose every snip prompts an unzip, until the fad of romantic commitment brings his free-wheelin' ways to an introspective end.

Call George a sexual kind of time traveler. In Act One, he's immersed in a universe of free love, motorcycle rides and strobe-light–happy parties; by Act Two, he's lost in a world of tortuous self-examination, questioning the value of hedonism and entertaining doubts that as a model for living, it will hold. By Act Three, he's the last hold-out of his generation, everyone around him either settling for the staid or otherwise transitioning. "Grow up, George!" Jill (Goldie Hawn) screams at our tortured hero. But poor George, though slowly aging out of his mile-high shag, low-cut shirts and skin-tight wide-legs, can't seem—stammer, stammer, stammer—to do it.

And when he finally attempts it (get ready to cue the closing credits), it's too late; the woman who has won him over most, Jackie (Christie), announces that she's leaving him for a stuffy establishmentarian. As the joke on the street had it at the time: "Just when I'm ready to sell out, nobody's willing to buy!"

The character of George is, arguably, the quintessential Beatty role. With it, he brought to the screen the persona that the public, through the tabloids, had already cast him in. Beatty, thereby, created a new male cinematic archetype: the hip, modern playboy. That said, it was also a case of same old, same old: Again, as he had since his big-screen debut in Elia Kazan's *Splendor in the Grass* (1961) and continuing through more dimensional, self-made variations, Beatty was playing the man-boy, the overgrown adolescent trapped in a world with a limited tolerance for his self-indulgent shenanigans, leaving him to suffer the overdue angst of maturation.

Like Paul Newman, Beatty had made a career out of playing low-key, charismatic

---

31. Pauline Kael, *5001 Nights at the Movies* (New York: Henry Holt, 1991), 670–671.
32. David Thomson, *The New Biographical Dictionary of Film Updated and Expanded* (New York: Alfred A. Knopf, 2010), 778.

rubes convinced that they were the smartest ones in the room, only to find, in the baffling, painful end, that the room was smarter than they were. And Beatty, at least the on-screen version, never did grow up. In the successive films in which he was ringmaster, he infantilized himself even more, playing more innocent, less complex characters in simpler, old-fashioned properties such as *Heaven Can Wait* (1978) and *Dick Tracy* (1990).

Shampoo was directed by Hal Ashby. As with all Ashby films, the verb "directed" is used loosely. Even in his own time, though his string of hits throughout the '70s is as impressive as any American auteur's, Ashby remained, to the critics, a puzzle. Was he simply a well-connected craftsman who could be counted on to accommodate the powers that be (in this case, producer Beatty and co-scenarist Robert Towne)? Or was a talent in its own right at work, as affirmed by the ably offbeat hits *The Landlord* (1970), *Harold and Maude* (1971), *The Last Detail* (1973) and *Being There* (1979)?

It's a debate still raging, as the revisionists (like me) struggle to secure Ashby's rightful reputation. Again, we turn to David Thomson and his *New Biographical Dictionary of Film*, this time on *The Last Detail*. Thomson categorizes it as Ashby's best film (an arguable contention, strong as that picture is), citing Ashby's realization "that living is a set of prisons."[33] Further, Thomson calls Ashby's post–Vietnam melodrama *Coming Home* (1978) "a film about self excuse and the isolation that learns to forget mistakes and problems."[34] With these assessments, Thomson has correctly identified Ashby's two signature motifs (though he fails to mention the man's equally steady love of the false messiah), each of which is a major thread running through Ashby's horny coming-of-age comedy *Shampoo*. So acknowledged, the film becomes as much Ashby's as Beatty's or Towne's.

Does *Shampoo* hold up? Yes, but in ironic fashion: not, as was intended, as a timepiece of the '60s but as one of the decade in which it was produced. Like its premature release date, its angst, about how the times-they-are-a-changin'-back, isn't '60s but '70s. By '75, we, like George in the film's purported '68, were walking a tightrope we could feel giving beneath our feet. Where might we land when the fall, proving more and more inevitable, came?

First, though, like George in the film's final frame, perched high atop the dappled sprawl of L.A. while, stripped of our ideals and self-amusements, we pondered the future, we would take solace in our sunny geography. Starting with *Shampoo* and progressing through the comedies of the next half of the decade, California, with its promise of a laid-back lifestyle, would steal the cultural spotlight from oppressive New York, taking us from high-octane angst to depressurized innocuousness.

Smile

Plot: A satirical examination of small-town America conducted through a teenage beauty pageant in Santa Rosa, California. **Director:** Michael Ritchie. **Script:** Jerry Belson. **Cast:** Bruce Dern, Barbara Feldon, Michael Kidd, Geoffrey Lewis, Melanie Griffith. United Artists. 117 minutes.

---

33. David Thomson, *The New Biographical Dictionary of Film Updated and Expanded* (New York: Alfred A. Knopf, 2010), 38.

34. David Thomson, *The New Biographical Dictionary of Film Updated and Expanded* (New York: Alfred A. Knopf, 2010), 38.

As America's Bicentennial neared, more and more indigenous artists, filmmakers included, took to the molecular examination of a handful of all–American institutions. Robert Altman topped all practitioners with his masterful *Nashville* (1975), using the grassroots world of country music to express the broken spirit and vain, showy optimism of America at 200 years of age. But another cinematic anthropologist, with technical chops almost as good and a satirical streak just as irrepressible, was out to draw the same conclusions by looking at a sub-world just as pathos-riddled and patriotic: the underrated Michael Ritchie, tackling the long-standing phenomenon of beauty pageants in *Smile*.

That said, *Smile* is more than just a listen to the dysfunctional heart of the Santa Rosa Young American Miss contest. In exposing the absurdity of the tired, corny conventions of such affairs, the film casts its vote for the feminist movement, a phenomenon hitting, at the time of *Smile*'s release, full stride. (One of the contestants, in all of her old-fashioned finery, calls Women's Lib "kinda silly.")

Gender equality, circa 1975, was just beginning to infiltrate mainstream American cinema; the adaptation of Ira Levin's bestselling pro-feminist sci-fi-satire *The Stepford Wives* was released that summer. A major aid had been the publication, a year earlier, of film critic Molly Haskell's seminal *From Reverence to Rape: The Treatment of Women in the Movies*. While comedy would go on, throughout the remainder of the decade, to boast few feminist stars, by its conclusion, vehicles for women eschewing the stereotypes identified by Haskell had become a staple of on-screen drama.

Until comedy caught up, there was *Smile*, advancing the cause by antiquating, scene by scene, the expectations placed on women since their casting as sexual objects and agents of servility. Hence, the Young American Miss Pageant, promoting yesterday's female today. See nubile Aryans, in outfits alternately coy and clingy, parade themselves for God-fearing family audiences, before bringing their can-do spirit to a culminating talent show. Watch them give tips on how best to pack a suitcase, play amateurish piano while spotlighting their mawkish paintings, or brazenly belt out, through a mouthful of braces, "Delta Dawn."

With moments like these, why push? So, writer Jerry Belson, while a sitcom veteran, and director Ritchie don't—or at least, not much. Their occasional violations include a poke at fast food culture (Major Weenie—just place your order with the talking dog) and a night spent in the company of the all-male contest sponsors, who, in the guise of a benign KKK, commit adolescent hijinks rather than lynchings.

The film's other major target is suburbia, specifically, the California variety. Again, we have a writer, Belson, who is a transplanted New Yorker, casting a wry Eastern eye on the quirky quotidian quality of Cali. And while Belson does a yeoman's job of showcasing the everyday self-importance that drives the community behind the pageant, he ultimately brings real heart to the proceedings—first, in a fine little backstory he provides Big Bob Freelander, the pageant's car-dealing sponsor, then, with his chronicle of Santa Rosa's hermetic toil on the Mother Hen's harried husband, driven to suicidal drink by pageantmania. In both instances, we are afforded a genuine look at the compromised soul of prototypical middle-class Americans, and thus, the country's.

The name "Freelander," by the way, is not a coincidence. It's a declaration of subtextual intent: Belson-Ritchie's pageant is a metaphor for America as a whole, a country which, at the end of a long, dysfunctional day, can only, as it does in the aforementioned Altman film, anthemically chant *It Don't Worry Me,* or in Ritchie's film, smile.

Smile was converted to a Broadway musical in 1986, with '70s middle-of-the-road powerhouse Marvin Hamlisch behind it. No smile was solicited.

The Sunshine Boys

Plot: A pair of aged vaudevillians pick up their lifelong rivalry when they attempt to reunite for a TV special. **Director:** Herbert Ross. **Script:** Neil Simon, from his play. **Cast:** Walter Matthau, George Burns, Richard Benjamin, Lee Meredith. United Artists. 110 minutes.

Comedy was at a divide. The 20th century's first comic generation, raised in vaudeville and popularized by radio and early TV, was settling into a tony, respected clique of Grand Masters. Meanwhile, a younger, edgier generation, spawned by socio-political wits Lenny Bruce and Mort Sahl, were embodying the spirit of the young, their more permissive material gaining rapid popularity through private forums like record albums and college amphitheaters. Benny-Berle-Youngman vs. Carlin-Pryor-Klein.

Arguably, the most representative demonstration of this charged polarity took place in 1975, when Milton Berle—with whom, as TV comedy's first star, the Baby Boomers had grown up—guest-hosted the hippest new show on television, *Saturday Night Live.* So embarrassingly incongruous was Berle's appearance, in which he insisted on undermining the material with Old School ad libs, showrunner Lorne Michaels permanently put the episode on ice. To this day, it has never been rerun.

Neil Simon, unequivocally stating that he was no performer yet maybe also rattled by the unsettling Berle appearance, turned down several overtures to front *SNL*. He was, after all, a card-carrying member of Berle nation, having cut his teeth under Uncle Miltie's immediate successor, TV sketch god Sid Caesar.

Looking to pay tribute, for better or worse, to this dying breed, Simon wrote his first exercise in nostalgia (many would follow): *The Sunshine Boys,* an extended sketch in which two aging vaudevillians take up their career-long war while rehearsing for a TV retrospective.

From a studio standpoint, it checked a lot of boxes: Simon's name, despite the staid film adaptation earlier that year of his *Prisoner of Second Avenue,* still held weight; 1930s nostalgia, pioneered by *The Sting* (1973), continued; old-fashioned, feel-good properties as remedy for troubled times were still considered box-office. Such was the momentum for the latter two that the original idea was to stunt-cast two members of comedy's gilded age. The problem was, which two? For a while, the trades had it that *The Sunshine Boys* would mark the return to the big screen of the reclusive Red Skelton. Check that. It would instead mark the comeback of the little-seen Phil Silvers' (the DVD release features silent scenes from Silvers' screen test). Finally, it was announced that at least one of the parts would go to Jack Benny, the other, maybe, to his long-time friend and pseudo-rival, George Burns.

In the end, Burns, who had been living off of the coattails of name friends since the 1964 death of his wife and professional partner Gracie Allen, was cast. He'd play the straight man, of course, a capacity he had fulfilled with wry relish since his first days on the stage. So, who for the cantankerous counterpart, the whirling dervish with the lingering resentment, out to undermine the ballyhooed reunion?

It would take the infantile energy of a Skelton, the benign bark of a Silvers, the see-through vanity of a Benny. (Simon, by the way, advocated for Jack Albertson. Albertson had played the part on Broadway and was then starring in the TV hit *Chico and the Man*, 1974–78.) Stumped, the powers-that-be went "young," casting an up-and-coming buck named Walter Matthau. Matthau already had the build, with his trademark stoop, shuffle-step walk and jowly visage; all he needed was some convincing makeup. It was a providential lesson in perfect casting. Instantly, Matthau and Burns fell into a sustained groove, their easy one-upmanship masking an unmistakable *noblesse oblige*.

The rehearsal process was marred by the presence of Harvey Keitel, the studio's nervous concession to the younger audience, a newcomer whose low-key fire proved to fit Simon's verbose hokum like extra-strength paprika on a rubber chicken. Calling a spade a spade, Keitel was wisely replaced in the role of the peacemaking nephew-agent by no-trouble, angst-comedy veteran Richard Benjamin. Old School neurotics only, please!

If *The Sunshine Boys* is one of Simon's best plays and best screen adaptations, the triumph is foremost contextual: Who better to constantly spout one-liners than a pair of old

George Burns (left) and Walter Matthau in the film adaptation of Neil Simon's *The Sunshine Boys* (MGM/United Artists, 1975). The movie revived aging vaudevillian Burns' career (he earned a Best Supporting Actor Oscar) and catapulted him to the status of America's grandfather (MGM/United Artists/Photofest).

vaudevillians? For once, the clown shoe fit. The remainder of the film's spoils belong to Matthau and Burns. Matthau's sibilant deadpan and Jewish music energizes much of the humor; it even makes the lesser lines, including the straight ones, funny. Of Simon, Matthau always maintained, "He writes the way I talk."[35] Matthau proves it definitively here.

Providing pitch-perfect contrast is Burns. His gravelly deadpan and careful, reflective style, with its quiet, certain rhythms, won America's heart (and, sentimentally, an Oscar). Aided by the death of most of his confreres, Burns was rediscovered as the Golden Age of Comedy's last living (or at least working) icon, enjoying unprecedented popularity as an Old School raconteur and, through successive films and endless TV and stage appearances, becoming America's grandfather. Benjamin's role as the beleaguered go-between is effectively thankless but he uses his squeaky fluster to make at least a little something of it.

As far as adapting the property, it's one of Simon's better efforts. He divides most of the long scenes into smaller, palatable moments, disarming the cloying quality of previous films. In the bargain, he, director Herb Ross and the location scouts nicely showcase many famous New York show biz landmarks. And the film climaxes, as did the play, with an excellent replica of inspirational vaudeville comedy team Smith and Dale's rapid-fire Dr. Kronkheit routine (though vaudeville would have never tolerated the double entendres).

Simon's work is never really about much. But this one has a distinct message: the self-destructive quality of hate. Simon mines it, comedically and dramatically, for all its worth, including a genuinely moving moment when Matthau, after a crippling heart attack, has a nice semi-goodbye scene with nephew Benjamin. Like most of the rest of the film, unless genuinely warranted, it's smartly underplayed. This is a rare case of an entire filmmaking collective doing Simon's material cinematic justice, falling into the proper tempo and rarely losing it.

1976

In 1976, the small, raggedy, semi-realist New York comedy was officially eulogized—ironically, the same year that President Ford told that economically ailing metropolis, looking for a desperately needed federal hand-out, to "drop dead." (Hence this book's title. Did you catch that?)

The big Hollywood-based studios, buoyed by the mega grosses of *The Godfather* (1972), *The Exorcist* (1973) and *Jaws* (1975), were back. So, as a consequence, were the classic genres for which they'd always been known: the romcom, the thriller, the Western.

Car-crazy L.A. was further represented when a new genre of macho, gas-guzzling comedy, aimed largely at the sizable drive-in market, began to leave its mark on the industry like a set of mile-long tire tracks.

But how would the quality of the comedy fare in the great New York–L.A. migration?

---

35. John Podhoretz, "The Unlikeliest Star," *Washington Examiner*, Feb. 28, 2000.

The Bad News Bears

Plot: An alcoholic ex-pitcher is coerced into coaching an eclectic team of Little Leaguers. **Director:** Michael Ritchie. **Script:** Bill Lancaster. **Cast:** Walter Matthau, Tatum O'Neal, Vic Morrow, Alfred Lutter. Paramount. 102 minutes.

"We must be doin' somethin' right the past 200 yearrrrrs...."

So sang, with see-through cynicism, the countrified crooners of Robert Altman's pre–Bicentennial *Nashville* (1975). That music-filled masterpiece was just one of the many films which, in anticipation of America's 200th birthday, devoted itself to the examination of iconic, all–American institutions. While Altman chose that revered right-wing soundtrack, country music and, later, with his *Buffalo Bill and the Indians* (1976), the venerable Western, to tell less political, more playful Michael Ritchie went America's national pastime: baseball.

Ritchie wouldn't be the only one to pick up the bat and ball: That same summer, John Badham released *The Bingo Long Traveling All-Stars & Motor Kings*. But Ritchie would be responsible for the decade's last great behavior-based comedy, scoring a sleeper hit besides.

The film's selling point was the unlikely coupling of grumpy mid-lifer Walter Matthau with temperamentally teenaged Tatum O'Neal—a new kind of Odd Couple. Matthau is awarded the most fitting character name of his career: Morris Buttermaker. He's a beer-swilling fallen jock (the first part is easy to believe ... the second?), coerced into making a bunch of in-fighting pre-teens into a Little League powerhouse. To that end, he recruits his estranged pseudo-stepdaughter, convincing her to suppress her budding femininity and break out her blazing fastball.

Sounds corny, cloying and crowd-pleasing. To everyone's surprise and delight, the first two didn't apply. Bill Lancaster's carefully crass screenplay and Ritchie's amiably experimental directing combined to provide a proudly realistic look at modern kids, attitude, language and all. It might have been prompted by the precedent established by Martin Scorsese's fun, feminist *Alice Doesn't Live Here Anymore* (1974), the rambling, realistic chronicle of a smart-mouthed single mom and her equally loose-lipped son, played with un–self-conscious aplomb by Alfred Lutter.

Lutter appears here too but this is no reprise of his part in *Alice*. He's lost in the shuffle of the more vocal kids, who have inherited his foul-mouthed mantle. In fact, he and the rest of the big-name child stars—the aforementioned O'Neal and budding bad boy Jackie Earl Haley—do okay but are all outshone by the long-haired, snot-nosed supporting horde.

Matthau is their Fagin, teaching them, in his own reluctant, homemade way, how to best the establishment, i.e., the other teams, squeaky middle-class kids from seemingly functional families. Here again, for one of the last times, the hippie vs. square stand-off serves as the dramatic engine, even if by now, it's the junior version, the former children and the latter parents. It's also urban, Jewish New York, represented by Matthau and his spirited, angry young charges, vs. idyllic, even-tempered California, represented by the conscientiously staid heads of the opposing teams. That sunny, leisurely and formal land was still held, by comic film, as a strange, vacuous, self-serving place, devoid of crisis, culture or color. In time, it would be heartily embraced. For now, it remained the indignantly uninteresting place you wanted to shake up.

And the kids do—well, mostly. As charmingly authentic as Lancaster's screenplay is, this film is made with editing and sound design. Ritchie proves himself a master of post-production, staging periodic orgies of on-field misplays (the precursors of today's ubiquitous ESPN fillers?) to snatches of classical music, particularly *Carmen*'s "La Habanera," smartly contrasting the lofty with the (pardon the pun) base.

Matthau, as their perpetually Pilsener-ed leader, wisely plays it low-key, hamming it up but on occasion. His avuncular slovenliness has rarely been put to such good, unforced use. Dependably defensive Vic Morrow is also perfectly cast, and for all of the Matthau-Bears momentum, he has the film's best scene with his dad-coach's surprise attack on his pitcher-son. O'Neal proves largely ill at ease, but fortunately, her story arc—the integration of a hold-her-own female into a rowdy male universe, a tailor-made sub-plot in this year of the Susan B. Anthony dollar—plays serendipitously in her favor. And

By the mid–70s, New York–based comedy was out; more and more films were set in its loopy, happy alternative, California—like Michael Ritchie's sleeper hit *The Bad News Bears* (Paramount, 1976) with Tatum O'Neal and Walter Matthau (Paramount Pictures/Photofest).

the film goes easy on the heartstrings, conceding, in O'Neal's scenes with Matthau, just a little.

Given Morrow's big scene, you'd think the film would play as an indictment of parental overzealousness. But it's something much deeper: a comment on the nature of American leadership. Post–Nam-Nixon, America was looking, like the lost little Bears, for a leader, only to come up with a tolerable fumbler: for the Bears, Walter Matthau, for the country, Gerald Ford. It might not be much, announces the film, but it beats the alternative. Another film released that year provided America with something resonantly better: a fumbler made good in the persona of Rocky Balboa. By the '80s, Rocky had gone from working-class hero to corporate fitness-craze icon, prompting comedian George Carlin to insightfully surmise, "America has lost its soul so it's trying to save its body."[36] *Rocky* (1976), despite its many parallels with *Bad News Bears*—the underdog heroes, the crusty mentor, the climactic loss—would, with its sincere-cum-synthetic simplicity, pave the way for the retro, white hat vs. black hat battles of *Star Wars* (1977), perfectly in sync with the primitive politics of Ronald Reagan.

After Ford, another good-hearted goofus, Carter. No wonder Reagan. No wonder less and less comedies, like *Bad News Bears*, about the corruption of American values at the hands of faulty leadership.

The Bad News Bears, the anti–Disney feel-good family film, proved such a success that it spawned two sequels (still a new phenomenon at the time), a TV series and, unfortunately, a 2005 remake wherein Lancaster's original screenplay was crossbred with forced macho jokes at the insistence of star Billy Bob Thornton.

Faulty leadership indeed.

The Big Bus

Plot: A parody of disaster films wherein a nuclear-powered bus travels from New York City to Denver. **Director:** James Frawley. **Script:** Lawrence J. Cohen, Fred Freeman. **Cast:** Joseph Bologna, Stockard Channing, John Beck, Ned Beatty, Sally Kellerman, Ruth Gordon. Paramount. 88 minutes.

By the time the '70s arrived, the world was, simply put, a disaster. Throughout the '60s, generations had warred, political assassination had become common practice, the death toll in Vietnam had peaked, and Charles Manson had run bloodily amok. Quotidian existence had become equally corrupted. You could get mugged, raped or murdered taking a walk, have your trash aspire to the sky thanks to labor strife, or be hijacked or otherwise threatened boarding a flight.

Cashing in on widespread fear of the latter was novelist Arthur Hailey who, in 1968, penned the popular *Airport*, a Bible-thick paperback putting the fate of a cross-section of ordinary Americans in the hands of a despondent bomber. The film version was released in 1970. Despite mixed reviews (even star Burt Lancaster knocked it), it was much loved by the public, who recognized its overblown mix of melodrama and action as a metaphor for the circumstantially sideswiped state of the nation.

Recognizing a collective anxiety waiting to be played upon even further, sci-fi TV king Irwin Allen self-financed the turtle-tempered luxury liner *The Poseidon Adventure* (1972), then got two studios to go Dutch on his flaming pie-in-the-sky *The Towering Inferno* (1974).

The national nervosity that Allen, nicknamed "the Master of Disaster," was preying on, a collective mix of fear and self-pity, lingered until the dissipation of the decade, at which point such films, separated from the times, would be exposed for what they were: Pavlovian cash grabs anchored on technically absurdist premises, soft casts and tired interpersonal dynamics.

A handful of movie buffs, however, had grown wise early—the parodists, of course. Hence, *The Big Bus*, a scattergun spoof of a burgeoning genre that for some reason, was of little interest to master of mockery Mel Brooks. The task fell instead to writers

---

36. George Carlin, *Brain Droppings* (New York: Hachette, 1998), 5.

Lawrence J. Cohen and Fred Freeman and to director James Frawley, TV veterans all. Makes sense. While the '70s marked the advent of big box-office cinematic parody, the small screen had been kicking its big brother in the pants for a long time, starting with the Sid Caesar–fronted *Your Show of Shows* (1950–54) and continuing through *The Carol Burnett Show* (1967–78). *The Big Bus* owes to both, especially the more spontaneous spirit of the former. Star Joe Bologna, in fact, went on to send up Caesar himself in *My Favorite Year* (1982); it's impossible not to note, throughout *The Big Bus*, just how many of his stances and shticks echo Caesar's.

The poster posited *The Big Bus* as: "The first disaster movie where everybody dies … laughing." Quite a promise—and yet, it delivered, skewing each of the genre's conventions with invention, accuracy and, let's say it, hilarity.

All aboard the world's first nuclear-powered bus (wonderfully designed by production man Joel Schiller) as, with much fanfare, it sets out on "history's first non-stop bus ride from New York to Denver." Small prob for the archetypes—the religious figure, the senior citizen, the bar buddies, the movie star—on board: A bomb has been planted, thanks to a James Bondian villain out to protect the interests of big oil (a play on the then unfolding energy crisis). Other archetypes—namely, the driver-hero with a past and his on-off love interest hostess—to the rescue! Meanwhile, there is comic panic of commendably consistent order, relieved by quintessential lounge act Murphy Dunne, and a rewarding climax playing on the technical absurdities of the genre. Further, it's all set to David Shire's spoofily spot-on score, brimming with the overblown sweep and hard-sell tension of such soundtracks.

The Big Bus, while modestly priced, proved to be the Big Bust. Bafflingly, that didn't deter the underwriting studio, Paramount, from trying the same thing again four years later. The result, *Airplane!* (1980), grossed close to $200 million. The difference? Likely that at the time of the former, the disaster genre was alive and well. Time had yet to expose its inherent follies. The bus in question, then, may have been adorned with an array of eclectic amenities (including a wonderfully tacky Bicentennial lounge) but a crucial one had been missing: a rear-view mirror.

The Bingo Long Traveling All-Stars & Motor Kings

Plot: A baseball team made up of ex–Negro League players proves so successful, it's challenged to a contest to re-enter the league or break up. **Director:** John Badham. **Script:** Hal Barwood, Matthew Robbins. **Cast:** Billy Dee Williams, James Earl Jones, Richard Pryor. Universal. 110 minutes.

Nineteen seventy-six was the year of the blockbuster TV mini-series *Roots*, an adaptation of the hefty Alex Haley bestseller dramatizing his painstakingly researched heritage. Hitherto, African Americans knew little of the trials and tribulations of their forefathers, the socio-political mechanics of slavery, and the true emotional weight of the Colonial experience. A genealogy craze ensued (long before today's .com tools made this kind of thing easily accessible), placing a widespread cultural premium on unheralded black figures past and present.

Thrown into the mix was cinema's first full-length look at Negro League baseball, a key component of 20th-century black history: the colorfully (and lengthily) titled *The*

Bingo Long Traveling All-Stars & Motor Kings. Buoyed by the success of Sidney Poitier's comedies and the uber ratings of *Roots*, *Bingo* helped to ensure decent budgets, wide distribution and industry-standard marketing for films aimed foremost at African American audiences.

Let it not be forgotten, however, that the true symbols of studio faith (despite the film's being produced by Motown founder Berry Gordy Jr.) were the ivory-toned hands into which the key creative reins had been placed: veteran writing team Hal Barwood and Matthew Robbins, along with a promising young director, John Badham.

If the film was but a modest success in its day, it's for myriad reasons: Its core subject, baseball, had long fallen out of fashion with the younger audience, having labeled it an antiquated establishmentarian symbol. (They'd come around in the 1980s, so much so that baseball films became, for a time, a veritable genre); the release of the aforementioned *Bad News Bears*, monopolizing those who *did* care for the subject; a lack of name casting, though each of the featured talents is nothing less than top-notch.

Then, there's the style of comedy. Badham, at least in the early years of his career, made a habit of embedding himself in self-serving subcultures, examining them with color, energy, personality and realism. The following year, the disco set catapulted him to go-to status. And indeed, *Bingo* features a lot of the elements the energetic Alabaman would put to more successful use in *Saturday Night Fever* (1977): the company of high-living young oafs out to have a good time, lots of bonding and drinking and dancing, love-hate relationships with women, and a climactic contest (realized, in *Bingo*, in slow motion, one of the film's few concessions to sports film cliché). The emphasis, in both cases, isn't on character or dialogue. In fact, you expect a lot of the *Bingo* scenes to play out longer than they do, to extend either comically or dramatically. But they don't.

The priorities here are pace, bits of business and, mostly, high spirits. *Bingo* bounces, rolls and skips like an errant grounder. Its Dixieland and gospel score is a great aid in sustaining this cockeyed, happy-go-lucky feel, as is the inspired editing, with its unceasing wipes, dissolves and graphic transitions; the film's a catalogue of late '70s motion graphics.

As the tale of a barnstorming baseball team, *Bingo* is also a road movie, and for the times, a good one. No lobotomization of the seminal American experience that is cross-country road travel—a hipster rite of passage (ride of passage?) and prime male bonding experience from the days of Kerouac through to *Easy Rider* (1969)—à la *The Gumball Rally* (1976) and its drive-in–aimed, gas-guzzling kin. The emphasis here is on bonhomie, a look at the pleasure and price of the brotherly bond. And what brothers they are: Billy Dee Williams, as Bingo, was never used better (sorry *Star Wars* fans). Both the role and Badham's direction bring out his Poitier style leadership and his Eddie Murphy–esque brashness. James Earl Jones, as a formidable batter based on black baseball legend Josh Gibson, establishes the jokey pugnaciousness that continued to play remedy to his exercises in gravelly gravitas. (Jones visited baseball repeatedly, on stage in *Fences* and on film in *Field of Dreams*, 1989.) And Richard Pryor enjoys his most amusing on-screen stint up to that time as a chatty journeyman convinced he can break the restricted major leagues by posing as a Cuban.

Together, they're the group of ragtag youths who go up against greedy establishmentarians (in this case, the team's owners)—so, yes, once again, as in a lot of '70s cinema, it's a case of socialism vs. capitalism. Interestingly, though, *Bingo* is not also a case, as expectation would have it, of black vs. white. It's black vs. black. When the team's black owners ask the players to clown it up to appease Caucasian audiences, there's but a modicum of protestation—then, acceptance and delight. As such, the film eschews an overly familiar racial storyline and happily settles for another ideological identity.

It's great fun, one of the true treasures of the age.

Buffalo Bill and the Indians

Plot: Friction develops between Buffalo Bill Cody and Chief Sitting Bull over the nature of the former's Wild West show. **Director:** Robert Altman. **Script:** Robert Altman, Alan Rudolph, suggested by the play *Indians* by Arthur Kopit. **Cast:** Paul Newman, Will Sampson, Burt Lancaster, Joel Grey, Harvey Keitel, Pat McCormack, Shelley Duvall. United Artists. 123 minutes.

After his masterpiece *Nashville* (1975), Robert Altman continued to expose the rampant dysfunction beneath America's patriotic show biz veneer. "He was fascinated by the whole role of putting on a show"—producer Matthew Stieg, from Mitchell Zuckoff's 2009 oral biography of Altman—"the whole tradition of showmanship, whether it's a con or not and how very American that tradition is."[37]

Altman's target this time was the Old West, or rather its mythomaniacal echo: Buffalo Bill Cody's Wild West Show, a ragtag extravaganza running on the inflated reputation of a faded cowboy hero. A worthy choice but a less relevant one. The cultural tide was clearly turning. With the conclusion of the Vietnam and Watergate debacles, old-fashioned American patriotism, and the classic male archetypes that went with it, were making a slow but certain comeback, signaled by the surprise success of the low-budget *Rocky* (1976). A shame, as Altman at this time was at the peak of his powers, a bona fide, dazzling auteur and an international darling. Such was the buzz around him that *Buffalo Bill* was underwritten by super-producer Dino De Laurentiis, who was also financing the year's most anticipated blockbuster, the feminist *King Kong*. Instead, *Buffalo Bill* proved the starting gun for a race to cinema's lower ranks, Altman proving prone to the same things that were derailing the American auteur movement as a whole: too much on-screen and off-screen self-indulgence. Ultimately, he baffled the critics who had played kingmaker and alienated the paying public.

The film, narratively, is beautifully framed, in a smart, subtle parody of American lyricism by Burt Lancaster, by now the respected elder statesman of the arty set (a precedent set by his work for Bernardo Bertolucci). Within are the components of Arthur Kopit's play *Indians*, a straight-ahead power struggle between all–American crass capitalist Buffalo Bill and the Zen-like Siting Bull, whom Bill wants as part of his ensemble. (Again, it's the blowhard, clued-out establishment vs. the quiet, driven hippies.) But by trying for something more panoramic, with his signature cutaways, offhand bits of business and periodic camera pushes, Altman repeatedly gets in the central dynamic's way.

Miraculously, the two central performances—by Paul Newman as Cody and Will Sampson as the silent Sitting Bull's spokesperson—survive. Newman, a conservative,

---

37. Mitchell Zuckoff, *Robert Altman: The Oral Biography* (New York: Alfred A. Knopf, 2009), 312.

brooding actor, is visibly pushing himself, living it up as the alcoholic, impotent, egotistical Cody. Given Cody's shaggy locks, iconic beard and party-hearty behavior, one has to ask: Was this Altman, through Newman, exercising self-parody?

Regardless, Newman has one of the best scenes he's ever done: the Shakespearean climax, wherein he delivers a charged monologue to Bull's taciturn ghost. Sampson brings a weighted dignity to his role, informing us that for all of its bluster, this is essentially a comedy of manners, contrasting the ways of the buffoonish Western stereotypes to those of the cool-headed Natives.

Comedy writer-cum-comic actor Pat McCormack momentarily delights as walrus-faced, empty-headed Grover Cleveland, playing Oliver Hardy to Stan Laurel–like First Lady Shelley Duvall. Joel Grey manages to hold his own as the show's MC, and you'll even find tough-as-nails Harvey Keitel as Bill's servile nephew, before subsequent screen roles toughened Keitel up.

But while this meditation on legend, entertainment, and the fight for recorded history aspires in comic tone and revisionist bent to *Little Big Man* (1970), the latter is clearly the more clever and more focused film.

Car Wash

Plot: Episodic comedy about life at a Los Angeles car wash. **Director:** Michael Schultz. **Script:** Joel Schumacher. **Cast:** Franklyn Ajaye, George Carlin, Professor Irwin Corrie, Richard Pryor. Universal. 96 minutes.

In America's Bicentennial year, two forms of cultural expression were rising like a July 4 fireworks display over the nation's capital: stand-up comedy, with clubs like The Improv and Catch a Rising Star anointing the next generation of TV and movie comedy talent (Jay Leno, Robin Williams, David Letterman *et al.*) and disco, destined for ubiquity the following year with the release of *Saturday Night Fever* (1977).

A popular joke among the comics became one of the most accurate, hippest summations of the Los Angeles of that time, likening it to a bowl of granola: What ain't nuts and fruits is flakes.

Out to affirm that thesis was screenwriter Joel Schumacher, later a high-concept Hollywood darling, and director Michael Schultz. Their *Car Wash* (cue the famous bass riff kicking off the title song—disco, naturally) is a comic sociological X-ray of the less than angelic City of Angels, concentrating on the marginalized, the deracinated and the otherwise adrift.

The film was conceived as a Broadway musical (it retains a few numbers) until Universal fell in love with it as a plain-faced comedy, recognizing, in the eponymous location's largely African American staff, the black audience appeal of Schultz's earlier *Cooley High* (1975). Like that film, *Car Wash* bristles with jive-talkin' bonhomie, adolescent practical jokes and dysfunctional, dead-end sex, as we watch the working-class heroes of the Dee-Luxe Car Wash cross paths with the surrounding population over a single, 89-degree day, from uppity Beverly Hills housewives to high-toned televangelists.

The template that had constituted *Cooley High*'s progenitor, George Lucas' *American Graffiti* (1973), was alive and well at Universal, its studio execs still counting the sizable take from those two films: the picaresque, multi-character narrative, the compressed time span, the DJ-hosted soundtrack, and the largely unknown cast, though two big stand-up stars, Richard Pryor and George Carlin, found themselves among the mix. (Schultz and Pryor reteamed to expound on the aforemetioned preacher character in the even crazier *Which Way Is Up?*, 1977.) What's missing here is the nostalgia factor, Schumacher and Schultz being more interested in, to use the patois of the day, "telling it like it is"—or at least, an exaggerated version of it.

The bona fide star of the film is the vibe. In that woozy time, in the wooziest of places, ordinary life took on a surreal, unformed quality. Free of Vietnam (Saigon had fallen the year before) and the corrupt Nixon presidency, American life had become, yes, free, but also unmoored. If we are not democracy's shining example and international defender, who are we? Just some idle society, it seemed, ridiculously going through the motions, with the only true form of transcendence left being self-amusement. No place in the country exuded this deliriously depoliticized posture more than Los Angeles, with its premium on recreation, its promise of easy, accidental success, and its hip resignation as answer to New York's signature hysteria. Schumacher and Schultz, particularly the latter, were tuned in to it. In its self-deprecating way, *Car Wash* is a love letter to a city, to a people, to a time.

The Duchess and the Dirtwater Fox

Plot: In 1880s San Francisco, a dance hall girl in possession of stolen money eludes a pack of villains with the help of a hapless gambler. **Director:** Melvin Frank. **Script:** Melvin Frank, Barry Sandler, Jack Rose. **Cast:** George Segal, Goldie Hawn. 20th Century–Fox. 103 minutes.

It was comic god Groucho Marx who, after a particularly chancy joke in *Monkey Business* (1931), addressed the camera directly to announce, "Well, they can't all be good. You've got to expect that every once in a while!"

It's also a fine summation of the status of *The Duchess and the Dirtwater Fox*, a Western comedy which, despite name stars, is a legitimately forgotten '70s catalogue item.

While the comic cinema of the time boasted three big voices (Woody Allen, Mel Brooks, Neil Simon), a handful of semi-auteurs, some ambitious African American talents and a supporting cast of underrated workmen, it also featured some of the last lions of the Studio Era. Each of the latter had just enough gas left in the tank to put out a film every couple of years. Foremost was the aging Billy Wilder; foreleast (have I just coined that?) was Melvin Frank. He followed up the surprise hit *A Touch of Class* (1973) with his functional if staid version of Simon's *The Prisoner of Second Avenue* (1975)

On *Duchess*, he tried for the lighthearted spirit of yore made contemporary by use of sex—but the sexual humor, due to its obviousness, comes across as crude and incongruous. The film purports to be a complete entertainment, a high-spirited mix of tried-and-true elements—Western, romcom, adventure—but it's plodding rather than deft. You're periodically bucked off of each mode, like the insistent running gag wherein cocky cowpoke George Segal's misbehaving horse defies its servile stereotype to play the miscreant.

Segal, the eponymous Dirtwater Fox, has stolen $40,000 from some roughnecks.

His escape dovetails with that of Goldie Hawn, the eponymous Duchess, a sexy saloon singer trying to rise above her lowly station. Segal, reliably, brings a lot of smarmy zeal to the role of the unscrupulous gambler. But he's such an inherently urban type, he's tough to buy as a Western stereotype. Hawn, also happy, visibly relishes the range her role offers: blowsy showgirl, Julie Andrews–style nanny (a disguise) and take-charge adventuress. And she and Segal enjoy evident compatibility. Still, these actorly indulgences are not enough to make us forgive the film's failings.

The score too tries hard to add the proper spirit but, like the performers, it can't. And it's seriously undermined by the song plastered over the romantic interlude and closing credits, which wins, hands down, for worst movie composition of the maudlin '70s (warbled by Bobby Vinton no less!). This genre of offbeat schmaltz was made popular with the insertion of "Raindrops Keep Fallin' on My Head" in the mega-hit *Butch Cassidy and the Sundance Kid* (1969), becoming a necessary evil of each succeeding comic Western. This tune was so bad, though, it finally ended the practice—one of the few good things you can say about the movie.

No. There's also this: a romantic, moving scene at a Jewish wedding, where Duchess and the Fox momentarily hidden out. It sounds incongruously awful but it's a piece of parachuted pathos that, surprisingly, works, although too soon, it's sacrificed for everything else.

The Gumball Rally

Plot: Broad stereotypes take part in an illicit coast-to-coast road race. **Director:** Charles Bail. **Script:** Leon Capetanos. **Cast:** Michael Sarrazin, Raul Julia, Gary Busey. Warner Bros. 105 minutes.

The high-speed chases that wowed audiences in *Bullitt* (1968) and *The French Connection* (1971) had helped to make that convention, by the mid–70s, a subgenre, loosely labeled "the car movie." As the decade progressed, there was a veritable traffic jam of these films, inspired not just by the aforementioned titles but by the influence of that cornpone, mythomaniacal daredevil Evel Knievel and an endless procession of cape-clad imitators. (Knievel's low-budget, laughable biopic, *Viva Knievel!,* was released the following year.)

Then there was the CB radio craze (that too had a film, based on a Top 40 novelty record no less: *Convoy*, 1976) busily inspiring America's vast yahoo sector to outrun "smokeys" while calling each other, though grown men, "Teddy bear" and "coffee pot." In addition, an oil crisis loomed. As America was running out of gas, audiences grew increasingly eager to vicariously live out flights of automative fancy.

As for *The Gumball Rally*, well, the foley must have been fun: roaring engines, screeching tires, metallic smash-ups. As these things go, this one tallied more crashes than most, the whole thing playing, arguably, as a metaphor for the military-industrial wreck that had been Vietnam.

This lampoonish take on a real-life cross-country road race—the titular rally from New York to Long Beach, secretly staged throughout the '70s—was produced, its discount look aside, not by Roger Corman but by First Artists, the lofty, self-serving production company headed by Barbra Streisand, Paul Newman and Sidney Poitier. Who knew that they were also Fast Buck Artists? The writer, Leon Capetanos, was soon to become one of Paul Mazursky's key collaborators.

"In this country, you're nothing if you don't have wheels," writes, in his screenplay, Capetanos, who should have added, "and stereotypes." Cultural caricatures, start your engines! In Capetanos' defense, broad ethnic humor, legitimized by TV's *All in the Family* (1971–80), the stand-up comedy of Don Rickles, and bestselling joke books ribbing the Polish were, at the time, all the rage.

In the end, though, as usual, to the blue-eyed, light-skinned hero—in this case, cool, coiffured Michael Sarrazin—the spoils. After all, that's for whom they made these films.

Mother, Jugs and Speed

Plot: Chronicles of a discount ambulance service in Los Angeles. **Director:** Peter Yates. **Script:** Tom Mankiewicz, story by Stephen Manes and Tom Mankiewicz. **Cast:** Bill Cosby, Raquel Welch, Harvey Keitel, Allen Garfield. 20th Century–Fox. 98 minutes.

"I don't have to tell you people times are tough. You read the papers; the country's going to Hell. You take inflation, recession, welfare—there's nothing we can do about that. But thanks to muggings, malnutrition, assassination and disease, we've got a chance to make a buck!"

The Gospel according to Allen Garfield, in one of the periodic parodies of locker room rah-rah he's asked to bark in one of the great cinematic curios of the decade, *Mother, Jugs and Speed*.

"The crippled, the junkie, the wounded, and the dying. Society calls them all worthless. But they're not worthless. Each one is worth $42.50, plus five cents a mile."

Garfield heads a corrupt, cheapjack ambulance service, proudly perched on capitalism's lowest rung. He and his loose-lipped, high-flyin' charges are living off the dying, the last monetary opportunity left in the decaying civilization that is Bicentennial America. How to classify these peculiar paramedics? As excusable, workaday practitioners of the American way? As professionals plain and simple, dutifully doing a dirty job that needs to be done? Or as irrefutable evidence that America has lost its last shred of humanity?

Enter, into this ragtag ensemble—which includes Larry Hagman as a nasal-voiced nerd and Dick Butkus as a cowboy hat–wearing outlier (!)—a pair of bleeding hearts who, experience by experience, begin to ask themselves these very questions. He's a Vietnam vet with a conscience; she's a budding feminist with a soft side: two shiny new archetypes of the Left. They will win small victories: He'll pull off a climactic act of heroism before leaving for the more stalwart world of law enforcement; she'll be permitted to boldly transcend the "female driver" stereotype then still at large. But in the end, they'll lose the emotional vs. functional war.

They are, respectively, Speed (Harvey Keitel) and Jugs (Raquel Welch, naturally). The one who sets them straight is Mother (Bill Cosby), using the same mix of loose conviviality and low-key morality then powering his hit cartoon series *Fat Albert and the Cosby Kids* (1972–85).

Sound eclectic? It is. That loaded adjective that often serves as a kindly synonym for uneven.

You can start by blaming the tricky premise, provided by animation magnate-executive producer Joe Barbera, then point the finger at screenwriter Tom Mankiewicz. Rather than play the whole thing as a dark comedy (as Martin Scorsese's *Bring Out Your Dead*, 1999, wisely did), Mankiewicz opted for something more ambitious, converting his dense research into a mix of slapstick (some of it worthy of the then-unfashionable Jerry Lewis), sex jokes, romance and social commentary. Good luck to any director in charge of sustaining the right tone. That assignment fell to action man Peter Yates, who proves in all ways a limited talent. There's no feel for any of the comedy, no facility with the actors, and surprisingly, no verve to the car chase.

Floating above it all is Cosby, by virtue of his happy naturalness. His light cool is the lazy eye of this cinematic shitstorm. It's almost enough to reinstate a soupcon of our reverence for his pre-criminal persona—until the scene where an immobile drug victim is almost raped by the film's baddie (Hagman, as yet another of his defeatist braggarts). We end up asking ourselves, shouldn't that have been Cosby's scene?

Murder by Death

Plot: Classic film detectives are called to the mansion of a reclusive millionaire for an evening of murder and mayhem. **Director:** Robert Moore. **Script:** Neil Simon. **Cast:** Peter Falk, David Niven, Maggie Smith, Peter Sellers, Eileen Brennan, James Coco, Truman Capote, Elsa Lanchester, Alec Guinness, Estelle Winwood. Columbia. 98 minutes.

New York, as a comic mecca, was done. The ultimate proof: the migration of its leading comic spokesperson, Neil Simon, to California. Go west, disgruntled middle-aged man! And so Simon did, in the company of then-wife Marsha Mason (together they became a talk show staple), leaving the stage, temporarily, for the movies. Original ones, too, not just adaptations. But this tack would not signify a return to the tenor of *The Out-of-Towners* (1970) or *The Heartbreak Kid* (1972). Rather, it marked another kind of return, perhaps prompted by the style by which ex–co-worker Mel Brooks was enjoying unprecedented (aka enviable) success: Old School TV sketch comedy.

In the parodic vein, of course—in this instance, a spoof of Agatha Christie's book and film *Ten Little Indians* (also known as *And Then There Were None*). You know it: The members of a group of notables, invited to a posh island outpost by a mysterious millionaire, confess secret transgressions and are thus subject to the threat of murder. Simon's twist is that each of the guests is one of the world's greatest detectives, plucked from the movies and books on which he had grown up. There are comic variations on brand-name busybodies Nick and Nora Charles, Charlie Chan, Sam Spade, Hercule Poirot and Miss Marple.

The style of humor is established by the opening joke, when we're informed that the mysterious millionaire's name is Lionel Twain (Lionel Trains, get it?). Further, that his address is 2–2 Twain (no need to explain that one, I hope!). Corny, forced, repeat. The closest the script comes to suggesting anything hip are gags about flatulence and homophobia, plus a couple of racial slurs. So why is the all-star cast so evidently bemused?

Nobody, except *Goon Show* alumnus Peter Sellers, has the proper pedigree to pull the material off. Sellers, as the Chan parody, enthusiastically offers, yes, a politically incorrect persona. In his defense, what he's actually offering is a parody of a stereotype. Call it grandfathered racism. It's hard to forgive Sellers today for the ethnic rogue's gallery by which he became an international star. But as frequent collaborator Blake Edwards maintained, in each of Sellers' portrayals, he always meant well, a view supported by the reverence, relish and humanity (even here, a tad) he consistently afforded his parts.

The other performance of note, by its sheer novelty, is that of author Truman Capote as Twain. The producers were stumped as to who to cast, so the role went to that impressionists' staple Capote, one of the last author-celebrities standing after that phenomenon's ubiquity in the vocal '60s. Small problem: While the diminutive, dough-faced Capote is showy enough, he simply has no facility for jokes.

Robert Moore's direction is the very definition of perfunctory. He seems to have problems with visual segues between scenes. Then again, as the script rigidly adheres to sketch form, with most of the action taking place in a single set, where to cut?

The whole thing should have played darker, borrowing more of the sensibility promised by the man responsible for the wittily spooky title design, cartoonist Charles Addams. Nevertheless, audiences loved it. In fact, the Spade variation got his own film (*The Cheap Detective*, 1978), plunging Simon once more into the sketch-based breach.

Network

Plot: A desperate news anchor boosts his ratings by threatening to kill himself on the air. **Director:** Sidney Lumet. **Script:** Paddy Chayefsky. **Cast:** William Holden, Faye Dunaway, Peter Finch, Robert Duvall, Ned Beatty, Beatrice Straight. MGM. 121 minutes.

For what shall it profit a man, if he shall gain the whole world's viewership, but lose his soul?—Chayefsky, 1976

And so, on-air, that man—trusted anchor Howard Beale—attempts to regain it, expressing the collective ire of his fed-up generation on his nightly newscasts. His cohorts categorize it as a nervous breakdown; he calls it the word of God, who comes to him in his sleep to cast him as his primetime Moses. The business of America, and especially television, being business, the sympathizers are given the squeeze and the broadcasts a boost. A precedent is set. In time, the whole "respectable network" becomes a "whorehouse," shamelessly serving up exploitative, knee-jerk programming verging on the absurd. At least, absurd in 1976, before the Tabloid TV craze of the 1990s (Jerry Springer, anyone?) and the introduction of Reality TV on which, infamously, respectable middle-class Americans ate vermin for cash prizes.

Just as people feared at the time of its release, *Network* indeed proved prophetic. After all, there was already evidence of TV's systematic deterioration: That season's big new hit was *Charlie's Angels* (1976–81), unleashing what was then termed T&A TV, in which the medium that had once given us Edward R. Murrow, *The Twilight Zone* (1959–64) and *Sesame Street* (1969–present day) was now taken over by bikini-clad Amazons with gleaming teeth and feathered hair, chasing criminals simply to set their sculpted body parts a-jiggle—all, of course, in pursuit of the mighty advertising dollar. A few years earlier, as remedy, a new, donation-based model was launched, Public Television, offering fare that harkened back to the medium's auspicious, intellectual infancy. While welcome, it ultimately proved a novelty; today, it struggles to survive.

By 1978, a book positing *Four Arguments for the Elimination of Television* was a bestseller. Still, its author, Jerry Mander, proved no Howard Beale; his Gospel, unlike Beale's, found few disciples. "It's all going to happen," prognosticated screenwriter Chayefsky in interviewer John Brady's *The Craft of the Screenwriter*. "I wrote a realistic drama."[38]

Uhhhh … yes and no. What Chayefsky wrote was a broadcast industry-set rehash of his earlier *The Hospital* (1971): messianic madman does the world a service by spreading the gospel of existential frustration inside a decaying, money-obsessed institution, while a doomed May-December couple battles for his, its and their own souls—as vocal (very—some of the speeches run longer than a night of Wagner) lament for the once simple and discriminating medium by which Chayefsky had made his name. Plus, we're led to believe that Beale's nightly cries of unquiet desperation are contagious, energizing us, like him, to stick our migrained heads out our windows to regurgitate the Great Truth that he's distilled to a proletariat catchphrase: "I'm as mad as hell and I'm not going to take it any more!"

Instead, however, the generation for whom this was written simply went on watching, if semi-sourly, television. They were mad, Chayefsky had gotten that right, and yet they took it. Why? Because TV is a far more passive medium than Chayefsky had attempted, back in '76, to convince us, a point made even more obvious by the subsequent emergence of more participatory communications vehicles like talk radio and social media. The ones doing the actual Beale-like screaming over the state of the world back then were, ironically, the TV-raised generation, just as put-out by soul-eroding life conventions like vapid entertainment, poisonous fast food and unmanageable world affairs. In dingy clubs in the East—New York's CBGB—and West—L.A.'s The Masque— they donned torn T-shirts, spiked their hair, put pins through their skin and screamed anarchic anthems: an unmusical musical movement called punk rock. Therein lies the true courage of mid–70s conviction.

As for its aesthetic worth, *Network* offers a lot less with which to argue. At the helm is the largely dependable Sidney Lumet, with his cheeky cinematography (courtesy of another ol' pro, Owen Roizman) and his healthy respect for acting. Australian Peter Finch was an odd choice to play a Middle American public father figure but proves credible and electric; William Holden plays another one of his "pessimistic optimists," as he liked to label his signature persona, suitably aged and lightly salted; Robert Duvall brings his emphatic gravitas to the proceedings, as the piece's business-suited Simon Legree, the exec who hijacks the network news division to appease the ever-enterprising, implacably unfeeling stockholders. And Ned Beatty has an enjoyably hammy cameo as Big Business incarnate.

The film's "nerve center," as David Thomson rightly cited in the ultimate edition of his *New Biographical Dictionary of Film*, is Faye Dunaway, as the full-speed-ahead career woman who is the witchy spirit of TV.[39] "I know the first thing you're going to ask me," Lumet recounts saying to her in pre-production, in his 1995 filmmaking primer-memoir *Making Movies*. "'Where's her vulnerability?' Don't ask it. She has none…. Furthermore,

---

38. John Brady, *The Craft of the Screenwriter* (New York: Simon & Schuster, 1981), 69.

39. David Thomson, *The New Biographical Dictionary of Film Updated and Expanded* (New York: Alfred A. Knopf, 2010), 288.

if you try to sneak it in, I'll get rid of it in the cutting room, so it'll be a wasted effort."[40] And still, she makes us care, subversively humanizing what's little more on paper than a leggy, loquacious symbol.

Network was, arguably, the climax of establishmentarian ire on film. That same year, a surprise low-budget hit, *Rocky,* beat it out for the Best Picture Oscar, signifying a switch to narrative simplicity, the return of hero worship, and the appeasement of a younger demographic. The albatrosses that were Vietnam and Watergate had, at last, cleared America's skies (both Saigon and Nixon had fallen) and the limbo period that was the Ford administration was now officially over (Jimmy Carter had been elected the month of the film's release). Cue *Star Wars* (1977) with its vision of a future as simple and fun as a B-Western and its hordes of ticket-buying teens and 20-somethings.

Next Stop, Greenwich Village

Plot: In the late 1950s, an aspiring actor leaves his Brooklyn home for Greenwich Village. There, to the consternation of his cloying mother, he falls in with a group of eclectic bohemians. **Script/Director:** Paul Mazursky. **Cast:** Lenny Baker, Ellen Greene, Shelley Winters, Antonio Fargas. 20th Century–Fox. 110 minutes.

"Joking is the American actor's disease. It's the American *person's* disease," constructively qualifies satirically-mouthed Larry Lapinsky's acting teacher, the estimable Herbert Berghof, as the conduit that will shape Larry's histrionic restlessness and bring him those salvific American commodities, fame and fortune. His guru specifies: "Because what you're doing is, you're keeping reality out. So that it won't touch you. The worst kind of joking you can do is to keep life out. Commenting, editorializing, joking … don't do it. It's fatal."

The voice, and words, may belong to the bogus Berghof (hypnotically performed by Michael Egan) but what it's channeling is writer-director Paul Mazursky's artistic conscience, as he shares with his audience the Berghof-influenced aesthetic mantra responsible for his cinematic style.

Like the other New York–born comic auteurs of the '70s—Simon, Allen, Brooks—Mazursky made films crowded with the caliber of quotidian eccentrics the movies would have us believe constituted the entire population of the Big Apple.

As his filmmaking philosophy attests, however, Mazursky was never looking, like Simon, to whittle them down to size to accommodate his TV-friendly one-liners. Nor, like Allen, was he out to reduce them to the marginalia surrounding his egocentric adventures. And, unlike Brooks, he had no intention of exaggerating their accents and ire. In Mazursky's New York–set films, the oblique denizens of NYC are vividly restored to an earthy earnestness, each one proudly awarded a beating heart.

In Mazursky's semi-autobiographical *Next Stop, Greenwich Village,* even that most tired of stereotypes, the overbearing Jewish mother, is rescued from the relentless barbs of Old School comics and the Oy Veyness of Philip Roth. Yes, she remains a shrew, a hysteric and a smotherer, all over her 22-year-old son Lenny like fat on a chicken. But she retains an artist's soul and can be hip, playful, sexy and movingly nostalgic. So

---

40. Sidney Lumet, *Making Movies* (New York: Alfred A. Knopf, 1995), 41.

humanized, and so perfectly played by Shelley Winters, she almost steals the show from the equally eclectic klatch of misbehaving bohemians with which her precious Lenny keeps controversial company.

Like all Mazurskian heroes, Lenny the aspiring actor is a seeker. (Mazursky's previous film, the picaresque *Harry and Tonto*, 1974, concentrated on a seeker of the senior citizen variety.) Made itchy by existence under his mismatched parents' roof in Brownsville, Lenny sets out in search of something larger and elusive that will justify, he humbly hopes, his anonymous existence. In this case, it's the flip side of the frigid '50s, a baby-step free-spiritedness that is the cultural antidote to the Brooks Brothers' conformity of polite middle-class society, or in Larry's case, of blue-collar Brooklyn society.

Nirvana is a mere subway ride away, in the Village, where Lenny—a one-man show waiting to break out, wandering the streets performing Brando impressions, reciting pseudo–Shakespearean soliloquies and improvising comedy bits that sound like they're copped from Lenny Bruce—fits right in. Mazurskian heroes may be separated from the pack by their aspirations but they are never entirely alienated, each destined to play a part in the filmmaker's sociological obsession with community. As protagonist in a Mazursky film, you inevitably form fast friendships and/or hook up with easy lovers, each of whom, in their small, searing way, will mark you forever.

Lenny falls in with the sexily hermetic Sarah (played by the cinematically underused Ellen Greene), the ghoulishly egotistical Robert (a young Christopher Walken, billed as Chris Walken), gay, black, self-loathing Bernstein (another underrated talent: Antonio Fargas) and others. They love, laugh and lacerate one another, like younger, hipper John Huston characters, as life's only alternative to the dull and dysfunctional upbringings they left behind.

Like the films of Billy Wilder, one of Mazursky's proportionate leitmotifs is deceit: Few are who they so proudly purport. And yet, these poseurs do not succeed in keeping us, by virtue of their remade identities, at a distance. Rather, in so pretending, we are brought closer to them. The masquerade is an admission of pain.

It is this concentration, balanced with the mother-son dynamic, that buoyantly rescues the film from a mere Oedipal seriocomedy. With its diverse, ingratiating cast working at the behest of a sincere feel for time, place and sensibility, it plays like lighthearted Kerouac. This is the Village, man, where we improvise theater games at parties, dance together in the streets, and talk life, art and death in musty cappuccino joints.

It's where we periodically have that great '50s no-no, too: loose sex, which can lead to everything from friendship-terminating jealousy to clandestine abortions. Despite the repeated imposition of the maternal monster, the film's true bad guy is the beast with two backs. And yet, attitudinally, this is not Puritanism at work. The film is no cautionary tale. Rather, it's a mature acknowledgment that "sex is serious," as Lenny philosophically maintains, the ultimate arbiter of human relations. It's been a Mazurskian bromide since his career-making *Bob and Carol and Ted and Alice* (1969).

In the end, poor, lost, limelight-looking Lenny indeed finds what he's searching for—by way of participation in the movies, a Mazurskian metaphor for the creation of art as remedy to existential unrest. Further, Lenny is sent packing for the West Coast, exactly where America, circa 1976, was migrating to find post–Vietnam-Watergate renewal. Everyone, then, had become the Lenny of the film's final frames, bittersweetly strolling the streets of their home turf one final time to a best-of-Dave-Brubeck score before going off to where salvation was bathed in sun and surf.

Nickelodeon

Plot: Slapstick hijinks set in the formative days of American cinema, as a trio of hapless filmmakers compete with the mighty Edison. **Director:** Peter Bogdanovich. **Script:** Peter Bogdanovich, W.D. Richter. **Cast:** Burt Reynolds, Ryan O'Neal, Tatum O'Neal, Brian Keith. Columbia. 121 minutes (director's cut: 129 minutes).

On March 17, 1975, Peter Bogdanovich improbably guest-hosted Johnny Carson's *Tonight Show* (1962–92), fulfilling opening monologue duties with Rich Little–style impressions of the Hollywood legends from whom he had made a living, first by interviewing them, then by copying their styles as a director. This incongruous TV stint was yet another manifestation of his controversial role as Tinseltown's top imitator.

The film he was planning to make while fulfilling this surprise, mostly promotional assignment (go-to starlet-girlfriend Cybill Shepherd was a guest) was *Nickelodeon*, a tongue-in-cheek comic epic on the formative days of American cinema, back when it was a high-flyin', fly-by-night cottage industry.

Though an original screenplay had been fashioned by the rising W.D. Richter, one producers Robert Chartoff and Irwin Winkler had highly prized, Bogdanovich predictably re-fashioned it into a grandiose act of personal hero-worship, creating a Fordian-Hawksian-Sturgian pastiche.

This extremely well-intentioned but overlong (and too often, overly labored) love letter to the cineastes from both the silent days and the Studio Era would serve as Bogdanovich's last gasp as perpetuator-recreator of his cinematic forebears. It also signaled, in the tradition of silent film slapstick, a resounding, ignominious fall.

Worse—by now, the imitator was beginning to imitate himself. Ryan O'Neal is here again, in the Harold Lloyd–ian specs he had donned in *What's Up, Doc?* (1972), as, once more, a deadpan innocent unwittingly drawn into a world for which he is unprepared. Further, he is reunited with daughter Tatum, this time playing a too-smart-by-half production assistant to Papa's waffling film director. Together, they enjoy a watered-down version of their to-and-fro from *Paper Moon* (1973). O'Neal the director is plagued by his uppity star, Burt Reynolds. Their emotional-physical rivalry, largely over the love interest (a skeletal beauty named Ellen Hitchcock; "Whatever happened to...?"), is reminiscent of the central Cain-Abel dynamic in *The Last Picture Show* (1971). There's a suitcase mix-up in the first act, a clear rehash of ... ad infinitum.

Still, it's the replication of the signature styles of the Studio Era giants that Bogdanovich is out, first and foremost, to apply his hand to. There's a lengthy knockabout fight out of Ford, a crazed industry Christmas party in the tradition of Sturges, scenes played at the breakneck verbal speed of Hawks, and plenty of silent-era sight gags, as O'Neal & Co. attempt to hold their own as a filmmaking unit while dodging studio-sent goons looking to put them out of business.

A film, then, for the cinematically savvy, a sizable sector in the '70s but still one whose size Bogdanovich vastly overestimated. For the proletariat, *Nickelodeon* offers but a plug nickel. On the whole, it's thin, overly familiar, and makes little of its star power. (In Bogdanovich's defense, he didn't want it to be a star vehicle; his wont was for a younger cast, headed by John Ritter, star of the then-new sitcom *Three's Company*, 1976–84, and Jeff Bridges.) O'Neal and Reynolds, like the rest of the cast, are but archetypes, stripped of their signature personas but not in the name of anything new or substantial.

O'Neal, then, comes across as boring while Reynolds, though he plays a surprisingly good rube, as perpetually put-out for the sake of being perpetually put-out.

Still, the film might have worked. After all, many years on, the Coen brothers made this kind of thing sing—mind you, by satirizing while subserving, replacing Bogdanovich's sweetheart sensibility with devilish delight. But it doesn't work. Chartoff and Winkler weren't happy, nor was the studio. Reynolds fought his director all the way, legend has it, ultimately lampooning him in *Hooper* (1978). Hollywood, scalded by Bogdanovich's appropriation of their "tricks," happily expressed its schadenfreude. Small wonder the film is about the indignities of being a director.

For all of that, Bogdanovich's reverence for the movies never wanes. The film climaxes with generous clips from D.W. Griffith's *Birth of a Nation* (1915), the audience oohing and ahhing reverently. This is followed by a slow-zoom-in speech by the blustery Brian Keith, as the scenery-chewing head of the indie outfit for whom hapless director O'Neal toils (a role originally designated for Bogdanovich book subject-cum-mentor Orson Welles), gilding the noble art of moviemaking.

One has to wonder, though, if Bogdanovich wasn't offering more, consciously or subconsciously, within these parting gestures. Was the film's "end of days" bent signaling not only the end of American cinema's infancy but, metaphorically, the termination of Bogdanovich's reign as king of the nostalgic castle? And maybe too a sense of the general public's waning taste for such unabashed expressions of cinematic reverence?

The movies would still offer parodies and homages of its heyday as the decade progressed but, as Westerns became car chase movies and sci-fi serials became the *Star Wars* franchise, the emphasis would be on revitalization, not replication.

The Pink Panther Strikes Again

Plot: Inspector Dreyfus goes mad and builds a doomsday machine. His lifelong nemesis, the bumbling Inspector Clouseau, must foil Dreyfus' plan to destroy the world. **Director:** Blake Edwards. **Script:** Frank Waldman, Blake Edwards. **Cast:** Peter Sellers, Herbert Lom, Lesley-Anne Down. United Artists. 103 minutes.

The Bicentennial wasn't the only thing being celebrated in 1976; so was the much-anticipated return of that flipside Hercule Poirot, Inspector Jacques Clouseau.

Two years earlier, he had returned after a decade-long hiatus, reviving the careers of writer-director Blake Edwards and character actor Peter Sellers. In *Return of the Pink Panther* (1974), the series' bumbling hero was re-imagined, slightly, into a parody of his initial incarnation. Here, with Clouseau promoted to chief inspector in the wake of his superior's nervous breakdown, Edwards and Sellers (and co-scenarist Frank Waldman) lampoon that lampoon. This is Clouseau plus: the quotable accent now sounds like he's nursing a cold ("Do you have a ruuuuuuuum?"), the facial reactions to the consequences of his actions take on a silent film quality, and many of the pratfalls come with the kinds of wails once emitted by Jerry Lewis. Everything else has grown broader too: The set-ups are more languid, the slapstick more deliberate, the pauses for laughs much longer. Over time, Edwards and Sellers would take this much too far, creating a collective conceit that the material was much funnier than its creators were purporting. For the moment, though, it all worked, buoyed by a palpable boys-at-play sensibility bobbing giddily beneath the surface.

Many consider *Strikes Again* the best film in this overlong series. You can see why. The set pieces it's built around are very strong: Clouseau's first encounter with his ex-boss, on a waterside bench at the asylum where the latter (and that dangerous commodity, a rake) is kept; an interrogation scene in which alibis are dismantled as antiques are disfigured; the unskillful storming of a castle where the former chief inspector, now a madman armed with a world-destructing ray machine, is holed up.

And, of course, the impromptu fights between Clouseau and manservant Cato, which by now have become series highlights. This one incorporates a poke at the popular, posthumous releases of martial arts deity Bruce Lee, the laughs boosted by playful switches of film speed.

If the film holds up today, it's a tribute to the timeless nature of well-wrought slapstick, which constitutes the bulk of the picture. Its other touches—parodies of bumbling, Band-Aid President Gerald Ford and cold-blooded consort Kissinger, the frequent gay and cross-dresser jokes (though they might have inspired Edwards' more sympathetic *Victor/Victoria*, 1982) and the scheme to obliterate the U.N. building in exchange for the murder of Clouseau (cringingly reminding us today of 9/11)—ring comparatively hollow. Otherwise, this is Edwards at his mid-career height, the playful, unabashedly commercial stage before he began to explore more personal territory.

To wit: the film's explosively funny "money shot," a parody of James Bond codas featuring Clouseau in *Full Monty* (1997) mode, before Cato makes it an unwitting *ménage à trois*, sending a Murphy bed through a high-rise wall, and all and sundry into the Seine.

The Ritz

Plot: A heterosexual businessman, seeking refuge from his homicidal brother-in-law, hides in a gay bathhouse. **Director:** Richard Lester. **Script:** Terrence McNally, based on his play. **Cast:** Jack Weston, Rita Moreno, Jerry Stiller. Warner Bros. 91 minutes.

By 1976, America's central cultural vibe was going West. So, are we there yet? No. We're still in New York, not L.A., for one of the last of the film adaptations of a distinctly New York–ese play, and curiously, not a mega-hit. Something, instead, that was hoped to register with the new, younger audience, including those from the cultural spectrum seriously underserved by mainstream American cinema. All they had had thus far had been *The Rocky Horror Picture Show* (1975). Now, there was this, Terrence McNally's busy bathhouse farce *The Ritz*.

Playwright Mart Crowley's bold, moving stage play *The Boys in the Band* had served as mainstream American cinema's first honest look at that close, campy, cannibalizing community. Worthy as it was, the 1970 film version proved but a curio, a one-and-done look at an interesting, growing subculture. The mainstream would have to be brought to a broader acceptance of the gay community through less earnest, less confrontational means. Enter broad comedy.

McNally, as both playwright and screenwriter, had reached that conclusion long before Hollywood. To score with the masses, he realized, he would have to present his people as the outside world saw them: the stars of a New Age circus, as had, with a generous nod to vintage chiller films and Hollywood musicals, *Rocky Horror*. But McNally was looking for something bigger than cult success. To that end, he would happily commit to a conspiracy of commercial concessions. Foremost, he would frame his dramatic agenda within the confines of genre—namely, the old-fashioned bedroom farce. Further, he would focus on a prototypically American avatar: a head-scratching businessman from central Ohio, thus also accommodating another cozy narrative device, comedy's "fish out of water" formula. Then he'd populate the property with well-worn comic stereotypes—the shrewish wife, the hot-headed mobster, the fallen chanteuse— and award the entire exercise the manic feel of the beloved Marx Brothers. His bets securely hedged, McNally would bring contemporary gay culture, in all its gaudy, giddy glory, from the bathhouse to the playhouse, then to the movie house.

Who to direct this ultra-manic tale of a middle-aged innocent on the lam from his murderous brother-in-law, introduced to an alternate sexual universe when he hides out in an East Side bathhouse? Richard Lester, of course, pioneer of the edit-crazy, gag-happy, distinctly cinematic style of film comedy that had caught the zeitgeist of the energetic, anything-goes '60s.

Small problem: By 1976, the old boy was seriously mellowing out. He might have just converted the exploits of Dumas' famed Musketeers into a pair of commercially successful comic adventure films, and given a hearty go at George MacDonald Fraser's Harry Flashman books, but he was not interested in offering the same treatment to another folkloric hero, Robin Hood. Instead, his *Robin and Marian* (1976) marked a new, more mature direction. While accomplished, the film was earnest and autumnal, Lester's clear, clean break from the cinematic excesses of his youth. Perhaps the surprise and disappointment of both critics and audiences are what prompted this return to his no-holds-barred roots.

But he doesn't. While he certainly services the comedy, Lester shows little impetus to augment it. Was he done with that kind of thing, or was it simply that he recognized that there was no need for it here, the script alone providing more than enough mania? Whatever. Largely, he stays out of the way; Richard Lester as Herbert Ross. The thinking too must have been that the cast, imported from the stage production, would weave the same cockeyed charm as it did on the boards. Quite a chance to take, as there wasn't a marquee name among the bunch. So, on the whole, it's effectively a filmed record of the play.

But film is not a particularly servile mistress. While the Broadway show had a nice, gritty spark to it, it has been largely lost in translation to film. Despite moments of genuine Marxian madness, it suffers the emasculation that is almost part and parcel of the stage-to-screen phenomenon (a fate poor Neil Simon knew all too well).

That said, each member of this most uncommercial of casts has his or her shining moments: piggy, proletariat Jack Weston, in the only film in which he enjoyed star billing; the underrated Rita Moreno, in her first full chance to show off her comic chops (though she was simultaneously plying them on TV's *The Electric Company,* 1971–77); Jerry Stiller as a squatty, sweaty Sonny Corleone, the scenery chewer's scenery chewer. And a special shout out to F. Murray Abraham as the bathhouse's bad-boy tour guide, accomplishing what the play-film dare not: the sending-up of gay culture without sacrificing its dignity.

Today, much of the play-film serves as a disco-era heirloom. That hedonistic, music-based lifestyle, pioneered by the dance-centric gay movement, was just getting going. The whole disco phenomenon, music included, is today categorized as anthemic, the first cultural mass movement born of the alternative lifestyle set to cross over to the general populace. While there is some validity to that, it need be remembered that such thinking is largely an act of historical revisionism. Here's what disco really was and why it rose: a much-needed, self-indulgent respite from an oppressive, divisive timeline that ran from the assassination of JFK to the evacuation of Saigon. After suffering the rigors of being part of a combative united front, the Boomers, no longer hippies but not yet reconciled to the family-based lives that their parents had led, were taking time for themselves, hence the media-spawned label The Me Generation. This was not, however, a mass conversion—at least not musically.

Many volubly abhorred the coming of disco stars such as K.C. and the Sunshine Band and Donna Summer and the sweaty, sex-and-drugs after-hours clubs in which their hits were heard. Today, such dissenters are looked upon as homophobic rednecks. The truth is that the battle was strictly musical: disco vs. rock'n'roll. Fans of the former resented the usurping of popular music by something that sounded facile and repetitive just when rock, both musically and lyrically, had hit the height of technical and lyrical sophistication.

As the movement surged, Hollywood, looking to cash in, promoted it as it once had big-budget musicals. The results proved even thinner than the music.

Silent Movie

Plot: A director pitches a desperate movie studio on producing a silent movie. **Director:** Mel Brooks. **Script:** Mel Brooks, Ron Clark, Rudy De Luca, Barry Levinson. **Cast:** Mel Brooks, Marty Feldman, Dom DeLuise, Bernadette Peters, Sid Caesar. 20th Century–Fox. 87 minutes.

In 1976, Mel Brooks was at the height of his directorial fame. The double-whammy of *Blazing Saddles* (1974) and *Young Frankenstein* (1974) created a fashionable cultural argument over the identity of America's leading comic auteur: Brooks or one-time co-worker Woody Allen, then between his comedic masterpiece *Love and Death* (1975) and his groundbreaking seriocomedy *Annie Hall* (1977). The intellectuals, of course, endorsed the latter, while the popular vote went to the baser Brooks.

It hardly hurt Brooks' reputation as the comic filmmaker of the common people that his films were rooted in something much more familiar than the I.Q.-crossing pastiches of Allen: parody. It was a tradition Brooks had been practicing since his days as writer on TV's *Your Show of Shows* (1950–54) and *Caesar's Hour* (1954–57). Small-screen audiences, circa 1976, were still being fed it via *The Carol Burnett Show* (1967–78). The Burnett show, in fact, is where Brooks began to mine writers, including Ron Clark, Rudy De Luca and soon-to-be-auteur in his own right Barry Levinson. Together, they'd begin not so much by sending up a genre but by employing its conventions to good-naturedly skew Hollywood, then in the early stages of a foreboding transformation: *Silent Movie*.

The moment the premise was announced, prospective audiences began to envision another film, like *Young Frankenstein* (1974), shot in black and white. It would also, of course, be set in the 1920s and feature Keystone Cops–like gags.

But in a commendable act of bait and switch, Brooks opted for color and a contemporary context; and while, yes, the gags aspired to those of the Chaplin-Keaton era, rooks' premise traded the reverential for the self-referential.

Brooks, who also stars, plays writer-director Mel Funn, who cannot secure backing for a modern-day silent movie from a troubled studio head desperate for a hit (a role played by Brooks' old boss Caesar, who soldiers through commendably despite, at the time, a climaxing battle with alcoholism). Convinced that their film is the solution to the studio's dilemma, Brooks and his sidekicks (Dom DeLuise and Marty Feldman) crisscross Tinseltown wooing stars (a veritable Hollywood A-list, each member happy to self-parody) in hopes of staving off a New York–based takeover

The premise is rooted in the changing of the guard then underway in Hollywood. In the wake of the eye-popping grosses generated by *The Godfather* (1972) and *Jaws* (1975), New York–based conglomerates began taking serious interest in the West Coast–based movie mills. Auteurs like Brooks were left to read the writing on the wall—hence *Silent Movie*, a playful fantasia in which the creatives triumph over the suits.

While the film's primary comic influences are the great silent film clowns, it offers nods to a bevy of talents from succeeding periods: In the dancey synchronicity of Brooks, DeLuise and Feldman, we see the influence of the Ritz Brothers, the comic song-and-dance trio often cited by Brooks as a primary influence; in Feldman's irrepressible lechery, we recognize the primary sexual drive of Harpo Marx; in the middle-act romance between Brooks and the vampy Bernadette Peters (a curvaceous stooge set up to foil Funn's scheme, for naught of course), Brooks wages parodic war on the gaudy grandiosity of MGM musicals.

It all makes for a sufficiently lively, if only occasionally inspired, mix. The entire film, in fact, has a sunny, facile quality to it—and that's not to be pejorative. Previous attempts to capture the tenor of the silent comedy era, most notably the big-budgeted *It's a Mad Mad Mad Mad World* (1963), suffered, as many a critic pointed out at the time, from the addition of sound, adding a bombast to the gags which inflated their throwaway quality. Here, Brooks settles largely for silence (violated only by the odd sound effect), reverently restoring their happy unimportance.

That said, the film has its implacable detractors. And yes, it isn't worthy of Brooks' best work. Still, it's Mel in a happy, capricious mood, taking a fun gamble and scoring a sufficiently sizable win.

Silver Streak

Plot: Hitchcockian ode in which a book editor uncovers a murder on a train from Los Angeles to Chicago, embroiling him in an action-packed joy ride. **Director:** Arthur Hiller. **Script:** Colin Higgins. **Cast:** Gene Wilder, Jill Clayburgh, Richard Pryor, Patrick McGoohan, Ned Beatty, Ray Walston. 20th Century–Fox. 114 minutes.

By the '70s, Film Studies programs were an academic mainstay across college campuses. No course on auteurism was without its screenings and lectures on the work of Alfred Hitchcock, the prolific British thrillermeister who became an intellectual darling when the critics cum filmmakers behind France's *Cahiers du Cinema* fell in love with him back in the '50s, at which time he was grinding out big-budget capers in Hollywood.

The most accomplished of those films was the sexy, clever *North by Northwest* (1959), its Ernest Lehman screenplay juggling suspense, romance and action with exemplary aplomb. Make that "unsurpassable," as its many imitators have repeatedly proven.

The most popular of these forgeries was a film that dealt with forgery itself: *Silver Streak*, which generously borrowed *North by Northwest* elements and recast them to fit the zeitgeist: Romantic tension became broadly metaphoric sex talk, the kind you'd find on TV's *Match Game* (1973–79); suspense became moments of prolonged expository dialogue, worthy of detective shows like *Columbo* (1971–78); action became sequences influenced by the Roger Moore Bond films or vehicular cat-and-mouse games that were played in almost every action film of that time.

Still, it passed. Such was the appetite of mainstream audiences for old-fashioned fare that even hollow imitations, as remedy from urban American realism and European-influenced subtext and technique, would do.

The forgery within the forgery is attributable to Patrick McGoohan, one of *Silver Streak*'s many Hitchcockian stereotypes: the smooth villain. Looking to cover up a Rembrandt-based scandal, his sangfroid millionaire knocks off a naysaying professor. But the crime is witnessed by a genial everyman (Hitchcockian stereotype number two, in case you're keeping count) who in turn becomes targeted. All of this takes part, in the tradition of *The Lady Vanishes* (1938), on the eponymous Silver Streak, though few, by 1976, were traveling distances the length of L.A. to Chicago by rail.

Comparing Hitchcock to Arthur Hiller, *Silver Streak*'s director, is like comparing Ingmar Bergman to Ikea; the obliquely cerebral vs. the purely functional. Hiller was a director only as good as his script; Paddy Chayefsky, on more than one occasion (*The Americanization of Emily*, 1964, *The Hospital*, 1971) made him look like a genius; here, Colin Higgins (of *Harold and Maude*, 1971, fame) makes him look like something closer to his true identity.

The chanciest element of the film was casting: Gene Wilder, not long before a pudgy-faced hysteric, as the romantic everyman; prettily proletariat Jill Clayburgh as a flirtatious blonde (Hitchcockian stereotype number three); Midwestern Ray Walston as a tough-talking gunsel.

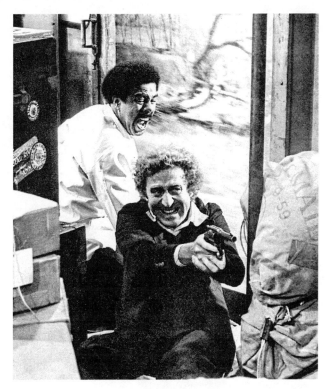

Richard Pryor (top) and Gene Wilder in *Silver Streak* (20th Century–Fox, 1976). The movie paid tribute to suspense master Alfred Hitchcock, a touch that became a common, and lucrative, practice in mid–70s film comedy (20th Century–Fox/Photofest).

Thank God for the role of the car thief on the run, who befriends Wilder after one of the many times he is thrown from the title train: Richard Pryor. Pryor brings hip and zip to the role, in a superimposition of modernity that ups the interest and entertainment quotient more than the climactic and overlong chase sequence (which wowed audiences, even though the film's ad campaign had unabashedly given it away).

Buoyed by *Silver Streak*'s commercial success, Higgins tried knitting the same Hitchcockian pieces together once again, this time with himself as helmsman. The result, *Foul Play* (1978), proved the imitation that would fool even the jaundiced eye.

1977

With the move to placid, stable California, movie comedy circa 1977 no longer belonged to the self-pityingly disenfranchised, but to slightly put-out suburbanites (*Fun with Dick and Jane*). New York–based angst comedy became the monopoly of a single filmmaker, Woody Allen. When his masterpiece *Annie Hall* won the Best Picture Oscar, it was both the genre's crowning achievement and its last bow (though Albert Brooks was in the wings, waiting to bring it back in his own, more conceptual way).

Allen, as lovelorn comedian Alvy Singer, was looking, post–*Annie Hall*, for something to believe in. So was Burt Reynolds as the Bandit, even if it was only a good time, and John Denver in *Oh, God!* While, yes, the quirky seeker had been a film comedy archetype since the unmoored '60s, by 1977 he had broadened his search—as had the public, obsessively rifling through self-help books and joining controversial movements like the Moonies. The goal was no longer to transcend; everyone had tried that in the '60s and had crashed like Icarus. It was to feel present and alive, the way that self-gratifying disco culture was teaching us.

Lily Tomlin, in Robert Benton's *The Late Show*, spoke for everyone with her obsession with "what's real." The social institutions that had held us in their protective hands for so long were in ashes and the peace-love-music thing was now too. The hunt for whatever the hell came next was on, pulling us in more crazy directions than Richard Pryor in the aptly titled *Which Way Is Up?*

Annie Hall

Plot: A neurotic comic has an ill-fated romance with a kooky singer. **Director:** Woody Allen. **Script:** Woody Allen, Marshall Brickman. **Cast:** Woody Allen, Diane Keaton, Tony Roberts, Paul Simon, Carol Kane. United Artists. 93 minutes.

Boy meets girl. Boy loses girl. Boy makes philosophical reflection.

Such, with the odd deviation, was the formula for every Woody Allen film going forward after the smash success of *Annie Hall*.

By 1977, Allen had firmly established himself as America's leading comic voice. He had become, to use a '50s ad industry buzzword that was not revived 'til the millennium, a brand. His films were in constant re-release and widely shown on television; collections of his comic essays consistently climbed bestseller lists; his bespectacled face stared back at grocery shoppers and bookstore browsers from the covers of *Time* and *Newsweek*; a comic strip based on his romantic adventures went into syndication; his best one-liners were quoted in the press, in anthologies and at parties. He had become, in one, our Chaplin and our Twain. Gapping the Angst Age and the Me Generation, Allen became the perfectly nervous, hopelessly self-absorbed poster boy for the times.

Next milestone: auteur. It was a lofty standing Allen had aspired to for years, inspired by the work of his non-comic (and how!) idol Ingmar Bergman. Sights set, Allen and fellow writer Marshall Brickman set about crafting an ambitious break from the pseudo–Bob Hope vehicles Allen had hitherto been making: a four-hour comic epic on the state of contemporary America, framed by a medium close-up of Allen providing stand-up style continuity.

One small problem: It didn't work. Even in spite of a reliance on veteran editor Ralph Rosenblum, who had given shape to many a previous Allen effort, organizing loose gags and seemingly incongruous scenes into works of coherence and impact. (Rosenblum, it can be argued, was the biggest unsung hero of the comic films of the age, having shaped the formative films of two of its two leading talents, Allen and Mel Brooks.) Being an auteur, a comic Bergman, was tougher than it looked.

Charmed by Diane Keaton's performance in what they had shot, it was decided to concentrate on the central love story. This Hail Mary, or Hail Diane, clicked. Soon, everyone would be hailing her, the film and Allen. Keaton established a signature persona that served her the rest of her long career, the film beat out *Star Wars* for the Best Picture Oscar (baffling toy-buying nerds for decades to come), and Allen was indeed knighted an auteur, a standing that inspired him to create an admirably chancy but disappointingly mixed oeuvre.

Such was the regard for *Annie Hall* that even after Allen went on to suffer the slings and arrows of the MeToo movement, prompted by a troubled romantic history and fuzzy allegations of child molestation, the film remained largely exempt from the feminist retro-ire in which his work was reframed.

Why has it survived?

Myriad reasons. Foremost, its validity as a time piece. *Annie Hall* represents the climax of the angst comedy age. The proof is that after its success, few bothered with said style of humor any more. True, the American tenor was palpably transitioning but *Annie Hall* had rendered the style that had hitherto defined the era with such panache, nobody felt that they could top it. As a result, Allen was awarded an angst comedy monopoly, while others went on to express themselves in other ways.

Two, the film's innovation. *Annie Hall* is chockablock with cinematic conventions—subtitles, double exposures, split screens, etc.—that had never been used for comic effect before (and not much since). So, standout. Then, there's Keaton. It's an Allen film, no question, but her quirky naturalism radiates throughout. "Oh, she was just playing herself," became a common criticism. But the trained eye sees more: the smart, conscious exacerbation of her best inherent qualities as well as an actorly transition from caterpillar to butterfly that is expert and exemplary. The film is rightly named after her (Hall is Keaton's real name).

Finally, the central relationship. While the romance of comedian Alvy Singer and

Woody Allen and Diane Keaton in *Annie Hall* (United Artists, 1977), one of the comic masterpieces of the decade and one of the few comedies to win the Best Picture Oscar (United Artists/Photofest).

aspiring chanteuse Annie Hall follows the classic '70s line—let's make a go of this without the albatross of marriage and family and see what transpires—the film has proven trans-generational, a perfect sample of the classic start-up relationship, usually bittersweet, chanced by all.

Annie Hall may also have lasted because, on a grander scale, another precarious and precious relationship is at work within the film. It's a tale not just of two people but of two Americas: the puritan, bucolic and celebratory, personified by naïve, happy Wisconsinite Annie, vs. the modern, urbanized and troubled, in the person of You Know Who. Annie's journey, then, is the nation's, from the liberated and enthusiastic to the bound and bereft.

How to get back to the Garden? "California, Max…"

The Bad News Bears in Breaking Training

Plot: Under a new coach, their star's estranged father, the Little League Bears travel to Houston to play at the Astrodome. **Director:** Michael Pressman. **Script:** Paul Brickman. **Cast:** William Devane, Clifton James, Jackie Earle Haley. Paramount. 99 minutes.

In 1967, superstar pitcher Sandy Koufax, the Brooklyn boy who had broken in with the Dodgers' first incarnation, suffered an arm injury curtailing the Hall of Fame career that had been ignited with the team's move to Los Angeles. SoCal baseball, as a result, went into a decade-long tailspin.

By the mid–70s, however, it was back, buoyed by a show biz manager and a soon-to-be-legendary infield. L.A.'s second favorite team, though, owed more to the Dodgers' lovable loser roots than to its new, glitzified edition. They were *The Bad News Bears*, the pugnacious, pint-sized stars of the sleeper hit of 1976, the film rescuing the on-screen depiction of children from the castrating clutches of Disney to deliver it to the dysfunctional maw of modernism. That said, in the end, there was no escaping family-friendly whitewashing—and so the Bears fell to cliché, sentimentality and blandness in the unambitious *Breaking Training*. (They fell to greater depths later, in Japan).

Bears had proven so popular with children, Hollywood took it upon itself to devote the follow-up entirely to their on-screen avatars. (Poor *Jaws 2*, 1978, suffered a similar fate with teenagers). Adults are in short supply here, and certainly, nobody who can steal a scene or otherwise upstage a bunch of showy kids, like Walter Matthau. So, the Bears set out for a big game at Houston's Astrodome on their own, until necessity prompts the presence of coach William Devane (who, yes, once had something of a film career), the team bad boy's befallen father. Devane straightens the kids out, reconciles with his son, and … uh, do I need to go on?

Just as the Bears are bereft of a coach, the film too has lost a guiding hand of consequence. A different Michael is at the helm: Pressman, not Ritchie. It explains the film's lack of cinematic panache—the frenetic editing, the handheld camerawork, the classical soundtrack (revived, okay, a bit)—and the less than potent fireworks between the kids.

Pressman's pedigree was the stagey world of theater and the equally staid world of series TV. But even as serviceman's work, this is decidedly subpar. Clunky would have been better, outright bad might have been too; at least there might have been accidental pleasures.

It's hard to believe Paul Brickman, responsible for that same year's *Citizens Band* and for *Risky Business* (1983), was behind this, even if he was simply playing studio stooge. The film's dramatic through-line is the "Where were you when I was growing up?" shtick, familiar to the point of saturation in that divorce-happy era, as opposed to the indifferent Matthau, is the very model of the late '70s, feminist-influenced sensitive male. He's not there to promote toughness but to instill, in sincere, soft-spoken tones, understanding. Whatever your politics, you'd rather he drank beer, scratched his belly and called the kids derogatory names. The script's other dramatic offense is its unabashed subscription to the "Do it for the Gipper!" bent, which it sets up with a clip of the famous sentimental pep talk by Pat O'Brien from *Knute Rockne, All American* (1940). Ugh!

This is not simply Bad News. It's bad everything.

Citizens Band

Plot: Examination of the CB radio craze, including stories about a truck-driving bigamist and a self-appointed regulator of the airwaves. **Director:** Jonathan Demme.

Script: Paul Brickman. **Cast:** Paul Le Mat, Candy Clark, Bruce McGill, Roberts Blossom. Paramount. 98 minutes.

"That's a big 10–4, Hot Coffee. What's your 20?"

Such was the patois of truck culture circa 1977 as the CB radio craze took over the American supply and delivery trade.

Four years earlier, a crippling fuel shortage had begun to take root. To quell the crisis, a nationwide speed limit of 55 mph had been imposed. America's truckers, frustrated with both developments, began to install CB radios in their 18-wheelers as a secret form of driver-to-driver communication, primarily to trade prescriptive tips on fully stocked gas stations and upcoming speed traps.

Much like English criminals with their rhyming slang ("apple and pears" for "under the stairs"), the truckers developed their own insular lingo: cops were "smokeys," a speeding ticket was a "bear bite" and "10–7" meant you were signing off. The trend spread across car-crazy and deeply communal America. CBs could be found in Volkswagen Beetles ("pregnant roller skates") and private residences. People no longer had proper names; they had "handles."

It was proof positive of America's identity crisis. After Vietnam and Watergate, and now a shortage of natural resources, the country had lost its standing as an exemplary, self-sufficient society. Ashamed of who they had become, citizens took to reinventing themselves. Through CB radios, they could reclaim the spirit of solidarity and lawlessness that had forged the country; they could go back to basics. Plus, ironically, conspiracy was cool. Watergate may have shocked the nation, but it had also legitimized the secret society. The CB radio craze was a way to use Nixon's example for the good. (Years later, the practice of technology-based fraternalism took up all over again with the advent of social media.)

By 1977, the fad had been celebrated in song (one-hit-wonder C.W. McCall's "Convoy," a country-pop crossover in 1975) but not yet on film. The low-budget *Citizens Band* got there first, followed by the much more successful *Smokey and the Bandit* (1977) and a take on the McCall hit directed by Sam Peckinpah, *Convoy* (1978). Though a resounding flop, *Citizens Band* left the other films in "the Granny lane," the one film legitimately in tune with the psychology behind the phenomenon.

The primary reason for *Citizens Band*'s aesthetic success (critics loved it) was its creative personnel, mainly screenwriter Paul Brickman, who reached exalted status with *Risky Business* (1983), and director Jonathan Demme, who also flourished come the '80s. These men's pet themes run throughout *Citizens Band*: the wide-eyed innocent who gets a real-world education, the girl next door–femme fatale heroine, the prickly politics of family and community.

Each of these bents touches on the great cultural friction at the core of American society: the puritan vs. the permissive. It's best exemplified in *Citizens Band* by Paul Le Mat (who worked with Demme again in the latter's breakthrough film, *Melvin and Howard*, 1980), the frustrated private citizen who takes it upon himself to play a one-man FCC, busting CB users hijacking the airwaves for their own, self-serving purposes. Le Mat is a variation on the classic Western hero, boldly attempting to impose order on a dangerously open society. He's no victor, though, even if he gets the girl in the end.

The girl in question is Candy Clark, another player from *American Graffiti* (1973). *Citizens Band*, very visibly, owes more than just a few cast members to George Lucas' nostalgic hit. *Citizens Band*'s loose crosscut of narratives, its emphasis on car culture, and its busy sound design all smack of derivation. They even cop *American Graffiti*'s famous cable stunt, if less effectively.

For all of that, the film is highly original. Brickman and Demme's shared take on character (largely, two love triangles: a pair of brothers in love with the same girl, and a bigamist trucker and his two wives) is singular. It captures the quotidian lunacy of subcultures as if it were *cinema verité*. Or as the astute J. Hoberman wrote in a colorful piece collected in *Jonathan Demme Interviews*, the film treats "white-bread America with benign post-hippie oh-wowism."[41] The world Demme and Brickman create is so all-of-a-piece—its characters, its dialogue, its rhythms—that any attempt to impose conventional film structure upon the proceedings, like the film's incongruous search-and-rescue ending, strikes us as a glaring violation.

Citizens Band's real climax is a moving single-take in which Le Mat presents his taciturn father (Demme favorite Charles Napier), who only comes alive via his CB radio, with a birthday cake. In so doing, LeMat inadvertently tells the old man that he loves him—the kind of personal connection the characters can only make through their airwave avatars. That this is the true ending speaks to everything that's artistically right about the film and commercially wrong. How to market small, ragtag ensemble comedies? In the Hollywood sense, there's no story, no big moments, no stars. In the case of *Citizens Band*, there wasn't even an auteur to sell, like Altman. To its credit, the producing studio, Paramount, tried hard: It released the film twice, the second time under a different title (*Handle with Care*). The critics still raved, the public still stayed away.

Like the characters at the core of *Citizens Band*, the film was trapped between two worlds—cast in, as critics throughout the director's career loved to pun, a Demme-monde.

Fun with Dick and Jane

Plot: A fallen upper-middle-class couple, fed up with inflationary times, avenge themselves on society by pulling off a heist. **Director:** Ted Kotcheff. **Script:** David Giler, Jerry Belson, Mordecai Richler. **Cast:** George Segal, Jane Fonda, Ed McMahon. Columbia. 99 minutes.

Let's start with the Canadian connection: director Ted Kotcheff and screenwriter Mordecai Richler. Canada, America's neighbor to the north, is geographically predestined to cast a cold (literally) eye on the U.S., a behemoth that subsumes most of the former's popular culture. Canadians are perfectly positioned to both accept and objectify the tenets of American society, thus living in a constant state of comparative study. Of such cozy (Canadian spelling: "cosy") critical distance is comedy concocted. As a result, starting when the madness of daily American life began, in the early '60s, to politically contrast the essential placidity of Canadian existence, the offering of good-natured comic commentary on the American scene became one of the sexiest jobs in the Great White North.

---

41. J. Hoberman in Robert E. Kapsis, *Jonathan Demme Interviews* (Jackson: University Press of Mississippi, 2009), 33.

A non-stop array of Toronto-, Montreal- and Winnipeg-spawned comic talent began to either flourish at home or to make its way into the U.S., not simply to enjoy, like most Canadians, some much-needed sunshine, but to function as a working part of the vast American comedy machine. This noble lineage can be traced from groundbreaking stand-up Mort Sahl through to contemporary late-night commentary queen Samantha Bee.

Richler, Canada's premier comic novelist, felt no such call. Occasionally, though, his ol' bud Kotcheff (they had worked together on TV dramas in Britain, then on the 1974 film adaptation of Richler's *The Apprenticeship of Duddy Kravitz*) drew him Stateside. Point in case: *Fun with Dick and Jane*, Kotcheff's thinking probably being that a Canadian would be best qualified to pen a sweet-and-sour look at the fall of American prosperity and its toll on the souls being robbed of it.

The archetypical couple affected by this economic erosion is a modern-day (circa 1977) incarnation of that happy WASP reading primer duo Dick and Jane. Now, they're upper-middle-class Californians whose God-given lifestyle is being taken away by forces grown beyond accessibility. In time, Dick and Jane become working-class heroes, sticking it to the institutions that have nipped them: phone companies, televangelists, corrupt corporations. A polite society Bonnie and Clyde.

It's light comedy disguised as relevant satire, but it's a near-miss in all ways. It aspires to be sophisticated entertainment but is clearly aimed at a middle-brow audience, helmed, incongruously, by a blue-collar director. Its attempted wit is peppered with schoolboy sexism and facile racism, habits seen in Richler's otherwise enjoyable literary canon. And the pace is often too languid for what should be zippy fun.

George Segal—Dick, the fallen NASA executive, a sad echo of America's finest technological achievement and a living symbol of its smarting, post-astronaut program pride—gives us, well, George Segal. Jane Fonda, as this other Jane, a comeback role for her, sticks to a rusty, glib delivery. It's an all–American haughtiness that becomes, over her next few films, a signature style and an acquired taste. She's enjoying her lines too much, pressing on the gas in what's supposed to be a breezy ride. The big surprise is Ed McMahon as George's unscrupulous, insider ex-boss, the embodiment of all that's wrong with America. Who knew that under the bulgy skin of America's favorite drunken uncle, a bona fide character actor resided?

Dick and Jane are here—but where's the fun? (The film was remade, not renewed, in 2005.)

The Goodbye Girl

Plot: A struggling actor moves in with a single mother and her precocious daughter. **Director:** Herbert Ross. **Script:** Neil Simon. **Cast:** Richard Dreyfuss, Marsha Mason, Quinn Cummings. Warner Bros. 110 minutes.

By 1977, Neil Simon was America's brand name comedy writer, one of the few whose name was deemed fit to appear above the title. His only rival was ex–co-worker Larry Gelbart, riding high as showrunner for the top-rated *M*A*S*H* TV series (1972–83) and garnering, as a result, the odd film assignment.

The Goodbye Girl subscribes to the comic template that had been a staple of the era: Jew vs. WASP and/or hippie vs. Establishmentarian. In this case, it doubles as the quintessential Simon dynamic: two distinct personality types in an apartment, fighting out their differences. But it didn't play with edge any more. So, here it is again, tempered and sugar-coated, reinvented as an old-fashioned romantic comedy.

As a struggling single mom burdened with a precocious (naturally) eight-year-old, the vivacious Marsha Mason (so sexy-funny in *Cinderella Liberty,* 1973) might still look good but she's desexualized. Simon and director Herb Ross have turned her into a modern frump. Starting with this, and over her next few films (most written by hubby Simon), Mason earned a new reputation as the Queen of Cry, enough to be parodied by TV's then-popular *SCTV* (1976–81). While other actresses—Streisand, Hawn, Fonda, Clayburgh—were expanding women's roles, Mason was going in the other direction. Here, she starts as an independent, nobly struggling mother, then is converted to dependency by being coerced into tending to the hero's wounds, followed by his lust. Older audiences, by which the film made the bulk of its money, loved this, deeming it Old School in the best kind of way. The younger set saw right through it.

But it isn't Mason's film. It's called *The Goodbye Girl,* but it should be *The Gabby Guy.* Your appreciation of the film depends entirely upon your tolerance for Richard Dreyfuss. His puckish chutzpah, as the single, smarmy actor with whom poor mother-daughter are forced to share their apartment, comes at you like a spritzing comic in hipster guise. He displays tremendous energy; was he high on coke at the time? (Eventually, he'd ditch this then chic habit.) His punchy bravura, accentuated by Henry Higgins–esque directives, fooled most of the people most of the time; he was awarded the Oscar in a surprise win over long-snubbed Richard Burton (for *Equus*). Still, Dreyfuss never manages to steal the film from Mason or Quinn Cummings, creating a springy, if pat, balance. Ross, to his credit, keeps the whole thing going at a good gallop, rescuing us from too many play-like scenes set in a single setting (in a nicely art-directed apartment but uh, where do two struggling artists get that kind of money?). And as usual, he expertly juggles the sticks-to-handheld ratio.

Despite such filmic aspirations, however, the shenanigans still retain their sitcom vibe. By 1977, the prime moviegoing audience was fast becoming the first generation to be raised on television, and even the older set had seen almost three decades of it. Moviegoers, particularly when it came to comedy, were beginning to settle for less wit, less edge, less bravura.

The film's comic centerpiece is a long anti-gay joke, with Dreyfuss cast as a lisping Richard III. While he certainly wouldn't be comic cinema's sole offender, Simon here demonstrates a Milton Berle–era sensibility about homosexual subculture, on par with his old-fashioned take on women. In his play-film *California Suite* (1978), he broadened his perspective on both, only to demonstrate an offensively cartoonish view of African Americans. Smartly, he became, come the '80s, a devoted nostalgist, setting most of his plays in earlier eras when such notions could be interpreted simply as conventions of the time. Curiously, though, it would be in those contributions where his political tolerance would prove broadest.

High Anxiety

Plot: In this parody of Hitchcock films, a respected psychiatrist is set up as a murderer. **Director:** Mel Brooks. **Script:** Mel Brooks, Ron Clark, Rudy De Luca, Barry Levinson.

Cast: Mel Brooks, Madeline Kahn, Cloris Leachman, Harvey Korman. 20th Century–Fox. 94 minutes.

It purports to be an homage to Master of Suspense Alfred Hitchcock, but not in as strict a sense as *Young Frankenstein* had put paid to Universal's horror films. Rather, Mel Brooks' *High Anxiety* is Hitchcock tokenism in the service of a TV sketch sensibility. Brooks even recruited Barry Levinson (later the famed director) and Rudy De Luca, then staff writers on the top-rated *Carol Burnett Show* (1967–78), to help write the script, making use of both their film spoof sensibilities (a staple of the Burnett series) and their workaday sketch chops.

There's an element of personal nostalgia to this: Through them, Brooks was no doubt reliving his halcyon sketch-writing days for Sid Caesar in the early '50s. Diminutive Howard Morris, one of Caesar's stooges, is even here as a stock Viennese psychiatrist and there might have been some thought to having Caesar himself play the ultra-physical Charlie Callas part, a patient who believes he's a dog. There's also a distinctly '50s attitude toward psychology, back then a major cultural plaything, morphed, by 1977, into Me Generation form.

With *Silent Movie* (1976), Brooks set out to make himself the star as well as the writer-director. He repeats that here, playing Dr. Richard Thorndyke, a world-respected shrink with a fear of heights. He's set up for murder, possibly by the unscrupulous team behind the institution into which he's been newly parachuted. A plot, then, that's mostly a mix of *North by Northwest* (1959) and *Vertigo* (1958).

There are big problems with *Anxiety*. First, Brooks plays the straight man. It's a terrible waste of a major comic talent, given the caliber of his earlier film cameos. He's no longer looking to be loved as Mel the Spritzer; he wants to be loved as Mel the Everyman. Fortunately, he breaks with this misguided agenda on two occasions, both of them major highlights: when he showily croons to Madeline Kahn, as a Hitchcockian blonde, in a ritzy piano lounge, and later, when he pulls out his comic stock-in-trade, the little old Jewish man, for an angry fracas, again with Kahn, now disguised as his shrewish wife.

Then there are the inevitable send-ups of iconic Hitchcockian scenes, including a salute to *The Birds* (1963) involving, you guessed it, bird poop—a necessary if predictable bent, Brooks being the father of big-screen scatology. Even the film's most clever notion, the periodic integration of purposefully faulty camera moves, proves a hit-and-miss affair.

Fortunately, some veteran sketch performers are there to compensate: the impeccable Harvey Korman, the surprisingly strong Cloris Leachman (Korman's nervy sneer and Leachman's brutish slur make a nice comic contrast) and of course, Kahn the ever-reliable, who adds cool to her quirk and manages to again be simultaneously funny and sexy.

High Anxiety was Brooks' last hurrah of the decade. He set foot in the '80s with a self-indulgent vaudeville show, his *History of the World Part One* (1981). He bided the rest of his time as a producer of dramatic material until the *Star Wars* (1977) phenomenon became a veritable genre, allowing him to spoof another day with *Spaceballs* (1987).

The Last Remake of Beau Geste

Plot: A parody of *Beau Geste* (1926, and, more famously, 1939), the desert-set action film in which the blue-blooded Geste brothers find themselves enrolled in the French Foreign Legion. **Director:** Marty Feldman. **Script:** Marty Feldman, Chris Allen.

Cast: Marty Feldman, Michael York, Ann-Margret, Peter Ustinov, Trevor Howard, Spike Milligan, Roy Kinnear. Universal. 94 minutes.

After suffering the effects of a thyroid condition that altered his looks, Marty Feldman became comic eye candy. A passably bad joke, I'll admit—the kind that Feldman would have made himself, and did, repeatedly. (He even titled his posthumously published autobiography *eYE, Marty*). If his googly-faced visage, along with his beakish nose and wiry frame, relegated him first to the writers' room, then to sidekick roles, that was fine by Feldman. Anything beat his formative years as a struggling jazz trumpeter, sleeping on park benches while trying to crack the dying English music hall circuit.

But stardom came to Feldman nonetheless, through a string of self-named BBC TV series that made their way across the Pond. What sold the humor in those shows was their universality. Long a fan of Buster Keaton, Feldman made a habit of interpolating episodes of silent film comedy, demonstrating an unbridled enthusiasm and innate understanding of the form. He demonstrated it again in *The Last Remake of Beau Geste*, the film he was awarded by Universal as part of the industry-wide search for the next Mel Brooks. (Brooks, of course, had ingratiated Feldman to American audiences even more through *Young Frankenstein*, 1974 and *Silent Movie*, 1976.)

The Keatonian homages in *Last Remake* are the undisputed highlights of what is otherwise a hit-and-miss mix of Brooksian genre parody, English hokum, naughty schoolboy humor and a touch of Hope and Crosby. It's not simply the black-and-white sequence where, in a slapstick jailbreak, Feldman convinces us that he might have ranked among the greats back before cinema could speak. There are other notions right out of Keaton's influential *The Cameraman* (1928), in which Feldman messes admirably with form. In a desert mirage sequence, for example, he cuts himself into director William Wellman's 1939 version of *Beau Geste* to share a joint with Gary Cooper. More of this and Feldman's film might have ranked as retro chic. Not what the studio wanted, of course. "You were supposed to imitate Mel Brooks," they would have yelled, "not some dead clown only film nerds remember!"

That admonition never happened. Feldman gave them, at least in part, what they wanted: a send-up of the '39 *Beau Geste*, in which a pop-eyed nebbish (guess who?) follows his dashing, daredevil brother (Michael York) into the French Foreign Legion. There, they hold the fort against Arab bandits (unforgivably played by contemporary standards) while harboring a family jewel everyone is seeking.

The studio let Feldman keep the odd bit of cinematic surrealism. Whatever else may have been there that might have been unique was cut behind his back. In *eYE Marty*, he wrote: "It was essentially an average film, not horrible, not epic and nowhere in between."[42]
While he's a little hard on it, one does long for the full Marty.

The Late Show

Plot: An aging P.I. is forced to collaborate with a spacey earth mother to solve the mystery of his partner's murder. **Script/Director:** Robert Benton. **Cast:** Art Carney, Lily Tomlin, Bill Macy, Eugene Roche, Joanna Cassidy. Warner Bros. 93 minutes.

Robert Altman wasn't just busy as a director throughout the '70s. He also produced. Here, he plays mentor to Robert Benton, the talented Texan still living off the laurels of

42. Marty Feldman, *eYE Marty* (London: Hodder & Stoughton, 2015), 243.

his narrative contribution to the universally respected *Bonnie and Clyde* (1967). Altman also lent Benton his editing team; if you can bring coherence to an Altman film, helping out a novice director should be a breeze! Some of Altman's sound tricks show up, too, though that may have just been a matter of influence.

Despite these endorsements, Benton does not produce smooth work—in fact, though his Oscar-winning directorial career would end up lasting over three decades, he never did. (Instead of arguing with me, watch his botched *Billy Bathgate*, 1991.) Nevertheless, the bulk of Benton's catalogue, including this kooky rookie effort, works relatively well. *The Late Show* is an off-noir (should we call it a gray?), a self-made subgenre Benton revisited repeatedly (*Still of the Night*, 1982, *Billy Bathgate*, 1991, *Twilight*, 1998).

This one subscribes to a double "fish out of water" formula, as the last of L.A.'s hard-boiled detectives meets the last of the thinning hippie movement. It works, as it should, on the chemistry of the odd pairing: Sam Spade goes to Woodstock. Old School morality vs. modern touchy-feeliness—yes, that again! But the polarity here is more charmingly offbeat than most. The central characters purport to be generational and cultural archetypes. Instead, each has almost completely played out their respective personas; they're running on fumes, their battle weariness their humanity.

He—Ira, golden ager P.I.—wears a hearing aid, drinks Alka-Seltzer and walks with a limp. She—Margo, hippiedom's last heroine—sees a shrink, pushes grass and meditates. He's all school-of-hard-knocks tough talk. She speaks Me Generation psycho-babble. It's the old clichés vs. the new. She hires him on a flimsy pretense, only to fall into a Nick and Nora arrangement, a May-December vibe that, wisely, never spills over into romantic improbability.

Art Carney as Ira plays the tough surprisingly well. He also has a nice scene where he's forced, due to a perforated ulcer, to show his human side, a gumshoe no-no. Lily Tomlin, as Margo, distinguishes herself in a big scene where she runs the gamut from high to low, pitching lone wolf Ira on a mutually beneficial liaison. Bonuses: smart, colorful supporting characters played by wily vets; a soundtrack made up of old torch songs and a minor-key, *Chinatown*-inspired horn; sepia-tinged cinematography, full of atmospheric touches that might have worked even better in black and white; and nice pieces of business, like using a swimming pool for a watery holding cell, which helps to break up the expository dialogue that is the soupy necessity of these kinds of things. (The climax is one of those long, tell-all scenes with all of the main characters in a room, followed by the inevitable confessions and the ensuing gunfire.)

The film was critically acclaimed (Benton's script was Oscar-nominated) and deemed, despite its roots in genre, highly original. Though it wasn't a money-making machine, it may even have influenced the ubiquitous TV detective shows that followed, all of which featured offbeat pairings (*Moonlighting*, 1985–89, *Scarecrow and Mrs. King*, 1983–87, etc.). The legacy of those shows makes the film, today, seem less than what the press had originally lauded.

Oh, God!

Plot: God returns to earth to spread His message through a grocery food manager. **Director:** Carl Reiner. **Script:** Larry Gelbart, from a novel by Avery Corman. **Cast:** George Burns, John Denver, Teri Garr. Warner Bros. 98 minutes.

In the late '60s, God had been officially declared dead in the *New York Times*. Come the 70s, he remained at rest. After all, what evidence was there that a protective hand was at work? War was raging, prices were rising, politicians were scheming. The Christian belief system, long a binding thread in the American fabric, was unraveling just like everything else.

Plus, a loose network of undermining foreign agents, which had infiltrated popular culture in the previous decade, remained at large: Eastern mysticism, introduced by the Beatles; drugs, both soft and hard, as a form of non-institutional transcendence; psychiatry and psychoanalysis, helping the quick-fix paperback usurp the Bible.

Longtime believers began to grow militant: The Rev. Jerry Falwell founded the Moral Majority; singer Anita Bryant a pro–Christian, anti-gay crusade; televangelists hijacked Sunday TV. Then, slowly but surely, a portion of the young took their side, a small but growing faction whose primary form of public expression was, as had always been their generational wont, music. Andrew Lloyd Webber and Tim Rice made a pop icon out of the son of God with *Jesus Christ Superstar* (stage 1970, film 1973), which begat *Godspell* (stage 1970, film '73), which begat the Top 40 hits "Put Your Hand in the Hand" (1971) and, sung by an actual nun no less, a musical rendition of the Lord's Prayer ('73). By 1977, this spiritual renaissance became known as the Born Again movement, an unorganized front of North American under–30s, and a few over, unabashedly espousing Old World answers to New World problems. Even Bob Dylan, anti-establishmentarian folk deity, succumbed to it, putting out a succession of Christian-themed albums. And why not? No one else seemed to be coming up with anything else that worked.

It was in this climate that in 1971, a middling novelist named Avery Corman fashioned *Oh, God!*, in which a nondescript grocery clerk in Tarzana, California, is handpicked by the Almighty as his messenger *du jour*. Given the lightness of its touch, the book caught but a small spray of the new religious wave (unlike an even more hubristic attempt, *Jonathan Livingston Seagull*—book 1970, film 1973—in which life lessons from on high were imparted to a bird!).

By '77, *Oh, God!* was ripe for cinematic adaptation. Even the hippies were un-hippying, their anger dissipating, their ideals being left behind. The new directive was to get back to basics. The search for a simple, incorruptible life philosophy was on, one that would see us, one and all, through whatever the hell came next.

Enter George Burns.

After re-ingratiating himself to the world through *The Sunshine Boys* (1975), Burns became culturally ubiquitous. There wasn't a talk show you couldn't find him on, a variety program on which he wasn't billed. The last cross-generational Old World icon, Burns, America's kindly, wisecracking grandfather, generously dispensed a raspy-voiced gospel of vaudeville anecdotes and good-hearted folk wisdom. Who better to play that showy sage, God?

The original idea was to employ Corman's novel as a vehicle for big-name stunt casting: Mel Brooks as a vocal, riffing God and Woody Allen as his doubting Thomas. But Allen dropped out in favor of his own projects and Brooks, although the film was slated to be directed by his old friend Carl Reiner (usurping screenwriter Larry Gelbart), followed suit. So again, enter George Burns ... but who to play the modern Moses?

The folk craze of the '60s had given us a deity of a musical sort, the singer-songwriter. Some used their acoustic guitar–harmonica combination to offer political commentary, others personal reflection. A smaller school, however, concentrated on what would later become a leading *cause célèbre*: the environment. Leading that pack was a myopic nebbish from Colorado, John Deutschendorf, who became one with his pet subject by renaming himself after his home state's bucolic capital.

Denver's simple, apolitical melodies, backed up by his backwoods "Aw shucks!" vibe—a kind of hippie Andy Griffith—made him the long-haired (sort of) troubadour acceptable to the older generation. As a result, his greatest hits album went on to become, for a time, the biggest-selling record in RCA history. Then came the revelation of his other colors, an affirmation of his fanbase's greatest fears: a well-publicized marijuana bust, revealing that this hitherto "good hippie" was "just another one of *them*."

Looking to reinvent himself, Denver decided to try his luck as an actor. He already had a bit of a TV presence (appearances with the Muppets, for instance, whose Scooter he cannily resembled). In *Oh, God!*, he would be joining other TV-bred talents: two Sid Caesar alums (screenwriter Gelbart and stooge-writer-cum film director Reiner) and of course Burns.

The film has a TV-esque feel to it. It was happening, inevitably, to more and more big-screen fare, particularly comedy—so much so that by the next decade, the Hollywood Film Directors' Who's Who would comprise an exhaustive list of one-time sitcom stars. As, essentially, an elongated piece of television then, the film subscribes to the same safe approach to subject matter by which the small screen had always abided to sell Tide. Gone is almost every ounce of satire or indictment, save for a fun appearance by the hammy Paul Sorvino in the third act, wherein writer Gelbart wages war on televangelists. Absent too is any sense of spoof or subtext aka anything Brooksian or Allen-esque. And despite the involvement of Reiner, Gelbart and Burns, anything else that might be constituted, comedically, Jewish. This is a God-man dialogue for WASPs, the Gospel according to the white, middle-class moviegoer.

And—surprise!—it works. Very little of it, particularly when one considers what we might have gotten with the original talents, is forced. (That said, it's not the most energetic of comedies either.) Reiner directs like he's just relatively content to be there. He's almost as removed an overseer as the film's eponymous character, Burns, who spends much of his on-screen time expostulating simple American percipience with self-amused ease.

Gelbart's script is careful with the one-liners, just long enough on the marital squabbles as poor, incredulous Denver tries to convince his wife (Teri Garr, at her sexiest in an unsexy role) that he's of sound mind, and, best of all, light-footed on the soapbox. In God's big message—"You've got to make it work"—Gelbart found the perfect philosophical middle ground, one that wouldn't offend the Holy Rollers nor their non-believing counterparts. The film's popularity was proof that the hippies were ready to concede to the generation against which they had so vociferously rebelled. At last, everyone found themselves subscribing to the same ethos: Let's just love each other and create a new and simpler world.

It's a symbiosis cozily personified by the Denver-Burns dynamic. The former's Mountain State bumpkin quality (remember his wide-eyed catchphrase "Far-out!"?) serves the role to a tee; after all, he's playing a hermetic who has his eyes opened by forces bigger than himself. That force, of course, is Burns, the other half of this father-son— well, more like grandfather-grandson—combination. Needless to say, the picture is largely his. With his monkey's build (accentuated by comically plain clothes), his thick glasses and his gummy smile, scenes are stolen before he even opens his mouth.

But open his mouth, of course, he does—and again, to the script's credit, just enough. He has a single lengthy scene: a nice verbal climax in a hotel room, where, disguised as a bellhop, he helps his judiciously challenged charge offer proof positive of their relationship by answering a selection of Big Questions—with one-liners, of course.

The picture was a hit of Biblical proportions, the sixth highest-grossing film of the year; keep in mind that it was released late (October) and that this was the year of *Star Wars* (1977). What could have been at work too was the search, after it had long been out of fashion, for a reliable authority figure, a guiding, decent-hearted, trustworthy paterfamilias. Nixon had been anything but, Ford had proven a buffoonish successor, and Carter, not even a year in office, was already overwhelmed. The way was being paved for Reagan. In the meantime, though, George Burns would do.

With the success of TV's *M*A*S*H*, Larry Gelbart, another Sid Caesar alum, became one of the top screenwriters in Hollywood (photograph by Kim Carlsberg/ Photofest).

A Piece of the Action

Plot: A pair of thieves work at a career center for delinquents. **Director:** Sidney Poitier. **Script:** Charles Blackwell, story by Timothy March. **Cast:** Sidney Poitier, Bill Cosby, James Earl Jones, Denise Nicholas. Warner Bros. 135 minutes.

You'd think, as the audience did back in the day, that *A Piece of the Action* would be the last member of the loose trilogy that had started with *Uptown Saturday Night* (1974). It isn't, though the film was marketed as such—no doubt a nervous studio trying to milk their cash cow before people discovered the truth: that this was a sober-faced polemic framed within comic caper conventions, about a new, disenfranchised generation of African American youth. Media-age babies, these kids were raised with celebrity role models like stars Sidney Poitier and Bill Cosby and were struggling (according to the film) with whether or not those icons represented something to aspire to or were just a duo of white capitalists in, essentially, blackface.

Confusion over what they represented to the young may well have been the emotional impetus behind this Poitier-Cosby collaboration, in which they play reformed thieves forced to work at a youth center. What price, they may have considered, upward mobility? Cosby would suffer the same slings and arrows all over again a decade later, over his TV sitcom. It's an interesting question, but in *A Piece of the Action*, superficially probed; a lot of the film resembles the then-popular *ABC Afterschool Specials* (1972–97) crossbred with Cosby's then-popular animated series *Fat Albert and the Cosby Kids* (1972–85). It might have also been that Poitier, after taking a shit-kicking from the critics for trying his hand at broad comedy, was looking to get back to what they had liked best.

Much of it unabashedly resembles *To Sir, with Love* (1967), one of Poitier's biggest dramatic hits. That said, here, Poitier indeed proves that he can still command, as he does when he bribes a roomful of disenfranchised teenagers into conducting a mock job interview.

The film also suffers from a distinct lack of chemistry, hitherto the series' main asset. The scenes between Poitier and Cosby are few, the movie concentrating instead on individual storylines. Looking to break with comic precedent even more, they each give themselves romantic subplots. It's semi-familiar territory for Poitier but completely new for Cosby. While neither actor embarrasses himself, these subplots don't add up to much either.

The good things: James Earl Jones is in it, his voice put to good use as a bullying detective. (It was used just as effectively again that same year, in a retro sci-fi wild card called *Star Wars*.) There's eye-catching Denise Nicholas as a fellow teacher. Okay, she'd been in *Let's Do It Again* (1976), but was she awarded her role here because she had been a teacher in TV's *Room 222* (1969–74)? The bad Titos Vandis, the token Greek of the era, gets his biggest role to date; it's a shame that he wastes it, chewing scenery.

The theme is a familiar one: the lengths you have to go to as an African American to get ahead. It's a message that was first brought forth by the blaxploitation phenomenon. From militancy, then, to sanctimony.

Semi-Tough

Plot: Love triangle between two football players and the team owner's daughter. **Director:** Michael Ritchie. **Script:** Walter Bernstein, from the novel by Dan Jenkins. **Cast:** Burt Reynolds, Kris Kristofferson, Jill Clayburgh, Robert Preston. United Artists. 108 minutes.

Who better to counterbalance the testosterone renaissance being promoted with fisticuffs and Mack trucks by Clint Eastwood and Burt Reynolds than Michael Ritchie? Throughout his career, Ritchie had often delved the soul of the all–American male, usually through the realm of sports.

So yes, *Semi-Tough* is a sports film—in this case, pro football—but in the same "sort of" way his *The Bad News Bears* (1976) had been. Together, *Bears* and *Semi-Tough* helped Ritchie usher in a new kind of sports flick, one that eschewed the homer-in-the-ninth, "Win one for the Gipper" clichés in favor of greater attention to culture and character.

This one came out of the sports branch of the "New Journalism" and frank, hip tell-all autobiographies like *Paper Lion* and *Ball Four*. (Ritchie partly parodies it through the character played by Jim McKrell, one of two TV game show hosts in the film. Remember *Celebrity Sweepstakes*, 1974–77?) At work was a collective search for the true dysfunctional energy of whichever game was under the microscope, including the off-putting, demythologizing, entertaining contradictions of those who played it.

This investigative school's athletes were, as a group, microcosms of the counter-culture, high-living yahoos whose discontent and unorthodox behavior were fueled by being under the thumb of the runaway corporate mentality. It's best exemplified in *Semi-Tough* in the well-played scene where the team's owner, played with offbeat panache by Robert Preston, forces star player Reynolds to crawl around his office like a rabid baby to promote better on-field coordination, the disgruntled Reynolds literally having to stoop to his boss' level.

If that scene sounds like cockeyed fun, predicated on woozy character dynamics, you got it! *Semi-Tough* is, at heart, an offbeat relationship comedy. The central one is a weirdly drawn triangle: a Southern-fried running back and a Zen-headed wide receiver enjoying a benign, flirtatious *Jules and Jim*–style arrangement with the owner's broad-minded daughter. These three people only understand each other, a precarious bond so unique, it's perpetually threatened by conventions old and new.

Hitherto, Reynolds had made Southern culture a major on-screen commodity. Here he does it again with an obliging swagger, but in the service of a smart contrast with Kris Kristofferson, his teammate and romantic rival. Kristofferson too is flogging an old behavioral horse—the hippie deity—but with a wider palette and in his most constructive context to date. Jill Clayburgh, as the rope in this romantic tug of war, tries hard in her role but she simply isn't the type. She's naturally wan and at best cute rather than sexy-funny. (Wasn't Marsha Mason available?) They're flies busily buzzing around the film's big question, the then-familiar one about the value of monogamy. To marry or not to marry, as neither option seemed to represent spiritual fulfillment. If the film speaks better than most on behalf of its romantically adrift generation, it's because novelist Dan Jenkins, screenwriter Walter Bernstein and Ritchie leave their thematic concerns not just with the film's boys' network but spread the subtextual wealth across genders.

The film's other major agenda is satire, serving as a grand-scale parody of the then-burgeoning self-help movement, particularly an egocentric practice called EST (here called B.E.A.T.). It's aptly represented by a surprisingly commanding Bert Convy (the film's second game show host) foreshadowing Tom Cruise's take on the reincarnation of the phenomenon in *Magnolia* (1999). It's a bent that hadn't been a part of Jenkins' novel. Still, after Ritchie pushed it, Jenkins gave it his blessing, recognizing that its reflection of Me Generation angst was in line with the rest of the film's ethos.

Semi-Tough helped to rebalance the waning but still present generational divide with its ultimate contention that the new mores could corrupt just as well as the old. Life's only satisfactory recourse, it finalizes, is middle-ground companionship, then labeled "living in sin." As such, the film perfectly captures the transitional period in male-female relations when the self-serving '70s began to give way to the back-to-basics '80s.

Many, especially given the ad campaign, wanted a pure football film, not some raggedy, loose-lipped *ménage à trois* with scant on-field action, save for a Super Bowl that today looks like an inflated high school game. Still, *Semi-Tough* was no semi-success. Theatrical only: $37 million.

Slap Shot

Plot: A struggling minor league hockey team resorts to on-ice violence to promote itself. **Director:** George Roy Hill. **Script:** Nancy Dowd. **Cast:** Paul Newman, Michael Ontkean, Melinda Dillon, Strother Martin. Universal. 122 minutes.

Like the consumer revenge fantasy *Fun with Dick and Jane* (1977), *Slap Shot* is a look at the ordinary American's anger at the social forces keeping him underfoot. In this case, though, its heroes don't steal from the institutions responsible for their diminished lifestyle; they steal the puck from opposing players.

The ailing, low-rung Charleston Chiefs hockey team is no more than a tax write-off, a white-collar plaything, just another whimsical folly of capitalism. Just as director George Roy Hill once sent desperate, dumber-than-he-looks Butch Cassidy to piss-poor Bolivia to rob banks, here he leads the Chiefs to a means just as laughably desperate: a plan to draw fans by drawing blood, thus boosting the team's salability and salvaging the players' sagging careers.

At the time of the film's release, there was much criticism over the increasingly violent nature of sports. The casualty-heavy war in 'Nam, coupled with the country-wide rise in inner-city crime, had begun to spill into hitherto innocent pastimes, which had staunchly represented model American values like fair play and egalitarianism. (It was around this time that bone-crunching football began to eclipse pastoral baseball as America's most popular sport.) Drama had begun to examine this infiltration with the interesting, offbeat *Rollerball* (1975). With *Slap Shot*, comedy suited up and hit the social commentary ice.

It's possible writer Nancy Dowd was only out to provide an insider's look at low-end hockey, but Hill makes something grander out of it without killing that idea's pulpy fun: a comic take on America's bloodlust. Hill was aided by the times. Knockabout humor, *à la* John Ford, had been long out of fashion due to objections over the war and the rise of anti-testosterone feminism. By 1977, though, the macho disco ethic was in full swing, creating audiences ready to laugh at violence anew.

And yet, in its way, *Slap Shot* is a feminist treatise. Maybe only a woman could have provided such a frank, comic take on animalistic male behavior. (Dowd's insights came from following her hockey player–brother Ned around. In the film, Ned plays über goon Ogie Ogilthorpe.) And, again attributable to the gender of the writer, the film's few female characters aren't just blue-collar eye candy. They're as endearingly goofy as the guys, best exemplified by bare-chested Melinda Dillon in a moving cameo as a free-spirited goalie's wife.

As for Newman, the team's concerned, aging captain, he's looking trim and agile for his age. Newman was a smart guy who loved to play dumb. Here, he gets a golden opportunity to show off his trademark opportunistic chump. He wears Don Cherry haberdashery and a perpetually perplexed expression on his bruised, befuddled face. Was this the beginning of Newman's last great persona, the broken man? Succeeding roles included *Absence of Malice* (1981), *The Verdict* (1982), *The Color of Money* (1986), *Nobody's Fool* (1994) and *Twilight* (1998). Each role was about faded glory, the burden of remaining in the mix, familial regret, and the onset of aches, pains and loneliness— many issues that, as a fading star trying to keep his name on marquees, were no doubt personal.

Friction between Old School Newman and young, intellectual Michael Ontkean, the team's token, disgruntled Ivy Leaguer, was probably meant to look, when Dowd's script was first fashioned, like that iconic early '70s struggle, the Greatest Generation vs. the Baby Boomers. But in '77, with the hippie thing officially over, it played, and plays today, like something more universal: the classic American conflict of the self-made man vs. the educated egghead.

A further affirmation of the demise of the counterculture is the conversion of the film's young anti-heroes, Ontkean and his equally brainy, put-out screen wife Lindsay Crouse. Ontkean and Crouse win the day not by proverbially beating 'em but by resignedly joining 'em. Crouse conforms to the team-directed zeitgeist by becoming a tarty hockey wife, and Ontkean, with his contemptuous on-ice striptease in sync with the team's desperately showy ethic, by trading the ideal of fair play for low showmanship. The under–30s, now the almost-30, were officially ready to sell out.

Hill is very patient with the script, fully aware that it's essentially a pastiche of small comic moments. He knows when he has a good joke. He frames it and lets it play out; he's not out to kill it with grandiosity or earnestness, like an Altman. In the tradition of the best American screen comedies, he keeps the scenes short and tight. Further, there's good, repeated use of ground-level camera on the ice. And the film builds to a truly hysterical climax, a free-for-all championship game. It's like the Marx Brothers' football game in *Horse Feathers* (1932) with blood.

Hill also demonstrates a great feel for the rust belt, with its underlit motel rooms, flimsy wood paneling and pinball machine–populated dive bars. This is the under-subsidized '70s, seldom seen on film outside of fraying New York City. But in this darkness, light: The film is about how something as flimsy as a game can sustain. Call it the importance of illusion aka America's much-ballyhooed "pursuit of happiness."

Hill made a career out of spotlighting see-through legends, comic heroes who pulled a fast one over the world to gain overinflated reputations and sometimes, *inter alia*, the right to survive: Butch Cassidy, Waldo Pepper, etc. The Chiefs do too, joining the ranks of *Rocky* (1976) as America's new breed of working-class hero.

Slap Shot received mixed reviews in America. Given its quality, that might have been due to the low-rank hockey holds on the roster of the country's cultural indulgences. In puck-mad Canada, it's a Bible.

Smokey and the Bandit

Plot: A pair of high-flyin' bootleggers illegally transport 400 cases of contraband from Texarkana to Atlanta. **Director:** Hal Needham. **Script:** James Lee Barrett, Charles Shyer, Alan Mandel. **Cast:** Burt Reynolds, Sally Field, Jackie Gleason, Jerry Reed. Universal. 96 minutes.

Said Jackie Gleason: "This is the worst script I've ever read. I'll do it."[43]

In the great Gleason's defense, the veteran TV comic was at an extremely low ebb—thanks, ironically, to the audience that would prove receptive to this, the surprise big-screen hit that revived his career.

43. Jack Bristow, "My Favorite 'Guilty Pleasure' Movies," *Huffpost*, Nov. 8, 2016.

With the emergence of the phenomenon of TV ratings in the early days of the decade, it was revealed to CBS, one of the powerhouses of that three-network era, that it had skewed too much of its programming to a bucolic audience. Looking to lure big-city hungry advertising, the network purged almost all of its prime-time comedy. This included the aging Gleason's variety hour, long a staple. Gleason may have been biding his post–TV time in bars and on golf courses, but his audience never forgot him. He was particularly loved by Floridians and their fellow Southerners, as, by insistently locating his variety show in Miami, Gleason had boosted civic pride and had nationally promoted the area as a prime tourist destination.

One member of said audience was the Georgia-born Burt Reynolds, fast climbing Hollywood's Most Bankable list. He handpicked Gleason for the role that appears first in the title of the film: a harried Southern sheriff who'd play Coyote to Burt's Road Runner. So signed, Gleason's sheriff would spend the film chasing a modern-day soldier of fortune running contraband beer across state lines.

Sounds thin, as Gleason had been the first to acknowledge. The second naysayer was Sally Field, another Reynolds casting whim. Convincing both Field and Gleason that they could circumvent the wanting dialogue by generously ad-libbing, this big-budget lark—a much-needed respite for Reynolds, sick of working with uppity directors like Peter Bogdanovich—went into 18-wheel motion.

What ensued was the most popular "car movie" made to that time, catapulting the low-cost, fast-buck genre into a financially respected, wide-release commodity. The South went to it and the North went to it. Hollywood went to the bank.

This giddy celebration of Southern folkways ranked second at the box office that year, after *Star Wars* (1977). This is significant. It marked the end of socially relevant American cinema and ushered in an era of mindless, high-spirited blockbusters, placing the narrative emphasis on action, pace, peril and mayhem—not far from the fun, facile feel of silent-era serials like *The Perils of Pauline* (1914) and the adventures of the Keystone Cops. For a long time, the movies had made us think (and the European ones had made us *really* think!). Now they were once again a relief from that practice, a return to their roots as pure, popular, popcorn-friendly entertainment.

Smokey and the Bandit is a cross-stitch of many commercial fibers: the buddy film, the car movie, the CB radio craze, the macho man–disco thing—and that most venerable cinematic commodity, the Western. Note the Remingtonian fresco painted on the side of the contraband-carrying truck and the endless verbal references to on-screen cowpokes past. Field, a runaway Eastern bride picked up by the Bandit, is the character that metropolitan audiences are invited to identify with, the book-reading, culturally savant everyperson given a whirlwind tour of the tenets of this cowboy-centric (though they be truckers) landscape. A wide-eyed mortal in, to use the Bandit's words, "redneck Heaven."

Reynolds here is completely in his element: trim, energetic and gum-chewing, with enough good ol' boy swagger to shame the Marlboro Man. It was a self-created image that proved, throughout his career, both a blessing and a curse: It made him a box office sure bet but limited his roles. For now, though, he was having great fun, as is the underrated Jerry Reed as his sidekick, who ignites much of the cornpone bonhomie (and provides the comfy tunes comprising the soundtrack).

Field proves a good sport, and the flirty vibe between her and Reynolds (the

The "macho man" ethic spawned by the phenomenon of disco made comic action stars out of Burt Reynolds, seen here in *Smoley and the Bandit* (Universal, 1977) and Clint Eastwood (Universal Pictures/Photofest).

beginnings of their famous off-screen romance) is palpable, its ad-lib tenor a faint echo of the improv-tinged comedies from earlier in the era. The only cast member seeming ill at ease, surprisingly, is Gleason, who looks positively belabored. Maybe the return to the screen, the big one at that (he had enjoyed two mini-careers in it earlier), had made him edgy, hence the security blanket of an Art Carney–style stooge on which he insisted.

With *Smokey*, for the first time in ages, the automotive carnage is not symbolic, representing, as it had for so long, America the military-industrial mess—though you could argue, with an inept Georgian president at the helm, it reflected the perpetually unlucky Jimmy Carter's innocent bungling. Truly, though, the film liberates the car from its metaphorical chains and posits it more simply as the trusty, speedy horse from the old Westerns. After all, first-time director Hal Needham was no satirist, no intellectual; rather, a veteran fight and action scene coordinator looking to make the venerable convention of the stunt a two-hour, stand-alone phenomenon. The film's famous "bridge jump" was so embraced by audiences that Needham built an entire film around it (see *Hooper,* 1978). TV, in turn, followed up on *Smokey* with *The Dukes of Hazzard* (1979-85), which later became a film in its own right (2005).

With *Smokey, Rocky* (1976) and *Star Wars* (1977), America was returning to uncomplicated heroes, cat-and-mouse narratives, and white hat-black hat morality. It was back to basics, paving the way for the dumbed-down politics of Ronald Reagan.

Which Way Is Up?

Plot: Americanization of Lina Wertmüller's *The Seduction of Mimi* (1972) wherein a hapless laborer falls into a muddle of union activism, romance and sex. **Director:** Michael Schultz. **Script:** Carl Gottlieb, Cecil Brown. **Cast:** Richard Pryor, Lonette McKee. Universal. 94 minutes.

With *Cooley High* (1975), director Michael Schultz demonstrated a propensity for low comedy, bawdy sexuality, political commentary and light humanitarianism. Who better to adapt the work of Italian auteur Lina Wertmüller, whose sexual-political farces were, at that time, hallowed staples of the American art house circuit?

In reworking Wertmüller's *The Seduction of Mimi* (1972), veteran comedy writer Carl Gottlieb and African American co-scenarist Cecil Brown managed to keep the film's ideological milieu while accommodating classic American film comedy narrative. Leroy Jones Jr., the fruit-picking nobody at the eye of this verbal-physical hurricane, is a black edition of classic white comic heroes, specifically, Bob Hope: a sexually frustrated coward who unwittingly becomes a big man. In this case, our hero does it by joining the union movement and availing himself of its financial-sexual rewards—only to find himself the brunt of exploitation and hoisted, in the end, by his own egotistical petard.

Gottlieb's fingerprints are visibly imprinted on the narrative; flash-forward two years and you'll find a lot of the film's conventions—its working-class hero's meteoric rise and fall, its epistolary voiceovers, its dysfunctional sex—in the Steve Martin vehicle *The Jerk* (1979), another Gottlieb collaboration. But so are the political Brown's; he was on his way to becoming a respected black educator. The result is a broad, bawdy comedy with its eye on the proverbial prize.

It's also a star vehicle for Richard Pryor, his first, earned by his supporting splash in *Silver Streak* (1976). Hitherto, movie audiences had seen two Pryors: the nervy man-child in a string of small to midsize roles, and the foul-mouthed showman of his cult concert movies. When, fans were asking, might the two come together? It took Gottlieb, Brown (a friend from Pryor's struggling years in Berkeley) and Schultz to get him there. Collectively, they recognized, in Wertmüller's central dupe, Pryor's signature qualities: his unforced infantilization, his see-through ego, his propensity for verbal and physical hysteria.

Add to that his versatility: Pryor plays multiple characters here (the hero, his mealy-mouthed father, a two-timing preacher), a comedic privilege hitherto afforded white, largely British (Alec Guinness, Peter Sellers—with apologies to Jerry Lewis) talent, a precedent paving the way for future African American stars such as Eddie Murphy. Pryor rewardingly hams it up in all three parts, remaining careful, though, to keep his Leroy at bay from the clutches of soul-killing caricature.

But the film is more than just a combination comic showcase-political polemic. In its unintentional way, it was an affirmation that the legacy of the barrier-breaking '60s and early '70s was officially over. In *Which Way Is Up?*, free love is rebutted with physical disdain. The dead-end struggle of the union with which Leroy gets involved is proof positive that "power to the people" has become a limited proposition; black unity, subject to repeated violations, veritably implodes. When, in the end, battered, beleaguered Leroy at last learns to stand up for himself, it's the chancy triumph of the individual over the system, nothing more. The author's message, then, could not be more representative of the burgeoning Me generation.

Pryor was riding high (likely literally too) at the time of the film's release. He and Schultz had another collaboration out that year, the reverent biopic *Greased Lightning* (1977), plus, Pryor was busy with that unlikeliest of showcases, network television—a variety series doomed, predictably, to but a handful of episodes. The worst, except for more concert films, was yet to come: mainstream Hollywood, which would homogenize him to the point of busy hollowness.

This is Pryor, prior.

The World's Greatest Lover

Plot: In the 1920s, a frustrated baker leaves Milwaukee to try his luck as Hollywood's next silent screen heartthrob. **Script/Director:** Gene Wilder. **Cast:** Gene Wilder, Carol Kane, Dom DeLuise. 20th Century–Fox. 89 minutes.

The ad campaign posited Gene Wilder as a magnetic silent-screen heartthrob, the header inviting you to "Go ahead—laugh!," the footer anointing him *The World's Greatest Lover*. You might have laughed, had it been almost any other comic figure, from Charlie Chaplin through to Woody Allen. But Wilder, as his career evolved from the cherubic hayseed in *Bonnie and Clyde* (1967) to the fumbling-dashing swordsman in his writer-director debut, *The Adventure of Sherlock Holmes' Smarter Brother* (1975), had developed a heroic, even romantic dimension, first put to use in Colin Higgins' *Silver Streak* (1976).

And so, especially so soon after that particular mega-hit, presenting himself as a laughably sexual figure in the tradition of so many film comedians seemed a bit of a gamble.

The film, however, went out of its way to remind the world that within Wilder, Gerry Silberman, Wilder's true identity, remained alive and kicking.

Gerry-Gene is Rudy Hickman (the "hick" is significant), a Milwaukee-based neurotic, as was Gerry, screaming for a bigger life (bringing to mind Wilder's famous declaration in Mel Brooks' *The Producers*, 1967, "I want everything I ever saw in the movies!"). Just as the real Gerry-Gene had, Gerry-Rudy heads to Hollywood to be a star. He brings his wife along—the petite, wan Carol Kane, put to very good use here—and she promptly leaves him for, as the title has suggested, the world's greatest lover: not Gerry-Gene but Rudolph Valentino, the swarthy 1920s pretty boy who died at a tragically young age, thus emblazing his name in the ledger of Hollywood mythology. But Rudy, with Valentino's assistance, wins her back, becoming a star in the bargain, in a thin, playful plot with allusions to Fellini's *The White Sheik* (1952).

The real influences in this semi-autobiographical tale are Mel Brooks and the aforementioned Chaplin. It was Wilder's stints in Brooks' comedies, after all, that had won him his auteur deal with 20th Century–Fox, on the condition that Wilder provide the same style of humor, which doesn't seem to be much of a problem. (He even employs many of Brooks' stock company, from Dom DeLuise as a hotheaded studio despot to monkey-faced Ronnie Graham as a nervous director.) Chaplin's influence can be detected in the film's nod to *City Lights* (1931), when Kane mistakes Wilder, in disguise, for Valentino, the same way that the blind Virginia Cherrill mistook Chaplin for her handsome, successful benefactor. Wilder had always aspired, in his films, for a combination of comedy and pathos, never quite managing to successfully blend the two. Here he comes as close as he ever did, even if, like a lot of the film, it's but nobly wonky.

Still, a lot of the picture lands. Its best comic asset is Wilder's ability to consistently award himself choice bits of comic business, most of which he makes good on, from nervously mumbling his words to ridiculously seducing a makeshift clothes dummy in public view. He's good to himself in all ways, never setting himself up for anything he can't handle, unlike in the more ambitious *Smarter Brother*.

As for the supporting players, except for Kane, Wilder asks them to play, well, Wilder; each has a go or two at Wilder's signature slow burn (in DeLuise's case, you stop counting), visibly showing the audience the creeping surge of blood pressure that converts a milquetoast to a madman. None can best the master, of course, so if Wilder, in the end, is not, as the poster puffily proclaims, *The World's Greatest Lover*, he is at least the world's angriest.

1978

As we inch our way to the climax of the decade, a distinct shift in audience takes place. The sons and daughters of '70s comic cinema's first audience, still called "War Babies" ("Baby Boomers" came later), begin to have their tastes and values, from rock'n'roll to recreational drugs, increasingly reflected in sanitized, mainstream form (*I Wanna Hold Your Hand*). While none of these films resonate at the box office the way that their role model *American Graffiti* (1973) had, the beginnings of a new era are visible.

A taste remains for nostalgic properties, but the successful ones start to boast hipper stars, like *Saturday Night Live*'s Chevy Chase. Stuff based on Broadway plays and parodies has gone flaccid, Change to "paralleling" the ubiquitous white remakes of soul hits then dominating the radio (James Taylor, Linda Ronstadt, etc.). Meanwhile, the Macho Man sensibility on display in downtown discos keeps Burt Reynolds in skin-tight jeans and finds a new, improbable comic champion in action star Clint Eastwood. An alternate male identity, formed by feminism, contrasts it in films featuring Alan Alda (*Same Time Next Year*) and a de-sexualized Warren Beatty (*Heaven Can Wait*).

Oh—and there are more comedy releases than any other year of the decade. Not incidental. America was ready to laugh again, to let loose, to surrender to base pleasures. Part of the return to the sensorial, along with club-hopping and recreational drugs.

Animal House

Plot: The eccentric members of a troublemaking college fraternity are expelled, prompting them to wreak havoc on the homecoming parade. **Director:** John Landis. **Script:** Harold Ramis, Douglas Kenney, Chris Miller. **Cast:** John Belushi, Peter Riegert, Tim

Matheson, Kevin Bacon, John Vernon, Donald Sutherland, Verna Bloom, Tom Hulce. Universal. 109 minutes.

A siege took place in the summer of '78: The first wave of the Baby Boomers took over America's movie theaters.

The theaters should have seen it coming. After all, a leading Boomer mouthpiece, *National Lampoon* magazine, an offshoot of the *Harvard Lampoon*, had been providing dark, hip takes on politics and popular culture since the late '60s, eventually becoming a newsstand staple. In time, it had spawned a popular syndicated *Radio Hour* and a number of bestselling comedy albums, voiced by a ragtag bunch of improvisers from Chicago who'd be handpicked for the original casts of *Saturday Night Live* (1977–present-day) and its Canadian-produced equivalent *SCTV* (1976–83). Now, *National Lampoon* had secured money for a movie, a behavior-gag hybrid based on their bestselling parody of college yearbooks circa 1962.

Unlike the era's earlier *American Graffiti* (1973), the film would be devoid of anything genuinely elegiac. Like its counterpart, however, it would offer plenty of hijinks, if of the more manufactured variety, owing to the Marx Brothers (including a trial scene aspiring to *Duck Soup*, 1933) and even more to the Marxes' dimwitted cousins, the Three Stooges. Plus, more originally, plenty of canonization of the recreational excess marking the best part of the college-going experience.

Up until this point, American film comedy, predicated on examining and

The smash success of *Animal House* (Universal, 1978) in the summer of '78, starring John Belushi, marked a seismic shift in the audience for movie comedies (Universal Pictures/Photofest).

championing the underdog, had largely cast Jews as its outsiders. Grodin, Segal, Allen *et al.* rebelled, complained or floundered against the impenetrable wall that was WASP society. Now, in *Animal House*, it was WASP vs. WASP; marginalized white kids (the wimps, the blimps, the slobs, the nerds) took over the role of the doormat, as Delta House, the worst frat outfit on the Faber College campus, set out to repeatedly get one up on their oppressive betters and eventually, the entire school.

Broad as it is, *Animal House* came from a real place: the writers, *Lampoon* staffers plus a few ringers, created Delta House from an amalgam of notorious fraternities across their collective experience. Together, they romanticized-exaggerated each of the houses' basest rituals: Hoovering cafeteria food, consuming copious amounts of grain alcohol, and playing Peeping Tom. Then they invented new ones like the famous toga party, replicated to this day whenever 18-to-25s gather.

As for plot, there's but a soupcon: Our oppressed boys are browbeaten to an ultimate state of rebellion until they "fight for their right to party" by explosively sabotaging the climactic homecoming celebrations. Cue the film's only true parallel to *American Graffiti*: a postscript on the post-film fates of the characters.

Animal House's primary aim is the celebration of anarchy, something it pulls off with fittingly crude panache. The gags are piled so high, it's not hard to envision the first choice for director: Richard Lester. (The ending in particular owes a lot to him.) Instead, the assignment went to the largely unknown John Landis, of the cult hit *The Kentucky Fried Movie* (1977). Landis demonstrates a crisp way with a joke and a passing interest in anything else (a bit of romance, that's it). In this, Landis proved a genuine throwback to the pre–screwball comedy helmers, studio hacks who knew how to get a laugh and get out.

It's Carter-era comedy, the president of the college being, like the Delta boys, a quirky, decent-hearted type who, despite his best efforts, laughably messes up on a constant basis. Delta House, White House—what's the diff? John Belushi, the slob-deity in this film whose star was already on the rise via *Saturday Night Live* (1975–present-day), famously stated that the message of his generation's comedy was that it was okay to mess up. Unfortunately, that entailed a right to make half-hearted movies. And so *Animal House*, instead of spawning a new era of equally high-spirited comedies, gave license to films with thin premises, cursory plots, crude gags and infantile sexuality, all presented without the same energy or sense of purpose. Hence *Porky's* (1981), *Police Academy* (1984) and too many films based on the catchphrase-spewing *SNL* persona *du jour*.

In *Paradise Lost*, as *Animal House*'s lone hipster teacher (Donald Sutherland) reminds us, Milton maintains that "it's more fun to be bad than good." And America in '78 wanted to be bad again, at least in an innocent way. The political thing was over; America just wanted to party. Good, goofy fun was the new protest. Bring on the village idiocy of Steve Martin, the benign bacchanalia of the Muppets, and the Stoogey self-destruction of beer-swilling, girl-ogling Belushi.

There are brownie points for you if you can name the trio of ill-fated sitcoms based on the movie.

The Bad News Bears Go to Japan

Plot: A small-time hustler brings a team of Little League misfits, the Bad News Bears, to Japan as part of his scheme to pay off his gambling debts. **Director:** John Berry. **Script:** Bill Lancaster. **Cast:** Tony Curtis, Jackie Earle Haley. Paramount. 91 minutes.

In 1978, the crass, combative New York Yankees, soon to be nicknamed the Bronx Zoo in a tell-all book by reliever Sparky Lyle, rose above their headline-hogging infighting to improbably repeat as World Series champions. The team that most resembled them on-screen, however, the equally colorful-quarrelsome Bad News Bears, definitively reaffirmed what their first sequel, *The Bad News Bears in Breaking Training* (1977), had more or less asserted: that they were incapable of recapturing the magic of their initial success.

Like many a fallen ballclub, the Bears had exhausted such team-binding, audience-winning tenets as energy, chemistry and showmanship. What was once a game-clinching clutch hit was now a dying—nay, a dead—quail.

Even a major change of setting couldn't adjust their luck. The team, under the unscrupulous tutelage of a fallen Hollywood sharpie (played by Tony Curtis, a fallen Hollywood sharpie), is brought to Japan to take on a team of Asian counterparts in a contest sure to settle their new figurehead's Mount Fuji–sized gambling tab. But it is we, the audience, who are conned—twice. Not only are we treated to not much of the Bears—well, what's left of them, with half the original cast gone or replaced and the rest maturing to near unrecognizability—we barely get Japan, the film giving equally short shrift to its second agenda as a big-screen travelogue.

Most of the picture is taken up by Curtis, by now balding (this was just before his mile-high toupees) and sporting a drinker's nose well-suited to his Bronx accent. Despite the odd comic success throughout his career, nobody would categorize him as the caliber of comedy star who could carry a picture. Curtis dutifully schemes and pleads throughout but each action is a sour reminder of the imprint committed, back in 1976, by the perfectly cast Walter Matthau. Matthau, had he been coerced to coming back, might have done with this script what his drunken coach had done with the first edition of the Bears: make something out of nothing.

One return did happen: screenwriter Bill Lancaster, who had penned the original. Here, though, Lancaster disregards his refreshing sociological instinct in favor of Hollywood-friendly (i.e., overfamiliar) narrative, giving us the staid, the sentimental and even—the film's least forgivable offense—the soppy: an improbable romance between tough kid Jackie Earle Haley and a teenage geisha.

With each eye-rolling convention, we are made aware of just how much the charm, spark and integrity of the first film was the brainchild of director Michael Ritchie (who simply produces here, handing the directorial reins over to John Berry, one of Hollywood's least distinguished directors despite a surprisingly long list of credits).

The Bears contend all right—for worst comedy of the decade.

The Cheap Detective

Plot: Parody of Humphrey Bogart films in which legendary detective Sam Spade deals with a number of shady dames while trying to clear himself of his partner's murder. **Director:** Robert Moore. **Script:** Neil Simon. **Cast:** Peter Falk, Marsha Mason, Madeline Kahn, Eileen Brennan, Louise Fletcher, Stockard Channing, Dom DeLuise, Sid Caesar, Ann-Margret. Columbia. 98 minutes.

After the murder mystery spoof *Murder by Death* (1976) proved a sizable hit, writer Neil Simon, swayed, one supposes, by Peter Falk's easy impression of Bogart in that film, sat down and returned yet again to his parodic roots, back when he was grinding out weekly send-ups of classic and contemporary films for Sid Caesar & Co. on *Your Shows of Shows* (1950–54). This time, Simon comedically mixed-and-matched a trio of Bogart's best-known pictures: *The Maltese Falcon* (1941), *Casablanca* (1942) and *The Big Sleep* (1946).

The result is a cut above the forced, overrated *Murder by Death* but, for all of its merits, suffers from the same anti-comedy deficiencies: overinflated belief in the quality of the material, staid episodes, a hit-and-miss cast.

The legitimate comic talents—Madeline Kahn, Dom DeLuise, the aforementioned Caesar—have an untroubled time of it, while the newbies to the form—Louise Fletcher, John Houseman, Marsha Mason (of course!)—struggle to find the necessary lightness to make their lines work. It's clowns vs. actors, with the baggy pants beating the leotards. (It should be said that the cast features a number of surprises: Fernando Lamas, caricaturing Paul Henreid, and Ann-Margret, sending up her sultry image.)

Falk, who deftly compromises both traditions, is the anchor, blowing cigarette smoke, cracking wise and warding off dames—a lot of dames; the picture even stops to indulge in bedroom farce. This intrusion of writer Simon and director Robert Moore's stagier instincts, evident here and a bit elsewhere, bogs the production down. Suddenly, we're not throwing things away as we should; we're attempting to create moments.

Other graduates of the Sid Caesar school of comedy writing—Mel Brooks, Larry Gelbart and, though he was growing decidedly out of it, Woody Allen—were doing this kind of thing a lot better, as was TV's *The Carol Burnett Show* (1967–78). Still, the picture was a hit, proof positive that the '70s premium on parody had not yet peaked.

The End

Plot: A depressed real estate salesman, looking to end it all, regains the spark to live after a stint in an asylum. **Director:** Burt Reynolds. **Script:** Jerry Belson. **Cast:** Burt Reynolds, Sally Field, Dom DeLuise, David Steinberg, Joanne Woodward, Myrna Loy, Kristy McNichol, Pat O'Brien, Robby Benson. United Artists. 100 minutes.

In her famous poem "Resume," Dorothy Parker, after having audited the flaws inherent in every possible means of suicide, concluded, "[Y]ou might as well live." Extending Parker's poem to screenplay form, veteran comedy writer Jerry Belson, whose career extended from *The Dick Van Dyke Show* (1961–66) to *Tracey Takes On* (1996–99), concocted a dark slapstick farce equal parts Woody Allen, Mel Brooks and TV sitcom.

It was Allen who had legitimized death as a genuine comic subject, one, like sex, taboo until the mid–60s. With the exception of the odd joke, the big studios remained wary of the subject (there'd be no *Weekend at Bernie's* until 1989). It took the clout of Burt Reynolds, coming off of the mega-hit *Smokey and the Bandit* (1977), to push the project through—a concession made only after he agreed to do another macho man exercise, *Hooper* (1978).

But Reynolds saw a lot in Belson's script: foremost, an opportunity to eschew type and extend his range. As the unscrupulous real estate salesman and failed family man Sonny Lawson, determined to terminate his own life after being diagnosed with a rare blood disease, Reynolds cries, rages and pleads—the whole Kübler-Ross gamut. Further, he gets to indulge in a different kind of physicality, not bar fights and sex scenes but pratfalls and double takes. And he enjoys long takes with other actors, mostly Dom DeLuise and then gal-pal Sally Field, instead of zippy filler fit to accommodate a car chase.

So enamored was he with these possibilities that he insisted on directing too, so that he could keep himself in frame long enough to show the world what he could do. He gets a little fancy with the shots here and there, as Sonny traipses from loved one to loved one semi–saying goodbye until a botched episode with pills lands our lead in the loony bin. But for the most part, he affords the other performers the same lengthy leash he affords himself.

And it pays off. While some (Joanne Woodward as Sonny's ex-wife, old hands Pat O'Brien and Myrna Loy as his aging parents, the hopeless Robby Benson as a gawky young priest) fail to distinguish themselves, others, like Reynolds, rise to new heights. The ubiquitous DeLuise, as a showy schizophrenic who becomes the institutionalized Sonny's friend-in-suicide, hams it up shamelessly—bringing the film to new manic heights. The third act is almost all DeLuise and Reynolds playing two-man comedy team; a kind of angst-age Laurel and Hardy. While the gags aren't bad, the synergy and bonhomie between them are positively palpable. Up to this point, we're classifying what we're seeing as cute; by the time these two are done, we're pronouncing it hysterical. (They went on to work together much too often and never as successfully.)

The rest of the film is too Jewish for the mostly WASPy cast, suffers from mawkish, TV-influenced sentimentality (teenaged Kristy McNichol is even there as Sonny's estranged daughter), and has nothing particularly deep to say about its primary subject. Still, when Sonny's girlfriend Field (a token appearance) tells him, "You're not funny," Sonny-Reynolds insists, "Yes, I am!"

He's mostly right.

Every Which Way But Loose

Plot: A brawlin' trucker, along with his pet orangutan, roam the American West in search of the country singer for whom the former has fallen. **Director:** Clint Eastwood. **Script:** Jeremy Joe Kronsberg. **Cast:** Clint Eastwood, Sondra Locke, Ruth Gordon, Geoffrey Lewis. Warner Bros. 114 minutes.

We're here again, in the *Smokey and the Bandit* (1977)–spawned land of male-oriented blue-collar bucolic comedies built around car chases and bar fights. Good ol' boy hero, chummy best bud, come-and-go love interest, cross-state journey.

Now, for the variations: Clint Eastwood instead of Burt Reynolds, Sondra Locke instead of Sally Field, an orangutan instead of … uhhh … how 'bout this: an orangutan instead of the whiskery "Gabby" Hayes, with Eastwood playing the classic Western hero in a white T-shirt instead of a white hat?

The *Smokey*-style truck is here—Eastwood is a trucker-fighter rolling through the San Fernando Valley, with a thing for apes and female runaways—along with the unabashed endorsement of heartland values (country music, beer drinkin', bare-knuckle brawlin') and right-wing fundamentalism. It's a redneck fantasia wherein we can reclaim our dangerous, deviant world through traditional values and grassroots folkways. Reynolds broke this ground but playfully; Eastwood stomps on it like it's a hapless biker's head. Makes sense. It's the same shtick that he'd endorsed as *Dirty Harry* (1971), the Smith & Wesson Superman taking out the worst members of the Manson-influenced counterculture, only transposed to comedy.

Too bad Clint has little clue as to how to set up and pay off a gag. But he does know how to stage and shoot a fight scene. Half, literally, the battle.

The only thing you might find amusing in this derivative, disjointed dust-up is Eastwood career appendage Sondra Locke. She wins hands down for the least talented or otherwise interesting presence in '70s cinema, a limited actress, a marginal sex symbol, and a terrible singer.

She's like the film: Every which way but good.

FM

Plot: The integrity of an FM radio station in L.A. is threatened by corporate involvement. **Director:** John A. Alonzo. **Script:** Ezra Sacks. **Cast:** Michael Brandon, Martin Mull, Cleavon Little, Cassie Yates, Eileen Brennan, Alex Karras. Universal. 104 minutes.

In 1967, the Beatles released *Sgt. Pepper's Lonely Hearts Club Band,* rock'n'roll's first concept album—which, in 1978, spawned one of the decade's great cinematic embarrassments. Back to the record: Its popularity marked rock's transition from dance music to a listening experience, the same leap jazz had made after World War II with the advent of bebop. But how was radio, pop music's store window, now going to get album-fixated audiences their fix, obsessed as the medium was with the three-minute single?

The answer was on an alternate frequency, FM. FM was an audio Wild West on which DJs could play cuts as long as Wagner operas if they so desired, make their own mixes if they dared, and otherwise operate outside the rigidity of their commercial counterpart. By the mid–70s, the cult of FM radio was beginning to go mainstream, with more and more listeners lured by its low-key, smoky-voiced on-air personalities introducing epic cuts from LPs new and obscure in voices at once conversational and conspiratorial. Relaxed as, in its way, it may have been, FM radio was making a bold statement: the reclamation of the music from corporate overlords.

Hence, *FM* the movie, and its tight band of ragtag radio staffers looking to save their much-loved little station, Los Angeles' QSKY, from the clutches of the avaricious suits. If that premise sounds, at least a bit, like TV's *WKRP in Cincinnati* (1978–82), it's because both TV and film that year were racing to the pole. (For the record, *FM* got there first, though *WKRP* was by far the bigger hit.) In '78, everybody wanted in on the rock phenomenon, especially the movies. Other releases included *American Hot Wax, The Buddy Holly Story* and *I Wanna Hold Your Hand*—not a great track record, but better when put up against the effort to cash in on rock's simplistic rival, disco: *Disco Fever, Thank God It's Friday* and, in 1979, *Disco Godfather.*

With the exceptions of *The Buddy Holly Story* and *I Wanna Hold Your Hand*, all of these films together constitute a late '70s cinematic subgenre: the movie that's an excuse for a soundtrack. While *FM* the film failed to win the box office, *FM* the album, a sort of late '70s Greatest Hits compilation, went platinum.

The movie, aspiring to be a seriocomic look at the up-and-down lives of FM DJs (then considered the coolest job an under–30 could have), is neither serio nor comic.

The situations, both the straight-faced and the funny, are thin, predictable and forced. There's no rescuing it with performance either. Director John Alonzo, the reputable cinematographer whose credits include *Chinatown* (1974), showed no facility for getting anything out of his low-rent cast. The closest the film comes to a resonant moment is when hipster comic Martin Mull—then on TV fronting the sequel to *Mary Hartman, Mary Hartman*, the mock talk show *Fernwood Tonight* (1977)—has a self-pitying breakdown on-air, a situation remedied by a comic conclusion. Like a lot of the film's big scenes, however, this denouement is seen but not heard, a wallpaper of pop usurping the dialogue—yet more proof that the soundtrack's the thing.

And for a film about rock'n'roll, where's the energy? Even its aspirations to the concert film genre are half-hearted: Linda Ronstadt and Jimmy Buffett—talented, yes, but not exactly Led Zeppelin and The Who. (Adding insult to injury, Tom Petty's in the film but he doesn't sing!)

The film's promotional tagline, as well as its Steely Dan–penned title song, announced, "*FM*—no static at all." Make that "*FM*—no pleasure at all."

Foul Play

Plot: An ode to Alfred Hitchcock in which a divorced librarian is embroiled in a plot to assassinate the Pope. **Script/Director:** Colin Higgins. **Cast:** Goldie Hawn, Chevy Chase, Burgess Meredith, Dudley Moore. Paramount. 116 minutes.

It may have been Mel Brooks, with the previous year's *High Anxiety* (1977), who was out to comedically salaam Alfred Hitchcock—but it was the younger Colin Higgins, late of penning *Silver Streak* (1976), who succeeded. After that film's unprecedented success, Higgins asked, naturally, to direct. With his initial effort, the generically titled *Foul Play*, he officially became the comic keeper of the Old Masters' legacy, plus an auteur (if a minor one) in his own right.

Foul Play, like *Silver Streak*, throws in everything but the kitchen sink; it's another film best classified as a thriller-comedy-romance. While both, as such, are deeply indebted to *North by Northwest* (1959), *Foul Play* cherry-picks from other items in the Hitchcock catalogue: its setting, from *Vertigo* (1958), its climax, from the 1956 version of *The Man Who Knew Too Much*, and its musical motifs from all of the above (Barry Manilow's operatic theme song aside).

Foul Play stars Goldie Hawn as a librarian who, after a chance encounter with a dying hitchhiker, is sent off on a MacGuffin-based chase, pairing her with an offbeat detective. Hawn, since her early days as a ditzy dancer on TV's *Laugh-In* (1967–73) and continuing throughout her mounting film career, had always proved a cross-generational darling: The old folks wanted to mother her while the young wanted to party with her. Still, Higgins likely remained unsure that an old-fashioned property with an establishment-approved star might keep away the younger generation. He took a flyer and cast TV's newest star, Chevy Chase, as the detective. He got lucky. Chase, in his first commercial release, looks uncomfortable but it works perfectly within the film's context; he's supposed to be the baffled establishmentarian in this suddenly off-kilter world, a reversal of his usual comic powers. It comes across as a bemused Zen demeanor: the straight man as the funny man. As such, Chase became a foot soldier in the new style of comic leading man that was developing: No longer the Jewish, middle-aged New York–based grump but the cooler, WASPy California-based Baby Boomer, sufficiently well-meaning and tolerably flawed. In *Foul Play*, it created a nice contrast to Hawn. His straight-faced egging and her wide-eyed incredulity make them a hipster Burns and Allen. (Such was the pairing's success that they reunited in another Old School comedy, *Seems Like Old Times*, 1980, penned by Neil Simon. Seems like a package deal.)

If that wasn't serendipitous enough, first-time director Higgins got even luckier with the casting of slumming British comic Dudley Moore, a last-minute replacement and an unknown in the U.S. (save to a savvy few). Moore was awarded a small turn parodying the macho-disco ethic of the times. He made so much of it, he quickly became a star in his own right. He replicated the shtick, with a few small variations, in succeeding comedies before insistently showing his shallow, sanctimonious side.

Higgins also awards fun set pieces to blowsy Rachel Roberts and to the always-game Burgess Meredith, who was then enjoying a career renaissance (*The Day of the Locust*, 1975, *Rocky*, 1976) as America's tough old bird. In so doing, Higgins replaced Hitchcock's

Along with Barbra Streisand, Goldie Hawn, pictured here in *Foul Play* (Paramount, 1978), became a feminist force in film comedy, often shaping her own vehicles (Paramount Pictures/ Photofest).

stodgy Britishness and playful wryness with a spirited, sunny feel and an oblique California wit. His direction never reaches surehandedness but it's competent, occasionally even buoyant.

Forgive the film its '70s sins—the climactic car chase–crash, the parody of the then-popular John Denver, that Barry Manilow song (though a sizable hit)—and it plays just as winningly today.

Heaven Can Wait

Plot: In this remake of *Here Comes Mr. Jordan* (1941), a reincarnated football player finds himself in the body of a murdered millionaire. **Director:** Warren Beatty, Buck Henry. **Script:** Warren Beatty, Elaine May, based on a play by Harry Segall. **Cast:** Warren Beatty, Julie Christie, James Mason, Charles Grodin, Dyan Cannon, Jack Warden, Vincent Gardenia. Paramount. 101 minutes.

After announcing herself as America's first bona fide female comic film auteur, Elaine May spent considerable time in the woods on the troubled *Mikey and Nicky* (1976), a fiasco she would repeatedly recut over the next 40 years. Her star having fallen with her exasperated underwriters, Paramount, May was rescued by one of the few forces with enough clout to restore it: long-time admirer Warren Beatty, then the top Hollywood ladies' man. After his self-pitying self-parody in *Shampoo* (1975), which, despite its exposition of the heart behind the hard-on, only affirmed his reputation as the Man Who Shagged Hollywood, Beatty was looking to palliate his playboy image. His next film, he had strategically decided, would be a kindly comedy—further, one in which he'd overcorrect his signature persona to the highest possible degree: He'd play an angel. Riding the last 1930s nostalgia wave, Beatty talked Paramount into remaking Columbia's *Here Comes Mr. Jordan* (1941). *Jordan* was a crowd-pleasing piece of whimsy wherein a simple-minded boxer, killed in a plane crash, returns to Earth in the body of a murdered millionaire. He exposes the killer, gets the girl and finds, ultimately, "Heaven on Earth." Pleasingly soft stuff—maybe too soft, Beatty figured, cocking a snook at the studio and calling on the acerbic May. In addition, another writerly talent cut from the same satirical cloth was brought into the fold—though curiously, as co-director: the edgily impish Buck Henry (who also appears as a celestial bureaucrat).

So buoyed, Beatty confidently undertook his first feature as a triple threat. The result, *Heaven Can Wait*, proved a sizable hit (despite a bad review by *The New Yorker*'s Penelope Gilliatt, who questioned its mid–70s relevance: "One can see why there were films about transmigration and reincarnation during the war, but not now"[44]). As for credit, let's spread the wealth: the film, discerningly dissected, is equal parts Beatty, May and Henry.

Beatty: as Joe Pendleton, the L.A. Rams quarterback cum unscrupulous industrialist, Beatty gets to display a variety of signature bents in particularly palatable form—foremost, his "overgrown innocent" persona, an on-screen image painstakingly self-gilded since the outset of his career; his notoriously leftist politics, with the kindly, clued-out Pendleton rewriting each moneygrubbing agenda put forth by his alternate

---

44. Penelope Gilliatt, ."The Current Cinema," *The New Yorker*, July 10, 1978

identity; his pretty-boy looks, enhanced by a quarterback's physique and his iconic coiffure, both of which he gets to keep despite the switch of bodies. May: primarily, the nervous, chattery dynamic between Charles Grodin (star of her *Heartbreak Kid*, 1972) and Dyan Cannon, as the millionaire's scheming in-house murderers, emitting a distinctly Nichols-May vibe. There's also some darker stuff—the freshly deceased Joe being made witness to a series of on-the-job accidents while choosing his new body, for instance—that is no doubt attributable to her dark sensibilities. Henry: his welcome cameo and the careful if occasionally unsure co-direction. (It earned him a solo stint: the much broader and less successful *First Family*, 1980.)

To use a perfectly apt football analogy, as dumb jock Joe is prone to do in shareholders' meetings: It's a winning team. That said, on its roster are a number of contributors who try a little too hard, both in terms of ingratiating the film to an audience and, again, in the mission to puritanically reframe the Beatty image. The former: old hand William Fraker's insistently lambent cinematography, which is nothing short of cloying, and, same criticism, Dave Grusin's squeaky, minor-key score. The latter: the purposeful desexing of literally all of the on-screen women (even the football game is devoid of cheerleaders). Poor, perpetually pining Julie Christie, as the people's advocate responsible for Joe the Capitalist's political conversion (also, of course, the love interest), finds herself fitted with tweed suits, offensively sensible shoes and, worse, Julie Andrews' priggishly pious tongue. Dyan Cannon fares a bit better—they cut her loose, a bit—but again, she is carefully corseted in button-down browns and Bea Arthur–caliber loungewear.

Given, then, its genre, its star and its complete lack of sex appeal, what to draw the male demographic? The football, naturally, with Joe deciding, despite his ill-suited new identity, to resume his old job as Rams quarterback. The NFL, at the time, had hit its first sustained peak, thanks to the emergence of a handful of perpetual Super Bowl contenders—the Cowboys, the Steelers, the Raiders—who were helping, along with impressionists both professional and amateur, to make mealy-mouthed Howard Cosell a household name. While, in the end, estrogen triumphs on-screen over testosterone, its addition indeed helped to engineer cross-gender appeal. Throwback romcoms shot with diffused light do not earn $100 million on the female ticket alone.

In the year of the shock-to-the-system that was *The Deer Hunter* (1978), *Heaven Can Wait* proved the counterweight (counter *Wait*?), the lighthearted yin to the jungle-dark yang. It's fluff of the first order, as self-satisfyingly insubstantial as it comes. Still, one might pry for a smidgeon of subtext: Was the administrative hash responsible for Joe's out-of-body experience supposed to reflect the incompetency of the Carter Administration?

Hooper

Plot: A look at the life of Hollywood's stunt community. **Director:** Hal Needham, **Script:** Thomas Rickman, Bill Kerby. **Cast:** Burt Reynolds, Jan-Michael Vincent, Brian Keith, Sally Field, Robert Klein. Warner Bros. 99 minutes.

The surprise success of *Smokey and the Bandit* (1977) made Burt Reynolds the #1 box office attraction and Hal Needham Hollywood's hottest director not named George

Lucas. A second pairing, no matter how thin, ill-conceived or personal, would be an easy sell. Given that rarest, most coveted of industry commodities, carte blanche, Needham indulged himself with a crony-filled pet project: a salute—well, more like a showcase—for Hollywood's stuntmen, the unsung heroes responsible for the rise of stars like Reynolds.

It fit. *Smokey* had affirmed that thanks to the rise of the physical-sexual ethos of disco culture, the testosterone-fueled backlash against peaking feminism, and the crippling oil crisis creating a countrywide nostalgia for the good ol' days of recreational gas-guzzling, America had reacquired its politically subverted taste for the world of the Village People's "Macho, Macho Man."

Like *Smokey*, *Hooper*—the name of the aging, eponymous stunt legend—posits the return of the traditional American male as a reincarnation of movie cowboys past. The only semblance of a plot is a clichéd Western dynamic: the old gunslinger (Hooper) threatened by the emergence of a talented young buck looking to sully his reputation. And even that isn't played out, the film opting instead for a *noblesse oblige* that, I guess, better represented the stuntman's sense of community.

Hooper has a notion, not a premise; dynamics, not relationships; stunts, not motivations. There's lots of overlapping dialogue for overlapping dialogue's sake (was it supposed to simulate a sense of reality or was this Needham, of all unworthy candidates, aspiring to Altman?) and jokes the Keystone Cops knew not to tip off. Put positively, it's a catalogue of well-worn classic stunts, strung together by Southern-friend chumminess and Fordian knockabout humor.

It's a shallow pool but it does have a deep end. Like many films of the time, *Hooper* ponders the value of monogamy vs. the single life, with Reynolds playing that question's grand inquisitor. While it spoke for many, still wary of falling into the staid life patterns of their parents but left empty by the new premium on after-hours carousing, it was obviously a dilemma close to Reynolds' heart. When he discusses it on-screen with fatherly co-star Brian Keith, the exchange has an unmistakably autobiographical feel.

Lord knows how Sally Field, here again in a Reynolds vehicle she must have felt beneath her, felt about this as his real-life gal pal (Burt aired their dirty laundry again that year in *The End*). Still, here she is, the return of the blue-jeaned trophy. Field later reported that when she started to get breaks as a legitimate actress, Reynolds balked. Of course he did. Why would one expect any less from *Smokey-Hooper*?

While these films certainly had their audience and broke up the New York–Los Angeles comic film tug of war by appealing to the middle and Southern states, it's easy to argue that it is largely their inclusion (intrusion?) that waters down the comic film catalogue of the '70s and prevents that decade's roster from being considered the, or at least one of the, greatest eras of the genre.

As that conclusion has yet to be reached, however, read on!

House Calls

Plot: A respected doctor and a socially conscious divorcee have a complicated romance. **Director:** Howard Zieff. **Script:** Alan Mandel, Charles Shyer, story by Julius J. Epstein and Max Shulman. **Cast:** Walter Matthau, Glenda Jackson, Art Carney, Richard Benjamin. Universal. 98 minutes.

Romcoms are, traditionally, predicated on contrast. In this one, it's class vs. brass: haughty, perfectly English Glenda Jackson taking on common, Jewish-American Walter Matthau.

The sexual revolution comedy, which had flourished between the late '60s and the mid–70s, was now petering out. *House Calls* was one of its happier Hail Marys. Narratively, it sticks to the tried and true: A product of the Greatest Generation finds himself immersed, this time by the premature death of his wife, in the younger, looser world. But *House Calls* is marked by an interesting late '70s distinction, a true sign of changing times: In this version, the squares win.

Matthau, a single surgeon, may be looking to belong to the youth set, but instead he settles for the moral, monogamous mores of old, a twist that hadn't been deemed acceptable in well over a dozen years (see *Cactus Flower*, 1969).

Indeed, the entire movie, while unique in certain ways, subscribes to a nostalgia for its pre–late '60s-early '70s brethren: the "meet-cute" (Matthau fixes Jackson's fractured jaw, only to be only to be mouthily attacked by her on television); the premium on verbal jousting, accelerated to a *His Girl Friday* (1940) fever pitch; the *I Was a Male War Bride* (1949) cross-dressing climax; Henry Mancini's over-honeyed (almost Mantovanian) score.

With its retro grace notes, *House Calls* serves as an early warning sign of the coming '80s, a notion boosted by the film's evident nostalgia, its new conservatism and its AIDS-aided valuation of the institution of wedded bliss. (Not to mention its insertion of the Beatles' "Something," previewing the usurpation of the art of film scoring at the hands of the Baby Boomer hit parade.)

Was director Howard Zieff, after his *Hearts of the West* (1975) failed to win big audiences, looking to go mainstream? The king of quirk, he's very inobtrusive here, trusting his seasoned cast. He deserves credit, though, as do the principals, for their collective engineering of the film's most memorable scene: a good-natured slapstick centerpiece wherein, again echoing earlier genre entries, Matthau and Jackson try to make love while each keeping a foot on the floor.

It's the best example of the film's habit of playing on Matthau's natural flirtatiousness and the comic conceit of him as a ladies' man, a capacity he first culled as the wily, leering lawyer in Billy Wilder's *The Fortune Cookie* (1966). He must have been flattered too to have a bevy of on-screen ladies refer to him throughout as handsome, cute and a catch. Still, he's not out to rewrite his image. The film is also proof positive that Matthau knew full well by this time that his offbeat physicality had become a major asset. He uses it for comic effect in various circumstances; often, it even elevates "nothing" sequences (like the time-filling love montage), converting them to comic highlights. Jackson, meanwhile, knows exactly how to play off of him, fully cognizant of when to pull in the reins and when to set things loose (they'd be paired again as a casting stunt in *Hopscotch*, 1980).

As always in Zieff's work, there's a strong and memorable supporting cast: Richard Benjamin plays the happy straight man (okay, again!) as Matthau's sounding board of a co-worker, while Art Carney, as the obliviously officious head of the hospital, dutifully perpetuates a late-career comeback.

Lest we seem to write it off as fluff, the film purports a second agenda as a polemic on social medicine. At this time in America, malpractice at the hands of self-serving doctors was becoming epidemic. By calling the medical profession on the carpet, albeit secondarily, *House Calls* takes its place as a lighter (much!) version of Paddy Chayefsky's smarter, darker *The Hospital* (1971). In addition, the film's political eye allowed Jackson, fast becoming a ministerial animal, to exercise a side of herself that would climax in an off-screen stint as a member of Parliament in the U.K.

House Calls is not one of the true comic gems of the era but as the genre goes, it's a lot less cloying than much of Neil Simon. It's California WASP with a soupcon of New York Jew, one of that comic school's last faint echoes before Woody Allen went on to enjoy a monopoly. It was enough to make it a sizable success, grossing over $29 million and scoring that questionable industry compliment, a TV series.

I Wanna Hold Your Hand

Plot: In 1964, a group of teenage misfits attempts to see the Beatles' first appearance on *The Ed Sullivan Show*. **Director:** Robert Zemeckis. **Script:** Robert Zemeckis, Bob Gale. **Cast:** Nancy Allen, Bobby Di Cicco, Mark McClure, Susan Kendall Newman. Universal. 98 minutes.

The surprise hit of 1978 was *The Buddy Holly Story*, a star-less, low-key bio of the pencil-necked country-rocker who co-pioneered a new, youthful style of music, until his life was tragically cut short in a plane crash—a cultural event romanticized in the early '70s through folkie Don McLean's elegiac mega-ballad "American Pie." That same year, Steven Spielberg, the rising young genius who had helped to revitalize the box office with the New Age epics *Jaws* (1975) and *Close Encounters of the Third Kind* (1977), tried his hand, for the first time, as executive producer for someone else: a Chicago-born eager-beaver fresh out of USC film school, Robert Zemeckis. Zemeckis, like his mentor, was a Baby Boomer, part of the vast postwar generation that had grown up as members of the leisure class, weaned on such innocuous conventions as television, fast food and kitschy, whiz-bang merchandise. The '60s had come along and politicized that generation. They had fought that fight, nobly and fiercely, and had partially won: Saigon had fallen and Nixon had been evicted from the White House.

But now, announced Zemeckis-Spielberg, it was time to get back to when life was fun, those uncomplicated, energetic and indulgent days when our hands held a baseball bat, not a protest sign, and we attended re-releases of *Pinocchio* (1940) and *Bambi* (1942), not films like *Medium Cool* (1969) and *The Sorrow and the Pity* (1969).

And so, the first salvo in cinema's prolonged adolescence movement was put into production: *I Wanna Hold Your Hand*, a manic teen comedy about a bunch of New Jersey misfits out to see the Beatles' first-ever North American appearance on that Sunday night, black-and-white TV staple, *The Ed Sullivan Show* (1948–71).

But as the success of *The Buddy Holly Story* had affirmed, '50s nostalgia, born of fellow Boomer George Lucas' *American Graffiti* (1973), was still in the throes of echoing. (*American Graffiti*, though set in '62, was clearly a look at the preceding decade.) As such, '60s nostalgia had to wait its turn, even the baby-step kind concentrating on the decade's earliest years. And so *I Wanna Hold Your Hand*, despite a modest two million dollar budget and the benefit of an all–Beatles soundtrack (a rarity, as Beatles songs were just beginning to be licensed for the movies), failed to make its pennies back. Had the film been released a decade later, when what Zemeckis and Spielberg were celebrating would be widespread, it would have likely been a hit.

That said, the film suffers from other commercial restrictions: a soft cast (Nancy Allen, who had co-starred in the horror hit *Carrie*, 1976, was the only semi-name), and mostly female, creating the false impression that *I Wanna Hold Your Hand* was a chick flick. Hardly. This is a high-octane teenage bedroom farce, spiritedly cross-cutting a quartet of wild goose chases in hotel rooms, elevators and back alleys, as the kids scheme and scheme again to personally encounter their mop-topped idols at the New York City hotel in which the band's. Each scenario, cleverly engineered, is a cog in a Rube Goldberg-ian narrative machine. This kind of precariously mechanized mania became a Zemeckis specialty: Within a few years, he would perfect perfected it with the back-to-back mega-hits *Romancing the Stone* (1984) and *Back to the Future* (1985).

While *American Graffiti* had scored with many of the same elements, no such narrative overlord was at work; instead, its teenage hijinks were enveloped in an "end of days" pall. (The same later with *Holly*.) But *I Wanna Hold Your Hand* was something new. This was not a long sigh, emitting a melancholy, "Ah! Those were the days." It was, more innocently, a bold, happy scream; a generational war cry, in effect, chanting "*Let's keep the spirit we had then alive today!*" So, while the film accomplishes what it sets out to do—capture the unbridled brio of the early Beatles years—it is also clearly offering a new spiritual-cultural template for everyday existence: a break with post–60s cynicism and its aftermath, a funereal feel, in exchange for a new kind of guiding hipness, innocence. Cue the Muppets, with their no-consequence violence, cue Steve Martin, the cool rube, cue Ronald Reagan, more icon than authority.

Further, *I Wanna Hold Your Hand* offered audiences (the few that attended) something else that was new: the first full glimpse of a comic archetype that would rise to full prominence in the '80s: the nerd. Undersized, bespectacled, physically awkward, obsessed with trivial pastimes and overprized junk culture memorabilia. Here, played with great comic aplomb by Eddie Deezen (whose resulting typecasting would land him in a much bigger nostalgic hit that same year, *Grease*) as a self-righteous, self-proclaimed "Beatles genius," we see what we had once seen, in part, from the fallen Jerry Lewis—but not as putz or schlemiel; rather, as an able assistant or outright hero, suffering the same indignities of comic characters past (bullies, cops, unrequited love) but surviving, thriving even, by holding fast to himself. In time, this archetype's on-screen fortunes would rise and endure, through films like *Revenge of the Nerds* (1984) and TV series such as *The Big Bang Theory* (2007–19).

Spielberg's influence is on the film too—not simply his sharing in the Baby Boomer ethos but in its cheeky representation of the Beatles themselves. We see the Fab Four only in bits and pieces—pairs of Beatle boots here, backs of shaggy-haired heads there—a convention borrowed from the effectively piecemeal representation of the shark in *Jaws* (1975), itself possibly borrowed from Howard Zieff's *Slither* (1973).

Perhaps the film's most telling scene is the conversion of the aforementioned Allen from old-fashioned, marriage-fixated good girl to all-out Beatles aficionado when she surrenders her engagement ring in favor of joining her cohorts in the balcony of the Ed Sullivan studio. Therein the film's ultimate pronouncement: the value of teenage spirit above all life conventions, a form of restorative hedonism that paperback sociologists had begun to call "the Me generation," which was being exercised on dance floors across North America to the simple-minded beat of disco music and, more dangerously, being consumed via vials, capsules and lines of uppers, downers and cocaine.

Movie Movie

Plot: A parody of Studio Era double features consisting of two one-hour film spoofs: a boxing melodrama and a splashy musical. **Director:** Stanley Donen. **Script:** Larry Gelbart, Sheldon Keller. **Cast:** George C. Scott, Barry Bostwick, Barbara Harris, Ann Reinking, Eli Wallach, Trish Van Devere, Red Buttons, Art Carney. Warner Bros. 106 minutes.

When the TV adaptation of Robert Altman's *M*A*S*H* hit the top five in the all-important Nielsen ratings in 1973 (it remained a Top Ten show for the remainder of its 11-year run), the man responsible for the conversion, showrunner Larry Gelbart, became scriptwriting's surest bet.

It wasn't true, of course: Gelbart's next series, *United States* (1980), flopped, and an ensuing film career was a hit-and-miss affair. Still, there were the big-screen successes *Oh, God!* (1977) and *Tootsie* (1982) and, in between, something that was successful critically but unsuccessful commercially: *Movie Movie* (written with long-time on-off collaborator Sheldon Keller).

For whatever reasons, the film's hook—a parody of Studio Era double features, the first hour a black-and-white boxing drama, the second a color musical—baffled the marketing team. "If we call it *Double Feature*," the script's original title, "people will expect a double feature!" fretted the suits. So, explained the eventual poster, "*Movie Movie* is one new movie. Twice the fun twice the action twice the entertainment." Further, it had an on-screen introduction in which one of the last living spokespeople for the Good Ol' Days, the much-loved George Burns, contextualized things with his raspy warmth. Uh, I know Americans are a literal people but … really?

If *Movie Movie* lost money, it's likely because, by 1978, both nostalgia for the 1930s and the practice of genre parody had been seriously homogenized. *Paper Moon* and *The Sting* (both 1973) were a long time ago, Gelbart had been at the parody game since his days as a staffer for TV's Sid Caesar, and *Animal House* (1978) had announced that it was the succeeding generation's turn to revel in days of yore, specifically, the '50s and '60s. (That ball was already rolling, with releases about Baby Boomer icons like *The Buddy Holly Story* and remakes of '50s classics like *Invasion of the Body Snatchers*).

A shame, as *Movie Movie* represents the apotheosis of both bents. Unlike Neil Simon's ventures into the territory (1976's *Murder by Death,* for example), it doesn't push or cloy; unlike Mel Brooks', it isn't scattergun or self-conscious. This is studied, hermetic work, a focused attempt to stay within the simple-minded, sentimental narratives, galloping pace and quotable moviespeak of the films on which the creative team grew up—a time when, as Burns explains in his brief, friendly introduction, "the boy always got the girl, crime never paid, and the only four-letter word in the movie house was 'Exit.'" (That intro is relegated to the Special Features ghetto on the DVD release due to widescreen incompatibility issues.)

The first film within the film is *Dynamite Hands,* a pastiche of classic boxing films like *The Champ* (1931), *Golden Boy* (1939), *City for Conquest* (1940) and *Body and Soul* (1947). Joey Popchik is a delivery boy for his Hungarian family's deli. When he accidentally knocks out the world's #2 heavyweight contender, Joey good-heartedly commits to a life in the ring to help his sister get an eye operation. In the end, of course, he's asked to take a dive, putting him at the crossroads of integrity, family and money.

After a brief coming attraction for the World War I actioner *Zero Hour* (*Movie Movie*'s original script had plans to include a newsreel and cartoon), we're treated to *Baxter's Beauties of 1933*, a colorful mini-musical borrowing from *42nd Street* (1933) and other show biz yarns of the Depression era. Broadway impresario Spats Baxter is given a month to live, due to a rare disease that mainly attacks show people (due to their finer nerves). He decides to put on one last show in hopes of leaving money for his estranged daughter. She ends up being the young ingenue who takes over from the drunken starlet on opening night, of course, allowing Baxter to die after the closing curtain with a smile on his face.

The similarities in story and sentiment between the two one-hour films are as much a pokey perspective on 1930s American cinema as anything else in the picture. Despite its other accuracies—the chiaroscuro, the art deco sets, the lightning-fast montages—the best comment of all is the dialogue. Gelbart and Keller appropriate Studio Era screenwriter-ese and mix metaphors, camp up clichés and play loose with logic. "Go ahead and shoot," a character tells a gangster, "but killin' me never solved nuthin'."

Hedging their bets against the violation of authenticity, Warners hired an old hand to helm: Stanley Donen, who, in his own musicals, had both employed and played with the tropes of vintage Hollywood narrative. (Donen's *Singin' in the Rain*, 1952, you can argue, was his first parody of the form.) Donen, along with Billy Wilder, Melvin Frank, Melville Shavelson and Blake Edwards, was a member of the old guard struggling to transition to post–Studio cinema. His attempts to hybridize the old and new, like *Lucky Lady* (1976), had proven disastrous. Here he was given the opportunity to return to his element, if with discernible cheek. He does, and rarely misses a step.

The cast, too, is totally in tune with the vibe. To the star, however, go the spoils: Powerhouse George C. Scott, as an aging fight man in the first film and the doomed kingmaker in the second, surprises and delights by never making a meal of anything. He lets the sensibility and the writing carry the day, fully aware that they're the film's main attractions.

Scott had co-champions there: Gelbart and Keller's screenplay was awarded the Writers Guild of America's Best Screenplay Award. But a twin bill whose first film was in tough-sell black-and-white and whose second was a musical when the only acceptable versions of the form were filmed rock concerts like *The Last Waltz* (1978) and post-modern takes like the coming *All That Jazz* (1979) was not going to register a Spats Baxter–style success.

The One and Only

Plot: An aspiring actor finds success as an eccentric wrestler. **Director:** Carl Reiner. **Script:** Steve Gordon. **Cast:** Henry Winkler, Kim Darby, Hervé Villechaize, Gene Saks. Paramount. 97 minutes.

"Ayyyyyy! Sit on it!"

One of the iconic catchphrases of the era, along with "Dy-no-mite!" and "De plane, boss! De plane!"

In 1973, a diminutive, dyslexic graduate of the Yale School of Drama auditioned for a part he had scant chance of getting. By adjusting his physicality and voice, he bested the competition (including Mickey Dolenz of *The Monkees*, 1966–68), earned himself a star on Hollywood's Walk of Fame, and saw his on-screen wardrobe appropriated by the Smithsonian.

Would that Henry Winkler's versatility had extended beyond the famous Fonz. Whether it was movies that were made-for-TV or the cinematic variety, Winkler never again succeeded in subverting his kindly, spindly nature as he had in *American Graffiti*'s (1973) TV cash-in, *Happy Days* (1974–84).

A shame, as now and again, he was afforded other larger-than-life parts. Case in point: *The One and Only*, a light pseudo-biography of 1950s wrestling showman Gorgeous George.

Winkler, in the film, is an irrepressible show-off, desperate for public attention. He jokes, he sings, he breaks into bad impressions. People are shocked, appalled and then, of course, strangely charmed. He marries his childhood sweetheart (the underrated Kim Darby, wasted yet again) and whisks her on a shoestring to New York City where he tries his luck as an actor. When a chance meeting (with *Fantasy Island*'s Hervé Villechaize, of "De plane!" fame) lands him in the wrestling ring, an unlikely legend is born.

Sounds a lot like Winkler's own story. This time, though, there was no triumphing against type. Winkler, throughout, remains a square peg in a Calcutta-sized hole. The part demands the ADD-energy of a Robin Williams (why didn't they get *that* TV star, then breaking in on *Mork and Mindy*, 1978–82?), who might have also had the build.

Yes, there are moments when the action slows and shtick gets exchanged for schmaltz, allowing Winkler to spend at least a few minutes in a zone in which he's much more comfortable. But then he's back trying to tackle something for which he's clearly overmatched.

This was Carl Reiner's next film after the mega-hit *Oh, God!* (1977) and was considered, rightly, a big letdown. It's not inspired work. Reiner directs as if he's still working in television; then again, writer Steve Gordon had come from there (having worked for Reiner on *The New Dick Van Dyke Show*, 1971–74)—as had, of course, Winkler.

The only thing that stands out is Gene Saks, the Broadway comedy veteran who, as a cranky wrestling promoter, is awarded the kind of choice one-liners you'd think they would have given the lead.

If you ever find yourself wrestling with the decision to watch this, sit on it!

Rabbit Test

Plot: Controversy develops when a night school teacher becomes the world's first pregnant man. **Director:** Joan Rivers. **Script:** Joan Rivers, Jay Redack. **Cast:** Billy Crystal, Roddy McDowall, Paul Lynde, Doris Roberts. Avco Embassy. 84 minutes.

After two decades of toiling in nightclubs, a homely housewife from Larchmont, New York, finally broke through as one of stand-up comedy's few female superstars. By the time her self-deprecating wit evolved into catty show biz insider patter, she'd be in line to take over from Johnny Carson on *The Tonight Show* (1954–present), America's premier late-night showcase. Before that, though, Joan Rivers (*née* Molinsky) vied for candidacy to be the film industry's next Mel Brooks-Woody Allen, writing and directing (but not appearing in) *Rabbit Test*.

The film's critical failure (as well as that of a follow-up, the obscure *A Girl Called Banana*, 1980) left a sizable hole in the fabric of American comic cinema. With feminism, by 1978, in full flower, the timing was perfect for a female comic auteur. *Rabbit Test*, then, was a golden opportunity for Rivers to provide what earlier in the decade, the talented but self-destructive Elaine May could not.

In *Rabbit Test*, Rivers strangely, perhaps detrimentally, attributes all of the burdens of her gender that had been such a part of her act—sexual attractiveness, separation from the mother figure, pregnancy—to a man. Billy Crystal, then an up-and-coming sitcom player (remember *Soap*, 1977–81?), is cast as the proverbial nice Jewish boy (whose last name is Carpenter!). He's smart, accomplished and perfectly passable looking—also naïve, anonymous and overdue for love.

He's the spinsterish Rivers, in other words, the careerist who didn't find love and family until middle age. When our hero finally stumbles upon affection, he becomes, with virtually no explanation, the world's first pregnant man.

It's a hook that, in smarter hands, could have offered a searing commentary on the male mentality, with, in the end, the hero graduating from a stereotypical understanding of the world of women to a sympathetic and pro-feminist one, *à la Tootsie* (1982). But Rivers was no political animal. Predictably, all you get are the kinds of one-liners that constituted her act—broad sex jokes, pokes at pop culture (circa 1978) and plenty of politically questionable ethnic humor—strung generously upon a clothesline of overly familiar plot conventions.

Was it foolish to expect more? Perhaps. But even Rivers' diehard fans found themselves disappointed, as this stand-up routine cum feature comedy came without the snap and spite of her personal appearances.

A self-made type, Rivers financed the film herself, an admirable gamble which, like her later stints on the fledgling Home Shopping Network and the red carpets of those film and TV award shows, paid surprising dividends. On a budget of under $2 million, *Rabbit Test* brought in $12 million. What it failed to bring was the timely, much-needed presence of American comic film's Ms.-ssiah.

Revenge of the Pink Panther

Plot: The bumbling Inspector Clouseau, believed to be dead, seeks revenge on his purported assassins. **Director:** Blake Edwards. **Script:** Frank Waldman, Ron Clark, Blake Edwards. **Cast:** Peter Sellers, Dyan Cannon, Herbert Lom, Burt Kwouk. United Artists. 98 minutes.

Its production history reads like Clouseau was responsible: an impossible assignment, plagued by unforeseen booby traps, exacerbated by physical misfortune. By the time spring was suggesting itself in 1978, United Artists found itself without a big summer release. Who, in a mere ten weeks, to write, direct and otherwise oversee the kind of production so anticipated, audiences would line up outside their favorite one- and two-screen theaters instead of attending the public pool or the sex-happy disco? Cue the twitchy Herbert Lom: "Oh no! You don't mean … Clouseau?!"

And so, though each was battling respective ailments and had grown so short with each other that they spoke largely through production assistants, Blake Edwards and

Peter Sellers hastily reunited. Money talks, especially with a funny French accent. An extremely broad one, it should be added, to go along with the uber-exaggerated everything else; for example, the iconic musical theme, now unabashedly disco-ized. (Elsewhere in the film, Henry Mancini even tries his hand at an original dance number, "Move 'Em Out." Suddenly, you long for his schmaltzy strings.) The role of Cato is blown up to Charlie Chan–Number One Son proportions (racism intact); the sight gags are now so overwrought, they suggest the hand of Rube Goldberg. What happened? Perhaps the new help: *Carol Burnett Show* (1967–78)—Mel Brooks foot soldier Ron Clark, who brought a sketch-like sensibility to the mix.

The bigger culprit, though, may well have been audience expectation. By now, Clouseau was the stuff of legend. He's even fawned over in the film: an entire crime syndicate is atwitter about him and the clerks in the costume shop where he purchases his disguises treat him like a deity. What to do then but to offer same old-same old on a bigger scale?

The only new elements are the inclusion of a subpar super car, referencing Edwards' *The Great Race* (1965), whose archetype-based sensibility a lot of this film shares, and Dyan Cannon. Cannon at least, as a peppy bad girl who leads Clouseau to the kingpin who wants him killed in an act of mob rivalry one-upmanship, adds a breath of fresh air, even if she and Sellers don't really connect. Then again, the hermetically harried Sellers connected with so few of the women with whom he was paired. On screen as in life, one supposes.

That said, and though on the whole Sellers looks tired, there are moments in which his happy participation is palatable: a Laurel and Hardy homage in which he and the now prominently billed Burt Kwouk (Cato, you fools) attempt to scale a building, only to crash into a bakery, and a bit in an oversized gangster get-up in which he pulls off the climactic bait-and-switch, triggering a Keystone Cops–style car chase topped by a fireworks explosion at a Hong Kong shipyard.

By production's end, Sellers began to fashion the next Clouseau scenario, one he hoped to produce without Edwards' participation. Instead, it was Edwards who would usurp Sellers, perpetuating the series well past the actor's death until, like Clouseau, the films would become known for their embarrassing ineptitude.

Same Time, Next Year

Plot: This adaptation of Bernard Slade's Broadway play chronicles a 25-year affair between a housewife and an accountant. **Director:** Robert Mulligan. **Script:** Bernard Slade, from his play. **Cast:** Ellen Burstyn, Alan Alda. Universal. 119 minutes.

Canadian Bernard Slade was another veteran of the Golden Age of Television whose facility for formulaic plots, offbeat archetypes and snappy dialogue was elevated by the Broadway stage. In 1975, this scriptwriter cum showrunner (*The Flying Nun*, 1967–70, *The Partridge Family*, 1970–74) came up with a narrative hook that middle-brow audiences who frequented the Great White Way swallowed like the Great White Shark then gracing movie screens in *Jaws* (1975): an extramarital affair conducted once a year over a 26-annum span. Again, it was an excuse to measure the effects of the socio-cultural changes America had undergone from the early '50s through to contemporary times,

Slade's George and Doris running the gamut of culturally influenced identities from uptight establishmentarians to post-hippie senior citizens.

At the time, the appetite for Neil Simon–esque stage properties was extremely high. Simon was still a regular on Broadway, a staple of the regional and amateur theater scenes, and a name-above-the-title presence at the movies. He had many outright imitators and other talents who were visibly influenced.

But Slade, at least with this, his first play, proved genuinely worthy of the Simon mantle. He had made a good living as a practitioner of the same TV-honed wit, and as such, had already been piggybacking on his hero (Slade's first TV series, the brief but well-remembered *Love on a Rooftop*, 1966–67, had been unapologetically based on Simon's 1964 play *Barefoot in the Park*).

But by the time *Same Time, Next Year* was available for adaptation into film, the "Simon thing" had hit the saturation point. Stage, film and TV audiences had had, like Slade's Doris ruining one of her and George's annual romantic respites by showing up eight months pregnant, a bellyful. A creative production team would have to be put behind the project that could make a splashy fashion statement out of what was fast becoming old-hat. Sadly, Slade's play was afforded the dutiful rather than the daring.

The original stage production had benefited from perfect casting: the nervy-stuffy Charles Grodin as the wimp-to-windbag George and the earthy, open Ellen Burstyn as the ditzy-to-demure Doris. Burstyn, as an Oscar winner, was rubberstamped for the film transference of her role; Grodin, whose film career, post–*Heartbreak Kid* (1972), had fallen to supporting parts, wasn't considered box office enough for the male lead. He was bumped by prime-time TV's top seriocomic star, *M*A*S*H*'s Alan Alda—an interesting but obtrusive substitution.

Alda, seemingly more flattered than inspired, tries hard but his trademark persona doesn't fit any of the personalities within his character's chronological evolution. The pugnacious piety by which he had converted his TV show from a high-flying service comedy to an increasingly sober look at the fragility of humanity undercuts the early George, another manifestation of the neurotic American male now becoming, thanks to a lot of Jack Lemmon and Woody Allen, a cliché. Worse, it instills a holier-than-thou inaccessibility in the latter version of the character. It's as if Alan was playing a sober-faced parody of his alternate public identity, that of vocal political advocate (albeit for leftist causes). As such, the play/film's high points—the death of George's son, and, later, his wife, the couple's climactic near–break-up—don't register as they should and are thus exposed for what they are: conventions incorporated simply to ensure that the audience is awarded its fair share of highs and lows.

Burstyn, who, mind you, had the advantage of familiarity with her role, transitions from suburban innocent to grandiloquent grandma with expert control. An innate understanding of each of her personas is vibrantly present, as well as an acute, stage-tested awareness of where, within her lines, the laughs are kept.

So, while it's not a fair fight, it still might have been enough to satisfy—but the film is doomed from the get-go by the heavy-handed sentimentality of the production team, headed by veteran director Robert Mulligan.

Paired, as he was in his early days, with the darker sensibilities of producer Alan J. Pakula (later a seminal '70s director in his own right), Mulligan was responsible for a series of confrontational dramas marked by integrity and spark. Much later in his career, along came the surprise smash *Summer of '42* (1971), the nostalgic tale of a romance of convenience between a gawky teenager and a mysterious war widow, set to music by the operatically wistful Michel Legrand. Mulligan, as a result, rebrands as American cinema's leading old-fashioned sentimentalist.

With the film's theme being the enduring nature of true love, Mulligan is out to reaffirm his latent label with *Same Time, Next Year*, going so far as to belittle snap with sap. Much is made of the *Summer of '42*–style milieu: a cozy seaside cottage framed by veteran cinematographer Robert Surtees, who is asked to go heavy on the gauze. Then there's the theme song ("The Last Time I Felt Like This"), commissioned by then king-queen of the Middle of the Road court, Alan and Marilyn Bergman, and co-sung by a pair of romantics old (Johnny Mathis) and new (Jane Olivor). In its defense, this mushy melody provides the film's biggest laughs, incongruously plastered over passage-of-time stills of Joe McCarthy, Nikita Khrushchev and Richard Nixon.

The film was just enough of a hit to prop up this kind of thing for the remainder of the decade. Same Thing, Next Year.

Up in Smoke

Plot: A pair of slacker-stoners elude the law and compete in a rock band contest. **Director:** Lou Adler. **Script:** Cheech Marin, Tommy Chong. **Cast:** Cheech Marin, Tommy Chong, Stacy Keach. Paramount. 86 minutes.

The hippie thing, dethroned by disco, was over—save for a pair of chummy, rambling holdouts who served as the feel-good generation's Laurel and Hardy: the alliterative Cheech and Chong.

The Latino Cheech and the Canadian Chong met on the comedy club scene in the late 1960s. By the early '70s, they were cult heroes, largely through a series of bestselling record albums which garnered much FM radio play. Their humor, largely drug-based, often reflected the style of roundabout conversations people had after sharing a joint. While this should have played as "you had to be there" humor, instead, it took on its own off-rhythm, red-eyed wit.

Given the cultural dividing line that was drug use, TV was never going to touch Cheech and Chong, no matter how many albums they sold. But the more morally relaxed medium of the movies would, even if cult hit might be the likeliest outcome. Instead, on a budget of just $4 million, *Up in Smoke* took in over ten times that amount, making its joint-rolling heroes, along with stand-up Steve Martin and *Saturday Night Live* (1975—present-day) fave John Belushi, the era's last comic film commodities.

California was the happy new center of American culture. Part of its "feel good" promise had always been, and was now more and more, drug use. Acid, post–Ken Kesey, had had its day; cocaine was the new rage but affordable only to the elite. Marijuana, though—low cost, small side effect, egalitarian—remained a constant. Good thing, too. Otherwise, Cheech and Chong's "stoner" humor might have already served as a time piece, like peace symbols and flower power. Instead, it appeased a wide, underserved demographic in the same manner that *Animal House* had validated the experiences of college-educated Baby Boomer nostalgists.

The wit and wisdom of Cheech and Chong served as America's last drug culture battle cry. (Cheech: "I am stoned." Chong: "So go with it!") Then the "Just Say No" Reagan era drove recreational drug use underground until its medicinally driven, state-by-state legalization.

In this set piece–happy road movie—as plotless as an agenda derailed by a dope session—Cheech and Chong not only indulge their audience, as they had on their records, verbally, but develop their own brand of slapstick, inhaling salami-sized doobies and snorting Kilimanjaros of Ajax. That said, the film's humor isn't rooted in anything new. The speeded-up car chases might remind you of the Keystone Cops, the crazy courtroom scene of the Marx Brothers.

It's only that it seems fresh when brought into the loosey-goosey drug fraternity. It's topped by a generous dollop of shit humor, made permissible by the new premium on crudeness that had been established by the success of *Blazing Saddles* (1974).

California may have been the promised land

While some doubted that cult comics Cheech (Cheech Marin, right) and Chong's (Tommy Chong) stoner humor would transfer to feature film, *Up in Smoke* (Paramount, 1978) was the first in a number of hits ("hits"—get it?) for the doped-up duo (Paramount Pictures/Photofest).

but this film, in its innocent way, was one of the first to show its other sides: Latino low-life (Cheech's East L.A.) and Caucasian elitism (Chong's Beverly Hills). More credit: its small concessions to politics (Cheech and Chong were never particularly political) featuring Tom Skerritt as a deranged Vietnam vet. Believe it or not, this is one of the first mainstream releases to look at the post-traumatic effect of that conflict, along with *Coming Home* (1978). By the '80s, examination of that phenomenon had become a veritable genre. And, while relegating women to just another party favor, the film scores extra political kudos for endorsing the LGBTQ movement at a time when taking its side was controversial and unpopular.

Most critics, cut from a moth-worn cloth, didn't get it. Gene Siskel, just then becoming a TV commodity, awarded it half a star out of four. "One of the most juvenile, poorly written, awkwardly directed pictures I have ever seen," wrote the conservative Siskel. "And my guess is that even if you saw it in a pleasantly altered state whether from grass, a banana daiquiri, Frango mint milkshake, or a Weight Watchers' Veal

Parmigiana frozen dinner, *Up in Smoke* would still be a real downer."[45] He later put it on his year-end list of the worst films of 1978.

Whatever, man.

Who Is Killing the Great Chefs of Europe?

Plot: A divorced couple is brought together again as sleuths as they attempt to finger the killer of Europe's top culinary talents. **Director:** Ted Kotcheff. **Script:** Peter Stone, from the novel *Someone Is Killing the Great Chefs of Europe* by Nan Lyons and Ivan Lyons. **Cast:** George Segal, Jacqueline Bisset, Robert Morley, Jean-Pierre Cassel. Warner Bros. 111 minutes.

I'd love to resist the temptation of the workaday critics of the time and spare you any cooking metaphors. Unfortunately, there's no getting around such analogies, because without argument, the ingredients here truly don't blend.

That said, making an ambitious property like this one work is an extremely tall task. It would be tall for a sophisticate, let alone a Philistine. After all, what we're looking at is a light-dark hybrid: an archetypical American screwball romcom at the heart of a dark-humored, European-style murder mystery.

While it's based on a novel, only one screenwriter can be responsible for such a thing: Peter Stone, the urbane wit and self-proclaimed puzzle aficionado whose screen credits go back to the loved-hated *Charade* (1963), a Hitchcock-influenced goose chase dignified by the verbal sparks between Cary Grant and Audrey Hepburn. *Chefs* aims to give us some of the same, set against a culinary backdrop. One by one, Agatha Christie–style, Europe's top cooks get murdered in the manner of their specialties. A brash American food magnate and an uppity dessert maven are at the center of things, re-piecing their broken marriage while playing amateur sleuths.

More than the cooking, it's the central couple, metaphorically, that best represents the dysfunctional schizophrenia of the film. George Segal is no Grant and Jacqueline Bisset no Hepburn. The film tries hard to glamorize them (all of that gauzy cinematography) and to put meat on their funny bones. Still, they never connect. Segal comes across as simply yakky and Bisset as hopelessly unyielding, even when the tension between them begins to soften and they end up frolicking together in a hotel bathtub. Just as disparate are the film's major modes, its brash, brutalist plot, and its dry European drollery.

The latter is largely carried by Robert Morley, the ubiquitous English character actor who, by 1978, had become the ranking icon of stuffy Old England. Here, as an influential gourmand, the sizable, windy Morley gets to indulge in unabashed self-parody, stuffing his face with delicacies of all sorts while spouting bon mots and put-downs as dry as overdone Beef Wellington. While Morley's relish is palpable, his exacerbated manner, and Stone's small, oblique wit, remain an acquired taste. As such, all of this blustery self-amusement is not enough to raise the film like a prize-winning souffle. (I've officially slipped into it, haven't I?)

Classify it, then, an ambitiously kooky "food film" whose elements never quite cohere.

---

45. Gene Siskel, "Cheech & Chong Are One Big Drag in Juvenile 'Up in Smoke,'" *Chicago Tribune*, Sept. 26, 1978.

1979

The closing of an era. "The last dance, last chance for love," as Donna Summer sang (spawning a flimsy, forgettable film of the same name). The Neil Simon-Mel Brooks thing was over thanks to increasingly tepid material; *The In-Laws* marked a return to angst-based comedy but had to be wrapped in action flick swaddling to be viable; Streisand had her final gasp as a major film comedienne with *The Main Event*; Altman had his last call as a comedy filmmaker (*A Perfect Couple*); Allen started a new phase as an experimental filmmaker (*Manhattan*); and the *Animal House*–like success of *The Jerk* clearly announced the appropriation of movie comedy by a WASPy, collegiate generation. They dominated the genre for the next few decades, until giving way to the slacker-hero era of film comedy's contemporary king, Judd Apatow.

But it's a nice send-off: an electric mix of the dry and small, the insistently commercial, the culturally questioning, the charmingly unappreciated, the slightly chancy, the "That is soooo over!," the goofily populist, the winningly offbeat.

And if you don't agree with me, then as 1979's newest film star would say, "Well, excuuuuuuse me!"

...And Justice for All

Plot: A volatile Baltimore defense attorney is coerced into defending his lifelong nemesis, a judge, on charges of assault and rape. **Director:** Norman Jewison. **Script:** Barry Levinson, Valerie Curtin. **Cast:** Al Pacino, Jack Warden, John Forsythe, Christine Lahti, Jeffrey Tambor, Lee Strasberg. Columbia. 119 minutes.

Comedy-drama, sometimes known as "dramedy," is hard to pull off. It's even harder to market.

The trick to the former is balance, the writer(s) having to provide each element in just the right proportions, at just the right times. *...And Justice for All*, one of the best screenplays of the decade (it was Oscar-nominated), does just that. It's a deft juggle of eccentric characterizations, smart dialogue and subtextual integrity, all in the service of a strong, intriguing plot: a volatile lawyer, having attacked an unscrupulous judge, is then blackmailed into defending him. The film promotes a pertinent, probing theme: the human cost of an askew judicial system. In addition, it provides lots of set pieces for its star, who gets to play logician, humanist, hysteric, romantic, speechmaker and, ultimately, martyr. The film ends with a bang, a triple-decker shit sandwich where legals and criminals alike go off the rails until our protagonist, in the ultimate thematic pronouncement, is forced to follow suit.

Which brings us to how to market these things: casting. By '79, people would pay to see Al Pacino in literally anything. He may have begun the decade as a virtual unknown but by its end, he had mesmerized audiences with his nervy quietude and streetfighter's volatility until his name was synonymous with quality. So respected, he could risk expansion into territory that seemed well out of his wheelhouse, a script as generous with absurdity as it was with integrity. Pacino pulls it off, of course, giving one of his all-time best performances as the increasingly frayed lawyer. He smartly settles for low-key, offhanded sincerity until he's encouraged to unleash his signature anger in the oft-quoted conclusion: "I'm out of order! *You're* out of order! This whole court is out of order!"

You'll have to forgive that his character's name is Arthur Kirkland, the least likely name ever for an Al Pacino character. It's an early tip-off that the film's humor is supposed to be in the Jewish-angst tradition. (The presence of Lee Strasberg, as Arthur's addled grandfather, affirms it.) It's a mark the film clearly misses—and yet, the laughs are still there.

The exemplary script was the brainchild of husband-and-wife team Barry Levinson and Valerie Curtin. While Curtin went on to explore acting, *...And Justice for All* proved a different kind of springboard for her partner. With this, Levinson graduated from gagman (Carol Burnett, Mel Brooks) to mature, visionary talent. The action is set (and shot) in his hometown, dysfunctionally diverse Baltimore. This set Levinson on a narrative path that went on to include his directorial debut, the boys-will-be-boys *Diner* (1982), and a string of other films devoted to the human marginalia of that marginalized metropolis.

As for the director of *...And Justice for All*, that was Norman Jewison, his first try at this kind of thing since *The Russians Are Coming! The Russians Are Coming!* (1966). Jewison rarely blows you away cinematically but he remains underrated as a director of actors. He's particularly good at two-person scenes featuring contrasting personalities (think Poitier-Steiger in *In the Heat of the Night,* 1967). They're all over this film. Though there's a nice, low-key playfulness to them, they're deceivingly spring-loaded.

Jewison had a strong supporting cast to work with too, from stalwarts like Jack Warden (who still tries too hard) and John Forsythe (Old School cool) to Christine Lahti (obliquely sexy) and the biggest surprise of all, Jeffrey Tambor in an operatic turn as Pacino's torn-to-pieces partner.

The film is so good, it survives a plethora of production violations: a sorry-assed centerpiece involving a helicopter joy ride (the lawyer at the hands of another, even crazier judge), technically lacking and anti-climactically concluded; a post-big-final-speech freeze-frame that's inexcusably awful; and the pre–Kenny G score and end song, "Something Going On," an embarrassment offering the thematic obviousness that the rest of the film mercifully eschews.

Being There

Plot: An abandoned simpleton, addicted to television, is elevated to the status of presidential confidante. **Director:** Hal Ashby. **Script:** Jerzy Kosinski, based on his novel. **Cast:** Peter Sellers, Shirley MacLaine, Melvyn Douglas, Jack Warden, Richard Dysart. United Artists. 130 minutes.

The behind-the-scenes story is legendary: Peter Sellers' decade-long hounding of source author Jerzy Kosinski, begging him for a chance to play the central part. Sellers even sent poor Kosinski correspondence written in the voice of the property's main character.

Why the diehard identification? No doubt because of the character's vessel-like quality. Sellers, as an impersonator, definitely saw himself that same way. Chance, aka Chauncey Gardiner, is a simpleton whose sole lifeline to the world has been television. Unleashed into society—in this case, Washington, D.C., with its uneasy mix of mean streets and high society—he functions but by, well, chance. His simple pronouncements, the product of a media-based infantilization of the intellect, are consistently mistaken for Old Man on the Mountain insights, reflecting America's infinite appetite for folk wisdom.

Of course, no man is a blank slate, Sellers' self-assessment to the contrary. Sellers biographies reveal a deeply scarring childhood (anchored on an emotionally incestuous relationship with his mother) resulting in irrepressible neurosis, volatile relationships and deep-set shame—not to mention a physical vulnerability which made this, tragically, his penultimate film (the forgettable *The Fiendish Plot of Dr. Fu Manchu* followed in 1980). His claim to fundamental invisibility was an act of wishful thinking, a core desire, like all actors, to perpetually transcend one's personality, to become, redeemingly, someone else.

That being the hard facts, the real Sellers, in his portrayal of the vacuous Chance, inevitably shines through—mostly, his inherently sad quality. It's in the vacant eyes, the stiff walk, the fine-as-baby-hair delivery. He can hold a scene with but a single expression—and does, repeatedly. The character, a symbol, should play thin. It doesn't, as Sellers brings a sustaining humanity to it

Sellers' performance was based, he admitted, on one of his comic idols: Stan Laurel (whose photo he carried with him for years). A lot of it, and a lot of the film, is steeped in an earlier, quieter mode of comic cinema: There are lots of wide shots, for example, emphasizing the character's isolation and boosting the audience's sympathy, *à la* Charlie Chaplin or Harry Langdon. (A lot of critics mistook this for lack of effort on director Hal Ashby's part, calling out the film for having a central vacuity.) It even has some nice silent film gags, including its famous ending (no spoiler this time; it's too good to ruin!). Many of these gags, predicated on an almost Slavic deadpan, play like those of French-Russian pantomimist-auteur Jacques Tati, though they're far less creative. The whole thing plays at a delicate, solemn level, unique for a comedy, particularly at a time when the genre was getting bigger and looser.

It's like Ashby's *Harold and Maude* (1971) with the broadness removed. Aiding its cause is Johnny Mandel's Satie-like score. The film also gets great comic mileage out of a funkified version of "Thus Spake Zarathustra."

The book/film's thematic target is television, suffering a tremendous volume of criticism at the time, as its post–Norman Lear content was transitioning to the T&A mentality. *Network* (1976) may have been the first big film to criticize that institution, but it presumed that TV could bring people to action. *Being There* provided a more accurate perspective: that TV pacified the masses into apathy, failing to reflect or prepare us for the demands of the real world.

And while the book was written in '70, it's hard, come '79, not to equate Chance, who rises to the status of pleasantly powerless god, with the good-hearted failure that was Jimmy Carter, especially when Chance comes to be looked upon as presidential material. The film also being about America's blind, instinctive attraction to simplicity in its informational and cultural content as well as in its leaders and celebrities, one can also see the coming of successors Ronald Reagan and, especially, George W. Bush.

But for all of its worth as a broadside, *Being There* is above all a droll, moving miniature. Try not to be touched by Chance's relationship with the dying father figure who takes him into Washington's moneyed inner circle, a homespun kingmaker played with naturalistic gruffness by veteran Melvyn Douglas. (How ironic is it that while Douglas was playing a dying man, it was Sellers who was literally dying?) Nor by that industrialist's flitty wife's genuine love for the oblivious Chance, in a gratifyingly giving performance by Shirley MacLaine.

The next time it's on its enemy, television, or available on Blu-ray or through streaming, be there.

Breaking Away

Plot: A group of teenage locals in small-town Indiana take on collegiate arrivistes in a ballyhooed bicycle race. **Director:** Peter Yates. **Script:** Steve Tesich. **Cast:** Dennis Christopher, Dennis Quaid, Daniel Stern, Jackie Earle Haley, Paul Dooley, Barbara Barrie. 20th Century–Fox. 101 minutes.

The film was lauded for its charming originality, but there's a lot that's borrowed in *Breaking Away*: the characters and vibe, both plucked from lightweight TV family drama (from such then-popular series as *Family,* 1976–81, and *Eight Is Enough,* 1977–81). Its humor, appropriated from TV sitcoms (shades of *Happy Days,* 1974–84, and the Bunkers). Then there was producer-director Peter Yates' pedigree in car racing, first called upon in the film by which he made his name, *Bullitt* (1968). Not to mention the fact that *Breaking Away* enjoyed a fixation with the underdog, the preferred Yatesian hero.

So the film, touted as fresh and novel upon its release, wasn't nearly the work it had fooled critics into hyperbolically huzzahing. Truth be told, it was the sociology they had gotten caught up in: first, the film's rare look at quotidian life in under-filmed Indiana (specifically, Bloomington), a quarry town that had fallen, like a lot of Middle America at that time, from industrial grace. Next, by the voice it gave to modern youth, focusing on the small sandwich generation between the children of the politically preoccupied '60s and those of the computer-fixated '80s.

Bereft of divisive causes, a meddling military to join or decry, or the prospect of an exciting new cultural plaything, these kids, the first to be raised on cartoons, fast food and minimum wage jobs, led an idle existence, a limbo state in which the most common colloquialism wasn't "What's happenin', man?" or "Grody to the max!" but, as the 19-year-old heroes in the film repeatedly ask themselves, "What the hell happens now?"

College is right out. In *Breaking Away*, the educated set is the enemy, an invading species taking over the town from the locals (called, after the quarrymen, "cutters"). Employment, when you can get it—car washes, car lots, etc.—is just as much of a dead end. How to rise above circumstance? Dream—as does the main character (played by Dennis Christopher, who, sadly, wouldn't resurface until Quentin Tarantino's *Django Unchained,* 2012). He attempts to duck circumstance by purporting to be a pro cyclist from Italy, a ruse that gets him in heartbreaking Dutch with a beauty from out of state.

The tension between these factions initiates the film's first plot point. It's a *Rocky*-inspired notion: that these rival subsectors take each other on in the Little 500, a bicycle race that passes for big stuff in Bloomington.

If the film is mostly '70s-style TV, it distinguishes itself by being just enough of an improvement; that much funnier, that much more colorful, that much more sincere. Screenwriter Steve Tesich, an immigrant, had attended the University of Indiana at Bloomington, where he had absorbed the local tensions as well as the legend of an Italian-influenced local boy who had made, aerodynamically, good. As a newcomer to the U.S., Tesich's heart naturally went out to the outsiders (ironically here, the townees), identifying with their upset sense of identity, their feeling of homelessness, their lives of shattered ideals.

The film also paved the way for the male coming-of-age films of the '80s, from *Diner* (1982) to *Stand by Me* (1986): a collection of stereotypes (usually the achy everyman, the itchy rebel, the compromised brain and the lovable nerd) living an amiably idle life until they're coerced into a grand circumstance destined to test their bond while promoting personal growth. Familiar stuff today; a new notion in '79.

Hence, the sleeper of the year—nay, the decade.

California Suite

Plot: A series of vignettes about characters staying in a West Coast luxury hotel. **Director:** Herbert Ross. **Script:** Neil Simon, based on his play. **Cast:** Alan Alda, Jane Fonda, Walter Matthau, Elaine May, Bill Cosby, Richard Pryor, Michael Caine, Maggie Smith. Columbia. 103 minutes.

By '79, quintessential New Yorker Neil Simon had been in Los Angeles for some time. Predictably, he was still having problems adjusting. Borrowing the sketch-triad form of his own *Plaza Suite*, he laid bare his take on the place and its people in *California Suite*. Together, the two plays-turned-films served as a comedic comparative study of the two warring cultures, a component of nearly every stand-up routine and sketch comedy show at the time.

"Nobody is happy in New York but they're alive," announces Simon, declaring the East winner over the West in the battle for cultural supremacy. As proof, he and the film's production designers offer a stultifyingly placid California. To wit: the David Hockney images used in the opening credits, along with Claude Bolling's low-key jazz score, and the opening-scene presence of soft-toned left-leaner Alan Alda; a conspiracy of offensively mellow '70s personalities. Like the contributions of Hockney-Bolling, everything—the lines, the look—is lightly parodic. This is not a jaundiced eye at work; it's a pastel one. Simon is out to gum, not bite. He's championing New York but has lost the electricity he's holding superior. Even the flat L.A. daylight, which should serve as an atmospheric social commentary, simply comes across as passably ugly. As for Simon's prime weapon, the rapid-fire badinage, that too is in a sorrily staid state. The best we get are clichés about New York vs. clichés about L.A.

Or was it simply that by this time, even Simon had grown tired of his shtick? He had played his talky game of two-handed love-hate so much by now, and had taken such critical flak for it, that here, he's grown painfully self-conscious. Between the one-liners now, the characters make one-liners about the fact that they're making one-liners. What purports, then, to be a parody of the modern West becomes a self-parody by the author himself.

Still, Simon does try to mix it up. With its various styles of comedy and its eclectic cast, the film is a litmus test of the range of Simon's writing: He's a forced melodramatist (a dour custody battle between Alda and Jane Fonda), a decent impersonator (of Noël Coward, in a forced but not unmoving battle of wits between Michael Caine and Maggie Smith), a garden variety bedroom farceur (a cheating-husband vaudeville between Walter Matthau and Elaine May) and a hopeless engineer of slapstick (a tennis match gone awry between Bill Cosby and Richard Pryor).

Let's dwell, as critics did at the time, on the last one. Simon adds a black cast, presumably to procure a new audience for his work. As expected, his banter, in their mouths, sounds incongruous, even his straight lines. So he balances it by taking the loose, hip, jive-ass comic sensibility of films like *Uptown Saturday Night* (1974) and sanitizes it—then he throws it to the wind with rhythmless slapstick. It painfully reminded critics of the broad comedy African Americans were restricted to in the early days of cinema. As such, the dramatic and socio-political boundaries pushed by Cosby and Pryor are here visibly, shockingly, devalued. Once again, it's a white man's world.

As for who comes out best, it's the Brits. Simon's dialogue is a tricky thing: It has to sound both like a joke and a real line. Some are good at this art, others have no predilection for it. (Fonda kills them with earnestness. Hadn't the casting director seen *Fun with Dick and Jane,* 1977?) But those from across the Pond, historically steeped in the art of verbal wit, have an unerring instinct for knowing what you bother to take seriously and what you don't. So when Caine and Smith, as a sham of a celebrity couple dealing with the implications of her Oscar nomination (ironically, Smith won one for this role), trade one-liners as expressions of subterranean tension, there's pith and pity perfectly placed.

With the adaptation, later in the year, of his autobiographical *Chapter Two* (1979), Simon's legacy within '70s American comic film was sealed. No other major voice's arc so represented the evolution of that catalogue, its journey from New York–based angst comedy to California-based tomfoolery.

Chapter Two

Plot: A widowed novelist struggles to make his second marriage work. **Director:** Robert Moore. **Script:** Neil Simon, from his play. **Cast:** James Caan, Marsha Mason, Joseph Bologna, Valerie Harper. Columbia. 124 minutes.

Neil Simon handled with care.

Too much care, unfortunately. After a commendably low-key beginning, this adaptation of Simon's sincerest work—a light-dark confessional about his troubled transition from widowhood to his second marriage—goes earnestly limp, undermining its dramatic intentions with myriad forms of overinflation (including that obtrusive score!). As a result, its premiums on introspection, confrontation and renewed romance are brought to a state of unapologetic cliché.

A shame. James Caan, as the spy-thriller novelist standing in for playwright Simon, and Marsha Mason, playing, as Simon's real-life second wife, herself, decidedly downplay the entire getting-to-know-you act. It's a welcome, and successful, change of stylistic expectation.

Then, though, there's Act Two: Caan's plunge into buyer's remorse, and worse,

Act Three: the obligatory happy ending, both as indulgently pat as they come (the latter especially, set to a wretched Marvin Hamlisch song called "I'm on Your Side"). In between, though, there's the exchange of heated speeches, the only extended scene from the Broadway show that Simon, still learning to make a film from a play (to his credit, this one's his closest effort yet), resists the urge to break up into cinematically savvy scenes.

Mason's tirade is, by Simon's own admission, a verbatim version of the one she gave him that inspired the play in the first place. Small wonder she demonstrates such facility with it (it helped her earn an Oscar nod). Its effectiveness is seriously lessened, however, by the fact that by this time, as a veteran of so many of her husband's productions, audiences had seen her cry and rail and cry and rail. Simon seems especially proud of putting her through it all again this time. Was it simply the quality of the "co-written" speech, one wonders, or did Simon consider it, in this time of films like *An Unmarried Woman* (1978) and *Norma Rae* (1979), a worthy contribution to cinematic feminism? Sorry, Neil. What you created is not a political romcom but something much more old-fashioned: a '70s version of the "women's weepy," a genre of over-the-top melodrama that studios used to produce in the '30s and '40s in which the heroine was put through episodes of operatic suffering aimed at bringing the female demographic to tears. You were a nostalgist, then, before you sat down to write *Brighton Beach Memoirs*.

Here to relieve the doom and gloom are comic macho man Joe Bologna and sitcom star Valerie Harper (both, by the way, looking proudly fit, as do Caan and Mason; the film doubles as a mid-life beauty pageant). They play the Caan-Mason sounding boards who experience a failed tryst of their own. The contrast allows us to appreciate just how lightly, at least through Act One, the marquee names treaded, Bologna and Harper offering the wait-for-laugh bombast more typical of a Simon product.

Though the picture was a surprise success, Caan went on to call it "a nothing."[46] Simon never appeared to think too much of it either, restricting his predisposition to its Broadway progenitor. Who can blame them, despite its opening 40 minutes? The film is yet another example of the generally short shrift the movies afforded Simon's stage work, more often than not coupling snap with sap.

Movie-wise it was Simon's last chapter of the decade. There'd be a little more of this cinematic ignominy to kick off the '80s, likely encouraging his professional shift from romcom practitioner to Depression-era nostalgist, a stage-to-screen transfer that fared, with a few staid exceptions, better.

The Frisco Kid

Plot: A Polish rabbi is forced to negotiate the Wild West with the reluctant assistance of a bank robber. **Director:** Robert Aldrich. **Script:** Michael Elias, Frank Shaw. **Cast:** Gene Wilder, Harrison Ford. Warner Bros. 119 minutes.

With its Western theme and the star presence of Gene Wilder, *The Frisco Kid* promised to be another *Blazing Saddles* (1974). The expectation was political irreverence,

---

46. Gene Siskel, "Movies: James Caan: Frustrated Star Talks Tough About His Career," *Chicago Tribune*, May 11, 1980.

cartoon-influenced slapstick and old-fashioned shtick. Instead, what critics and audiences received was a sweet-natured character study. The character in question: a Polish rabbi (Wilder) sent to head up a San Francisco synagogue. He's cut adrift in the Old West, however (a Gefilte fish out of water?) and, aided by a jaded young cowpoke (Harrison Ford, in one of his last supporting performances), must learn to preserve body and soul.

By '79, both the premium on Jewish wit and the subgenre of the comic Western had worn thin. The Mel Brooks-Neil Simon sensibility was critically and commercially tempering. (Woody Allen, their co-conspirator, was climbing high but by diversification.) In addition, the nostalgia movement responsible for the revival of venerable genres had moved on to science fiction with 1977's double-whammy of *Star Wars* and *Close Encounters of the Third Kind*. *Frisco Kid* still borrowed from both the Jewish comic tradition and the Western but in a low-key manner, the humor gentler, the action less bombastic. It was deeper too, delving producer Mace Neufeld's religious orientation.

The film's big question is the kind a wide-eyed scholar might ask a long-bearded elder: Is it possible for one to maintain traditional Jewish values in a classic American universe, with its emphasis on moneygrubbing and gun violence? The answer, rendered by Rabbi Wilder's struggles and triumph, is yes, but it's a rough ride, one requiring the odd, dramatic compromise (like when he shoots the villain in self-defense).

Further testament to the film's earnestness is its choice of director. Rather than someone with a sketch comedy pedigree or a background in funny TV commercials, Neufeld went with Robert Aldrich. No doubt a sure hand was wanted for the traditional Western elements—the horses, the guns, etc.—but the choice blatantly devalued the film's chancily genteel intentions. Not only that, it messed with its periodic concessions to broad comedy. Worse, the film is teeming with technical indifference, including amateurish editing and a corny score.

If the film isn't redeemed by intention, it is, in part, by Wilder's performance. It's a sensitive and sincere portrayal, with Wilder showing careful command of his patented bait-and-switch face, wherein wet-eyed innocence turns to unleashed mania.

Like the film, though, it went completely under the radar. Unlike the film, it was a fate undeserved.

Hot Stuff

Plot: Police detectives take over a pawnshop used as a fencing operation. **Director:** Dom DeLuise. **Script:** Michael Kane, Donald E. Westlake. **Cast:** Dom DeLuise, Suzanne Pleshette, Jerry Reed. Columbia. 91 minutes.

Throughout the '70s, there were a handful of comedians who were, well, just there. Everywhere. You'd see them on talk shows, variety shows, game shows and every other kind of show. They were TV comedy's foot soldiers, ready at a moment's notice for whatever assignment came along. Their weapons were a quirky, ingratiating personality, indefatigable energy, forgivably hokey gags and the ability, if pushed, to go manically off-script. They were much loved inside the industry, reasonably appreciated by the masses, and made a rat's nest of a living, often explaining their careers by claiming that they were just happy to be working.

High among their ranks was that high-strung cherub, Dom DeLuise. After breaking through in the '60s as a comic magician, he made a name for himself on *The Dean Martin Show* (1965–74) while being given the odd movie assignment. On the big screen, he occasionally rose above his station, exacerbating his signature qualities to better fit the format. In so doing, he managed to outright steal two films, *The Twelve Chairs* (1970) and *The End* (1978), by bringing a lunatic, animal quality to his roles that afforded both pictures, just shy of "meh," comic legitimacy.

In '79, the hunt for the next film comedy cash cow, after Woody Allen and Mel Brooks, was on. Every talent associated with either party, it seemed, was offered a star-writer-director deal. But DeLuise was a sizable (no pun intended, though he would certainly have made it) gamble. Sidekick-to-star is a big transition. Would there be enough there to sustain an hour and a half, let alone, as was the studio aspiration, a catalogue? The answer, predictably, was no. What the underwriters got was a series of TV-caliber sketches, played by a cast asking the audience to take or leave the jokes while appreciating how much of a good time the players were having—in other words, Dom DeLuise.

The only trace of originality in DeLuise's *Hot Stuff* is the plot. Master of the comic caper Donald E. Westlake was involved, no doubt accounting for the spark. After busting a pawnshop fencing stolen goods, a ragtag unit of undercover cops talk their sober-faced superior (DeLuise) into taking over the joint, in hopes of getting the unscrupulous trade on hidden camera. Having tallied umpteen arrests, they invite all and sundry to a party, where they plan to slap the cuffs on their clientele. By that time, though, they've pissed off the local mob, who show up and instigate a riot.

The rest depends on the characters and the jokes, both obstinately shortchanged. The dramatis personae is a parade of tired comic stereotypes—the town drunk, the Jewish mother, the fedora-wearing mobster, etc.—who come through the shop like an assembly line, each bringing but nervous energy and bits of business that don't build (though that dark, comic Gargantua, Pat McCormick, offers some choice ad-libs).

Worse, DeLuise doesn't even afford himself any opportunities to step into the spotlight and bring matters to a fever pitch, save for a small moment when he runs the emotional gamut after unwittingly sampling marijuana.

This is not hot stuff. It's tepid stuff.

The In-Laws

Plot: A dentist is coerced by his prospective in-law into a plot against a Central American dictator. **Director:** Arthur Hiller. **Script:** Andrew Bergman. **Cast:** Alan Arkin, Peter Falk, Richard Libertini. Warner Bros. 103 minutes.

With the authorship of *We're in the Money*, his 1971 book on Depression-era cinema, Andrew Bergman announced himself as the foremost critical-historical authority on 1930s movie comedy. Venturing into screenwriting (and later, directing), he borrowed many of that cinematic catalogue's best practices. Bergman's comedic talent was first exhibited as part of *Blazing Saddles*' (1974) vast writing team. After that, he was asked to pen a sequel to the equally successful *Freebie and the Bean* (1974). Instead, he came up with *The In-Laws*, a comic-action film maintaining the bully-buddy dynamic of *Freebie* while imbuing it with pretensions of Marx Brothers–influenced anarchy.

While elements of *The In-Laws* harken to the comedies of yore, the plot is firmly rooted in the real-life comedy that was '70s American foreign policy. Peter Falk is a rogue CIA man out to foil a Latin American syndicate plotting to collapse the Western economic. Alan Arkin is a family man–dentist forced to come along for the bullet-ridden ride. Can they wrangle their way out of jam after jam to see their kids get married? The film was a parodic play on America's most dysfunctional political talent, which, by '79, had wreaked havoc throughout Central and South America.

While *The In-Laws* was undoubtedly influenced by the Marx Brothers, it owes just as much to that tandem's true heir, Mel Brooks—in particular, Brooks' breakthrough film *The Producers* (1967). The resemblance is uncanny: Falk-Arkin's first meeting with a crazed Latino General (a lampoon of '70s dictators from Pinochet to Amin), echoing the Mostel-Wilder tête-à-tête with demented director Roger Debris; a funny set piece in a hotel lobby, where a nervous Arkin tries to bolt from impending danger, only to be tackled, repeatedly, by Falk, echoing the passive-aggressive Mostel-Wilder father-son dynamic; the climactic scene before a firing squad, wherein Falk comically begs for the sparing of his friend's life, echoing Wilder's climactic courtroom plea. We're back to late '60s-early '70s–style comedy: Circumstance is testing the limits of the human temperament, bringing ordinary, hard-working white-collar family types (Wilder-Arkin) to the

Throughout the 1970s, the anarchic spirit of the anti-establishmentarian Marx Brothers continued to wield influence over movie comedy, including *The In-Laws*. The Marxes' own *Animal Crackers* (1930) was theatrically re-released in 1974. Pictured from left: Harpo, Chico and Groucho (Photofest).

brink of their civility, until their Jewish angst breaks through like a song in a Broadway show.

Arkin co-produced. By this time, his star had fallen. No doubt he recognized in Bergman's style an opportunity to put the spotlight back on his patented form of hysteria. Plus, he saw sizable holes where he'd get to improvise (like in the firing squad scene), a chance to get back to his cabaret roots. He also saw the opportunity to work with Falk, whom he had long admired. Falk, looking to wrangle free of the straitjacket of TV's *Columbo* (1971–2003), jumped at the offer. Good thing, as these "buddy films" are predicated on chemistry. Falk smartly underplays his role, happy to leave Arkin, the great reactor, the repeated cutaways that spotlight his broad palette of incredulity—a rare case of the straight man being the funny one.

The In-Laws was directed by Arthur Hiller, a man of limited talents responsible for some sizable hits—proof positive that he was only as good as his script. This one isn't great, but it is very good, periodically hitting the heights of Marxian anarchy to which it aspires. Also, it proves that the old industry bromide is true: The best film comedy is often directed by the most unobtrusive of helmsmen. Gregory La Cava, Eddie Cline, Sam Wood … no film nerd would classify these Studio Era workhorses, responsible for so much classic comedy, as auteurs. Assemblymen, their job was to frame the talent and to stay on schedule and budget. While Hiller was not a product of their era, he did come up through TV drama, a system predicated on similar dictates.

Even without the added boost of a great director, *The In-Laws* contains enough choice moments to classify it as one of the best comedies of the second half of the '70s. Its flagship scenes, those that rise above the material, have a loose and loony feel. Utility character actor Richard Libertini, as the deranged Generalissimo, brings much-missed Second City savvy to the role. Then there's the film's famous "serpentine" scene, a comic rumba of actor and squib, which became one of the most memorable bits of comic business of the decade. Arkin spent the rest of his life having it annoyingly referenced by fans.

That said, *The In-Laws* is full of minor offenses. Another tie to Brooks, composer John Morris, wallpapers it with what sounds like discounted Neal Hefti. Then there are the embarrassingly underwritten female characters, who look and play like refugees from instant coffee commercials.

Critical reception to *The In-Laws* was mixed. Given Bergman's association with *Blazing Saddles*, the cognoscenti expected more. (The same fate was suffered by a Gene Wilder Western comedy released this same year, *The Frisco Kid*.) Over time, however, the film's rep, largely staked on its best bits, grew. By 2012, it was digitally cleaned up and lushly re-issued for DVD, as part of the highbrow Criterion Collection no less! In time, it was also chosen for a remake, Hollywood's highest honor and its basest instinct.

The Jerk

Plot: The rise and fall (and rise) of a naïve Southern bumpkin who achieves fame as an inventor. **Director:** Carl Reiner. **Script:** Steve Martin, Carl Gottlieb, Michael Elias. **Cast:** Steve Martin, Bernadette Peters, Jackie Mason. Universal. 95 minutes.

In August 1975, high school friend Bill McEuen started taping Steve Martin's act at a San Francisco nightclub called The Boarding House. Until then, after a childhood spent hawking venue maps and novelty items at Disneyland, Martin had been working on a stand-up routine for ten trying years. He was determined to develop something wholly original, eschewing such staples of the trade as one-liners, political commentary and observational humor. Inspired by the physical self-deprecation of Laurel and Hardy, the innocuous anarchy of Jerry Lewis, and the shock quality of the surrealist and Dada movements, he eventually succeeded not only in carving out a niche but, semi-strategically, in catching the wave of changing times.

Such was the word of mouth about Martin that McEuen's recordings, collected as the LP *Let's Get Small*, sold a million units before their public release in 1977. The album, buoyed by a rave review in *Rolling Stone*, served as the climax of the comic LP era, an age that had stretched from the caveman days of the suit-and-tie comedian (Shelley Berman, Bob Newhart, etc.) to the open-collar years (Mort Sahl, George Carlin, etc.). No home, it seemed, between '77 and '81, was without Martin on the turntable; he was as ubiquitous as the Bee Gees. No talk show—Johnny, Mike, Merv—failed to book him.

Momentum grew, until name venues from the Troubadour to the Nassau Coliseum enjoyed unprecedented numbers whenever he appeared (one show boasted 45,000 fans), making Martin comedy's first "rock star." Fans young and old screamed for him as if for Elvis (who, before his shocking death in August of that year, had counted himself a fan), rendering themselves giddily hoarse over the sight of Martin's milk-white suit and prematurely matching hair, usually adorned by a prop arrow or a set of bunny ears. Comedy hadn't seen this kind of worship since the advent of the aforementioned Lewis and his then partner, another Martin (Dean), back in the foofy '50s.

Retracing the road that got him there, Martin, in his 2007 book *Born Standing Up,*

In the late 1970s, stand-up comic Steve Martin rose to rock star status. When he brought his baser, wilder style of comedy to the screen, it paved the way for equally primal personalities Jim Carrey and Will Ferrell (Photofest).

reflected: "My act ... was becoming a parody of comedy. I was an entertainer who was playing an entertainer, a not-so-good one."[47] For all of its originality, then, Martin's act was essentially parodic—specifically, a spoof of the slick, self-aggrandizing show biz icons of the previous generation, then still dominating prime time variety and talk shows and passe venues like Las Vegas.

A product of the counterculture, Martin was sending up something else. The worst sin you could commit, in the insider's era that had been the '60s, was to be unhip. No matter how fundamentally naïve you were, you never (never!) wore it on your sleeve, lest you be laughed at. When you're a comedian, however, that's the goal. And so, Martin's act was a calculated case of the hippest guy in the room pretending to be the most unhip, which became, ironically, the hippest thing in the room.

If it struck, it was also because it reflected a sad, comic truth about Martin's generation, which could be admitted by '77: that the reason that the new world order advocated by the flower children hadn't worked was that too many young Americans had been Steve Martins, people who purported to be in the know but who, more transparently and agonizingly than they knew, fundamentally hadn't gotten it. For all of their pretensions, they hadn't been smart or libertarian enough to personally see the bold, experimental ethic of the times through. Now, in '77, Martin was speaking for this other "silent majority," in the only way that you could without creating a collective sense of shame and failure: comedy.

Martin represented something else, too: a musical-comedic fraternity that had been emerging, since the early part of the decade, out of the American desert. Now labeled "the California sound," artists such as Linda Ronstadt, the Eagles and Jackson Browne were helping to promote the West Coast lifestyle as the new way to be, an oasis—free now of threats like Charles Manson—from the urban nightmare of New York City. SoCal, specifically, was the place, having replaced San Francisco as the new Shangri-La (Shangri-L.A.?). Johnny Carson was writing love letters to it nightly through his monologue, Tommy Lasorda's L.A. Dodgers were constant contenders, and innocent pastimes suggesting a second childhood, like roller skating, were setting national precedents. In short, the California vibe was renewing the country. Goofy self-indulgence, a playful respite between the severing '60s and the establishmentarian '80s, was in. Martin, consequently, was in.

But not with the studios. Hard as it is to believe in our anything-for-a-buck age, it took some serious coercion for them to play ball with comedy's hottest commodity. The fear was that the simple movie-ization of a stand-up act, not to mention one that the whole world could already recite chapter and verse, would not, pardon the pun, stand up. Screen comics, like the still enormously popular Woody Allen, had long-ago graduated from such practices, leaping from string-of-gags vehicles like *Take the Money and Run* (1969) to sophisticated comedy-dramas like *Manhattan* (1979), a critical darling.

Universal finally took the plunge—a good one, it turned out, as Martin's *The Jerk*, produced for $4 million, ended up grossing over 100 times that amount.

The title is distinctly Lewisian, as is the film. Martin indeed fleshes out some of the best bits from his famous stand-up act, stringing them together on a thin rags-to-riches premise that includes, in another nod to Lewis, a childlike romance. (Lewis piggybacked

---

47. Ryan Vlastelica, "A Beginner's Guide to Steve Martin's Eclectic, Ground-Breaking Career," *AV Club*, Aug. 25, 2015.

on Martin's success: The clout of *The Jerk* earned Lewis another kick at the film can after a long absence. His film *Hardly Working*, 1980, even used the tagline "The original jerk is back!")

Martin is Navan Johnson, the white sheep of a black family who leaves his impoverished circumstance to find his people, discovering a string of Lewisian odd jobs instead (all of which he botches, naturally). Then he hits the jackpot: After being served with a class-action lawsuit, he finds himself on Skid Row, until the woman he loves (the multi-talented Bernadette Peters, in a criminally token role) comes to the rescue.

Enjoyment of the film is predicated on one's appreciation for the larval Steve Martin. In time, Martin—through film, music and literature—grew into a respected renaissance man, not an idol of the brainless but of the brainy, relied on by studios to bring a certain comic gravitas to otherwise lightweight properties. *The Jerk* was the infantile surrealism phase of his career in its purest, most extended form. Judge it as primordial pool or as precursor to a baser, wilder style of comedy, announcing the coming of equally primal personalities like Jim Carrey and Will Ferrell.

Along with *Animal House* (1978), *The Jerk* helped to announce that neurotic comedy, long dominant, was out (except for Allen, who would retain his audience) and that something far less psychological was in. These new comic heroes—Belushi, Martin—were not self-obsessed sophisticates but misfit primitives, ruled by base instincts and not much else.

It went with the other cultural rages: the simplicity of disco music and the premium on instant gratification like feel-good drugs and anonymous sex. The Martins of the world may have been sending up the products of this culture, but they were also, celebrating it.

Love at First Bite

Plot: Dracula, evicted from his castle, travels to New York City to quell his infatuation with a disco-dancing fashion model. **Director:** Stan Dragoti. **Script:** Robert Kaufman. **Cast:** George Hamilton, Susan Saint James, Arte Johnson, Richard Benjamin, Dick Shawn. American International Pictures. 94 minutes.

Long Hollywood's playboy mannequin, the stiffly urbane, perpetually tanned George Hamilton began to self-parody with his turn in the soapy *Once Is Not Enough* (1975). Looking to build on his untapped capacity for comic self-regard, he turned to friend Robert Kaufman, as much of a stereotype as Hamilton: the prototypical wisecracking New York Jewish comedy writer. Together they concocted *Love at First Bite*, a Mel Brooksian comedy casting Hamilton as an irresistibly romantic Dracula (a precedent set by Frank Langella in the Broadway restaging of a few years earlier).

His castle having been appropriated by the Romanian government as a training facility for its Olympic athletes, Drac the lonely lover relocates to New York City. There he searches for the woman he has pursued throughout the ages, personified as a flighty supermodel (played with great comic conviction by the underrated Susan Saint James). Looking to break them up is a contemporary Van Helsing, the model's therapist-boyfriend (Richard Benjamin, at his most Richard Benjamin) before the lovers, as bats, fly off into the night forever.

The result was wildly successful ($44 million on a $4 million budget) and justly so. Audiences responded, yes, to Hamilton but also to the film's comic take on the cultural impedimenta of the then blossoming Me Generation: disco, psychotherapy, feminism, recreational pharmaceuticals and one-night stands.

The flagship scene is the disco dance, where Drac and his leggy paramour parody *Saturday Night Fever* (1977) to the thumpy anthem that best-lauded disco's fundamental values, Alicia Bridges' "I Love the Nightlife" (replaced in subsequent releases due to a legal dispute). In the best book on the disco phenomenon, Peter Shapiro's *Turn the Beat Around: The Secret History of Disco,* the author wrote, "[D]isco dancing was the clarion call of sexual liberation,"[48] and encapsulated the genre's other qualities: "Disco may have had a hard gloss and an icy, metallic sheen, but it could still be warm and fuzzy when it needed to."[49]

Sex, style and romance—it's all there in the dance between Hamilton and Saint James. It could have been broader, like the *Saturday Night Fever* parody in *Airplane!* (1980), but director Stan Dragoti was not out to push. The jokes are broad, for sure, with that sketchy, scattergun quality (why else would Arte Johnson, as a sniveling Renfield, and Dick Shawn, as a tough-tender cop, be there?). But like Hamilton's vampire, a modicum of redemptive reserve rules.

Screenwriter Kaufman wasn't just out to play with Dracula's image, he was also out to play with New York's. Much of that—African American street toughs, low-rent Latino families, over-feminized homosexuals—plays even more stereotypically today. Mercifully, it's peripheral, the real comic concern being Drac's search for lasting romantic fulfillment.

Hamilton tried to perpetuate his newfound status as a comic entity in 1981's *Zorro the Gay Blade* (you can imagine the even more politically incorrect humor). While the film flopped, a line had been crossed. Forevermore, in commercials, on talk shows, or in anything else, he'd be a self-appointed figure of fun.

The Main Event

Plot: A perfume magnate becomes the manager, and lover, of a boxer on the comeback trail. **Director:** Howard Zieff. **Script:** Gail Parent, Andrew Smith. **Cast:** Barbra Streisand, Ryan O'Neal. Warner Bros. 112 minutes.

The Main Event is about Barbra Streisand and Ryan O'Neal. That's the main event.

At this point in her carefully cultivated career, Streisand was looking to take complete charge. She co-produced the film with her then partner (in all ways), hairdresser-to-the-stars cum egotistical studio head Jon Peters. Looking for a hit, she used the premise—an out-of-work marketing exec puts her savvy behind a Rocky manqué—to recycle many of the elements that had stood her in good stead in previous vehicles. It's not a Greatest Hits album but a Greatest Hits movie: the sexuality she exhibited in *The Owl and the Pussycat* in '70 (the diaphanous negligees replaced by form-fitting gym wear); the golden-haired goy toy from '73's *The Way We Were* (plus, it's

---

48. Peter Shapiro, *Turn the Beat Around: The Secret History of Disco* (New York: Faber & Faber, 2005), 189.

49. Shapiro, Peter, *Turn the Beat Around: The Secret History of Disco* (New York: Faber and Faber, 2005), 242

O'Neal, from that same year's *What's Up, Doc?*); the heroine's need for money, from '74's *For Pete's Sake*; and the rapid wit of her smash debut, '68's *Funny Girl*.

Put 'em all together and what do you get? On the surface, a disco-era battle of the sexes. There's lots of estrogen vs. testosterone between the leads, staging battles in the bedroom between the battles in the ring. It's dialogue that aspires to modernize Tracy-Hepburn (one critic called the film a reverse *Pat and Mike*, 1952) but it's flat, obvious and insistent. Plus, there's no genuine chemistry behind it; each actor appears too wrapped up in their protective ego. In comedy, unlike boxing, a good defense is rarely good policy.

And if O'Neal is the boxer and Streisand the manager, why does she show off her body more than he shows off his? A little more undress might have helped to redeem him, mercifully reducing him to an archetype. Bogdanovich, in *What's Up, Doc?*, smartly straitjacketed O'Neal in a Cary Grant impression. Left to his own devices, O'Neal is not only a bad comic, he's a bad straight man.

As for Streisand, Vincent Canby said it best: "She's become too much without being enough."[50] It's all here so it isn't. Was she simply spreading herself too thin (she even charted with the Paul Jabara disco theme)? This Jill-of-all-trades act reveals what the film really is: a big, flat, staid star vehicle—so much so that the whole script turns on plot points that are just there for twists' sake. The script cares little for what's natural for the characters; what it cares about is the provision of big, commercial-minded entertainment. To wit, the ending: first, Streisand seduces her golden ticket before the big fight (explain, please!). Then, in the ring, she throws in the towel, literally, giving up her feminist agenda for, if not chauvinism, then the opportunity to perpetually be forced to dismantle it—further, this is supposed to pass as fairy-tale romance.

Where's the usually unique Howard Zieff? He's in good soldier mode here, getting the cast to hit their marks and say their lines. He brings nothing of himself to it; he can't seem to get anyone to loosen up or go chancy. The only sign that he might be the director is the premise. Throughout his career, Zieff concentrated on talented, cocky innocents who had their swagger tested by dog-eat-dog superiors.

Goldie Hawn was originally slated to play the lead. It might have worked. Her less obtrusive brand of obsequiousness—the girlishly wide eyes doing most of the work— would have provided a greater contrast and might have even served to relax the contentedly removed O'Neal. Also, she would have been much more in tune with Zieff's signature style. Still, *The Main Event* was a big event. After all, it was about Barbra Streisand and Ryan O'Neal.

Manhattan

Plot: A middle-aged comedy writer falls in love with his best friend's mistress. **Director:** Woody Allen. **Script:** Woody Allen, Marshall Brickman. **Cast:** Woody Allen, Diane Keaton, Muriel Hemingway, Michael Murphy, Meryl Streep. United Artists. 96 minutes.

By the end of the '70s, New York was through as the hotbed of American film comedy—it was through, in fact, as pretty much everything. Los Angeles had become the

---

50. Vincent Canby, "Film: Streisand in 'Main Event,'" *New York Times*, June 22, 1979

center of American popular culture, its sunny veneer, like the laugh track on a bad sitcom, concealing much that wasn't working. Still, it was the place to be, exuding a happy, innocent vibe best represented by the goofy grimace of Steve Martin, the baseball field bonhomie of Tommy Lasorda, and the benign bile of *People* magazine. If L.A. was an adobe bungalow surrounded by palm trees, New York was the dark, decrepit tenement that had been razed to facilitate the upgrade.

For poor, downtrodden New York City, it was a long way down, status-wise, from a long-standing reputation as the greatest city in the world, the epitome of cultural sophistication, architectural genius and urban romanticism. Cinematically, New York was down to a single defender: Brooklyn-born Woody Allen, the quintessential New Yorker, urban, cultured, intellectual. At a time when the Statue of Liberty was on the brink of a much-needed, corporate-sponsored makeover, Allen decided to set about restoring the reputation of the city he so loved. As such, he would pull out all of the romantic stops: high-contrast black-and-white cinematography, a Gershwin score and a love story as much about a man and a place as about a boy and a girl.

Manhattan opens, famously, with a montage of New York street scenes, an arrestingly monochrome picture book instantly restoring the Big Apple's one-time reputation as America's "dream city." From there, we are immersed in a hermetic universe of self-obsessed, neurotic bluestockings, alternating their geography from tasteful, L-shaped apartments stocked with Franz Kafka and Virginia Woolf to iconic haunts like Elaine's, MoMA and the Russian Tea Room. Therein, they build up and take down their romantic scaffolding—most controversially, the wonky fit between Isaac, Allen's character, and Tracy, played by the flat-voiced, photogenic Mariel Hemingway; 42 vs. 17.

Not much was made at the time of Allen's character's involvement with a teenager. It was the film's other arrangements—such as gender-switching and same-sex parentage—that had then rattled the critics. Such are the vagaries, over time, of morality.

For the most part, the Allen-Hemingway dynamic got lost in the pile-up of the film's many merits: its Big City gloss, courtesy of cinematographer Gordon Willis; Gary Graffman's tasteful, almost formal adaptation of Gershwin's best compositions; the comic ease between Allen and Diane Keaton, building on *Annie Hall* (1977). Keaton's character, the Radcliffe-educated poseuse who breaks up the Allen-Hemingway tryst, is Annie if, after the conclusion of that film, Annie had stayed in New York and taken a wrong behavioral turn.

The interpersonal shenanigans (there's also Michael Murphy-Anne Byrne, Michael Murphy-Diane Keaton, Meryl Streep-Woody Allen and Meryl Streep-Karen Ludwig) owe a lot to the Russian literature Allen had so generously parodied in *Love and Death* (1975). Still, like many of *Manhattan*'s best sequences—foremost, a talky stroll through the New York planetarium—their petty, prickly quality serve to reinforce the film's primary contention: man's self-preoccupation as remedy for the cosmic meaningless of existence. Name another comedy that aspires to such grand statement. Chaplin's *The Great Dictator* (1940) maybe? Benigni's *Life Is Beautiful* (1997)? The point is, few artists have the audacity, intelligence and talent to expand the didactic scope of comic film. That alone qualifies *Manhattan* as Allen's most substantial comedy.

More American Graffiti

Plot: Cross-cut stories of select characters from *American Graffiti* (1973) as they negotiate the complicated '60s. **Script/Director:** Bill L. Norton. **Cast:** Ron Howard, Cindy Williams, Paul Le Mat, Charles Martin Smith, Candy Clark, Mackenzie Phillips, Bo Hopkins. Universal. 110 minutes.

The unexpected quality of *The Godfather Part II* (1974) did more than any other film to promote that now-unstoppable industry convention, the sequel. In the wake of its critical-commercial success, every box office hit followed up with a successive (and after that had been exhausted, regressive) narrative. Over the remainder of the 70s, the demon child Damien returned, Rocky held a rematch, the three musketeers morphed into a foursome, and the poor, plagued Poseidon endured another unfortunate adventure. Though it took a little longer, inevitably, sequel-mania came to comedy.

American Graffiti (1973) brought us the small-town California '50s, a nocturnal orgy, if a relatively innocent one, of sock hops, drag races and fretting about the future. Setting his sights on something larger, but that would speak to the same Baby Boomer audience, George Lucas set about producing a timepiece on the '60s, picking up the lives of a handful of the characters introduced in the first film.

Still reeling from having project-managed the cinematic success story of the decade, *Star Wars* (1977), Lucas hired Bill L. Norton, a fellow Californian responsible for the cult crime caper *Cisco Pike* (1971), to write and direct, with Lucas serving as executive producer (and occasionally, manning the camera, just for fun).

Instead of muscle cars and Bill Haley inaugurating time and place, here it's army-issue choppers and Martha and the Vandellas. We spend a quarter of our time in the jungle, trying to wrangle our way out of 'Nam with the manlier, more enterprising Toad (Charles Martin Smith), while flipping chronologically backward and forward (from 1964 to 1969 and vice versa) to spend equal time on the drag race circuit with a mellowed, lovestruck Milner (Paul Le Mat), on the music scene with a hippie-fied Debbie (Candy Clark), and in the midst of a long, feminism-spawned marital row between Steve (Ron Howard) and Laurie (Cindy Williams).

With its varied geography, alternating time periods and extended interactions between the characters, *More American Graffiti* is a decided break from its predecessor. While a bold, interesting choice, this violation of audience expectation cost it dearly. It was but a modest box office success. Writer-director Norton, as a consequence, was relegated to a career spent largely in television.

Taken on its own merits, however, it's respectable work; an episodic behavioral comedy sharing a directorial bent with two other up-and-coming talents, Robert Zemeckis and Jonathan Demme. It replaces sociology with situation but exhibits a wit and depth separating it from middlebrow TV. It's stylistically worthy, too, a veritable showcase of '60s visual culture.

Plus, while it's played, chancily, as a kind of hip service comedy, the Toad narrative goes out of its way to integrate the reality of Vietnam (including, though probably for budgetary reasons, documentary footage), aspiring in its own humble manner to breakthrough work on the subject like *Coming Home* (1978) and *The Deer Hunter* (1979). At the top of the decade, with the conflict still raging, Vietnam was, cinematically speaking, fought with kid gloves. As Wes D. Gehring noted in his 2016 *Genre-Busting Dark*

Comedies of the 1970s, commenting on the period of *M*A*S*H* (1970) and *Little Big Man* (1971), "Dark comedy and anti–Vietnam films had very much gone mainstream"[51]—yes, Wes, but only metaphorically. Now, enough time had elapsed that a bold-faced approach could be taken—and the *Graffiti* follow-up, in its own small way, wanted in.

Oh—and Lucas finally fixes that pictorial postscript. At the end of the first film, you'll remember, it catches us up on the fates of Toad, Milner, Steve and Curt—not, however, the female characters. So, at the conclusion of *More American Graffiti*, we learn that Laurie is rising through the professional ranks and that Debbie has forged a career as a country singer. (Richard Dreyfuss, now too big a star for this modestly budgeted sequel, has his character replaced by a younger brother.)

Interesting footnotes—as is the film.

The Muppet Movie

Plot: Kermit the Frog heads for Hollywood. Along the way, he forms the Muppets while dodging a shifty entrepreneur who wants him as a spokesperson for his French-fried frog legs franchise. **Director:** James Frawley. **Script:** Jerry Juhl, Jack Burns. **Cast:** The Muppets, Charles Durning, Austin Pendleton, Orson Welles. Associated Film Distribution. 95 minutes.

Package deals make for strange bedfellows.

In 1975, super-agent Bernie Brillstein tried to pair the counterculture comic actors on his roster with a family-friendly puppeteer he had rescued from a life of children's programming and TV commercials. The result was an on-screen mishmash and an off-screen war that was the first season of *Saturday Night Live* (1975–present-day). Cut loose from TV's hippest, hottest show, Jim Henson could console himself with his continuing contribution to *Sesame Street* (1969–present-day). Enter Britain's Lew Grade, provider of the proper demographic context, the cheaper, glossier means of production, the roster of internationally known middlebrow guest talent, and the entrepreneurial clout to penetrate worldwide markets. The result was *The Muppet Show* (1976–81), a weekly showcase for Henson's creations rooted in the innocence of vaudeville and the gentler aspects of the hippie generation. The show was an instant success around the globe.

But Grade wasn't finished. Sensing a lot more milk in the teat of this felt-and-wire cash cow, he next set out to conquer the movies, using the same elements and sensibility that had made the TV series a smashing success.

Grade stocked this breakout vehicle with many of his biggest stars. Further, he broke up the action with some commercially sentimental songs, modernized versions of the forgotten tunes the series was reviving. A family-friendly blockbuster then, the kind the movies hadn't seen since *Doctor Dolittle* (1967) and *Chitty Chitty Bang Bang* (1969).

Filmgoing as a familial ritual was in the throes of a long dormancy. The fall of the big studios in the early days of the decade had left that responsibility to its best practitioner, the Walt Disney corporation. While it too was ailing, the Mouse House

---

51. Wes D. Gehring, *Genre-Busting Dark Comedies of the 1970s* (Jefferson, NC: McFarland, 2016), 67.

performed its due diligence, concentrating mostly on less expensive live-action fare. But their core audience was diminishing. The traditional family was, after all, breaking up, another victim of the rising divorce rate and the politically preoccupied, anti-monogamy counterculture. It wasn't until the unprecedented success of *Star Wars* (1977), whose mix of innocence, action and magic owed as much to Disney as it did to Flash Gordon, that producers began to reconsider what had become an underserved audience. Grade's *Muppet Movie* affirmed its rise, helping to pave the way for the revival of the all-ages spectacle that would dominate the think-big '80s (until its amendment for the male, 18–30 demographic in the think-boy '90s).

While no outer space–set extravaganza (extravaGonzo?), *The Muppet Movie*'s opening minutes rendered audiences aghast with an act of technical derring-do: gang leader Kermit the Frog riding a bicycle, a pre–CGI miracle letting the world know, as *Star Wars* had, that as far as special effects went, the movies had left Ray Harryhausen in the dust. It was also, in its own small way, another harbinger that increasingly, technology and story were gravitating toward a symbiotic relationship, which the advent of computers definitively affirmed.

From there, Kermit collects Fozzie Bear, the Great Gonzo and Miss Piggy—both paragon and parody of the women's movement—on their way to show biz glory, all the while dodging a fast-food king determined to have Kermit as his spokesperson (spokesfrog?) by hook or by crook.

While the kindly kooks vs. the crass capitalists storyline had been dead for some time, in the hands of Henson, it took on a new, invigorating dimension. (The same can

As the 1970s mellowed, the tone of anarchy that had marked the early part of the decade was replaced by a benign version, best exemplified by the family-friendly Muppets, shown here in *The Muppet Movie* (1979). Pictured from left: Kermit, Gonzo, Camilla and Fozzie (Associated Film/Photofest).

be said of Milos Forman's adaptation of *Hair* released that same year, another subscription that should have played dated.) Henson was instrumental in keeping the best spirit of the '60s alive through the immediate post-hippie era, providing, through his puppets, power to groups of weird-looking but benign freaks subscribing to a friendly all-for-one, one-for-all ethic, keeping the notion alive that the world could still be saved through love and music. Fleetwood Mac, at that same time, was doing it too; you could argue that they were the Muppets of music, with the light, happy togetherness of their bestselling album *Rumours*. Their hit single "Don't Stop Thinking About Tomorrow" was, arguably, rock's "Rainbow Connection" (*The Muppet Movie*'s iconic theme), featuring the same optimistic message.

Like many a comic film before it, and the stars' hit TV series, *The Muppet Movie* is buoyed by much self-referential humor (Kermit: "Oh great! It's a running gag!") This too should have played tired but is again made anew by virtue of spirit. The human guest stars, while welcome, are a checkered affair, many smacking of tokenism. For one, though, it was an audition, an opportunity to see if, like The Muppets, his distinctly offbeat wit could make the leap from the small screen to the big: Steve Martin, reprising a bit from his film debut, the Academy Award–winning short *The Absent-Minded Waiter* (1977). He passed. Within the year, he was the second major comic commodity in tune with the turning cultural tide, from the tested and resigned to the oblique and ever-innocent.

The Muppet Movie, then, did a lot of things, not to mention its additional function as a baby step toward the revival of the movie musical, dead as a doornail in that rock-centric era except for concert films and the squeakified film version of *Grease* (1978). Having conquered both TV and the movies, Henson's empire grew until, ironically, it was appropriated by Disney.

1941

Plot: Comic war epic on Los Angeles' panicky reaction to Pearl Harbor. **Director:** Steven Spielberg. **Script:** Robert Zemeckis, Bob Gale. **Cast:** John Belushi, Dan Aykroyd, Nancy Allen, Tim Matheson, Ned Beatty, Lorraine Gary, Robert Stack, Murray Hamilton, Toshiro Mifune, Slim Pickens. Universal. 118 minutes (director's cut: 146 minutes).

With the made-for-TV film *Duel* (1971), Steven Spielberg, all of 25, announced himself as Hollywood's next *enfant terrible*. He subsequently wowed the critics with *The Sugarland Express* (1974), then press and public alike with the industry's first-ever summer blockbuster, *Jaws* (1975). After his equally showy *Close Encounters of the Third Kind* (1977), Spielberg quickly solidified a reputation as that most cherished of studio commodities: a sure bet. Whatever followed, it would arrive with rave reviews, sold-out showings and high anticipation over his *next* release. But just as Pearl Harbor was an unexpected disaster, so too was Spielberg's comic take on Hollywood's hysterical reaction to it: *1941*.

In *The Comic Mind*, Gerald Mast's 1979 analysis of the history of film comedy, he observed: "From the beginning, comedy has been bent on destruction—of objects, egos, social assumptions, society's leaders, and the goals of society itself. Similarly, the greatest comic artists in film ... are pure destroyers."[52] Words, perhaps, that Spielberg took too much to heart, without bothering to read on: "What, then, is the good of this purely destructive, negative thing?"[53]

Left to his own devices, as Spielberg is throughout the last two acts of this film, he stages countless fistfights, incites widescreen riots, and wages vehicular and aeronautic offensives on American soil. It's a proud, indulgent display of a sense of humor formed by knockabout interludes in John Ford Westerns and pell-mells like *It's a Mad Mad Mad Mad World* (1963) and *Those Magnificent Men in Their Flying Machines* (1966). It's also an expansive, and expensive, detour, glaringly marring what is otherwise a fun, charming and genuinely amusing Robert Zemeckis comedy (Zemeckis wrote the film with partner Bob Gale) in the tradition of Mr. Z.'s unheralded *I Wanna Hold Your Hand* (1978).

To wit, this bird's-eye look at the behavioral mania that gripped Hollywood post–Pearl Harbor retains the multi-narrative structure and much of the cast (mixed with those of *Saturday Night Live*, 1975–present-day, *SCTV*, 1976–83, and *Animal House*, 1978) of Zemeckis' aforementioned debut. And other Zemeckis signatures—the Rube Goldberg plot devices, the sexual hijinks and, most tellingly, the film's spirited, madcap feel—are just as evident.

Trimmed of the oversized Spielbergian interludes that interrupt this messy mélange, the underwriting studio, by committing that act of financial heresy, would have had another fun, quirky piece of Americana *à la I Wanna Hold Your Hand*. In other words, a smaller flop, though one appreciated by the critics. Instead, its deference to the Boy Wonder brought the kind of notices which, combined with poor box office, helped to apply the brakes to '70s cinema as it was then known: the Golden Age of American auteurism.

Plus, like a badly staged gag, the picture's timing was wrong. With the double whammy of *The Deer Hunter* and *Coming Home* in '78, Hollywood had begun to examine the horror that had been Vietnam. War was once again, as the protest signs over that conflict had originally maintained, hell. And here Spielberg and Zemeckis were, expensively convincing us that it was grand, innocent, admirable fun.

A Perfect Couple

Plot: A lonely middle-aged man from an oppressive family tries his romantic luck with a young singer in a traveling band. **Director:** Robert Altman. **Script:** Allan Nicholls, Robert Altman. **Cast:** Paul Dooley, Marta Heflin, Ted Neeley. 20th Century–Fox. 110 minutes.

Likely tired from having worked on such grand scales—*Buffalo Bill and the Indians* (1976), followed by the equally large and messy *A Wedding* (1978)—and perhaps still stinging from the slings and arrows brought on by it, Robert Altman decided to try his hand at the romcom. While he had built a solid reputation by paying but lip service to

52. Gerald Mast, *The Comic Mind: Comedy and the Movies* (Chicago: University of Chicago Press, 1973), 338.
53. Gerald Mast, *The Comic Mind: Comedy and the Movies* (Chicago: University of Chicago Press, 1973), 340.

formula—using it, at best, as a springboard for his free-for-alls—here, he would subscribe to it with as much devotion as his rebellious spirit would allow.

A Perfect Couple is an encyclopedia of classic romcom elements: the attraction of opposites, the introductory "meet-cute," the disastrous first date, the poetic
coming-together, the threat of separation, the happy ending. Despite all of this, the irrepressible Altman made each convention his own, converting the formulaic to the fine.
So much of it could have been forced, like the slapstick centerpiece in which a shoving
match breaks out between the characters. Instead, it's a uniquely delicate film, one of the
proverbial "little gems" of the era.

The title is, of course, ironic. This couple is anything but perfect. Or original; a lot of the script (by Altman and Allan Nicholls, though God knows how much
improv went on) owes a debt to *Marty* (1955). Paul Dooley (a big year for him, as he
was Oscar-nominated as the frustrated father in *Breaking Away*) is Alex, the overgrown
whipping boy of a Greek family determined to keep him in his lowly place. Lonely, he
takes a romantic gamble on Sheila (Marta Heflin), a going-nowhere backup singer in a
soul ensemble fronted by an egotistical band leader. Alex and Sheila fumble their way to
love while fumbling their respective ways to freedom.

While formulaic—the premise also conforming to the still-clinging establishment
(his world) vs. hippie (her world) dynamic—one can argue that *A Perfect Couple* is nonetheless an autobiographical work. Dooley's conversion from respectable middle-aged
man to love-and-music generation sympathizer can be seen to reflect Altman's own
journey, his fateful, once-upon-a-time decision to throw caution to the wind and make
hip, groundbreaking cinema after years as a respected industry workman. Like young,
pre–*M*A*S*H* (1970) Altman, the characters here are imprisoned, a state reflected by the
freight elevator doors to Heflin's loft, within which they are often framed. Their shared
enemy is patriarchy. Both Alex and Sheila are oppressed by father figures Old School
and New. Deep-set within them is a mutual need for recklessness, a soul-saving capacity
they're both too timid to go out and find—so writers Altman and Nicholls have the serendipitous winds of ill fortune find it for them.

It's nicely set up and nicely paid off. Heflin's wide, introspective eyes and
mile-long pout are a great natural contrast to Dooley's scattergun insistence, as are
her loose clothes and flowing scarves to his wide-lapelled, cream-colored suits. When
they're moved by an invisible, if clumsy, God from these differences into romantic union, each kiss cuts through the comedy without killing it; they are tender and
heartfelt.

But it's not just the way the romance is handled that makes *A Perfect Couple* stand
out. Uniquely, it's also half a concert film. The band in question (of which co-writer
Nicholls is both singer and songwriter) is a vocal group named Keeping 'Em Off the
Streets (headed by Ted Neeley, star of *Jesus Christ Superstar*, 1973). They sing blue-eyed
soul and funk with voracious verve and beady-eyed intent. As in Altman's *Nashville*
(1975), the music here is extremely personal, intrinsically tied to the characters and their
relationships. It consistently and resonantly underscores the subtext of the scenes, thus
allowing many small moments to play *sans* dialogue. In addition, it allows for a lovely
metaphorical climax, a melding of establishment and hippie when the band gets to play
at the Hollywood Bowl with the L.A. Philharmonic.

Upon its release, critics who had once so loved Altman viewed the film not as an act
of redemption nor as a respite from his chancier ambitions. Instead, it was deemed part

of the continuation of a downward slide, the cognoscenti mistaking this collection of small, mounting moments for just more messy filmmaking.

The Altman of the '70s, then, went down as an original, prolific, bravura force that came in with a bang and went out with a whimper. The truth is that he went out on his own, if humbled, terms, singing a sweet little song.

Real Life

Plot: A neurotic filmmaker sets out to chronicle, and complicate, the lives of members of a typical American family. **Director:** Albert Brooks. **Script:** Albert Brooks, Monica Johnson, Harry Shearer. **Cast:** Albert Brooks, Charles Grodin, Frances Lee McCain. Paramount. 99 minutes.

In 1972, PBS, a new, intellectual take on television, debuted a 12-hour documentary series called *An American Family*. This anthropological study of Californian suburbanites garnered the fledgling network one of its first major audiences. One of the many taking it all in was Albert Brooks, then transitioning from post-modern stand-up comic to experimental filmmaker. Like another writer-director with the same last name, Albert (*née*, incredibly, Einstein) recognized a premise ripe for parody when he saw one. The result, *Real Life*, was the first feature film of his sporadic, underrated and extremely funny oeuvre.

Part self-obsessed angst comic, part showy pseudo-intellectual, Brooks put himself at the center of the film, even though it purports to be a record of a year in the life of the Yeagers, a mom-dad-apple pie arrangement on the outskirts of Phoenix. In so doing, Brooks prophetically created the first and ultimate "photobomb," his neurotic, obsequious filmmaker–on-screen narrator disrupting the Yeagers' lives at every turn.

While ego—specifically, Brooks'—is the ultimate joke, the film is about a lot more, some of it retro, much of it futuristic. A product of the '60s, Brooks here, and in many of his subsequent films, plays that era's leading stereotype: the seeker, intractably mired in such philosophical quicksand as truth, substance and the nature of reality. As such, he joined but a handful of comic filmmakers who were exploring the same philosophical territory, including Paul Mazursky and Woody Allen. The answers to Brooks' questions, however, are answered from the get-go. After introducing the prospect of his groundbreaking cinematic mega-project to members of the community in which the filming will take place, he bursts into Vegas-like song to better ingratiate himself. In Brooksland, everything is show business. There is no reality, other than the reality of the ubiquity of the entertainment mindset. It's a distinctly American mix of hucksterism and chutzpah born of Brooks' Eastern European Jewish roots and his familial pedigree. (His father had been a radio star, and his brother Bob Einstein, another comic, earned fame sending up '70s daredevil Evel Knievel.)

As an amateur futurist, Brooks builds on the prophecy of the coming of the media age, as famously foretold in the '60s by public intellectual Marshall McLuhan. Here, cameras are everywhere (including headpieces the size of gumball machines that look like Salvador Dalí's take on *Star Wars*' Storm Troopers, floating in and out of dinner scenes and encounters on the streets). And, yes, everyone's a star, regardless of how maudlin their existences. It's the Reality TV phenomenon, parodied long before it got started.

Another kick in the pants: the earnestness of science. Brooks pontificates proudly as the marginally qualified host, then, throughout the film, argues heatedly with a panel of social scientists about the intellectual validity of his intentions. Again, asks Brooks, what is there to truly put stock in other than the self, a question he'll reposit in *Looking for America* (1983) and *Defending Your Life* (1991). Label him, then, though he also belongs to the conceptual and angst comedy schools, the ultimate Me Generation comic. "Let's think about me," Brooks insists, even when his project has tanked and he's begging his disheartened subjects on bended knee for personal sympathy.

And why wouldn't he subscribe to crass narcissism? Every major director at that time, it seemed, was as high on it as they were on cocaine, the auteur theory having gone completely to their heads. Francis Ford Coppola was shooting *Apocalypse Now* (1979) and Michael Cimino was making *Heaven's Gate* (1980), two overblown, self-indulgent productions plagued by runaway budgets, ego battles and mass, largely negative, publicity—the kind of personality-based shitshow that would soon bring an end to the directorial age and transfer power to the "boardroom-think" of the studios (nicely parodied by Brooks as a disparate voice).

While a lot of *Real Life* is carefully conceived, an exercise such as this one naturally entails improvisation (Harry Shearer had a hand in things), a form at which Brooks is equally adept, as is the rest of the cast. If you're looking for someone to simulate reality, you can do worse than to go with Charles Grodin (pre-toupee here), the anti-actor's actor, with his careful, almost inaudible voice and his instinctively minimalist style. Frances Lee McCain (who?) plays Grodin's wife, who falls into a cinematically disruptive affair with the ever-needy Brooks. The two-handers between Brooks and, in turn, Grodin and McCain are big-screen improv at its best, their success paving the way for the films of Christopher Guest.

Had Brooks been more prolific, and a tad more accessible, he might have taken his rightful place among the major comic auteurs of the last stages of the 20th century (Blake Edwards, Mel Brooks, Woody Allen, etc.). Instead, by proceeding as cautiously as he did, he created a small, memorable library of cult classics, becoming better known for voice work in family fare (finding first Nemo, then Dory).

Oh well ... that's show business—or is that reality?

Rock'n'Roll High School

Plot: A Nazi-esque high school principal wars with students over their love of the Ramones. **Director:** Allan Arkush. **Script:** Richard Whiteley, Russ Dvonch, Joseph McBride, story by Arkush and Joe Dante. **Cast:** P.J. Soles, The Ramones, Paul Bartel, Vince Van Patten, Clint Howard. New World Pictures. 93 minutes.

In November 1979, friction ran high between the United States and Iran. After Iran's deposed shah was admitted to the U.S. for cancer treatment, a group of militarized Iranian students demanded he be returned home to be tried for crimes against his people. They seized the U.S. Embassy in Tehran, holding 52 U.S. citizens hostage for what would end up being a nerve-wracking 444 days.

Up until then, the threat of anarchy had seemed so innocent. The closest thing to conflict America had had in some time was the war between rock, disco, punk and New

Wave; the closest thing to a missile strike, the blowing-up of disco records at Chicago's Comiskey Park one out-of-control night in July 1979.

Madness, as the runaway success of the anarchic *Animal House* (1978) had attested, was actually that less potent word, "mayhem." Even punk, with its insistence on nihilistic self-destruction, was cast with a comic eye; it was an import, after all, so something strange, inorganic and essentially amusing. Punk's American practitioners were appreciated but would remain, at best, an acquired taste—like the Ramones.

Looking to cash in on the spirit of *Animal House,* the underserved punk market and the growing phenomenon of the "midnight movie"—a tradition begat by *The Rocky Horror Picture Show* (1975) in which art houses, after showing the latest Kurosawa or Truffaut, would open their doors to a late shift of cult-loving 20-somethings—exploitation king Roger Corman gave Allan Arkush, an ex-cabbie who had been cutting Corman's trailers, a shot at a film that capitalized on all three.

Though born in 1926, Corman had always had a beat on the primal appetites of the American postwar teenager. When mainstream Hollywood was giving that demographic the sanitized sexuality of Sandra Dee, Corman was giving them bikini-clad scream queens; when it was giving them *The Sound of Music* (1965), he was letting them ride with the notorious Hell's Angels; when it was still producing films directed by the aging Studio Era guard, he was giving them young filmmakers (Coppola, Scorsese, Demme, etc.) who would grow to become the cinematic voices of their generation.

Nor was *Rock'n'Roll High School* the first time he had given them rock'n'roll. *Rock'n'Roll High School,* in fact, isn't much of a stretch from Corman's *Carnival Rock* (1957). It may be 1979, but as far as *Rock'n'Roll High School*'s sensibilities run, it's still the 1950s. Time has not erased the dividing lines between the button-down authoritarians and the fun-lovin' teens, who innocently promote the decay of civilization through their loud, blasphemous music. The Ramones, in fact, are a bit of a throwback, with their Elvis-issue leather jackets and their early Beatles mop tops, and the title song that they sing, on a soundtrack that includes Chuck Berry no less, has a facile 1950s quality to it.

The only thing that's changed is tone: The generational war is now played for laughs. The teaching staff at Vince Lombardi High is headed by a Nazi-esque she-wolf who demonstrates the ill effects of rock'n'roll by subjecting a lab mouse to a musical gamut running from middle-of-the-road one-hit-wonder Debby Boone to the resurgent Who, at which point the poor mouse literally explodes.

Corman may be borrowing from other cultural currents here but he's mostly borrowing from himself, creating a spirited self-parody of the throwaway teen film he helped pioneer. The Corman persona, in fact, finds avatars in the film's major female characters: bad girl cheerleader Riff Randell, who spreads her love of the Ramones throughout the school, and her nerdy BFF Kate Rambeau, who falls under her influence. Ideologically, they represent, as does the battle between the teachers and the kids, the puritan vs. the permissive aka America's behavioral tectonic plates.

But Corman himself has frequently described his personality as that of scrupulous businessman and capitalist monster, with the latter incarnation, in the end, winning. So when Riff shuts down the school and incites a riot in response to the school's burning of Ramones records, it's an ear-ringing self-endorsement for Corman the unapologetically base showman.

Like *Animal House, Rock'n'Roll High School* just skirts messy. Instead, like the school's namesake, the film wins ugly. The result is a cult classic and a reminder that, like the pre–Iran hostage crisis fumbling of Presidents Ford and Carter, high-tension culture clash was once inconsequential fun.

Scavenger Hunt

Plot: An eccentric game inventor sends his estranged relatives on a scavenger hunt. **Director:** Michael Schultz. **Script:** Steven A. Vail, Henry Harper. **Cast:** Richard Benjamin, James Coco, Scatman Crothers, Ruth Gordon, Cloris Leachman, Cleavon Little, Roddy McDowall, Tony Randall. 20th Century–Fox. 116 minutes.

In 1963, producer-director Stanley Kramer, hitherto known for self-important social dramas, set the top comedians of the day on a cross-country goose chase (propelled by capitalist America's signature sin: greed) in *It's a Mad Mad Mad Mad World*. Somewhere, a dying man's fortune lay, ripe for the tax-free taking. Solve the riddle of his final words, outfox your competitors, triumph over the follies of happenstance, and the money, a bucketful, is yours.

Kramer's film was, purportedly, an ode to the halcyon days of silent cinema, chock-ablock with car chases, slapstick, knockabout humor and a grand, parabolic finale. Further, it was fashioned to accommodate the widescreen-mania of the time (it was shot in one-camera Cinerama), film's atomic bomb in the war against television. To the savvier critics, it was overblown, bombastic, noisy and forced. To the common element, excusably episodic hysteria.

Either of those epithets would be welcome affixations to *Scavenger Hunt*. Where writer-producer Steven A. Vail found the temerity to aspire to *Mad Mad World* given his slim talents and meager budget is baffling, even in egocentric Hollywood. This is not a remake or an homage; there isn't even enough here to call it a riff. It's a misguided, see-through conceit.

The dying man here is a game board magnate (Vincent Price). True to character, he sets out a posthumous maze for his sorry, shallow relatives, forced to collect arcane objects and people (yes, people) assigned a numerical value; to the victor with the most points, the spoils. Not a bad variation, foreshadowing the coming video game craze. Too bad it constitutes the only clever (and I use the term loosely) notion in the film. And so, an all–B cast, including some '70s eye candy aimed at luring the teen set (remember Dirk Benedict?), fumbles, falls and fights its way to the prize.

So discount is this picture, the fundamentals are missing. The characters not only aren't characters, but they're also not even caricatures. They're just repositories of nervous energy, ticking and shticking. The pratfalls are ill-timed and ill-shot. And the verbal wit (again, I use the term…) is so off-target, you wonder why they even bothered.

The film was directed by Michael Schultz, the African American auteur responsible for the resonant *Cooley High* (1976) and Richard Pryor's best vehicle, *Which Way Is Up?* (1977). Hitherto, Schultz's sloppiness had served as a style, his rawness bringing a primal electricity to properties. Here, there's nothing and no one vital at the heart of things to excuse his lack of finesse. He stands exposed, self-made, and struggling.

It's a bad, bad, bad, bad film.

(There'd be another attempt at this kind of thing, *Rat Race*, in 2001. Not great either, but a considerable improvement over *Scavenger Hunt*.)

Starting Over

Plot: After he breaks up with his singer-songwriter wife, a despondent writer chances a romance with a nursery school teacher. **Script/Director:** James L. Brooks, based on the book by Dan Wakefield. **Cast:** Burt Reynolds, Jill Clayburgh, Candice Bergen. Paramount. 105 minutes.

Perhaps no visual look so dominated '70s cinema as the soft tones of Sven Nykvist, the Swedish cinematographer responsible for the signature look of the world's most popular foreign film director, the pensively pessimistic Ingmar Bergman. After a while, everyone solicited Sven, whether his style suited their film or not. You'd think the combo of his stark, silky skills and the dark, whispery bent of director Alan Pakula (*The Parallax View*, 1974, *All the President's Men*, 1976) would combine to cast oppressive clouds over a comedy, effectively killing the humor. Instead, much of *Starting Over* works, the approach serving to ward off the cautiously sunny, Neil Simon–esque feel that had become the industry standard.

And that's not *Starting Over*'s sole distinction. It also marks the arrival of a new voice in comic American relationship films: not neurotic Jewish but wonky WASP. James L. Brooks, as he had been demonstrating more loudly on TV as the man behind the MTM (Mary Tyler Moore) shows, was a writer with an instinctive knack for distilling characters to their contradictions—then, of switching their happy-sad-mad modes at lightning-fast speeds. The trick to this is to perpetually ensure that the action is properly, if idiosyncratically, motivated. The result is something rooted in an old acting lesson: Cry when your character wants to laugh, laugh when your character wants to cry.

Brooks is the writer (okay, the adapter) of this deceivingly simple tale of a divorced scribe torn between his feminist songwriter ex and a neurotic schoolteacher. Despite his TV pedigree, Brooks, looking for a style of long-form wit akin to the kind he was honing on the small screen, never cartoonizes his characters (was he saving that for his showrunner stint on *The Simpsons*, 1988–present day?), reduces them to Feydeau-like figures, robs them of I.Q. points, or otherwise excises their humanity. It's their restriction to their essential quirks, in fact, that humanizes them. The result is one of the best screenplays of the decade (along with *Hearts of the West*, 1975, and *…And Justice for All*, 1979).

Casting against type is always a dangerous proposition (actors love it, audiences don't) but it works marvelously here. Candice Bergen, as Burt Reynolds' ex, surprised the world by showing the true makings of a talented comedienne, one consistently willing to take chances (setting the stage for TV's *Murphy Brown*, 1988–98 and again, 2018; she even has a few small scenes with Charles Kimbrough, her future co-star in that series).

The film's funny songs, sung off-key by Bergen, are highlights, though the script goes to the well once too often. They're smart parodies of feminist anthems in both ballad and disco form. Amazingly, they never belittle the movement or reduce the character to a parodic device. That's because they're consistently framed in a context wherein the character is afforded her due, ably demonstrating what it is that women are forced to tolerate—infantile humor, outdated ideals, fear of commitment—at the hands of men.

Reynolds, who was looking for a break from his Good Ol' Boy shtick, is awarded a golden opportunity. He takes it, containing himself and proving that he can get laughs just as well by reacting as by overacting. In addition, he finds out that he can maintain his sexiness in professorial tweeds and corduroys just as well as in skintight Levis and weathered Stetsons. Pakula even manages to make something useful out of Jill Clayburgh's flitty, middle-class style, converting her to a bourgeois Diane Keaton (Clayburgh and Bergen were both Oscar-nominated). Reynolds' seduction of her is a classic, in which it's determined that romance is too mushy and that animalism is too offensive, affirming the film's prime inquiry: the search for what might exist in between. While that question—familiar by now but intelligently examined—is centered around the male hero, Brooks adeptly demonstrates its effect on the opposite sex.

In the end, the film settles for a pat answer: that the tried and true is okay, no matter how you get there. It's one of the film's few disappointments—like its minor-key electronic piano-folk flute and flugelhorn score and its pat comic climax when the torn-between-two-lovers Reynolds suffers a Neil Simon–esque panic attack at Bloomingdale's. Otherwise, the film stands alongside *A Perfect Couple* as proof that interesting, intelligent approaches were turning what had become a staid genre into smart, mature entertainments. Even some of Hollywood's oldest dogs were now willing, in the service of this shift, to essay new tricks.

10

Plot: A middle-aged man disrupts an elusive beauty's Mexican honeymoon. **Script/ Director:** Blake Edwards. **Cast:** Dudley Moore, Julie Andrews, Bo Derek. Warner Bros. 122 minutes.

It's a late entry into the Old School–nebbish-set-loose-into-the-throng-of-the sexual-revolution thing but by this stage, that premise had been made relevant again by the new premium on sexuality established by the rise of disco. Once again, as in the late '60s, the pre–World War II generation found itself surrounded by explicitly free-loving youth, only now, with feel-good drugs and anonymous, "take-me-now sex doubling not as political statements but standing alone as vessels of fun for fun's sake.

10 is the first of several Blake Edwards entries over the coming years in which he took time off from his childhood love of silent film–style slapstick to venture deeper into one of his major subtexts, the war between men and women—a war waged by his own patriarchal-generational biases.

Here, Dudley Moore as, effectively, Edwards, is a middle-aged man looking for the fountain of youth in the form of a distant beauty. His long-suffering wife, played by Edwards' real life-wife Julie Andrews, plays Jiminy Cricket to this morally exploratory Pinocchio.

In wake of the surprise popularity of TV's *Charlie's Angels* (1976–81) and in particular statuesque, feather-haired Farah Fawcett, TV and film would start grinding out bikini-clad SoCal poster girls like Pet Rocks, mood rings and macramé plant holders. It was labeled the T&A phenomenon, a new low for television, and a commercial intrusion on loftier cinematic inclinations. Edwards was one of the few filmmakers not to embarrassingly make a meal of it, recognizing instead how to make such titillating tokenism work, using this ballyhooed reduction-idealization of women to explore the personal theme of mid-life male malaise.

Edwards chose Bo Derek, an American Amazon and protégée of one-time male sex symbol John Derek, as his elusive on-screen object of desire. He set hurting, hapless Moore after her, a sexualized Coyote dogging a cock-teasing Road Runner. Though Derek, a kind of gentler Ursula Andress, wasn't asked to do much in the film, she nevertheless took a critical shit-kicking. The truth is, she comports herself quite well within the narrow parameters of her role. Her slo-mo emergence from the ocean became one of the iconic images of the era, and her cornrow hairstyle (Caucasian dreadlocks) became a major fashion trend. As for Moore, it was the precedent he set with his hit bit part in *Foul Play* (1978)—as an awkward Alice in a sexualized Wonderland—that earned him this, his first star vehicle. It's clear today that his nervy obsequiousness paved the way for the coming of the more photogenic Hugh Grant.

Plus, for the first time in American film, Moore got to play the drunk, the revival of a very old comic shtick that served him, film after film, quite well, with audiences howling at every wobble, weave and slur. (When Moore began to die of a degenerative disease, some thought he was still at it.) Julie Andrews is far too haughty to play what's supposed to be an object of sympathy and too stodgily old-fashioned to serve as a spokesperson for the modern woman (plus, we're forced to put up with the interminable, Helen Reddy–style songs she's given).

The film's climactic, "Bolero"-scored scene, full of comic *coitus interruptus*, is supposed to play as a statement on the incompatibility of the generations. For all of the aging man's desire to play the sexual bad boy, however, in the end, it's the puritan ethic that formed him that wins. Even in '79, it seemed, Adam and Eve had to be punished.

Sounds noble, but it's the way that Edwards gets us there: Moore is prompted to trade Andrews for Derek by virtue of the former's political intelligence, deemed oppressive and cloying. And when he makes this all-important choice, we're treated to a sanctimonious speech on generational superiority that makes William Holden's in *Network* (1976) feel like a sound bite.

It's not a very funny film either, even in the context of its time. Its enormous success (it was one of the highest-grossing films of the decade) was simply because it had caught the zeitgeist. Still, critics were more than kind. Roger Ebert listed it as one of the best films of the year while Gene Siskel (their weekly parry-thrust review show was just getting going on PBS) called it "a gentle essay on the problems of male menopause."[54]

The *mot* généreux, not *juste*.

The Villain

Plot: Live-action salute to the Road Runner-Coyote cartoons pitting an incompetent villain against a virtuous lunkhead. **Director:** Hal Needham. **Script:** Robert G. Kane. **Cast:** Kirk Douglas, Arnold Schwarzenegger, Ann-Margret, Paul Lynde, Foster Brooks. Columbia. 89 minutes.

In 1949, as America was transitioning to the postwar suburban dream, animator Chuck Jones developed the ultimate metaphor for the burden of keeping up

---

54. Gene Siskel, "'10' Is Not Just Another Pretty Film—It's Pretty Funny," *Chicago Tribune*, October 10, 1979.

with, fittingly, the Joneses. Against a desert background, he pitted an emaciated, pinch-faced coyote (a design inspired by a description of the beast by Mark Twain) against a species of ground cuckoo re-imagined as a kind of blue-gray ostrich with the speed of a sports car, horn included. In theatrical shorts produced over the next 20 years, the poor, enterprising coyote, looking for a quick meal, pursued his prey to no avail, more often than not hoisted by his own errantly engineered petard, usually mail-ordered from Acme.

The slippery bird, metaphorically, represented the frustratingly elusive entitlements of an affluent middle-class lifestyle: the raise that Dad could never get, the mink coat that Mom could only dream about, the latest TV-advertised toys the kids were told they didn't need.

In this, Jones had been preceded by other animators, who had made the cat-and-mouse dynamic, sometimes literally using cats and mice, a staple of the animation short. But the Road Runner cartoons proved its most resonant incarnation, coming as they did at the height of American opportunity and consumerism. The 48 shorts were packaged for television in 1962. By the late '70s, they had imprinted themselves on audiences like a nestling. An entire generation had seen the same cartoons so many times, there wasn't a mishap the demographic couldn't recount.

The makers of *The Villain*, therefore, began at a disadvantage. Looking to transpose the Road Runner–Coyote narrative to full-length, live-action form, they would be dealing with overly familiar material. Further, they'd be gambling on a thin, vignette-filled narrative to sustain itself for an hour and a half. The hope, one supposed, was that this chancy translation would award the gags, and the plot, second life. Hope may spring eternal but here, like the Coyote, we are reminded that it can also go hopelessly awry, landing with a resounding thud.

Playing on the desert background, we find ourselves in the Old West. Kirk Douglas, looking to revive his sagging career, plays the eponymous bad guy aka the Coyote. He's sent in pursuit of a wagonful of money, being driven by a young, incongruous Arnold Schwarzenegger aka the Road Runner. (He has a sidekick: Ann-Margret, back playing eye-candy after having established herself as a legitimate actress in Richard Attenborough's interestingly glum *Magic*, 1978.) And so, true to the film's inspiration, booby traps of all kinds are set up, to slapstick avail. As far as storyline goes, "Th-th-th-that's all, folks!"

Still, there's the nagging sensation through it all that it could have worked. Come the '80s, Baby Boomer filmmakers proved that the hybrid of cartoon and live-action, like Robert Zemeckis' *Who Framed Roger Rabbit* (1988), could be a fun and rewarding idea, not just some crazy elevator pitch. But that was years away. The assignment here falls to Hal Needham, the ex-stuntman whose humor extended to the action-based variety and, as he affirms definitively in this film, not much more.

In Needham's defense, the verbal wit surrounding the stunts is moldy and flat. The writer is Robert G. Kane, joke supplier to the Who's Who of Old School comics on that '70s TV staple, *The Dean Martin Celebrity Roasts* (1974–84). And the cast—Needham's films are riots of bad bedfellows—show no talent whatsoever for the idiom. It's up to the slapstick then, which you'd think Needham, of *Smokey and the Bandit* (1977) fame, would handle with facility. But the mess! Sequences that don't cut, stuntmen with no resemblance to the actors … even sound problems.

By '79, there was a feeling, with this, *1941* and (ugh!) *Scavenger Hunt*, that American film comedy had become unmoored. It had lost its way, narratively and technically. You could see it flailing, looking for direction, asking itself, "How do you make these things again?" To return to the realm of metaphor if I may, so was the country, still looking for a sense of purpose and renewal after Vietnam-Nixon, a problem that would come to be solved by the throwback conservatism of Ronald Reagan and the rise of hi-tech.

Meanwhile, there'd be poor, never-say-die Kirk Douglas, dying.

Conclusion

So... Drop Dead Funny?

FLASH FORWARD—PRESENT DAY (as a screenplay might explain):

We live in an age of analytics. It's only fitting then to cull the comedies of the '70s for content and quality, in order to determine a percentage by which to posit it in the firmament of film history.

The catalogue runs quite a gamut. It encompasses two major schools: low-budget Eastern angst comedy, born of the Jewish tradition, Broadway and urban blight, and big-budget California kookiness, born of a much-needed respite from the former. It accounts for two major audiences: the Greatest Generation and their offspring, at war and then, slowly, at peace. It legitimizes the blaxploitation movement and gives African American auteurs a chance—Davis, Schultz, Poitier. It speaks in dominant, decade-defining voices—Allen, Brooks, Simon—in interesting, offbeat asides—Altman, Ashby, Mazursky—for good, sometimes surprising, workmen—Ross, Schultz, Zieff—and for a handful of Studio Era holdovers—Edwards, Wilder, Frank. It makes a star out of the character actor—Segal, Matthau, Grodin—a feminist icon out of the starlet—Streisand, Hawn, Fonda—and reinvents the outlier—Pryor, Belushi, Martin.

But is it any good?

Excuse the busy, noisy interruption of the Burt Reynolds-Clint Eastwood car chase phenomenon, plus the odd clunker, and the answer is an unequivocal yes. Of the 130 commercial releases examined in this book, 85 can be classified as worthy. Close to 70 percent, which is more than can be said for any decade since. Not all were box office hits of course, but revisionist critical opinion bears out that while life in the 1970s was "funny" in the worst kind of way, its films were funny in the best.

And why wouldn't the percentage be so impressively high, especially for an era in which the big studios were in disarray, the star system had devolved, and the audience had splintered? Here was an era that contained the best work of no less than four iconic voices: Woody Allen, Mel Brooks, Neil Simon and Elaine May—a film comedy Mount Rushmore. Some of the best work by some of America's best screenwriters, including Paddy Chayefsky, Larry Gelbart, Barry Levinson and James L. Brooks. And on-screen personalities as large and magnetic as those from any era, from Barbra Streisand and Richard Pryor to Goldie Hawn and John Belushi.

And while those films were conceived, written, produced and released close to half a hundred years ago (time to donate those wide-leg jeans, people!), their echo indisputably reverberates.

The angst-based comedy of the primal portion of the decade was adopted by TV's

Larry David, cautiously with *Seinfeld* (1989–98) and then unabashedly with *Curb Your Enthusiasm* (2000–present-day). The woozy perspective on California that had marked the output of the decade's second half found keepers of the flame in *Entourage* (2004–11) and *Californication* (2007–14). The *Animal House*-style excesses of youth, which served as the decade's comic climax, seem to get re-worked for each succeeding generation, hence the *American Pie* franchise (1999–2012) and whichever film(s) will fit the next fit of nostalgia. Comedies for black audiences are a bankable commodity now. And while feminism, due to the rise of hip-hop culture, has taken a public hit, talented comediennes from Melissa McCarthy to Kristen Wiig are being either afforded their own vehicles or the opportunity to carry revamps of once male-dominated material.

Comic film of the 1970s has come a long way, baby.

Bibliography

Adamson, Joe. *Groucho, Harpo, Chico and Sometimes Zeppo.* New York: Simon & Schuster, 1973.

Allen, Woody. "Woody Allen on Love and Death." *Esquire,* July 1, 1975: 78.

Arkin, Alan. *Out of My Mind.* New York: Simon & Schuster, 2020.

Badham, John. *John Badham on Directing: Notes from the Set of* Saturday Night Fever, War Games, *and More.* Studio City, California: Michael Wiese Productions, 2013.

Balio, Tino. *The Foreign Film Renaissance on American Screens, 1946–1973.* Madison: University of Wisconsin Press, 2010.

Bennetts, Leslie. *Last Girl Before Freeway: The Life, Loves, Losses and Liberation of Joan Rivers.* New York: Little, Brown, 2016.

Berton, Pierre. *Hollywood's Canada: The Americanization of Our National Image.* Toronto: University of Toronto Press, 1977.

Bjorkman, Stig. *Woody Allen on Woody Allen.* New York: Grove Press, 1993.

Bogdanovich, Peter, and Orson Welles. *This Is Orson Welles.* New York: HarperCollins, 1992.

Brady, John. *The Craft of the Screenwriter.* New York: Simon & Schuster, 1981.

Burns, George. *Living It Up: Or, They Still Love Me in Altoona!* New York: Putnam, 1976.

Caesar, Sid. *Caesar's Hours.* New York: Public Affairs, 2003.

Carlin, George. *Brain Droppings.* New York: Hachette, 1998.

Corman, Roger, and Jim Jerome. *How I Made a Hundred Movies in Hollywood and Never Lost a Dime.* Boston: Da Capo, 1998.

Crowe, Cameron. *Conversations with Wilder.* New York: Knopf, 2001.

Edelman, Rob. *Matthau: A Life.* New York: Taylor Trade, 2002.

Feiffer, Jules. *Backing into Forward.* New York: Doubleday, 2010.

Feldman, Marty. *eYe Marty.* London: Hodder & Stoughton, 2015.

Foran, Charles. *Mordecai: The Life and Times.* Toronto: Random House Canada, 2010.

Frum, David. *How We Got Here: The 70's.* New York: Basic Books, 2000.

Gehring, Wes D. *Genre-Busting Dark Comedies of the 1970s.* Jefferson, NC: McFarland, 2016.

Gelbart, Larry. *Laughing Matters: On Writing* M*A*S*H, Tootsie, Oh, God! *and Other Funny Things.* New York: Random House, 1998.

Gottlieb, Carl. *The Jaws Log: Thirtieth Anniversary Edition.* New York: New Market Press, 2002.

Gray, Beverly. *Seduced by Mrs. Robinson.* New York: Algonquin, 2017.

Harris, Mark. *Mike Nichols.* New York: Random House, 2021.

Haskell, Molly. *From Reverence to Rape.* Chicago: University of Chicago Press, 1974 (revised 1987).

Hawn, Goldie. *Goldie: A Lotus Grows in the Mud.* New York: Berkley, 2006.

Heller-Nicholas, Alexandra, and Dean Brandum. *The Films of Elaine May.* Edinburgh: Edinburgh University Press, 2019.

Henry, David, and Joe Henry. *Furious Cool: Richard Pryor and the World That Made Him.* Chapel Hill: Algonquin Books of Chapel Hill, 2013.

Hirsch, Paul. *A Long Time Ago in a Cutting Room Far, Far Away.* Chicago: Chicago Review Press, 2021.

Horton, Robert, ed. *Billy Wilder Interviews.* Jackson: University Press of Mississippi, 2001.

Itzkoff, Dave. *Robin.* New York: Henry Holt, 2019.

Itzkoff, David. *Mad as Hell: The Making of* Network *and the Fateful Vision of the Angriest Man in Movies.* New York: Times Books, 2014.

Jacobs, Diane. *Hollywood Renaissance.* South Brunswick, NJ: A.S. Barnes, 1977.

Jewison, Norman. *This Terrible Business Has Been Good to Me.* Toronto: Key Porter, 2004.

Jones, Brian Jay. *Jim Henson: The Biography.* New York: Ballantine, 2013.

Jones, Chuck. *Chuck Amok.* New York: Farrar, Strauss and Giroux, 1989.

Kael, Pauline. *5001 Nights at the Movies.* New York: Henry Holt, 1991.

Kanfer, Stefan. *Groucho.* London: Penguin, 2000.

Kapsis, Robert E. *Jonathan Demme Interviews.* Jackson: University Press of Mississippi, 2009.

Kerr, Walter. *The Silent Clowns.* New York: Alfred A. Knopf, 1975.

Kotcheff, Ted, and John Young. *Director's Cut: My Life in Film.* Toronto: ECW Press, 2017.

Lax, Eric. *Woody Allen.* New York: Alfred A. Knopf, 1991.

Lear, Norman. *Even This I Get to Experience.* New York: Penguin, 2014.

Lethem, Jonathan. *More Alive and Less Lonely.* New York: Melville House, 2018.

Levy, Shawn. *King of Comedy: The Art and Life of Jerry Lewis.* New York: St. Martin's Press, 1997.

Lumet, Sidney. *Making Movies.* New York: Alfred A. Knopf, 1995.

Madison, William V. *Madeline Kahn: Being the Music, A Life.* Jackson: University of Mississippi Press, 2016.

Martin, Steve. *Born Standing Up.* New York: Scribner, 2007.

Mast, Gerald. *The Comic Mind: Comedy and the Movies.* Chicago: University of Chicago Press, 1973.

McGilligan, Patrick. *Funny Man: Mel Brooks.* New York: Harper, 2019.

Needham, Hal. *Stuntman! My Car-Crashing, Plane-Jumping, Bone-Breaking, Death-Defying Hollywood Life.* New York: Little, Brown, 2011.

Plaza Suite. Turner Classic Movies, 2006.

Richler, Mordecai. *The Apprenticeship of Duddy Kravitz.* New York: Little, Brown, 1959.

Sacks, Mike. *And Here's the Kicker.* Cincinnati: F & W Media, 2009.

Sarris, Andrew. *The American Cinema: Directors and Directions, 1929–1968.* New York: Dutton, 1968.

Shapiro, Peter. *Turn the Beat Around: The Secret History of Disco.* New York City: Faber & Faber, 2005.

Simon, Neil. *Memoirs.* New York: Simon & Schuster, 1996.

Smith, Bill. *The Vaudevillians.* New York: Macmillan, 1976.

Spoto, Donald. *The Art of Alfred Hitchcock.* New York: Anchor, 1991.

Thomson, David. *Have You Seen...?* New York: Alfred A. Knopf, 2009.

Thomson, David. *The New Biographical Dictionary of Film Updated and Expanded.* New York: Alfred A. Knopf, 2010.

Vlastelica, Ryan. 2015. "A Beginner's Guide to Steve Martin's Eclectic, Groundbreaking Career." *AV Club,* August 15, 2015. https://www.avclub.com/a-beginner-s-guide-to-steve-martin-s-eclectic-groundbr-1798284115. Accessed July 20, 2022.

Walker, Alexander. *Peter Sellers.* New York: Macmillan, 1981.

Wasson, Sam. *Improv Nation: How We Made a Great American Art.* Boston: Houghton Mifflin Harcourt, 2017.

Wasson, Sam. *Paul Mazursky.* Middletown, CT: Wesleyan University Press, 2011.

Wasson, Sam. *A Splurch in the Kisser.* Middletown, CT: Wesleyan University Press, 2009.

Wells, Ira. *Norman Jewison: A Director's Life.* Toronto: Sutherland House, 2021.

Wilder, Gene. *Kiss Me Like a Stranger.* New York: St. Martin's Press, 2005.

Yacowar, Maurice. *Loser Take All: The Comic Art of Woody Allen.* Oxford: Roadhouse, 1979.

Yacowar, Maurice. *Method in Madness: The Comic Art of Mel Brooks.* New York: St. Martin's Press, 1981.

Yule, Andrew. *Richard Lester: The Man Who Framed the Beatles.* New York: Donald I. Fine, 1994.

Zolotow, Maurice. 2004. *Billy Wilder in Hollywood.* New York: Limelight.

Zuckoff, Mitchell. *Robert Altman: The Oral Biography.* New York: Alfred A. Knopf, 2009.

Index

Numbers in *bold italics* indicate pages with photographs